Joy

GOD'S PLAN UNFOLDED

JACK·B·SCOTT

Tyndale House
Publishers, Inc.
Wheaton, Illinois

In quoting Scrip-
ture this book uses
the American Stan-
dard Version (1901)
but uses *Lord* in-
stead of *Jehovah*.

Library of Congress
Catalog Card
Number 77-93756
ISBN 0-8423-
1048-7, paper
Copyright © 1976
by Jack B. Scott.
Revised edition
copyright © 1978
by Jack B. Scott.
Revised edition
published by Tyn-
dale House Pub-
lishers, Inc.,
Wheaton, Illinois.
All rights reserved.
First printing,
revised edition,
April 1978.
Printed in the
United States of
America.

CONTENTS

Foreword   5

CHAPTER ONE
A View of the Whole
(Genesis to Malachi)   9

CHAPTER TWO
The Beginning of the People of God
(Genesis)   17
The Creation of the World (chs. 1,2)   Satan's Challenge to the Purpose of God (ch.3)   Tracing the Two Seeds to the Flood (chs. 4-8)   Man's New Start and His Old Problem (chs. 9-11)   The Growth of Abraham's Faith (chs. 12-22)   The Transition Period, Isaac's Life (chs. 23-28:9)   Jacob—from Sinner to Saint (chs. 25:19-33:20)   Jacob's Children, the Family of God (chs. 34-50)

CHAPTER THREE
The People of God Redeemed
(Exodus-Deuteronomy)   59
Redemption from Egypt (Exod. 1-19)   The Giving of the Law to the People of God (Exod. 20–Deut.)   The Ten Commandments (Exod. 20:1-17)   The Law as an Application of Justice (Exod. 21-24)   The Tabernacle (Exod. 25-31, 35-40)   Apostasy and a New Revelation (Exod. 32-34)   The Sacrificial System (Lev.)   The Years of Wandering (Num. 1-20)   The End of the Journey (Num. 21-36)   The Second Legislation (Deut.)

CHAPTER FOUR
The People Inherit the Land
(Joshua)   97

CHAPTER FIVE
The Spiritual Decline of Israel
(Judges, Ruth, 1 Samuel 1, 2)   105
The Book of Judges   The Other Side of the Story

CHAPTER SIX
The Revival and Prosperity
of the People of God
(1 Samuel 2:12—1 Kings 11)   117
The Dawn Breaks (1 Sam. 2:12–ch. 7)   The Making of a King–Saul (1 Sam. 8-15)   The Rise of David (1 Sam. 16-31)   The Reign of David (2 Sam. 1-24)   The Reign of Solomon (1 Kgs. 1-11)

CHAPTER SEVEN
The Age of the Prophets
1 Kings 12—2 Kings 25)   141
The Period of Stabilization (1 Kgs. 15-22)   The Period of Treachery (2 Kgs. 1-11)   The Last Great Period of Israel (2 Kgs. 12–15:7)   The Last Days of Israel (2 Kgs. 15:8–17:41)   The Last Days of Judah (2 Kgs. 18:1–25:30)

CHAPTER EIGHT
The Prophets of
the Ninth Century   165
Joel c. 850 B.C.   Jonah c. 800 B.C.

CHAPTER NINE
The Writings to Counter
Solomon's Folly   183
Ecclesiastes   Song of Songs

CHAPTER TEN
The Eighth Century Prophets   197
Amos   Hosea   Isaiah   Micah

CHAPTER ELEVEN
The Seventh Century Prophets   251
*Jeremiah   Lamentations–by Jeremiah
Zephaniah   Nahum   Obadiah   Habakkuk*

CHAPTER TWELVE
The Time of Purging
(586-400 B.C.)   289
The History of the Period   Ezekiel   Daniel   Esther

CHAPTER THIRTEEN
The Restoration and Future Hope
of God's People   327
1, 2 Chronicles   Ezra   Nehemiah   Haggai   Zechariah   Malachi

CHAPTER FOURTEEN
The Books of Devotion
and Practical Living for
the People of God   357
Job   Psalms   Proverbs

FOREWORD

THIS WORK is an *introduction to the content of the Old Testament* designed to lead the student of God's Word into a knowledge of the message of the Old Testament. It is a tool, nothing more. If the result of the use of this book is not a greater love of God's Word Written and a greater desire to study the contents of that Word, then the author has failed in his purpose.

The arrangement of the order of the books of the Old Testament in this book is basically, but not entirely, chronological. The purpose, where possible, is to give the historical background contained in Scripture, followed by the writings of the prophets in chronological order against that background. My chronological order may differ from others. It is my own, based upon my understanding of the content of the various books of the Bible and the general historical background of the ancient Near East.

No footnotes or quotations from other authors appear, not because other authors have nothing to say, but because I desire that the reader learn to study God's Word for himself. I have sought to be brief because, in the final analysis, appeal must be to God's Word alone.

May our Lord use this book for his children's better understanding of the Old Testament Scriptures.

His servant,
Jack Scott
Montgomery, Alabama
October 1977

ABBREVIATIONS
USED IN THIS BOOK

OLD TESTAMENT
BOOKS OF THE BIBLE

NEW TESTAMENT
BOOKS OF THE BIBLE

Gen.	Genesis	Matt.	Matthew
Exod.	Exodus	Mark	Mark
Lev.	Leviticus	Luke	Luke
Num.	Numbers	John	John
Deut.	Deuteronomy	Acts	Acts
Josh.	Joshua	Rom.	Romans
Judg.	Judges	1 Cor.	1 Corinthians
Ruth	Ruth	2 Cor.	2 Corinthians
1 Sam.	1 Samuel	Gal.	Galatians
2 Sam.	2 Samuel	Eph.	Ephesians
1 Kgs.	1 Kings	Phil.	Philippians
2 Kgs.	2 Kings	Col.	Colossians
1 Chron.	1 Chronicles	1 Thes.	1 Thessalonians
2 Chron.	2 Chronicles	2 Thes.	2 Thessalonians
Ezra	Ezra	1 Tim.	1 Timothy
Neh.	Nehemiah	2 Tim.	2 Timothy
Est.	Esther	Tit.	Titus
Job	Job	Philem.	Philemon
Psa.	Psalms	Heb.	Hebrews
Prov.	Proverbs	Jas.	James
Eccl.	Ecclesiastes	1 Pet.	1 Peter
Song of Songs		2 Pet.	2 Peter
(Solomon)		1 John	1 John
Isa.	Isaiah	2 John	2 John
Jer.	Jeremiah	3 John	3 John
Lam.	Lamentations	Jude	Jude
Ezek.	Ezekiel	Rev.	Revelation
Dan.	Daniel		
Hos.	Hosea		
Joel	Joel		

OTHER ABBREVIATIONS

Amos	Amos
Obad.	Obadiah
Jonah	Jonah
Mic.	Micah
Nah.	Nahum
Hab.	Habakkuk
Zeph.	Zephaniah
Hag.	Haggai
Zech.	Zechariah
Mal.	Malachi

c.	circa (about)
cf.	compare the following
ch.	chapter
chs.	chapters
f.	the following verse, chapter
ff.	several following verses, chapters
i.e.	that is
v.	verse
vv.	verses

A VIEW OF
THE WHOLE
Genesis—Malachi

THE UNFOLDING of the history of God's dealing with his people in the Old Testament era is itself a thrilling truth to behold. It is particularly thrilling when we realize that the history of God's people which is unfolded in God's Word is our history too if we have believed in the Lord. We also are the people of God.

What God said to his people thousands of years ago certainly shall have great significance for us today because God never changes and his people's need for him never changes.

Nor does the nature of man change except by the grace of God. Indeed the Old Testament revelation is the story of how God has changed a multitude of sinful people to be his own from among the peoples of the world. Since that work (begun in

Eden) continues today, the cloud of witnesses of past millennia say much to us today.

The book of Genesis tells us about the beginnings of the people of God on earth. It tells of the creative purpose of God and of his orderly creation of all things good, to his own glory. Here also is recorded the entrance of sin into the life of man and the consequent fall of man from fellowship with God. That in turn led to suffering and judgment. The record of the deterioration of man, leading to the awful judgment at the great flood, testifies to man's need of God and of God's grace and salvation. Thus, God, as Savior and Provider of hope through grace, becomes one of the great doctrines of Genesis and of the entire Word of God.

We can trace throughout the Old Testament one of the chief marks of God's children, namely, that sense of their need for God. So Jacob, Moses, David and Hezekiah, among a vast array of faithful men, learn above all to trust in God and to look to him for the answers to all of life's perplexities and trials.

These are the people of God who are called one by one into God's family, marked by their *faith in God.* Thus God calls a people to be his own. This calling is itself first seen in Genesis.

Abraham, Isaac, Jacob, Judah and his brothers are all called to faith in God. We also see that the faith which has come by the grace of God into the hearts of God's people grows in each individual. Scripture nowhere else, either in the Old or New Testament, offers a clearer view of the growth of one man's faith than it does in the recorded growth of the faith of Abraham.

At the same time, we also see another essential quality developing in the people of God. *Love* is begun. And love grows among those who were naturally sinful and hostile, after the grace of God works in their hearts. So we see the selfish and belligerent family of Jacob increase in the bond of love through trials and testing. We see this particularly in the lives of two men: Judah and Joseph.

In addition to faith and love, another marked characteristic of the children of God seen with increasing frequency in Scripture, is *hope.* This hope comes to God's people, especially to Abraham and his children, through the promises of God. These promises chiefly embrace two great hopes: the hope of a seed (a multitude of descendants); and the hope of an inheritance (a permanent place to live before God).

In the Old Testament we see the development of both of these hope concepts. The promise of a seed, first given in Genesis 3:15 and called the seed of the woman, later is renewed to Abraham.

He is given a son, Isaac, through whom all the promises of God to Abraham are channelled. Abraham is assured that that seed ultimately will become a multitude. And as the New Testament shows, the Seed promised to Abraham culminates in one person—the Christ (Gal. 3:16).

Similarly, the inheritance first promised to Abraham is in terms of the land of Canaan, a land of promise and of the dwelling of Abraham's seed. By the time of Joshua, the possession becomes a reality. By David's time, a thousand years after Abraham, the possession has increased to reach from the river of Egypt to the Euphrates. Nevertheless Israel, because of sin, is unable to retain that possession. Israel's empire shrinks until Jerusalem itself falls into enemy hands.

In the days of decline particularly, the Lord begins to introduce a new concept, a hope for a new heaven and new earth, a new Jerusalem. Now the eyes of God's people are lifted to hope for an inheritance that will not fade away, to which hope the New Testament continues to point (1 Pet. 1:3, 4; Rev. 21, 22). Though we call this a new hope, nevertheless the writer to the Hebrews makes it clear that even Abraham carried this higher hope with him to the grave, as did the other Old Testament believers (Heb. 11:9, 10, 13-16).

One important observation needs to be made about the people of God as they begin to be conscious of being God's people in the days of Abraham. God called his people not only to bestow his blessings upon them but also in order that they should become a holy people. They were to honor and glorify God by their lives on earth among all men. To do this, God called them to lives that honored God by obedience to his Word.

One of the clearest expressions of this continuing will of God for his people is to be found in Genesis 18:19, where the Lord is speaking of the very purpose of his having called Abraham. The Lord says: "I have known him, to the end that he may command his children and his household after him, that they may keep the way of the Lord, to do righteousness and justice; to the end that the Lord may bring upon Abraham that which he hath spoken of him."

Here we see plainly that God, in first choosing Abraham and calling him, had intended that he and his seed should faithfully live so as to reflect the will of God in their lives. The very working out of the planned blessings of God on his own people was dependent on this evidence in their lives, that they were indeed his children.

The terms *righteousness* and *justice* here describe throughout

Scripture the high expectation of God for his children. God never lowered this standard. Throughout the period of Old Testament revelation, he continually called his children to this life and to these standards. Prophet after prophet measured Israel by the standards of righteousness and justice.

The Lord says in one place to Abraham, "Walk before me and be thou perfect" (Gen. 17:1). God never lowers this standard. So Jesus much later says to his disciples, "Ye therefore shall be perfect, as your heavenly Father is perfect" (Matt. 5:48). No higher standard can be set for the people of God.

Later, the Lord at Mount Sinai told those who had come out of Egypt that they were his holy people. Immediately after that declaration in Exodus 19, in the *next* chapter he unfolded his will in the form of the Ten Commandments. The commandments therefore were given to the people of God as the expression of the kind of lives which God would have his people to show to the world.

Following these specific rules of conduct which embrace the whole of the revealed will of God, and which expound more fully God's will for his people—to "do righteousness and justice," God gave to them a multitude of examples or "justices" which affect all of life. So in Exodus 21—23, he gave numerous examples of everyday life and taught the people that every facet of their lives must reflect a conscious effort to do the will of God in keeping with the Ten Commandments.

It is here also that God introduced the sacrifices or the means of bringing the people to the realization of their sins and their consequent need of God's forgiveness. They would fall short of the high standard which God had set. Therefore the sacrifices were given to impress on them this fact and the seriousness of sin. Sin should break the hearts of God's children and make their hearts contrite before God as they learn to trust in him. The entire sacrificial system was the Old Testament means of humbling God's people and pointing them to trust in God. The sacrificial system furthermore pointed out their need of a Savior who could deal with their sin.

The tabernacle, also introduced in this period of revelation, was so designed as to show the spiritual need of God's people and to lead them to trust in the Savior whom God would send. The tabernacle itself showed the pattern of the work of Christ, as the writer to the Hebrews later testifies (Heb. 9, 10).

The book of Genesis also records for us the beginning work of Satan, the great enemy of God and of God's people. As God's plan and purpose for his people is revealed, Satan is shown to be in total opposition to God's purpose and plan. Satan succeeds in provoking man, whom God had created, to that same rebellious heart and nature which Satan possessed. Genesis records the temptation and fall of man and the beginning of the children of Satan who continued throughout redemptive history to oppose God and God's family, the children of God.

Satan begins at Eden but does not stop there. After the fall, we see Cain, the offspring of Satan, oppose Abel, his fleshly brother but a stranger in spiritual matters. Cain, as his father the Devil, seeks to destroy God's child. He succeeds in killing righteous Abel but is not able to defeat God's purpose. No sooner is Abel dead than God raises up, through Adam and Eve, another son, Seth, in whose days God's children began to call on the Lord. Thus, two strands of people appear and develop on earth.

In God's sight, there are but two classes of men: the children of God and the children of Satan. These can be traced throughout the Old and New Testaments—and to this day. Much of the riches of God's Word is seen in the biblical revelation of the nature of God's children and Satan's children, and of God's dealing with each.

Satan's opposition continues even after the great flood. We note, for instance, Abraham and his children facing continual hostility from the offspring of Satan who live in Canaan. Later in Egypt, the evil opposition of Satan's seed in the person of Pharaoh and the Egyptians is quite evident. As Israel leaves Egypt and moves again into Canaan, this hostility of the enemies of God increases. All of Israel's history is plagued with continuous enmities.

Tragically, we see the gradual infiltration of the children of Satan into the family of God's people, the Old Testament church. Soon there are as many or perhaps even more unbelievers than believers in the church. The developing hostility culminates in the Old Testament with the overthrow of Jerusalem and the ensuing Babylonian captivity. But the enmity does not end there. After the return, we find Jerusalem and Judea filled with enemies of God's people.

By the time of the New Testament, the church again is permeated by unbelief. Satan's agents in the church, the majority of Jews in Jesus' time, finally ally themselves with the secular power of Rome to express the ultimate hostility, the actual crucifixion of Jesus Christ, the Son of God.

The New Testament records even more of the continuing hostility between the people of God and Satan's offspring. The book of Revelation most vividly portrays this in chapter 12.

Having noted in the book of Genesis these major themes, we have shown how they can be traced throughout the Old Testament: man's need of God; the people of God called; the opposing work of Satan. The Scripture then traces the history of God's dealing with his people in the history of Israel. This history is written against the background of the history of the secular world. The rise and fall of nations and great empires is woven into the background of biblical history. God's work of redeeming a people was not isolated from the everyday reality of history all around Israel.

The history of God's people proves to be the record of the success and failure of Israel as she is more or less obedient to her Lord.

When Israel inherited the land of Canaan, she succeeded in prospering there only so long as she was submissive to God's Word and will. When parents began to neglect instructing their children in accord with God's express will in Deuteronomy 6:4ff, the whole nation suffered. So we read of the tragic days of the period of the judges.

When the people became broken by their enemies and reached the point of hopeless desperation, God raised up men like Samuel and David to call the people back to God. The examples of the leadership of Saul and David show the marked contrast between a faithless and a faithful shepherd of God's flock which is typical of the whole of Old Testament history.

When leaders fail, as they did in the time of Solomon and his successors, tragic results affect the whole church. Then all suffer—both the sinners and the saints. Both the offspring of Satan in Israel and God's true believers suffer the consequence of Israel's failures.

To counter the evil influence of those who led Israel astray I believe certain unnamed writers of God's Word withstood that evil influence by writing such works as the Song of Songs and Ecclesiastes. The study of these books shows how devastating the failure of the leaders could be for all in the church.

Further, to counter the evil influence of Solomon and his evil successors in Israel, God raised up a continuing flow of prophets. These prophets bravely faced the hostility of unbelief which existed in Israel in order to call those who trusted in God to continue faithful toward God.

From Joel in the ninth century B.C., who warns of spiritual decay, as the joy of serving God disappears from the hearts of the people; through the eighth century, with the great array of prophets who decry the social sins and injustices of their day; down to the seventh and sixth centuries of spiritual deterioration, God sends prophet after prophet to call the people to repentance and to a return to the Lord.

Amos rebukes their failure to love one another, while Hosea describes their failure to love God. Jonah exemplifies the reluctance of some of God's true children to obey God and become submissive to his purpose for the redemption of men. Jeremiah focuses on the sinfulness of the hearts of the people and points with hope to the ultimate solution by the hand of God—the changing of the people's hearts.

In captivity, such prophets as Ezekiel and Daniel record testimony to the continuing grace of God and how he sustains those who put their trust in him.

The doctrine of the remnant, which was introduced by the eighth century prophets, Amos and Isaiah, and later expounded by the prophets Jeremiah and Ezekiel, shows that though God's people must go through great trials and terrible ordeals, God will spare those who put their trust in him. Nowhere do we have a better and warmer expression of this hope than in the prophet Habakkuk, whose ministry was near the time of the fall of Jerusalem.

The remnant of God's people did return. Out from captivity in Babylon came a large contingent of those who sought to do God's will. This remnant returned to Jerusalem and built again her Temple and her walls. This era is marked by a great love for God's Word, particularly for the Law of Moses. It is a period of revival and return (or at least a desire to return) to those high standards which God set for his people in the Law of Moses.

In all of this time of spiritual rise and decline of God's people, there is a continuous flow of psalms, songs and proverbs expressing the faith of God's children who live through those ages. The authors of most of these writings are not known, but since their writings are retained in God's Word, we know that what is expressed here, as elsewhere in Scripture, is the Word of God.

Job expresses the faith of God's child, tested by his confrontation with most difficult trials, losses and suffering. It is a testimony to the longsuffering of God which is in turn instilled into God's child, enabling him to hold the faith even in times of the doubts of those closest to him.

The Psalms record beautifully the faith of many of God's children in addition to David the great psalmist. Perhaps the first Psalm is most typical of the content of all the Psalms. It declares the righteousness of God's people in contrast to the wickedness of those without faith. Here, as frequently elsewhere, God's child is portrayed as like a tree transplanted by the waters of God's

Word and grace. He bears his fruit in his season and never withers. It beautifully illustrates the utter dependence of God's child on God's Word and God's sustaining power. It also is in sharp contrast to the fruitless life of the wicked and his inevitable ending without hope and without inheritance.

In this introductory chapter we have only briefly sketched the developing content of the Old Testament message of God for his people. It is enough to show the great relevance of this ancient message from God for his people today. The contemporary quality of God's Word is beautifully expressed by Jesus himself in dealing with his own generation. On one occasion he retorted to the Pharisees: "Abraham rejoiced to see my day; and he saw it, and was glad . . . before Abraham was born, I am" (John 8:56, 58). As the writer to the Hebrews also states: "Jesus Christ is the same yesterday and today, yea and forever" (Heb. 13:8). The eternal Christ makes God's Word to God's people always contemporary and always relevant.

In the following chapters, then, we will be doing more than studying the life and learning of an ancient people. We will be studying God's revelation of his truth and will to his people, not for his people of an ancient time only but for his people at all times. In this study there is much for us to learn for our day and our daily life.

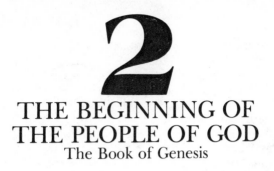

THE BEGINNING OF
THE PEOPLE OF GOD
The Book of Genesis

THE CREATION OF THE
WORLD
Genesis 1-2

THE OPENING WORDS of the Old Testament tell of the beginnings. The beginnings spoken of are the beginning of the creation of heaven and earth. From the time of this beginning, God is assumed as existing already. Scripture says little about what preceded the creation of the world because man's beginning is related to creation, so what preceded creation is not essential for man to know.

To our curiosity about such things Scripture does give two responses: one in the Old Testament and one in the New. First, in the Old Testament in Deuteronomy 29:29, God tells us that the secret things belong to the Lord but what is revealed belongs to us and our children forever. This is as much as to say that we should concern ourselves with what God *has* revealed and not be too curious about the rest. Enough is revealed to demand all of our concern and attention.

However, Scripture does reveal to us part of what was in God's mind concerning the purpose of creation which was in the mind of God. This concept of God's intent and purpose in creation is most important for us to know. Though throughout Scripture this purpose of God is implied, it is explicitly taught in Ephesians 1:4. Here we are told that God chose us in Christ before the foundation of the world, that is, before creation. The purpose of God for us is then given: that we should be holy and without blemish before God in love.

I realize that some translations place the phrase "in love" with the next sentence. (The Greek would allow either.) But the phrase is needed with the preceding concept and indeed completes it and is preferable, not only from the grammatical point of view but because it is consistent with God's truth as revealed throughout Scripture.

The teaching is as follows: God, before creation, purposed to have a people who would spend eternity with him, with whom he would share the blessings of eternity in his presence. This concept alone is staggering to us and beyond our full comprehension. It speaks of a God of love who in love included us in his eternal purpose. He specifically chose us to be with him forever. He purposed to accomplish our inclusion in his family by his Son, Jesus Christ. Here is implied the whole plan of salvation as Scripture unfolds it for us. The point is that God did this choosing in Christ *before* he created heaven and earth. Thus we see how God's prior purpose affects all that he begins to do in creation of the world and man in it.

There follows an explanation of the kind of people God purposed to have. They were to be *holy* and *without blemish*. The two words are not synonymous. "Holy" pertains to that which is set aside for God. These people were to be a holy people, exclusively God's people. "Without blemish" teaches us that they were to be sinless, flawless, since only such people could abide in the presence of God forever.

They were further to be *before God,* in his presence, in a relationship of *love.* God here expresses that essential relationship, love, which must be the bond among God's people and between God and his people. Love is frequently shown in Scripture to be a bond between the persons of the Trinity (John 3:35; 15:9;

17:23, 26). So man, who is to be created in God's image, must also possess this characteristic.

Ephesians 1:4 helps us to see what God had in mind when he began to create heaven and earth and to put man on it. We need this concept in order to see the marvelous unity of God's Word as we trace God's purpose in all his dealings with man. God is never thwarted from his initial purpose. In his determinate counsel he carries out to completion his original purpose. This is the thrilling story which unfolds in the revelation of God, the Scriptures of the Old and New Testaments.

The first paragraph of Scripture (Gen. 1:1-5) introduces the creative work of God. The word used here for "create" is a word of which God is alone the subject in Scripture. It means therefore exclusively that work of God which brings into existence what formerly had no existence.

In order further to reveal God's creative power, God brought order out of chaos and light out of darkness (v. 2). The second verse is a commentary on the first, not something in addition. For his own glory, God first created heaven and earth in a chaotic and dark state, and then he brought order and light to bear on what he had made.

The word used here for God is the generic term which is, in the Hebrew language, a plural form. It is rightly translated here as a singular because the Hebrew verb "created" is singular in form. The reason the form of the noun for God is in the plural is to express the majesty of God and perhaps also to indicate the plurality of persons in the Godhead. The same verse speaks of the Spirit of God as a person, thus implying a plurality of persons in the one Godhead. The doctrine of the Trinity is here implicit, however, and we must wait for the New Testament to provide the explicit doctrine of the Trinity. In other words, the use of a plural form for God and the introduction of the personality of the Spirit of God allows for, though it does not explicitly teach, the trinitarian personality of God.

It is worthy of note that the concepts here introduced (order out of chaos and of light out of darkness) are used in the New Testament to teach the redemptive work of God in our lives. In 2 Corinthians 5:17 we are told that if one is in Christ he is a new creation. The old is passed away and he is become new.

Again in 2 Corinthians 4:6, Paul alludes to Genesis 1:2 in saying that God who caused the light to shine out of darkness has also shined in our darkened hearts to give the light of the knowledge of the glory of God in Christ. Here he speaks of the work of rebirth or regeneration which occurs in every believer's heart, enabling him to know God and salvation. As the Spirit was involved in the original creation and in the giving of light, so too in our spiritual recreation into God's family, the Spirit is active. John 1:4, 5 similarly alludes to the light of God which subdues the darkness.

Another thing we need to point out here is that the sequence of evening and morning (Gen. 1:5) which is the biblical order of the twenty-four hour period, reflects over and over this triumph of light over darkness. We learn how God has built right into creation itself and into the order of night and day, a sermon reflecting God's creation of light to conquer darkness and the inevitable triumph of spiritual light over spiritual darkness. God's natural revelation begins with the very first day.

Verses 6 to 8 record the form of the earth as God first created it. It is important here to see specifically what is taught. The word "firmament" could better be translated "expanse." It refers to an area of living which God made for man on earth. Above and below that expanse, water was stored. We observe that this is not the way the world is today. We know of no such gatherings of water above and below the living area of man on earth. They do not exist today. This is the point. The world God made in the beginning was apparently different from the world as we know it. At the time of the flood, the world underwent a worldwide catastrophic change to become the world as we know it today. This was precisely the point of Peter when he was writing to the church in his latter days.

In 2 Peter 3:3-7, Peter refers to a time of unbelief when men, wilfully ignoring what God had done in judgment against the ancient world by the flood, would disbelieve in the return of Christ. They would contend that by their observations the world is pretty much the same as it was from the beginning. Peter insists in verse 5 that they *wilfully ignore* the doctrine of creation as recorded in Genesis 1.

The world before the flood, Peter tells us, was quite different from our present world. It was compacted out of water. Then in the flood by means of the great reservoirs of water both above and below the earth, the world that *then was* was destroyed. Peter contrasts that world with the present heaven and earth (v. 7).

It is important to see then that the world as God first created it was quite different from its appearance today. The vast reservoirs of water above and below the inhabitable earth were released at the time of the flood and brought such a catastrophic change to the earth that it altered radically the whole structure and appearance of the earth. We shall note later that the flood involved much more than rain for forty days and nights. It involved also the release of the fountains of the deep and the release of the waters of heaven (Gen. 7:11). Rain was merely the third element of the flood and probably the least significant in terms of damage done (Gen. 7:12. See also Gen. 8:2).

Thus Scripture is consistent with itself. We do not have here some ancient mythological concept of the earth's structure alluded to, but the clearly revealed Word of God, in both the Old and the New Testaments, testifying to the same truth. Those today who ignore the biblical revelation in their pursuit of the truth about the world's origin, are simply ignoring the creative work of God and the power of God to change what he has created. In their insistence on the necessity for billions of years to effect great changes on the earth, some ignore the catastrophic effects of the flood. While research scientists may discover many great truths about our universe which we can appreciate, we must nevertheless be guided by God's Word in the interpretation of those facts. I do not see how any Christian can do otherwise.

The rest of the first chapter, giving the order of creation (first light, then a place to dwell, then dry land and waters on earth to contain the various forms of creation) gives further evidence of the mind of God at work in an orderly fashion. After this, specific lights are made to shine on man. Next the waters and the land on earth become full of all kinds of creatures.

Verse 26 introduces man, the crown of creation, on the sixth day of creation. In all, we see the order and the plan of God as he unfolds his creative work. This in itself speaks of the orderliness of God and implies that before even beginning creation there was indeed a purpose in God's mind which led eventually to the creation of man for whom a world had now been prepared.

Man is described here as created in the image of God. Just what the image of God involves, we are not here told, but the broader revelation of God's Word teaches that man was made for God and to have fellowship with him. As we noted in Ephesians 1:4, man was made to live before God, in his presence in love. This suggests similar capacities in man which are present in God. To be in God's image, then, is to be capable of fellowship with God and to be able to experience mutual love with God, reflecting God's love toward us. Man then is unique, for of no other creature of which we know is this true.

We also see the phrase "Let us make man" and "our likeness" implying, though again not explicitly teaching, the plural personality of God.

God, moreover, gave to man a work to do and a responsibility before God. He was to replenish and subdue the earth, exercising dominion over all that God had created (1:28). When God had finished with his creation, he was pleased and pronounced all very good. This surely implies that the creation was flawless and that man, as made by God, was also very good (sinless).

At this point we pause to note that all of the factors stated in Ephesians 1:4 are, at the time of creation, present. God made man holy (for himself) and without blemish (very good) to dwell before him (in his presence and image) in a relationship of love. This latter is seen in the fact that God had now given to the first man commandments by which he would show, through obedience, his love toward God. As Jesus himself said later, "If ye love me, ye will keep my commandments" (John 14:15—Compare also John 15:14). Thus, obedience to God is ever a manifestation of the love of his children. The situation for the fulfillment of God's purpose in creating man was therefore established from the beginning. All of the essential elements for the continuance of God's purpose were present and instituted at the time of creation.

In chapter 2, verses 1 to 3, we are introduced to the Sabbath concept, the time of rest for God from his work of creation. This also suggests God's intent to bring all things which he had begun to their culmination. To impress this truth on man, it is here specifically stated that God rested on the seventh day and hallowed (made holy) that day.

Later, the writer to the Hebrews shows us that symbolically this seventh day was established to point to the final entering into rest and fellowship with God by his people (Heb. 4:3-11). Each seventh day therefore stands from the time of creation to recall God's great purpose of having a people before him forever. Each Sabbath day thereafter was to be a reminder to God's people of this hope and was indeed a sampling of eternity in a rehearsal for heaven itself; since on that day God's people would lay aside the profane duties of this world and be given totally to enjoyment of God. We shall see this doctrine as it later develops.

With chapter 2, verse 4, we are introduced to God in a personal sense. The personal name, Yahweh or Jehovah or Lord as some translations have it, is here seen for the first time. It is significant that it occurs here because the following verses' emphasis is on the personal care of God for man in providing all of his needs: physical, emotional and spiritual. Chapter 1 has given the order of creation, while chapter 2 lays emphasis on man the crown of creation and shows that in God's purpose all else was made for man, for his good. In the second chapter the logical, not the chronological order is therefore emphasized. Chapter 2 demonstrates the love of God for man whom he had made.

Verse 5 suggests that man is needed to complete the creation. Verse 7 details the creation of man to show both his humble origin from the dust of the ground and his lofty origin from the very breath of God himself.

Verses 8 to 14 tell how God so very abundantly provided for the physical needs of man, giving him on this beautiful earth a special place to call his own and providing for him every good fruit to nourish his body.

In verse 9 we are told of the two trees in the midst of the garden. They are introduced mysteriously and their nature is not explained except that one is called the Tree of Life and one the Tree of the Knowledge of Good and Evil.

Outside of this context (chapters 2 and 3), the latter tree is never mentioned again. Since it is called the Tree of the Knowledge of Good and Evil, it no doubt was placed there to test Adam's love of God by obedience. The issue was: "Shall man know good and evil by the revelation of God or by experimentation and independence from God's revelation?" The trees' very presence set up a choice which Adam would have to make—to depend on God's revealed will or to seek to exist independently of God. The former would manifest his love, the latter his hate of God.

God also met man's emotional needs. Man obviously was made to bear responsibility, being in God's image. Therefore God gave him a task to perform before God (vv. 15-17). Again specific commands were given by which Adam would show his love as he obeyed God.

Finally, God met man's need in a special way. He was made to have fellowship with God—but in a context of fellowship with men like himself. God, we are told, created man, male and female (1:27). Here in chapter 2 we have an elaboration of this creation of the female to show again how all of God's work was for man and for his good, out of God's love toward man.

The woman is here described as a helpmeet for him, answering to his needs. She was made for man to complete man. Man alone was incomplete and thus the mutual need of each is built into the very fiber of mankind.

God made the woman from the body of the man and ordained that thereafter men would be born of women, again stressing the mutual need and dependency of each toward the other which only the other can provide.

God then established the concept of the family which would be the way in which God would call his people and redeem them. The relationship between a husband and a wife would reflect the eternal relationship between Christ and his church (Eph. 5:22, 33).

We conclude this section therefore by observing once again that God's purpose, as expressed in Ephesians 1:4, is, in the time of the creation of man in God's image, fully expressed. Here we have a people who are holy and without blemish before God, in a state of love. But sinlessness and love must be tested. Above all, Adam's sense of his need for God must be tested if there was to be that eternal fellowship with God which God had purposed and desired.

SATAN'S CHALLENGE TO THE PURPOSE OF GOD
Genesis 3

The third chapter introduces the serpent, who is described as subtle and yet as one of the creatures of God. Nothing was therefore inherently evil in the serpent. He, like the other creatures of God, was created good. When he begins to speak to the woman we immediately see that more is involved here than a mere creature subject to man. A personality is revealed—a personality which is already hostile to God and detrimental to man. Though it is not specifically stated in this chapter, it is elsewhere clearly shown that this serpent was used by Satan as his entrance into man's world, to tempt man to sin. Revelation 12:9, in describing Satan, calls him "the great dragon . . . the old serpent, he that is called the devil and Satan, the deceiver of the whole world." Satan here and wherever he appears in Scripture is portrayed as one who opposes God and man's good by lies and with the motivations of a murderer (John 8:44). It is this Satan who is the dominant character here in the account of man's sin and fall.

Satan's intent is clear. He wants to foil God's good plan and purpose for man. He wants to make man, like himself, rebellious toward God. He no doubt chose to use the serpent as better suiting his purposes, being more subtle than other creatures.

Note the approach of Satan. "Hath God said?" He openly challenges the Word of God which is the rule and authority by which man is to live and by which he is to prosper.

The subtle quality of Satan's approach is in the way he sows seeds of doubt about God's Word in the heart of Eve. He misquotes or overstates the Word of God to imply the unreasonableness of God's having commanded anything to man. Sa-

tan's subtle addition to the Word of God is seen in the words
"any tree" and "all the trees." Satan knew what God had said but
he overstated God's Word here to imply harshness on God's
part.

It is important to note how Eve follows his lead. In answering
Satan, she at first quotes God accurately but then she adds to
God's commands by the words "neither shall ye touch it" (v. 3).
She too, following Satan's leading, now added to God's com-
mand; and thus she revealed her resentment toward the severity
of God.

It is no wonder that later God warns through Moses and then
still later through the apostle John, that we are never to add to or
take away from God's Word (Deut. 4:2; 12:32; Rev. 22:18, 19).
Both in the beginning and in the end of God's revelation to his
people, he sternly warns against any careless handling of his
Word. The fact that Eve here so carelessly handled the Word of
God shows already the rebellion that was in her heart.

Having now set aside the authority of God's Word, she was
helpless to outwit Satan. He could now feed her lies as he did in
verse 4. When God's Word is removed as the standard of truth,
then man is incapable of distinguishing between truth and a lie.

In verses 6ff, the woman's actions and thoughts give us a portrait
of sin at work in the heart. Eve saw that the tree was good for
food, though God had not said this. In Genesis 2:9, God had
carefully distinguished between that fruit which was good for
food and that which was not. Her judgment, no longer guided
by God's Word, was susceptible to sinful error. Her own desire
now took over. Fleshly pleasures and not God's truth guided her
actions after this. The tree and its fruit pleased her and this
became her standard for action. Finally, though her mind still
told her that it was forbidden, she brought her mind under her
lustful desires by reasoning a lie—that it would make one wise.

The overt act of taking the fruit followed, and is the culmination of the sin that first began in her heart when she determined
no longer to be led by the Word of God. It is profitable to
compare two similar New Testament portraits of sin in 1 John
2:16 and James 1:14, 15.

We are startled to learn that her husband had been with her
all this time and apparently never protested or took his rightful
place of spiritual leadership in the home. He merely followed
her spiritual lead, committing the same sin with her.

Adam's sin therefore can be summarized as follows: he did
not exercise that dominion over the other creatures which God
had commissioned him to do (1:26). The serpent was indeed

under Adam and therefore subject to him. Adam therefore was
without excuse. Further, he through his wife disregarded God's
specific word and God's revealed will concerning the fruit of the
Tree of the Knowledge of Good and Evil. Finally, he allowed his
wife to lead him spiritually, which was a reversal of the clear plan
which God had expressed in Genesis 2.

Much later, when Paul was to deal with the spiritual leaders in
the church, he would show how, from the beginning, God had
ordained the man and not the woman for this office (1 Tim.
2:11-15).

The consequences of this first sin of our first parents is spelled
out in bold sentences that follow (vv. 7-24). Their eyes were
opened and they knew that they were naked. Having now
known sin experimentally, it already drastically affected their
outlook on life. Original innocence was gone. Guilt had taken
over. Now when they heard the voice of God, they, who were
made to have fellowship with God, fled from him and hid (v. 8).

God's penetrating question—"Where art thou?" has more to
do with their spiritual state than their physical location. The
answer to the question is not to state where in the garden they
are but the fact that they are in hiding from God. That says it all
(v. 10).

The evidence of their newly acquired sinful nature is seen in
their feelings of guilt before God. Their desire to hide from him
and their tendency to blame others, even God for their sin, show
further their guilt (vv. 12, 13).

Following this, God now addresses all three personalities involved in this temptation and fall. First he speaks to the serpent
(Satan). The creature-serpent is cursed in a visible way more
than any other beast. From this time on, the serpent will always
be a visible reminder to man of the consequences of the curse of
God (v. 14).

It is verse 15 in which, while God is addressing Satan, he
nevertheless gives the first great promise and hope of redemption for man. Genesis 3:15 has rightly been called the first Gospel. Indeed all of the rest of Scripture is an unfolding of the
truth contained here.

The first concept we note in Genesis 3:15 is that of the two
seeds. "Thy seed and her seed" suggests two lines of descent
among men in a spiritual sense. Scripture never makes any other
distinction than this: the seed of the woman (God's children) and
the seed of the serpent (Satan's offspring). We can and should
trace through both the Old and New Testaments this concept of

two families of men, spiritually speaking, those of God and those of Satan. It is a most important distinction and concept.

It is apparent from the New Testament that our Lord continues to make the same distinction. This is quite clear from John 8:42-44. In this passage, Jesus speaks of God as the Father of those who love Christ (v. 42) and he speaks of the devil as the father of those who now resist Christ (v. 44). Similarly, John, in 1 John 3:8-10, speaks of the children of God and the children of the devil. Scripture knows no other distinction among men more important than this one. In Christ, all distinctions are erased, but among men these two categories of mankind continue: the seed of the woman (God's children), and the seed of the serpent (Satan's children). Much of the further revelation of God will pertain to the characteristics of each family among men, and the enmity that exists between them. In Scripture, the two seeds are generally distinguished by the terms "the righteous" and "the wicked."

Second, we note that the verse speaks of the enmity between the two. It is God who put that enmity between them to maintain the distinction. Whenever the two seeds make peace with each other, God's children lose. Scripture subsequently makes this quite evident to us. We shall see this enmity develop as early as the fourth chapter of Genesis and it can be traced throughout Scripture. In Revelation chapter 12, for instance, it is still very much apparent.

Finally, the verse tells us that the serpent will bruise (crush) the heel of the seed of the woman and the seed of the woman will bruise (crush) his head. This alludes to the suffering of the seed of the woman but also to his ultimate triumph over the serpent. (A crushed head suggests a fatal blow.) Thus too, throughout Scripture we read of the suffering of God's children at the hand of Satan and his offspring, but always there is a promise of ultimate triumph for God's children.

At this point it is imperative that we stress the final outcome of things as the verse here foretells. The seed of the woman pertains to God's children. Yet above all it pertains to the Christ. In Isaiah 7:14 we are told of One who is to be born of a virgin— One who is "God with us." In Matthew 1:18, 22, 23 this prophecy of Isaiah is applied to Jesus Christ. In Galatians 4:4, 5 we are told that in the fulness of time God sent his Son to be born of a woman. Finally in Romans 16:20 we have the promise that the God of Peace shall bruise Satan under our feet. All of these passages pertain to the Genesis 3:15 gospel. They point to that ultimate triumph by *the* seed of the woman, Christ, over

Satan. Here we should compare Hebrews 2:14, 15 where we see that Christ acts on our behalf as *the* seed out of many seed in his triumph for us over the devil.

In Christ's life on earth we see Satan's resistance and his attempts to destroy the Christ. At the cross we see both the wounded Christ and the crushing of Satan's head, as Christ both died and rose again to triumph over all of his and our enemies.

That is why Genesis 3:15 is rightly to be known as the first Gospel. It gives assurance and hope to those who look to God to provide the triumph over Satan and deliverance from his power.

Having thus directly addressed Satan and indirectly addressed all who put their trust in God, the Lord now addresses the woman. The inevitable judgment of God on her is twofold: she will bear her seed only by much pain; and she will now be subject to *sinful* man who will arbitrarily, even sinfully at times, rule over her.

Note, childbearing is not the punishment or the consequence of sin but childbearing *in pain* is. It was God's good plan that by the birth of a seed the deliverer should come. I believe this to be Paul's meaning in 1 Timothy 2:15. Childbearing is the office of woman by which ultimately through women, as at the birth of Christ, she and all shall be saved if they believe. It is a most noble office, therefore, and one in which all faithful women share, but because of sin it is a painful experience.

Note also that wives being subject to their husbands is not the consequence of sin. When God created woman and established the home—before sin existed God established this relationship, as we have already noted. However, now the husband is a sinner, and consequently his rule is often harsh, unfair, even cruel and certainly often unwise. Nevertheless the subjection of the wife is still God's will. Paul shows this is true even after salvation has come into the home (Eph. 5:22, 23).

Finally, the Lord addressed the husband, Adam. The consequences of his sin are that now, as he seeks to subdue the earth, the earth will resist. He can get a living from the earth only by the sweat of his face. Ultimately the earth he was to subdue will subdue him and he will return to it. Here death, the penalty for sin, is introduced as a present reality to Adam (v. 19) according to the warning God had made in 2:17.

Verse 21 states that the Lord made coats of skins for Adam and Eve. This, no doubt, means that before their very eyes animals were slaughtered to cover their nakedness. This was perhaps a preparation for the sacrificial system later to be practiced by men. However, we should be cautious about making too much out of this. It was basically an act of God's mercy and tender care for these sinners in need. The doctrine of substitutionary atonement is not specifically taught here. We shall discuss that subject where it is introduced, in Genesis 22.

The third chapter closes by telling us that God blocked the way of access to the Tree of Life so that man by his strength could never attain to it. This suggests that God was here showing to man that man could never regain the life with God which he had lost by his own effort. It could only be by God's grace, as we shall see.

The Tree of Life is in Scripture elsewhere symbolic of eternal life (see especially Rev. 2:7 and 22:2, 14). There, access is given to the Tree of Life only for those who have washed their robes (had their sins cleansed by Christ's blood). Compare Revelation 7:14.

The cherubim who guard the way of access next appear in Exodus 28:18ff, where they are figures hovering over the mercy seat in the holy of holies in the tabernacle. We will note further their significance at that time.

We see man now not as God had created him but as his own sin had marred him. He has become perverted from that good state in which God had made him and has utterly failed to be what God intended him to be. He is not holy, he does not love either God his maker or his fellowmen, and he is not able to live before God.

TRACING THE TWO SEEDS TO THE FLOOD
Genesis 4-8

In spite of man's fallen state into sin and death we see in the words of Eve at the beginning of chapter 4 a real expression of faith as she hopes in the promises of God. She understood Cain to be God's fulfillment of his promise to provide a seed of woman to triumph over the seed of the serpent. She was wrong about Cain but right in looking to God to provide the seed of hope.

In the birth of these two children, Cain and Abel, we have the beginnings of the two lines of descent from Adam: one the line of descent of the seed of the serpent, the unrighteous; and the other the line of descent of the seed of the woman the righteous. Here begin the two families of men which can be traced in a spiritual line throughout the history of man to this very day. All men belong at any given time to the children of God or the offspring of Satan.

The New Testament, as we have shown, teaches us of the two families. It precisely places Abel and Cain in the family of God and the family of Satan respectively (Heb. 11:4; 1 John 3:12).

In the act of making offerings to God, we are told that Cain brought of the fruit of the field and Abel brought of the flocks. There is no indication here that the material of the offering of Cain was displeasing to God. It is too much to assume that God had ordered blood sacrifices only. Scripture nowhere states this in connection with Adam and his generation. The point of concern is not the kind of sacrifices but the heart of the sacrificer. Scripture elsewhere and often allows for grain offerings.

The context here plainly shows that Cain's heart was evil, as I John 3:12 also testifies. Abel's heart was right with God. It was a heart of faith. Therefore, what he did (the offering he made) was acceptable to God.

Later on, God would reject the sacrifices of Israel not because they were not offering correct sactifices in terms of the materials brought to God but because their hearts were far from God (see Isaiah 1:11-20).

Clearly here Cain's heart was evil and it even showed in his attitude toward God and his outward appearance (4:5). Cain was apprised by God of his full responsibility before God not to sin. When he did sin, he would be held fully accountable to God (4:7). Cain's further action shows him indeed to be a child of Satan, a seed of the serpent. He, evidently, first in words, deceived his brother, though we are not told what precisely he said to him. Then later he killed righteous Abel, thus by his lies and murder fully reflecting the nature of his father the devil (4:8).

God in his question to Cain showed that Cain was fully responsible and accountable to God for all of his deeds. We *are* accountable for our brother. All sinners, though rebellious against God, are nevertheless ultimately accountable to him.

Here then we see the beginning of that enmity and hostility between the two seeds which can be traced through both the Old and New Testaments and down through man's history to the present time.

The sign of Cain given to him by God seems to have been unique (4:15). It is vain to try to identify it with any kind of visible mark or distinction on any people in the world today. The description of Cain as a fugitive and wanderer however does aptly identify every sinner in respect to God.

Verses 16-24 trace the line of descent of Cain, the seed of the serpent, for seven generations. Reference to Cain's wife has troubled some. The only possible explanation is that she was his sister (v. 17). Genesis records the names of only three of the children of Adam and Eve, though it tells us that he had numerous sons and daughters, as he lived more than 900 years (Gen. 5:5). It is important to note that among the descendants of Cain were many gifted men: inventors, artists, and developers of cultures. Satan's children have always done well in the world by the standards of men. They have been its leaders for most of history.

The most evident thing however is that, by nature, the children of Satan do not become better but deteriorate. Lamech, the seventh from Adam by Cain, illustrates the depths to which the unregenerate decline, as he not only kills, as Cain his ancestor had done, but far from having any regret, he boasts of his deed before his wives, even making up a little poem to sing in mockery of God's long-suffering shown toward Cain his ancestor (vs. 23-24)! He also is the first recorded bigamist or polygamist (v. 23). Here we see tendencies not only to violate God's will concerning love toward others but also to violate God's purpose in the establishing of the family, one man and one woman joined in flesh as one person.

The rest of the fourth chapter, having now traced Cain's descendants, shows us that God will not be thwarted by the wiles of the devil. God raises up another seed to take the place of slain Abel (v. 25). Again we see Eve's expression of hope and trust in God to supply her needs. In this line of descent, we find men of faith. The expression "they began to call upon the name of the Lord" is a biblical expression denoting faith. We see it elsewhere in Genesis in reference to the faith of Abraham (12:8) and the faith of Isaac (26:25). It is the prophet Joel who declares that "whosoever shall call on the name of the Lord shall be delivered" (Joel 2:32).

We have thus in the chapter which follows a tracing of the line of descent of the faithful in contrast to chapter 4. In the seventh generation from Adam through Seth we have mention of Enoch, who is in great contrast to the Lamech of chapter 4. Enoch walked with God and by God's grace was taken directly to be with God. Hebrews 11:4 tells us that he walked before God in faith and was therefore well-pleasing to God. If Lamech, the seventh from Adam by Cain, shows us the depths to which Satan's children decline; Enoch, the seventh from Adam by Seth, points to the heights to which God's children attain to God's ultimate purpose. By God's grace they attain full sanctification and the privilege of living in God's presence forever.

Though the genealogical sections of Scripture are often by-passed, they show much of the grace of God in dealing with his own. Seth's line is traced to Noah and his sons in the fifth chapter. Focus is, of course, on Noah because of his importance in the chapters that follow. He is the link between Seth and Abraham. The biblical figures here indicate that Seth lived until the days of Noah. Noah's name, like the names of many biblical characters, is significant to us as indicative of the man's character and life. His name means "comfort" (v. 29) and in a time of distress he would be man's comfort and assurance of continued life.

Finally, in regard to the fifth chapter, we need to point out that all of Adam's descendants, even those by Seth, were sinners like Adam. As God had originally made Adam in his own image, so now Adam's children were in his likeness (the likeness of fallen Adam). This doctrine of original sin simply means that all men born into the world are naturally, without the intervening grace of God, sinful and dead in sin as Paul so much later would express it (Eph. 2:1-3). Where faith does appear, it is indicative of the special grace of God at work in that heart. For, as Paul goes on to say, we are saved by grace through faith and this salvation is not of ourselves but it is the gift of God (Eph. 2:8, 9).

In chapter 6 we are introduced to the sons of God and the daughters of men. Intermarriage between the two follows. The question of who these people are has been a subject of discussion for centuries. Many have concluded that the sons of God are some kind of angelic beings and the daughters of men are earthly humans, but Scripture almost everywhere uses the term "sons of God" to describe God's children by faith from among men (Gal. 3:26, John 1:12, 13). Moreover, in the judgment that follows, it is evident that the sins committed are committed by men, not angelic beings. Far more reasonable, therefore, it is to assume that there the term "sons of God" identifies the line of faithful men traced in chapter 5, and is equivalent to the seed of the woman. Therefore "daughters of men" would identify those children of Satan described in chapter 4. The sin then is the intermarriage of God's children with Satan's children, the attempt to erase the enmity that God has established. When God's children make peace with the world and the sinners in it, God's truth is compromised and the church on earth is weakened. Later Paul soberly warns against such intermarriage of believers and unbelievers as detrimental to the whole church (2 Cor. 6:14-18), for it threatens the home, the bulwark of the church.

Again we note that while this was displeasing to God, nevertheless in the eyes of men the resultant generations were noble and mighty (6:4). Warning is therefore given to us not to judge as men judge but rather through the eyes of God's Word. What pleases men is not necessarily pleasing to God.

Beginning in Genesis 6:5 and throughout the next few chapters, through chapter 8, we find the record of God's judgment on the world of that day which, as we noted, Peter mentions in his second epistle.

First, the state of man is given. He is totally wicked and incapable of a thought pleasing to God. He can do only evil continually. The path of sin is always the same. Paul well demonstrates this in Romans 1:18-32. The phrase "it repented the Lord" in verse 6, like similar expressions elsewhere in Scripture, does not mean that God changes his mind or has to admit to error in the sense that men repent (1 Sam. 15:29). It is rather a strong expression frequently used to convey the utter displeasure of God with men. It stresses how completely men have failed to be what God purposed them to be. Neither does it mean that God was here admitting defeat. Instead, God would now intervene in the natural course of events, man having demonstrated that he could not better his lot.

Now we have God's judgment: "I will destroy man whom I have created" (6:7). There are no exceptions to this solemn pronouncement. Yet here we see God's intervening grace. In 6:8 we are told that Noah found grace in the eyes of the Lord. It must be assumed that Noah *naturally* was no exception to other men, but the grace of God took hold of his life and made him different.

In Scripture grace as an act of God is always toward the undeserving sinner. Grace inserted here plainly teaches us that Noah's salvation was not because of his good but rather because God changed him, saving him that he might do good works. The righteousness of Noah mentioned in verse 9, like that of Abraham, and of every child of God among men, is imputed through faith by grace. The good works follow. So Paul states this relationship between grace and faith and good works in Ephesians 2:8-10. Hebrews 11:7 also affirms that Noah's actions were based on his faith. Noah's obedience to God then well demonstrated his faith in God by which he lived (6:22).

In the early part of chapter 7 we find details of those who entered the ark before the flood came. Note that God invites Noah in because he has imputed to him righteousness (v. 1). By virtue of God's invitation to Noah, not only he but his entire household and specified animals enter. The logical explanation for the mention of clean animals here is that after the flood, God would allow men to eat the clean animals. They are saved in larger numbers, therefore, to supply the food necessary after the flood.

Most particularly, in chapter 7 and also in chapter 8, we are told that the nature of the flood, i.e., its sources, are not just rain from heaven. Indeed that is the third and lesser element of the flood. The two major sources are the stored up waters above and below the area where men live as we saw at creation (7:11, 12; 8:2—see Gen. 1:7). Remember, Peter called this the world that then was and which was destroyed. The catastrophic nature of such a release of stored up hydraulic power is beyond our ability to imagine. It caused the great upheavals of the earth that still mystify geologists today.

We learn here also that the flood was total, covering the whole earth. Archaeologists suggest that certain evidence of a great flood is found in Mesopotamia. However, that flood, they contend, was a local flood though of considerable size. It cannot, therefore, be identified with the biblical flood. The biblical flood covered the whole earth (7:19). In this judgment all outside the ark died (7:22, 23).

The eighth chapter tells of God's compassion on Noah as God dried the earth he had flooded. The account of the flood and the drying of the earth is very similar to other Near Eastern accounts of a great flood. This has given rise to the theory that the biblical account is but one of many such stories. A far better assumption is that in the Bible we have the true account as preserved by God for his people while elsewhere in the East the memory of this great distress was preserved, though in imperfect form, distorted by mythology and polytheism.

MAN'S NEW START AND HIS OLD PROBLEM
(Genesis 9-11)

As we begin to read chapter 9, we seem to be at a new beginning. Verse 1 sounds very much like Genesis 1:28, as though God were starting over with man. However, it is not as simple as this. The closing of chapter 8 shows us that man is still very wicked. He does not have the innocence of Eden any longer. Yet he is to continue to have responsibility and bear life on earth. It is a new start but the old sinful nature is very much in evidence.

The curse is also very much in evidence here. Man will not have dominion or be able to subdue the earth as well as God had intended that he should. Creatures will fear him but they will not be submissive (9:2). Now animals will be for food for man, again showing how they bear the curse which fell on all creatures at Adam's fall (Rom. 8:20, 21). In pronouncing the death penalty on all animals to feed sinful man, God was also, by sanctifying the blood of animals, reminding man of the sacredness of life, even that life which mankind so carelessly regarded (Gen. 4:8, 23).

At this point, the Lord established the death penalty for the murderer. The death penalty was not given in a context of disrespect for human life but in a context of the highest respect of God, for the lives even of sinners (9:5, 6). The law was given in the context of man's multiplying and replenishing the earth (9:7) i.e., in a context of life. Consequently the Law Giver had the best intent for mankind in mind.

The covenant mentioned first in 6:18 and now in 9:9 is a covenant with mankind in general (9:17). Noah and his seed here obviously include all men born after Noah. The covenant even includes the animals of creation which were preserved with Noah. Like most biblical covenants, it is for the good of those included. It is established by God, it is unconditional and it has a seal or a sign.

God is the establisher of this covenant to preserve life on earth. Its goal is to prevent men from deteriorating to the state to which they had deteriorated previously, before the flood. He lays no condition on man but commits himself to preserve men from utter destruction by the flood (9:15). Until the day of final judgment, God will never again wipe men off the face of the earth as he did at the flood.

This does not, of course, prevent God from local judgments by flood or by other means. Neither does it say that God will not, in the final day, judge the world. Peter makes it quite clear that he will once again judge the whole world, in 2 Peter 3:7. The sign of this covenant is the bow in the heavens visible both to man and God. It reminds men that God remembers his promise every time the clouds gather, reminiscent of the flood. In essence, the covenant declares that such total destruction as once befell mankind will not occur again until the end of man's history; not because men are better, but because God in his graciousness has so purposed to preserve men so long as time shall continue.

The old problem of man's sinful nature is graphically brought out again in the closing verses of chapter 9. There is no real change in the natural sinful inclinations of man. Even Noah, though righteous in his generation, is nevertheless still plagued by a sinful nature which is not totally subdued. After the flood,

Noah gets drunk, misusing the blessings which God has given him, and consequently lies sprawled in shameful nakedness before his sons, a disgraceful and distasteful figure (9:20, 21).

Ham, one of his sons, also displays his natural tendencies to sin. When he sees his father's nakedness, his reaction is one of ridicule, not love and compassion, which ought to exist between father and son. We are not certain what he told his brothers anymore than we know what Cain said to Abel, but in both cases Scripture disapproves and judgment follows. The tender love and respect of Shem and Japheth is in sharp contrast to the actions of Ham (9:23).

The prophecy which follows this incident pertains not to racial but spiritual history. It posits basically two categories of men. The first are the descendants of Ham (Canaan and his ilk). They are comparable to the descendants of Cain before the flood. They are the unrighteous whose unrighteousness is exemplified by the actions of their father Ham. The specific mention here of Canaan simply shows that the prophecy pertains to his seed as well.

The other category of men are the descendants of Shem, who are comparable to the descendants of Seth before the flood. They are the righteous whose righteousness is exemplified in the actions of Shem.

Canaan the seed of Ham is cursed. In the end, he is a servant of Shem and his descendants. Shem is blessed. The Lord is his God. The whole prophecy is spiritual and has to do with the two families of man just as we saw in the chapters preceding the flood.

But just as before the flood, in the eyes of men, Satan's seed seem to prosper and excel, so now also. In chapter 10 when the seed of Ham are traced, they seem to be anything but servants. Among his descendants we find the greatest ancient world empires: Akkad, Assyria, Phoenicia, Babylon, Egypt, the Hittites. As in all man's history, the offspring of Satan consider themselves the masters of the world. Yet in reality they are the servants of God's children.

We see this fact of who-serves-who illustrated in the way the Egyptians were used to preserve God's people in time of famine and to educate God's servant Moses for leadership of Israel. Later the Egyptians turned over their wealth to the Israelites as they left Egypt. Then God destroyed their armies when they were through serving Israel. Canaan served God's people by the development of the alphabet later used by Moses and his successors to write God's Word for God's people. Canaan also served to develop the land which Israel would take over, fully developed with vineyards and cultivated land and cities already built.

Later Assyria, Babylonia and Persia would rise and fall as God willed to accomplish his purpose for his people, to preserve that remnant who believed. Finally, we see the empire of Alexander the Great spread Greek culture and language throughout the world and Rome establish a world government all in preparation for the coming of Christ and the proclamation of the gospel to the ends of the earth.

None of these peoples and empire leaders had in mind any service to God or to the people of God, but in reality every empire and every nation of men and every effort of all men in inventions and art are used by God's people to the glory of God and for the good of God's people. Thus Ham and his seed are indeed servants to God's children.

Thus we see that the prophecy of Noah does not pertain to the races of men as we know them today nor is it a justification for the subjection of other races to the whites. Far from it! Japheth here represents not a separate category of men but those out of all nations who shall be called into God's family. It is therefore a missionary promise that out of all mankind, the people settled over all the earth, God will continually call a people unto himself.

In the Old Testament times, those of other peoples who joined Israel were few. With the coming of Christ this changed and the gospel spread rapidly to include people from every corner of the earth. These, therefore, are the blessed to dwell in the tents of Shem, i.e., to be a part of Christ's church to whom accrue all of the blessings of God's people forever.

Chapter 10 only briefly traces the descendants of Noah's three sons. First we see Japheth, to whom least attention is here given since his role in redemptive history comes much later. Second we see Ham, of whom we have already spoken above. Finally we see Shem, where the focus of attention is now to be given. It is with Shem that God has chosen to establish the promises and the blessings which ultimately will include men from all the earth.

The beginning of the blessing of God on Shem occurs in an act of God to scatter men over the face of the earth. By this means, God separated a people, the descendants of Shem by Arpachshad, one of his sons (10:22). The occasion of God's act here in chapter 11 is again the sin of man. Men sought to unite against the will of God and obliterate the distinctions which God had set between the righteous and the unrighteous, as was done before the flood. Again, it is apparent that their attempts to unite were motivated by godless people and godless desires. In their aspirations to build a great tower and a city and make a name for themselves, there is no place in their plans for God. "Let us" is their motto (11:3, 4).

God's response to man's "Let us build us a city" (v. 4) was "Let us go down and there confound their language" (11:7).

This act of God was in reality a blessing on men in general. It was an act of God's common grace, because evil, when concentrated, quickly corrupts to the point of destruction, as it did prior to the flood, and as can later be seen in the events at Sodom and Gomorrah. To this scattering of men by the confusion of language, we have the counterpart in the New Testament when God by the gift of tongues by the Holy Spirit at Pentecost united men of differing cultures and languages unto one church of which Christ is the head (Acts chapter 2).

Out of all the people scattered over the face of the earth, God chose one people, one family, that of Shem's son, Arpachshad, for special grace and attention. God watched over his descendants until the time of his beginning to establish a people on earth to be his particular people from among the families of men (11:10-32). Attention focuses on his descendants who are traced to Terah, who by this time was living in Mesopotamia at the ancient city of Ur (11:24-28). Among Terah's sons was one named Abram. The Lord finally called Abram to leave his background and people and become the Lord's child in the midst of an unbelieving world.

THE GROWTH OF
ABRAHAM'S FAITH
Genesis 12-22

It is important to remember the background of which Abram (or Abraham, as he was later called) came. When Abraham was still called Abram and lived in Ur, his father moved to Haran, which was to the northwest of Ur and on the way to Canaan by the most suitable travel route of that day. Terah, however, never got beyond Haran. But God intended that Abraham should. He would have to separate from his family to do so. This act of Abraham to separate from his family and go to Canaan was in itself an act of faith, as the writer to the Hebrews tells us (Heb. 11:8).

We must keep in mind that Abraham's ancestors were by now not worshippers of the Lord but of pagan gods, being intermingled with the unbelief of Ur. Joshua reminds us of this (Josh. 24:2). This means that Abraham's step in faith was against the traditions of his fathers. He had also to leave his father, a most difficult thing to do. The time of the life of Terah indicates that he probably lived on in Haran some 60 years after Abraham left there. All of this shows the great faith of Abraham to leave behind his culture and family and follow God's lead to an unknown world.

It is God who takes the initiative with Abraham as he did with Noah, calling him and promising to bless him. First, God promises to make of Abraham a great nation; but more than this, he is to be blessed by God. The word "blessed" carries with it special meaning of God's special grace. It is used of Adam before the fall and of Noah after the flood and of Abraham and his seed in faith. The Psalmist declares its special meaning for the righteous (Psa. 5:12).

The name of Abraham is singled out for special honor as God will make it great. (Abraham was to become the father of the faithful—Romans 4:11, 12.) Moreover, through the blessings given to Abraham, all the families of the earth would be blessed (12:3). Clearly here we have a promise of missionary proportions as God shows that from the beginning his intent has been to call a people from all the earth to receive his special blessing.

We should pause here to note that all of the great promises of God so far given with gospel implications, contain the hope of the salvation of men. In Genesis 3:15 the concept of a seed is first given, called the seed of the woman. This seed will triumph over the seed of the serpent (Satan). In Noah's prophecy (Gen. 9:25-27), God is identified with one people who are called the descendants of Shem, but room is made in that blessing for Japheth and his family also. Now here in Genesis 12:3 once more, not only one particular family out of Shem is chosen but still, through that family, blessings shall accrue to a vast multitude of peoples in all the earth. God's electing purpose narrows down from all humanity to a race (Shem), to a family (Abraham's); yet the impact of the blessing continues to reach to the ends of the earth.

Hebrews 11:8 tells us that Abraham went by faith. Genesis 12:4 reflects the first act of faith on Abraham's part. If he acted in faith, from where did that faith come? Ephesians 2:8, 9 gives us the only possible answer to the question. Our faith is a gift of God. It can exist only in one who is reborn of God. Further evidence of Abraham's faith is cited in verse 8, where he "called upon the name of the Lord." As we noted in Genesis 4:26, in Scripture this expression means that he exercised his faith toward

God. In Romans 10:12-15, Paul quotes Joel and declares that men call on the Lord only as believers. This is the biblical, if not the common, meaning of the phrase "to call on the name of the Lord."

This then represents for us the beginning of Abraham's faith. From this point we see it grow. Called out of paganism, his faith, though like a mustard seed, grows before our eyes.

Genesis 12:10-20 shows us the frailty of his faith when tested at an early time. Forced to go to Egypt, he seems to have doubted God's ability or willingness to protect him there. Perhaps he was awed by the reputation of this already ancient empire. His act of passing off his wife Sarah as his sister is inexcusable. To try to excuse it is to miss the whole point. His faith was weak and in his weakness he lied and acted the coward. In spite of it however, God protected him and continued to bless him.

In chapter 13 we see his faith emerge in considerable strength. He returned to Canaan and so prospered that he and his nephew Lot could no longer live together. Though Abraham was no doubt the stronger, he nevertheless was quite generous and offered to Lot the choice of the land in which they dwelt. By this he showed that he was not self-seeking. Love of others was already a fruit of the spiritual maturity showing in Abraham's life.

By contrast, Lot appears grasping and self-seeking and spiritually dull. Lot made a bad choice, choosing the apparent worldly prosperity of Sodom. His choice was bad because those people were sinners (13:13).

God was pleased with Abraham's show of faith here as he entrusted his future to God and not to men. Ironically, he promised to Abraham all the land, even what Lot had chosen. Here for the first time a seed is mentioned for Abraham. The promises to Abraham were for him and his seed forever (13:15). It is Paul who later points out that the promise of a seed to Abraham would ultimately culminate in one seed, the Christ, through whom all the blessings would come to fruition (Gal. 3:16). So by the New Testament we see that the seed of the woman of 3:15 and the seed of Abraham of 13:15 terminates in Christ and in those who believe in him.

Abraham is challenged to walk through the whole land which shall be given to his seed. Later Joshua was given a similar promise (Josh. 1:2-4) which became a reality in his day.

As for Abraham, the New Testament writer to the Hebrews tells us that he understood the promises to pertain to more than a literal land of that day. Scripture says, "He looked for the city which hath foundations, whose builder and maker is God" (Heb. 11:10). And again "They desire a better country, that is, a heavenly: wherefore God is not ashamed of them, to be called their God; for He hath prepared for them a city" (Heb. 11:16). In other words, Abraham by faith saw that the promise of a land terminated not in an earthly country but the heavenly eternal city of God and his people. Later it would be symbolized by Jerusalem; but the New Jerusalem from above was really the city of God's people, not earthly Jerusalem. This must be kept in mind today as we see in the return of the Jews to Jerusalem a partial fulfillment of Scripture. God's people are to look for the city coming down from above, not merely for the earthly city. (Compare Gal. 4:25, 26; Heb. 12:22; Rev. 3:12; 21:2, 10.)

Chapter 14 tells us of a most important lesson learned by Abraham in the growth of his faith. The occasion was an attack by some armies from the Mesopotamian area against Canaanite cities, among them, Sodom and Gomorrah, where Lot lived. Lot and most of the citizens of Sodom were taken captive (14:12).

The strength of Abraham was impressive and we see from 14:14 that he had indeed accumulated great wealth and a whole city of people who lived with him. He defeated the enemy however, not by his strength but by the power of God as he was soon to learn (14:15, 16).

As Abraham returned, the whole town, what was left, came out to greet him. Abraham was faced that day by two kings, the king of Sodom and the king of Salem, Melchizedek. The first represented the world and offered him fame and riches and the glory of men. The latter king instead offered praises to God, not Abraham, and taught Abraham that God, and not he, was the rightful hero that day.

Just who Melchizedek was, beyond being the king of Salem and priest of God, we cannot say. He is later identified as a type of Christ (Heb. 7:1f). That day he simply represented God's claim on Abraham.

Confronted on the one hand by the glory and praises of men and their rewards, and on the other hand by the claims of God on his own life, Abraham acted in faith, praising God as Melchizedek had taught him, tithing all which he possessed, and refusing to take anything from the king of Sodom. Abraham was jealous for the name of God (14:20-23). This was an act of his personal faith however, and he would not obligate those who did not have such faith. His faith would cost no one but himself (14:24).

By now, we are impressed with the rapid growth of Abraham's faith. Chapter 15 shows us that God was also pleased. After Abraham had turned his back on the rewards of this world, the Lord reassured him by the words, "I am thy shield and thine exceeding great reward." For whatever meager things of this world God's servant may give up, God compensates in spiritual riches beyond measure.

The one great concern of Abraham at this point was that he presently lacked a seed through whom all of these hopes could be conveyed (15:2). Tablets which have been discovered in the area of Mesopotamia and have been translated, have been found to record the customs of the days in which Abraham had lived in Mesopotamia. They show us that Abraham here expressed the common notion of that time that when one had no child, his servant became his heir, i.e., was adopted as a son. This problem now greatly concerned Abraham.

On the face of it, he found a problem he could not solve. His wife gave him no heir but God promised him a seed and a multitude of heirs (15:5). The response of Abraham to this supernatural promise of God was to believe in the Lord. That expression of faith pleased God and was reckoned or imputed to Abraham for righteousness. Paul later shows that indeed all who stand righteous before God and therefore are justified in his sight, are so by faith, as with Abraham (Rom. 4:3f., Gal. 3:6f.). Here then is established the great principle of faith-righteousness as over against works-righteousness. None is acceptable to God by his works, only by faith can we please God (Heb. 11:6).

Here a word needs to be said about the meaning of the biblical term, *faith*. The root word used here in the Hebrew Bible is a word which has the sense of something quite strong and certain and secure, like a man's arms cradling a baby (Num. 11:12) or the pillars of a building (2 Kings 18:16). In the passive form it means "to be made firm or sure or established" (Isa. 7:9). In the causative form it means "to cause to be certain or sure or firm." This latter form is in the Bible the common term for "to believe," i.e., "to cause to be certain, sure."

That same root was often used by Jesus in the New Testament when he would stress the certainty of a thing. In our English Bible he is often recorded as saying, "verily, verily." The word he used was this same Hebrew word. We too use this Hebrew word each time we pray and often at the end of our hymns. We say "amen," which is the same Hebrew word which means "certainty" and in one form means "to believe."

All of this is to say that the biblical concept of faith is not uncertainty but certainty. Some may say, "I believe it is true but I'm not sure." In biblical terms, this is an impossibility. To believe is to be sure, a certainty based not on human reasoning but on the authority of God's Word. When it says Abraham believed in the Lord, it means he was certain of the promises which God had given him based on the authority of God's Word.

In the context of this great affirmation of Abraham's faith, God gives to him a covenant (15:8-21). The covenant includes the revelation of suffering, redemption from captivity and rich inheritance in the land (vv. 13, 14, 18-20). Those experiences through which his seed would go would reflect the redemptive work of God for each of his people, when he brings each of us from sin and death to redemption in Christ and on to eternal inheritance. The 15th chapter then contains in the kernel much which points to the whole redemptive history of man.

After the great expression of Abraham's faith given in chapter 15, it is with disappointment that we read in the next chapter of the weakness of his faith. In the affair of Sarah's handmaid Hagar, Abraham did not act in faith.

Again Abraham, still very much a product of his culture, resorted to a practice commonly known from ancient writings, that of having a child by the servant of his wife. It was a human solution to the problem which Abraham had found in 15:2. It was not however of faith and what is not of faith is sin (Rom. 14:23).

In many respects the sin of Abraham here was like that of Adam. He did not heed God's word, he did not seek God's will and he let his wife lead him in this spiritual decision. He intended to help God but in the end brought misery on all concerned: his wife, Hagar, Ishmael, himself, and even on Isaac.

Sarah herself soon discovered the sin of what they had done and she reacted wrongly (16:6).

Yet God was not frustrated by the show of sin in Abraham's family. He did not lower his standards at all for Abraham but again he reiterated his goal for his children: "I am God almighty; walk before me, and be thou perfect" (17:1). God never, in all of his dealings with men, lowers his standards to accommodate the frailties of man. He always moves men on toward that high goal which he has set and by his grace all of his children shall in the end attain it. We are to be holy and without blemish before him in love. Every time we, as his children, fall short of this, God calls us back to that high goal which he *will accomplish* in us. Long afterward, Jesus, addressing his disciples, says: "Ye therefore shall be perfect, as your heavenly father is perfect" (Matt. 5:48). There is no higher goal. Paul also well expresses this in Philippians 3:12f: "Not that I have already obtained, or am already made perfect: but I press on, if so be that I may lay hold on that for which also I was laid hold on by Christ Jesus . . . I press on toward the goal unto the prize of the high calling of God in Christ Jesus."

Abraham fails here but God does not give up on him. He renews the promise and gives him a new name (17:5). Now with the covenant, God gives a sacrament, circumcision of the flesh, as an outward sign of that inward work of cleansing done by God. Here an important concept is introduced. Since the promises were not only to Abraham but to his seed, all the seed are to receive the seal or sacrament of the covenant promise. The outward circumcision did not save them. What was necessary for salvation was the inward circumcision of the heart, the cleansing of their hearts by God.

This was always the meaning of the fleshly circumcision. It was an outward sign of an inner work which only God could accomplish. To give it to one's child was to confess that only God could save that child by cleansing his heart. It was given to every child of believers who, by it, professed their faith in God and expressed the need of their children for the same cleansing. Circumcision of the heart is always the essential (Deut. 10:16; 30:6, Jer. 4:4; 9:25-26; Rom. 2:28-29).

The sacrament of circumcision in the Old Testament is in some ways comparable to baptism in the New Testament. Both are outward signs of inner work of the Holy Spirit necessary for man's salvation. In both, the cleansing of the heart is symbolized. Compare Hebrews 9:14; 10:22; Acts 2:38-41; Titus 3:4-7.

The action of Abraham in this time again shows that men of faith can falter. He pleads for Ishmael to be the seed of promise but God insists that it is Sarah who will bear the seed of promise. God gives the yet unborn child the name Isaac (17:19). This shows that to God the seed does matter. Not just any seed will do. All the true children of Abraham are chosen by God and the seed of promise terminates in Christ. God's plan for a people can only succeed by God's purpose and will. The unwise efforts and pleas of Abraham cannot alter the purpose of God.

The continued doubt of Sarah is seen in chapter 18 when Sarah laughs at hearing that she, who is too old from the natural point of view to bear a child, would indeed bear Isaac (18:12). Her son's name Isaac would always remind her of her unbelief that day. The name Isaac means "laughter." In essence, she and Abraham here had to learn that nothing is too hard for the Lord (18:14).

The incident at Mamre introduced in chapter 18, verse 1, tells of one of the most significant judgments of God in the Old Testament, second only to the flood. It is the judgment against Sodom and Gomorrah.

The three men who came to Abraham (18:2) were later identified as the Lord in some human form together with two angels (18:33; 19:1). Such anthropomorphic appearances of God in the history of men are rare. The occasion of this one is God's declaration of his intent for Abraham and his family on the one hand, and his purpose to judge evil on the other hand. These matters are introduced in Genesis 18:16.

The major subject of Genesis 18:16 through chapter 19 is the judgment on Sodom and Gomorrah. However, inserted into this account is that important revelation concerning God's intent and purpose for the believer and his family. We shall look at this first. It is found in verse 19.

On the basis of God's covenant with Abraham and his seed, God as though talking with himself or with the two others there, expresses his will for Abraham. He declares that he has known Abraham for a specific end or purpose. The word "known" means more than "to be acquainted with." It carries the full impact of choosing. That is, "I have chosen him to the end that . . ."

Next the purpose is given: "that he may command his children and household, that they may keep the way of the Lord, to do righteousness and justice, that the Lord may bring upon Abraham that which he hath spoken of him." Most significant here is the parental responsibility established in the believing home. Parents are to instruct their families in obedience to the Lord, i.e., the will of the Lord. This will is here for the first time expressed in terms of doing righteousness and justice. We shall see that these two words are hereafter used continually to express that will which God has for his people. They summarize God's will for his children. Only as the children reflect God's will, will God bring to pass his good blessings on them. In other words, righteousness and justice shall mark the lives of the children of God.

We have already seen that righteousness in the lives of God's children can come only on the basis of their faith. No works of their own are righteous unless they have first trusted in the Lord. To do righteousness therefore is to be a believer who, by faith, lives before God. All that the believer does in faith will be reckoned as righteous in God's sight, that is, acceptable. As for the meaning of the word justice, we shall consider this in another place.

The Lord shared with Abraham that day his purpose to destroy wicked Sodom. The state of Sodom at this time was comparable to that of the world before the Flood. But Abraham had no interest in Sodom because of the righteous ones who were living there (18:23). His plea to spare Sodom on the basis of a certain number of righteous people there is a reasonable one, but he was to learn an important lesson on evangelism that day. In the last analysis, the task of the believer in a world which is under judgment is not to try to save that world but to call men out of it. The Lord will judge the unrighteous. The world is stored up for judgment (2 Peter 3:7). As Peter said at Pentecost, "Save yourselves from this crooked generation" (Acts 2:40).

The wickedness of Sodom is seen in chapter 19 when Lot, by contrast, shows that he is God's child, displaying concern and love for these strangers (the two angels) (19:1-3). There is no evidence that at that point he knew them to be angels from God. The men of Sodom exposed their evil desires and intent for carnal knowledge of the strangers (19:5). The term "know" here, as often in Scripture, means "to know sexually." Lot's offer of his two daughters may seem drastic to us but Lot's intent was to protect these guests under his roof and to prevent more crime.

When Lot learned who they were and heard their call to get out of Sodom before it was destroyed, he lingered. The folly of Lot's choice now becomes evident. He was righteous, a child of God (2 Pet. 2:7, 8) but he had chosen to indulge in the worldly life. Jesus' words later would apply to Lot: "Lay not up for yourselves treasures on earth" (Matt. 6:19f.). It was hard for Lot to leave these worldly things (19:16). What is more, it was no atmosphere in which to bring up his family. Some of his own daughters apparently intermarried with unbelievers and were too involved in the world to hear their father's plea (19:14).

Only two unmarried daughters and his wife began to leave with him. Even his wife did not succeed in extricating herself from the lures of Sodom.

In 19:26, we are told that Lot's wife looked back, in disobedience to the angels. We should not consider this a mere act of curiosity on her part. The word used here for "looked back" is rare in the Hebrew Bible. It has a special sense of "looking in trust or expectation or longing." She, by this look, revealed her heart's desire to stay. She loved the world too much. This same word is used in the incident of the brazen serpent to which the Israelites had to look to be saved in the wilderness (Num. 21:9). The word is also used in connection with Jonah when he was in distress in the midst of the sea and looked in trust toward the

Lord's holy Temple (Jonah 2:4). In all cases, the sense of the word is "to look longingly toward," and this was the sin of Lot's wife. She looked longingly toward the sinful city of Sodom.

Lot and his two daughters were saved that day, not by their will but by God's mercy (19:16-29). The line of Lot in the family of God quickly runs out. In fact, his own sons, born to him by his own daughters, represent not those in the family of Abraham but those who later would be Israel's enemies (19:37, 38).

Chapters 20 and 21 describe two final strides in the growth of Abraham's faith. The incident in chapter 20 can only be described as a lapse in his faith. It gives evidence that there were still flaws there. Apparently in his growth in faith, he had failed to realize God's presence everywhere. Where God was not honored, Abraham apparently concluded, God was not present (20:11). His sin, like that described in chapter 12, is not excusable. Whatever is not of faith is sin.

In chapter 21, however, God teaches Abraham to depend on him always, by providing that long-awaited son Isaac. Abraham learns here a great lesson in the dependability of God (21:1). The birth of Isaac opened old wounds and reminded Abraham of less trusting days when, outside of God's will, he had acted in haste to have a child by Hagar. Now this earlier act of folly clashed with his present blessings from God and the result, as it always is with God's people when they act in unbelief, was sorrow (21:9-14).

In this time of sorrow, no doubt Abraham's faith grew. He learned obedience through suffering. He was now ready for his faith to be tested. This brings us to chapter 22.

Chapter 22 tells of the testing of Abraham's faith. It was a most difficult test. We have seen Abraham's growth in faith not as a smooth, steady incline upward, but jagged with setbacks from time to time. This is typical of the growth of faith in every believer. Now, for God's glory, that faith must be tested because the Lord had chosen Abraham to be the example of all believers.

The command to which Abraham must respond was most difficult. He was to offer his son as a sacrifice to God. The book of Hebrews tells us that he responded in great faith (Heb. 11:17-19). So well had Abraham learned his lesson about the dependability of God that he now believed that God, who had promised to bless his seed, would even raise Isaac from the dead should he now die (Heb. 11:19). Abraham never demonstrates any doubt about this matter at all.

When Isaac asked the question concerning the lamb for the burnt offering, again in faith his father answered prophetically:

"God will provide himself the lamb for the burnt offering" (22:7, 8). It was prophetic because it laid hold of the ancient promise of God to provide by the woman the seed to defeat Satan. And it looked ahead to Isaiah 53, that vivid description of God's lamb who would die for God's people. No doubt, John the Baptist had this prophecy in mind when, on one occasion, he said to his followers, "Behold the lamb of God, that taketh away the sin of the world!" (John 1:29). Whether Abraham understood this or how much he did understand we cannot say but surely his prophecy that day did point to the coming work of Christ.

The Lord's intervention in Abraham's act of obedience (22:12) indicates that it was never God's intent for Abraham to carry out the sacrifice but it was God's intent that he should be willing to do so. Here also, as though in partial fulfillment of Abraham's prophecy, God provides a ram as a substitution for Isaac (22:13). That day for the first time the major principle of animal sacrifice was given to Abraham. That principle was substitutionary atonement. Whatever animal sacrifices had meant to the offerer before, they now showed God's people that God would provide a sacrifice as a substitute for God's people so that they would not have to die for their sins.

Once more, in this most appropriate place, God renewed his covenant with Abraham in terms of the seed. The words "Thy seed shall possess the gate of his enemies" is a clear link with Genesis 3:15, the triumph of the seed of the woman over the seed of the serpent.

THE TRANSITION PERIOD, THE DEATH OF ABRAHAM AND THE LIFE OF ISAAC
Genesis 23—28:9

These chapters can be called the transition period. Isaac's life lacks the color and interest of Abraham and Jacob. He is somewhat like a valley between two mountain peaks. For Abraham, these chapters are somewhat anticlimactic. Chapter 23 relates Abraham's quest for a burial place for Sarah and shows his faith in God's promise. He chose to be buried in the land which God had promised him, though as yet he did not own any of it but was a stranger there still.

Chapter 24 tells of his seeking a wife for Isaac and introduces the family of Laban which would play a most significant role in Jacob's life. It also stresses the comprehension of Abraham concerning God's desires for a faithful seed. Abraham saw in Canaan no one fit to be the wife of this child of promise which God had given to him, for the people there were very wicked. He shared God's concern for a faithful seed and sent to his homeland for an appropriate wife for Isaac. But note that she had to be willing to come, leaving her family as Abraham had done, if she was to qualify as Isaac's wife.

The early part of chapter 25 relates the balance of Abraham's life and his death. Since Abraham lived to be 175 years old (25:7) and Sarah died at the age of 127, apparently Abraham had a rather long life with Keturah, his second wife (Abraham was just ten years older than Sarah and therefore 137 at the time of her death—see Gen. 17:17). Yet the whole latter part of Abraham's life is passed over in a few sentences. Isaac alone is the seed of promise, though Abraham had many other children (25:2).

The life of Isaac overlaps that of Abraham on the one hand and that of Jacob on the other. Very little is told of him exclusively. In fact, one chapter (26) is about all there is. From this chapter it can be surmised that Isaac was like his father in many ways. He made the same mistakes (26:1-11) but mostly he followed in his father's footsteps. Verse 18 well summarizes his life. He digged the wells his father had digged, and he named them by the names his father had given them. Although Isaac led a rather lacklustre life he is to be commended in that he followed in the footsteps of a great man. He was God's chosen seed. The Lord renewed with him the promises he had made to Abraham long before (26:23-24), and Isaac responded with the same faith which was shown by his father (26:25). (Compare 12:8.) The rest of Isaac's life is intertwined with that of Jacob and Esau, his two sons, to whom we shall now turn.

JACOB—
FROM SINNER TO SAINT
Genesis 25:19—33:20

We find often in Scripture that the Lord has, for a time, withheld children from godly women to test their faith. We saw this in the case of Sarah; we see it now with Rebecca. We shall see it too of Rachel and later of Hannah the mother of Samuel and also Elizabeth the mother of John the Baptist.

In each case the seed was a blessing and in each case the Lord proved himself faithful to those who looked to him for a seed. So here in 25:19f., we read of the birth of Jacob and Esau.

When God promised the two children to Rebecca, he told her of two nations to come. God himself made a choice between the two, making one greater than the other (v. 23). The phrase "the elder shall serve the younger" recalls the prophecy of Noah (Gen. 9:25-27). So again we have the distinction between the children of God and the children of Satan. This time the distinction is made between two who are children of the same human parents and even in the same conception!

It is God who makes a distinction and who chooses Jacob and not Esau. Paul, in Romans 9:6ff., discusses the important lessons of the election of God from this incident. Being of the fleshly seed (descendant) of Abraham does not make one God's child (Rom. 9:7, 8). Salvation is based on God's promises and according to God's will.

The "purpose of God" (Rom. 9:11) that he should have a people is based on God's election of some from the state of deadness in sin to eternal life (Rom. 9:11—compare Eph. 2:1-3). None can be saved by his works since the nature of all men is corrupt. Salvation comes only by the grace of God who works in the hearts of those whom he elects, to bring them from spiritual death to life in Christ (Eph. 2:4-9).

The differing spiritual natures of the two boys, Esau and Jacob, become evident in an incident recorded of their early life (25:27-34). Isaac's preference for Esau was based not on the revealed will of God (v. 23) but on fleshly desire (v. 28), and in the end it would result in great pain and sorrow to him personally and to his family.

The incident recorded here tells of a day when Esau desired for himself some pottage Jacob had prepared. His carnal-minded orientation shows when he is ready to sell his birthright for this moment of physical pleasure. It was a childish transaction, that could have no real validity in and of itself, but it revealed Esau's nature. The Bible says he despised his birthright (v. 34).

Jacob also does not appear too well in the incident. He seems to act selfishly in withholding something his brother needed. Nevertheless he did reveal a deep sense of and appreciation for the spiritual heritage of his father and grandfather (25:31).

This whole episode revealed Esau to be profane, i.e., a child of Satan in the family of the children of God. Later evidence of his nature reveals the same thing. When he chose wives, they were Canaanites (26:34, 35; 36:2, 3). When Jacob displeased him, his heart was filled with murder (27:41), reminiscent of another brother-murderer, Cain. The writer to the

Hebrews sums up for us the nature of Esau—profane (Heb. 12:16).

We reiterate here that God did not call and choose Jacob because he was naturally good. God chose Jacob according to his own good pleasure and remade Jacob the sinner into Israel the saint.

Jacob the sinner is shown in chapter 27. Isaac's continued stubbornness was the occasion for the unhappy incidents recorded here. Isaac chose Esau to bless, though God had not chosen him (27:1). This sin was compounded by the sin of Rebecca and Jacob plotting to steal the blessing from Esau. She knew God's will but she lacked patience and faith to wait for God. As Sarah and Abraham had done, she tried to help God, and to do so by devious means. Jacob was fully implicated in the sin, apparently fearing only getting caught (v. 12).

Rebecca's easy response to Jacob's fear, calling the curse on herself, brought more repercussions than she expected. She actually never again saw her son Jacob after this incident. What seemed to be a separation of only a few days (v. 44) turned into twenty years! By that time, she presumably was dead.

Jacob's sins mounted one upon another. First, he lied to his father (vv. 18, 19), then he blasphemed the name of God, attempting to implicate God in his own evil (v. 20). The pretense succeeded and Jacob received the blessing which God had intended for him but he received it by sinful means. When Isaac learned what had happened, he finally submitted to God's will (v. 33). Esau, as we mentioned, was not so submissive (v. 41).

Isaac's compliance is shown in 28:1f. When he sent Jacob away, he renewed the blessing to him, this time willingly. Thus Isaac seemed to have blamed himself rather than Jacob for the misdeed. The book of Hebrews tells us that Isaac blessed Jacob and Esau in faith (Heb. 11:20). Meantime, Esau continued in his carnal ways (28:9).

Jacob left Canaan far from a spiritual giant. At Bethel, he encountered God face to face in a dream while all alone (28:12, 13). The ladder here seen by Jacob is later alluded to as a type of Christ (John 1:51). The point here seems to be that God reaches down where man is in his need. Jacob fled in fear from Esau and was a sinner and was alone. God reached down to him where he was and made known his love of Jacob (vv. 13-15). In his words to Jacob, he gives both comfort and promise and this is the blessing that really counts, what God and not man gives.

Jacob's response leaves much to be desired. He sought to bargain with God in what seems to be a prideful manner—"If God will be with me . . . then the Lord will be my God . . . and of all . . . I will surely give the tithe unto thee" (vv. 20-22). How greatly this reaction of Jacob contrasts with Abraham's spiritual reaction to God's mercy (14:20).

Jacob the deceiver met his match and more than his match in his uncle Laban, with whom he stayed in Mesopotamia. Laban outwitted him coming and going, as chapters 29 and 30 reveal. There is something of poetic justice in the way, time and again, Jacob was deceived and forced to stay some twenty years as a slave to his uncle. Nevertheless, in the time of trial Jacob learned to trust in God and not in himself. He saw that in spite of Laban's deceits and without Jacob's trickery, God prospered him (31:7-13).

When Jacob fled with his two wives (31:17f.), Laban chased him and caught him. Again God intervened to prevent a clash between the two men. Archaeology helps us to understand the action of Rachel in stealing her father's gods. According to prevalent custom in Mesopotamia, the child who possessed such family gods had a claim on the inheritance. This time Jacob himself was innocent.

Again in Jacob's encounter with Laban he expressed his complete faith in God (31:38-42). When the two men finally parted ways, they erected a border marker between the two peoples to remind each not to pass over that border to wrong the other. Jacob called it Mizpah, or "Watchtower." Verse 49 is not a benediction, though it is sometimes so used. The context shows that these two men are not expressing to one another good will, but saying in essence, "God keep an eye on you while I can't watch you so you don't wrong me."

No sooner was Jacob free of the pursuit of Laban than he received news of Esau's approach to annihilate Jacob (32:1f.). In this moment, blocked from retreat back to Mesopotamia by his uncle Laban and faced with a hostile brother ahead of him, Jacob reached the heights of his spiritual stature. His prayer in 32:9 to 12 expresses a spirit of great humility and trust. His faith is now like the faith of Abraham. He does not hope or trust in his own cleverness now, but only in God's mercy. He bases his prayer on the promises of God which he recalls (32:12).

Alone that night, he had a strange experience with a man who wrestled with him all night (v. 22ff.). That night he was given a new name—Israel, meaning "he who strives (or wrestles) with God." The reason given for this new name is that Jacob had striven with men and God, and had prevailed. He had won over men, his enemies, not by his own cleverness but by his faith in God. He had won with God, not by his bargains but by his humility and submission, the only way we can ever "win" with God.

In summary we can say that God chose Jacob as he does all of his children, not because they are naturally good but because of his good purpose and will for them. He then remakes these sinners whom he has called to be what he desires them to be. As we review Jacob's life, we see how, by his trials and difficulties, God burned out of him all pride.

The encounter between Esau and Jacob in chapter 33 reveals that God indeed took care of all Jacob's enemies, even Esau. It also reveals once more the materialistic orientation of Esau. Esau expressed in verse 9 that he had enough and therefore was satisfied (with the possessions he owned). All along, apparently, his great concern had been that Jacob had cheated him out of his material blessings. When, however, he saw that this was not the case and that he had plenty of material things, he no longer desired to kill Jacob. Would that he had felt the loss of the spiritual blessings such as Jacob received, but he did not. He *was* profane.

JACOB'S CHILDREN, THE FAMILY OF GOD
Genesis 34—50

The last section of Genesis relates various episodes in the lives of Jacob's children. Jacob is still living but he is in the background now. The theme of this section may well be the question—Who shall have preeminence among the sons of Jacob? As each is tested, this question comes to the fore.

The first test of God's children, the sons of Jacob, comes in the affair of Dinah recorded in chapter 34. In her apparent curiosity, she became quite friendly with the Canaanite daughters of the city of Shechem. One of the young men there, also called Shechem, lay with her and fell in love with Dinah. The brothers of Dinah were rightly angered when they learned of the matter (34:7).

The proposition of Shechem's father for Israel's family to intermarry with the Canaanites was of course contrary to God's will (v. 9f.). We recall the sin of God's children prior to the flood and remember also Esau's sin in marrying Canaanites. Abraham had been very careful to avoid such a thing in respect to his own son Isaac. However, the brothers were equally wrong in their lies and deception of the men of Shechem (v. 13). Particularly implicated were Simeon and Levi, the second and third sons of Jacob (vv. 25-26). In short succession, the sons of Jacob committed lies, murder and theft (34:27-29), all without their father's consent (v. 30).

In spite of this, God nevertheless protected Jacob's family as they had to continue to dwell in the land of Canaan (35:5).

Chapter 35 contains several other things of note: the death of Deborah, Rebecca's nurse (v. 8); the birth of Benjamin, Jacob's last son (v. 18); and the death of Jacob's beloved Rachel (v. 19).

Perhaps in these anxious times, Reuben, the firstborn of Jacob, felt insecure and laden with responsibility. For whatever reason, we do read that he lay with his father's concubine. This act, familiar to us from other portions of Scripture, evidences the intent of the one who takes his lord's concubines to be head of the family or the land. It was therefore an arrogant act, not merely carnal lust. Thus by this time the three first sons of Jacob: Reuben, Simeon and Levi all had acted in a manner so as to raise serious questions about their fitness to be leaders of God's people.

Chapter 36 is given exclusively to the tracing of Esau's descendants, showing us that they now became a separate people from the Israelites. God had separated the two men while they were still in the womb. Each was on the way to being a whole nation: Jacob became the Israelites, Esau became the Edomites. Both nations have long histories in the land but they are quite different. A final account of Edom is expressed in the words of the prophet Obadiah, much later.

With chapter 37 we begin a new account, the story of Joseph, the predominant character to the end of the book, and of his brothers. The younger days of Joseph are rather inauspicious. We are told that he was his father's favorite (v. 3) but also something of a tattler on his brothers (v. 2). All of this quite naturally built up resentment in the hearts of the other brothers. Joseph's brazen relating of dreams about his lording it over not only his brothers but his parents as well did not help matters (v. 5f.). Added to this, we have the folly of Jacob, who sent Joseph to his brothers while they were far away from home. Here you have all the ingredients of a tragedy which indeed occurred.

God's intervention here by way of Reuben, the older son,

prevented the murder of their brother which they had contemplated. However, when they sold Joseph to the Ishmaelites who were traveling to Egypt, they never expected to see him again (v. 28). In this unsavory episode, two brothers stand out for some commendation: Reuben because he tried to save Joseph; and Judah because he prevented the murder of his brother (v. 26). But all were implicated in the lie which they told to their father (vv. 29ff.).

We will skip chapter 38 for the present, to trace the career of Joseph a little farther. Chapter 39 picks up the narrative and relates how he prospered in Egypt. It was a time of testing for young Joseph. He was handsome, strong-looking and appealing to his master's wife (39:7). When she sought to seduce Joseph, his answer revealed the deep faith which he possessed. To Joseph, having an affair with his master's wife was not merely a question of social impropriety but indeed a sin against God (v. 9).

Though he suffered for his stand, God compensated Joseph for his losses by blessing him in prison (39:21). In the providence of God, a way of escape from prison was provided when his reputation as an interpreter of dreams reached the king. Again we see that Joseph never acted for self-gain but always to glorify God (40:8, 41:16). We see a different man now from the 17-year old noted in chapter 37:2. God remembered and richly and highly exalted this man from the status of a prisoner in jail to be second in the land under Pharaoh (41:37f.).

This man of thirty now (41:46) was a man of authority and, by God's help, an able administrator to preserve Egypt in the time of the famine of which God had spoken in Pharaoh's dream (41:53-57).

Before going on with the account of Joseph's encounter with the brothers, let us now return to chapter 38, which tells of an episode in the life of Judah, one of Joseph's brothers who is the fourth son of Jacob. In this chapter we see Judah in a very unpleasant light. He married a Canaanite, contrary to God's will (38:2). He failed to rear his own children properly, resulting in their acts which displeased the Lord and brought their death (vv. 6-10). And he neglected the needs of his daughter-in-law, Tamar (vv. 11f.). As if that were not enough, he continued to lust after the harlots of the land, and even had an affair with his own daughter-in-law who had tricked him into providing her a seed.

Amazingly, in spite of this series of shameful acts on Judah's part, God humbled Judah (v. 26) and gave him by Tamar a son through whom God would later send blessings on Israel, Perez (38:29).

When the famine came of which God had forewarned Pharaoh by Joseph, the family of Jacob together with all in the land began to suffer. In the providence of God, therefore, the sons of Jacob went to Egypt and had to face Joseph, whom they thought to see no more. They did not recognize him because having been sold to slavery when he was a young boy, he was now a mature man (42:6f).

Joseph's game of cat and mouse with his brothers was doubtlessly the will of God. It was a time for their testing now as Joseph had formerly been tested. It is evident that the brothers, feeling the pressure which Joseph put upon them, showed signs of repentance and remorse for their past acts (42:21).

When the brothers returned to Jacob without Simeon and told him that the lord of the land demanded that they bring Benjamin back if they hoped ever to see Simeon again, Jacob naturally poured out the stored up bitterness in his soul (42:36).

At this point, once more Reuben, the eldest brother, was tested and failed. His response to his father's needs on this occasion can only be called cruel (42:37). He failed to persuade his father by his crude measures. Again Reuben showed that he was no leader of God's people.

At this time, Judah emerged to lead his brothers as the predominant one in the family. By contrast to Reuben, we see Judah compassionate and self-sacrificing, ready to be a surety for Benjamin, ready to lay down his life for his brother out of his love for his father (43:8, 9). Judah therefore shows spiritual qualities completely lacking in the others. From this point on, the phrase "Judah and his brethren" is frequent, indicating the new role of leadership which Judah had now acquired (44:14).

The spiritual growth of Judah is made evident in his encounter with Joseph, who is still unknown to him, in the matter of Benjamin's apparent misdeed (44:18-34). Judah fulfilled his promise to his father and showed his great love for both his father and Benjamin. He showed too the great change in attitude that had taken place in the brothers who once could coldly see their brother Joseph be sold to slavery. Now Judah was ready and willing to offer his life for Benjamin while thinking that Benjamin had done wrong (44:32-34).

Joseph too shows great change. The rather proud and vain young man of seventeen is now spiritually matured and humbled (45:5-8). His insight into the sovereignty of God in his life and that of his brothers (45:7-8), is comparable to Peter's declaration at Pentecost (Acts 2:23, 24). Peter was able to see that though wicked men with wicked hands had crucified the Lord of Glory, it had been part of God's purpose, for the ultimate good of God's people.

The blessing of Jacob after his arrival in Egypt and renewed fellowship with Joseph, is a summary prophecy reflecting much of what we have already seen (ch. 49). Reuben, Simeon and Levi are eliminated from preeminence in the family of Jacob (49:2-7) because of the serious flaws in their character. Attention centers on Judah who is exalted as leader (v. 8). Moreover, the prediction of his triumph over his enemy seems to refer to the promise in Genesis 3:15, indicating that from him the long-awaited seed shall come (49:8). The figure of the lion in verse 9 is later applied to God's people (Micah 5:2-8) and more specifically to the Christ of the house of David (Rev. 5:5).

Verse 10, which makes reference to the sceptre in the house of Judah, clearly foretells the coming of rule by kings among God's people. The name Shiloh may refer to the King of Kings. The word "Shiloh" may be translated "him to whom it belongs," i.e., the kingdom of God. Reference in verses 11 and 12 to blood and the red color may also have Messianic overtones and allude to the cross. One thing is sure. This passage gives to Judah the preeminence among the people of God and looks to Judah for the Deliverer.

After Jacob's death, the brothers' fears of Joseph's revenge were quickly allayed by Joseph himself in his words of comfort to them (50:19-21). The insight which Joseph had gained about the meanings of his own experience in the way the Lord had worked all for good, can appropriately summarize the whole lesson of God's people in this period of the Patriarchs—"God meant it for good, to bring to pass, as it is this day, to save much people alive."

While the people stayed in Egypt, the promise of God to Abraham became the hope of Israel.

We can see then in the beginning of God's working with his people that God's purpose to have a people holy, without blemish, before him in love, was not thwarted by the failures of men. God chose and called sinners, made them his children and molded them into what he desired them to be. From Seth to Noah, from Shem to Abraham, from Isaac to Jacob to Judah, God moved steadily on toward that Seed who should come to triumph over the enemies of God and God's people. God's good purpose was never overcome by the evils and failures of men. This first book is a great testimony to God's sovereign grace.

THE PEOPLE OF GOD REDEEMED
Exodus-Deuteronomy

REDEMPTION FROM EGYPT
Exodus 1-19

JACOB'S FAMILY had gone down to Egypt in the time of Joseph some seventy souls strong. The going down had been according to God's word long before to Abraham (Gen. 15:13). As Jacob had gone to Egypt to see his son, the Lord assured him that God would go with him and make a great nation of him there (Gen. 46:3). To Abraham, Jacob and Joseph, God gave assurance that he would bring his people back to Canaan (15:14; 46:4; 50:24).

Now, after several hundred years, the people are still in Egypt and in a state of slavery. In spite of this, God has richly blessed them and made them grow (1:7). As God blessed the people of

Israel, the Egyptians became increasingly hard on them. The reason given is the change in monarchies in Egypt. Those who favored Joseph and the Israelites were no longer ruling (1:8). The reference to a new king may refer to a new dynasty in Egypt, a new ruling family. Some believe that the rulers, when Joseph and his family came to Egypt, were the Hyksos, a Semitic people who did rule Egypt for a time. Being Semitic, they would be more favorable to the Semitic Israelites than would the native Egyptians.

At any rate, the Egyptians now were hostile to Israel and cruelly enslaved them (1:10-14). Their cruelty reached great extremes, even to the extermination of all male children (1:15f.) but the faithful in Israel prevented this (1:17).

One notable act of prevention to protect her son was the act of Moses' mother. This godly woman, having no strength herself to protect her infant boy, entrusted him to God, putting him in a papyrus boat on the Nile River (2:1ff.). By God's providence, this entrustment to the Lord was blessed and Moses was not only saved from being killed but he was brought up in the palace of the king. Above this, he was cared for by his own mother. Thus Moses was at the same time exposed to the best education possible in the ancient world together with the spiritual nurture of his own faith by his own mother. God had special work for this child to do.

In chapter 2 we are told of an abortive attempt by Moses to set his people free from their oppression (2:11f.). What he did, he did as an act of faith. The writer to the Hebrews tells us this (Heb. 11:24-26). Moses however did what he did abortively and was forced to flee Egypt. He was not yet ready for the great task God had for him, to liberate his people. He still needed some years of humbling and learning patience to trust in God alone. The Lord provided a place in the wilderness and circumstances for Moses to grow to that spiritual maturity which God required (2:16-22).

God in the meantime had not forgotten Israel or her suffering (2:24). He was preparing a way of deliverance in the person of the now matured man Moses (ch. 3).

Moses was a shepherd. It is notable how many of God's great leaders were shepherds before they led God's people. Of course, we think of Abel, Abraham, Isaac and Jacob, all of whom tended flocks. Later David would learn many of the basic truths of God's watchcare for his people while serving as a shepherd himself (See Psalm 23). Amos the prophet was also a shepherd and the prophets frequently referred to the leaders of Israel as shepherds. In the New Testament Jesus refers to himself as the

Good Shepherd and as an example of what all of God's appointed leaders of the people should be (John 10). It is Peter who refers to leaders of the church as shepherds of the flock (I Pet. 5:1-4. Compare Acts 20:28f.).

When Moses was about eighty years old, God encountered him at the bush in the wilderness of Sinai or Horeb as it is also called (3:1). We know his approximate age from various passages which we may compare (Exodus 7:7 and Acts 7:23). This would mean that for some forty years now Moses had been in the wilderness, tending the flocks of his father-in-law. A man with his education and background nevertheless had to be molded into the man whom God desired him to be.

In Moses' first face-to-face encounter with the Lord, God appeared as the God of his fathers, thus establishing a continuity with the covenant which God had made with the patriarchs (3:6). As God had before promised Abraham, he was now ready to bring his people out of bondage. In verse 10, he specifically tells Moses what his part is to be.

We see that now Moses has lost his vain self-confidence and in his years of humility has come to realize his own limitations (3:11). This is always necessary for God's servants. Yet God's answer was more than adequate—"I will be with thee" (3:12).

In this context, God goes on to establish his name by which his people shall know him (3:14, 15). The name he gives is best translated "I will be." In the context here, we can see that its significance is that God will be *with his people*.

It is not merely an expression of the being of God but rather of his presence *with his people.* In verse 12, he had said, "I will be with thee." Now in verse 14 he declares that his name is "I will be" (The verbal form in the Hebrew is exactly the same in both of these verses—the first person singular of the Hebrew verb "to be" in the imperfect or incompleted action form). Now when, in verse 15, he says that this is his name forever, we are to understand that God's people will hereafter know him as the God who will be with his people forever. Thus the personal name of the Lord becomes in the Hebrew language *Yahweh* (the third person, imperfect of the verb "to be"). Most Bibles write it either as Jehovah or Lord, i.e., "He will be with us."

Later the Lord will give to the people the pattern of the tabernacle as a visible sign of his presence right in the midst of the camp of Israel. Much later still, at a time of deterioration in Israel, when their enemies threaten them, God will declare that a son shall be born in Israel as a sign of hope and his name will be called Immanuel (God with us) (Isa. 7:14). When Jesus is born in

Bethlehem, Matthew tells us that this was the fulfillment of the
Old Testament prophecy of Isaiah. Jesus *is* God with us. Indeed,
Jesus' very last words to his church before his ascension to the
Father were, "Lo, I am with you always, even unto the end of the
world" (Matt. 28:20). See also Acts 18:9, 10 for his continuing
assurance of his presence with his people after his ascension.

The revelation that day to Moses was therefore to become the
great hope of God's people and the great answer to their every
need—God's abiding presence with his people. We shall see that
time and again he assured his people and true leaders that he
was with them. Nothing else makes possible the continued work
of the church today in the world other than this.

In spite of all this, Moses was still uncertain. His fear continued to be based on his feeling of inadequacy. He rightly
feared that the people would not listen to him or accept what he
said as from the Lord (4:1). God's answer was to give to him
miraculous powers that day to demonstrate God's presence and
approval of what he did and said (4:2f.). In verse 5 we are
explicitly told what the function of the miracles which God
worked by Moses was to be—it was to enable the people to
believe that Moses was sent of the Lord and not coming and
speaking in his own authority.

This passage is very important in showing the proper relationship between the Biblical miracles and revelation. Plainly, the
miracles were given to Moses to establish him as a spokesman of
God and to give him authority for what he taught. We note
furthermore that the miracles of the Bible come primarily at the
times of new written revelation. Certain clusters of miracles
come in this the first period of written revelation, the time of
Moses. Later in the time of Elijah and Elisha who were the
forerunners of the great writing prophets, we have another cluster of miracles and a lesser cluster in the time of Daniel.

In the New Testament the greatest cluster is around Christ in
the declaration of the gospel, and in a lesser degree, around his
apostles both before and after his resurrection and ascension.
God gave these miraculous powers to his servants for a specific
purpose and by them he established their authority as givers of
new revelation from God. It seems, therefore, sound to conclude
that the age of miracles closed when the age of new revelation
closed at the end of the Apostolic Age.

In spite of Moses' reluctance, God thrust him out of the wilderness and into the presence of Pharaoh (4:13, 5:1). Chapters
5-11 tell of the encounters between Moses and Pharaoh; and
while this second attempt to liberate God's people seemed destined to failure as his first attempt had forty years before, we see

now a different Moses. He does not again flee to the wilderness. He comes to God as a true mediator seeking God's assurance (5:22, 23). And God gives to Moses that assurance that God is indeed with him, recalling to Moses his name: God is with you (6:2f.).

The answer of God to Moses that day contained what can properly be called the vocabulary of redemption (6:6-8). It speaks of *deliverance from the burdens* of Egypt (v. 6—compare also Matthew 11:28); the *ridding from* the *bondage* (v. 6—compare Rom. 6:17—servants of sin); *redemption* (v. 6—compare Rom. 3:24); *adoption* (v. 7—compare Eph. 1:5); *knowing* or *believing in God* (v. 7—compare Hos. 4:6; Phil. 3:10; 2 Tim. 1:12); *bringing in* (v. 8—compare Matt. 25:21); and *the inheritance* (v. 8—compare I Pet. 1:4). The point here is that God that day told Moses of his immediate purpose for Israel but in telling he used a vocabulary which would become the essential vocabulary of God's people for communicating to the world the gospel of salvation. Chapter 7 begins to relate the series of miracles and signs to be worked by the hand of Moses. Again what Moses is to *do* is linked with what he is to *say*. The office of the prophet of God is here clearly given. As Moses was to Aaron, so God would be to his prophet. As Aaron would speak what Moses gave him to speak so the prophet would speak what God gave him to say (7:1, 2).

The reference here and elsewhere to God's hardening the heart of Pharaoh needs some explanation (7:3, 13, etc.). In Genesis 6:5 and 8:21 we are told that the natural heart of man is always evil and only evil. To assume, therefore, that God here makes Pharaoh's heart to be stubborn and rebellious when naturally he would have been inclined to obey God is erroneous. The word "hardened" used here is better translated "made to set." God did not make Pharaoh worse, he simply refused to restrain him from his worst. He let Pharaoh's heart set according to its natural evil tendencies. In the New Testament, Paul describes the same phenomenon in Romans 1 when he says of evil men that "God gave them up unto vile passions . . . a reprobate mind" (Romans 1:26, 28). God here simply did not intervene, as he so often does in men's lives, to prevent Pharaoh from doing the total evil which was in his heart.

Perhaps the reason why God allowed the magicians and sorcerers of Egypt to match some of the miracles of the Lord was to test the faith of Moses and Aaron, while at the same time, provoking the Egyptians' vain minds (7:11, 22, etc.). The acts of these magicians were probably real and not mere deceptions. The Scripture says they *did* them, but certainly not by their own power. They may have been as surprised as was the witch of Endor who, by God's help, later on would bring Samuel from the dead.

The next few chapters relate the various miracles which served to show God's favor for his own people (8:22, 9:4, 6, etc.) and humbled the Egyptians (9:20, etc.). But Pharaoh's heart continued to be hard right up to the end. While he seemed to fluctuate between submission to God's will and stubbornly refusing to let Israel go, there is no evidence that his heart was ever really changed from the hardness of heart that was naturally his.

In chapter 11 we read the climax of the miraculous plagues against Egypt. God's intent was both to bless his own people and to judge Egypt. To do so, he supplied riches to Israel and provided an escape for them from the judgment about to fall on the land. The riches were the spoils of the Egyptians' jewels and treasures (11:2, 3). The judgment was the slaying of the firstborn of all Egypt in a single night (11:4-6). The escape of Israel from this awful judgment was to be in connection with the Passover and the feast of unleavened bread (11:7, ch. 12).

The instructions for the slaying of the Passover lamb, given in 12:1-11, contain all the elements of redemption. There is first a *lamb* for a household, a male lamb *without blemish* (12:3, 5) comparable to the Lamb of God (John 1:29, 1 Pet. 1:19) whose *blood must be shed* (12:7, Heb. 9:22; 1 John 1:7). There is also *judgment against sin* (12:13, see also Matt. 23:33; Luke 21:36; Rom. 2:3; Heb. 2:3, 12:25). For those who obeyed God and trusted in him, the lamb was a *substitutionary atonement* (12:13, compare Gen. 22; John 1:29; 1 Pet. 1:18, 19). Finally a *sacrament* was established as a memorial of this event, a sign and seal of the work God has done (12:4. Compare Luke 22:20; 1 Cor. 5:7; 11:25; Rom. 3:25).

In the Passover event God also once more stressed the importance of parental instruction in relation to the knowledge of God among the children of believers. As he had told Abraham, so once more God lays upon the believing parents the responsibility to take every opportunity to give a reason for the faith in them and to glorify God before their children (12:26, 27).

The actual work of redemption is related in 12:29ff. The spoiling of the Egyptians, aided by God (12:35, 36), was in accord with God's ownership of all things. He entrusted these possessions to Israel that day. Israel would be required to give a good account of her stewardship of them as were the Egyptians.

We are told that some 600,000 men, in addition to the others, left Egypt. Some have estimated the total population of the Israelites living in Egypt to be close to 2.5 million (12:37).

The mixed multitude mentioned in 12:38 (see also Num. 11:4) may have been made up of Egyptians and other foreigners who had attached themselves to the Israelites in some 400 years of their history. However, a better explanation, it seems to me, is that the term "mixed multitude" refers to the spiritual mixture among the Israelites. Not all were God's children who went out of Egypt. Among those were many unbelievers. This is clearly shown in the testings which Israel endured in the wilderness. Paul apparently had this sense of the text (1 Cor. 10:1-11). We could also compare the words of the writer of Hebrews (Heb. 3:16-19) and of Jude (v. 5).

The time of the Exodus is still a great problem. In 12:40 we are told that the time Israel was in Egypt was 430 years. This is comparable to the 400 years of affliction God had foretold to Abraham (Gen. 15:13). Paul too makes reference to the 430 years as the time between the promise by faith and the giving of the Law. Apparently he counts the promise by faith to be what Jacob carried with him into Egypt which was held to by God's people over that 430 years' sojourn in Egypt (Gal. 3:17). 1 Kings 6:1 allows 480 years from the Exodus to the time of Solomon's fourth year.

Because of apparent inconsistencies in the dates which we have and our inability always to know the methodology of counting, conservative scholars have not all agreed on the date of the Exodus. Good arguments have been put forward for a date in the 15th century B.C. and also for a later date in the 13th century B.C. We shall not attempt here to try to settle a matter which has never been satisfactorily settled. It is not imperative to know the secular dates of this event but it is important to know that it occurred some 430 years after Jacob's entrance into Egypt. In that time, the family became a great nation formed in the womb of Egyptian oppression.

The meaning of the Passover experience is further unfolded in chapter 13. There we see that in saving the firstborn of Israel, the Lord thereby lays claim to them (13:2). Later, the Lord will take the Levites instead of the firstborn of all Israel to do his special service. The point is that the firstborn here represent the whole people. The judgment on the firstborn of Egypt is a judgment against the whole people. The salvation of the firstborn of Israel is the salvation of the whole people. Now God lays claim to the firstborn which is tantamount to his claiming the whole people for his service. They belong to God. Ultimately they are all to be a kingdom of priests (19:6).

The overthrow of the enemy, Egypt, is recorded in narrative form in chapter 14 and is poetically celebrated in chapter 15. In this event we see both the weakness of the people's faith (14:10-12) and the strength of Moses' faith as he leads them to trust in God (14:13-14). In the end, the goal was God's glory (14:18). The message of Genesis 3:15 is here recalled when God promises to defeat the enemies of God's people.

Moses' hymn of victory, recorded in chapter 15, praises both God's mighty works (1ff.) and his mighty power (6ff.). The hymn centers on the uniqueness of Israel's God (v. 11). It closes with a strong expression of confidence in God to carry out his purpose to bring his people to himself (v. 17). The closing verse (18) declares the kingship of God over his people forever. For the faithful there never is any King but the Lord.

No sooner had the people seen the overthrow of their enemies than they faced trials of their new faith in God (14:31; 15:22-26). Most of the sites or stopping places mentioned in the journeys of Israel through the wilderness are today not known to us for certain. Even the site of Mount Sinai is disputed. More important than the exact location of these sites is to know what God taught the people as they passed from place to place, forced to depend on the Lord.

The frequent murmurings of the people (15:24; 16:2; 17:3, etc.) indicate both the weakness of the faith of God's children at this point and also the existence of unbelievers among God's people.

The promise of manna for the people to eat is just an example of how God did provide their daily bread (16:4-15). The name manna itself comes from two Hebrew words meaning "What is it?" The people apparently gave it this name: "Whatever you call it."

It is significant that God spoke of the observance of the Sabbath to the people even before the giving of the Ten Commandments (16:22-30). This shows first of all that the Sabbath rest was already an ordinance among God's people. Its origin dates back to creation itself. Sabbath observance was God's will for all men. Secondly, as is shown here, the Sabbath observance is in the context of God's promises of enough for the family in six days in order that they may rest on the seventh from their ordinary concerns. No one therefore should have to work on the Sabbath out of his own necessity. This is in accord with Jesus' statement that the Sabbath was made for man and not man for the Sabbath (Mark 2:27).

In spite of the people's murmuring, the long-suffering of God is shown as he provides their needs (17:6) and delivers them from their enemy (17:8-16).

Chapter 18 illustrates how God's people put to use the learning of the secular world for the good of God's kingdom. The advice from Moses' father-in-law concerning his leadership was very sound advice (18:18-23). It is commendable to the wisdom of Moses that he responded favorably to this advice (18:24). Even men of Moses' stature could learn from others, even from lesser men. Any good leader must learn this.

Chapter 19 is the climax to the whole section (Exod. 1-19). As Israel arrives at Mount Sinai and Moses faces the Lord, God first reminds Israel of what he has done for them. The redemption from Egypt is described as a flying on eagles' wings to God. God also, at this time, expresses once more his purpose for a holy people, a kingdom of priests (19:6). Thus the formula: 1) what I have done for you; 2) what I call you to do and be—is given once more.

In the New Testament as well we see similar expressions of God's work followed by his expectations for us. Romans 12:1, 2 follows the long treatment by Paul of what God has done for us; 1 Peter 2:1-9 expresses God's purpose in terms quite similar to those found here in Exodus. We could also compare Revelation 1:6 and 5:10, which adopt the phrase "kingdom of priests" to express God's ultimate goal for his people. We see then that God's goals and purposes never really change.

We have then, first of all, the calling of the people to be God's special people, a holy nation, in accord with God's original purpose which was declared before the beginning of creation (Ephesians 1:4).

There follows God's plan or express will for conforming his people into the kind of people he desires them to be. This constitutes the second major section of the subject now before us: The People of God Redeemed; namely, the giving of the Law to the people of God.

THE GIVING OF THE LAW
TO THE PEOPLE OF GOD
Exodus 20—Deuteronomy

We shall consider the giving of the Law under eight headings: The Ten Commandments; The Law as an Application of Justice; The Tabernacle; Apostasy and a New Revelation; The Sacrificial System; The Years of Wandering; The End of the Journey; The Second Legislation.

The Ten Commandments (Exodus 20:1-17). Again let us stress the point that the Ten Commandments are given in a context of God's expression of his goals for his people, and are given to express God's will for his people. They are therefore a portrait of God's will for his children. And lest we think they are archaic or no longer relevant, we must remember that the New Testament does not destroy but upholds the Law of God for his people.

John, in 1 John 2:3, 4, 7, states that we are shown to be God's children by our conformity to his commandments. In Romans 3:31 Paul, after preaching the essence of the gospel, declares that the gospel does not make the Law null and void but, contrarily, establishes the Law, i.e., makes it possible for God's children to obey. Finally our Lord, in the Sermon on the Mount, states in no uncertain terms that the Law of God is very much a part of God's kingdom, and that obedience to it is expected of God's children (Matt. 5:17-19). He goes on to give us an exposition of the Ten Commandments so that there is no doubt about which law he means (See Matthew 5:21f.).

The Ten Commandments are introduced by a reminder once more of what God has done for his people. On the basis therefore of God's deliverance of his own out of the house of bondage, i.e., the expression of God's love for his people (20:2), they are now to express their love to him in obedience to his will (20:3ff.). It was Jesus who said, "If you love me, you will keep my commandments" (John 14:15 and 1 John 5:2, 3). Jesus also teaches us that the love of God and of our neighbor is a summation of the whole Law of God (Matt. 22:34-40). Thus once again we see the purpose of God to have a people holy and without blemish before him in love.

In *the first Commandment* (20:3) the wording would better be translated "besides me" meaning "in addition to me." The word used here never means "instead of." God is here requiring the whole devotion of his people. There can never be room in their lives for the Lord *plus* any other kind of god or object of devotion and commitment.

In the days of Ahab, the wicked king of Israel, Elijah suddenly appeared and called the people away from vacillation between the Lord and Baal. He accused them of limping between two sides (1 Kings 18:21). He exhorted them to choose to follow either the Lord or Baal but not to try to follow both. Jesus also, in very plain words, declares that we cannot serve God and mammon. We must despise one and cling to the other; hate one and love the other. We cannot serve two masters (Matt. 6:24).

James similarly warns against double-mindedness (Jas. 1:8). Paul relates sadly the fate of some who apparently sought to be in the Christian fellowship but whose god was their own belly (Rom. 16:18, Phil. 3:19). Finally, Jesus most graphically illustrates the folly of such attempts in the parable of the unjust steward (Luke 16:1-13). The point of that parable is that the sons of this world (Satan's offspring) consistently serve their god, mammon, while God's children are not so consistent and wise in serving the Lord (16:18). God calls his children to faithfulness to him which means to serve him only (16:10-13).

The second Commandment has as its object a right knowledge of God. The Lord consistently calls his own to know him truly and rightly (see Hosea 4:1, 6:6).

Men cannot know God by expressing out of their vain and sinful hearts their own concepts of God, whether by idols made with their hands or by their vain philosophical thoughts about God. God will not be known by man's thoughts or concepts about him. Time and again the Lord warns Israel not to make graven images, the imaginations of men about God (Exod. 34:14-16, etc.). When they disobeyed and did seek to make images such as in the golden calf incident (Exod. 32), it was with tragic results (see also 2 Kings 21:7-9).

When we read such ancient writings as the Babylonian mythologies about their gods, their creation story, or the myths of the Greeks, we see that men tended to create their gods in their own images, that is, like sinful men.

But if the second Commandment forbids our expressing in any way our own concepts of God from our own evil hearts, it also points to the true way of knowing God; namely, by his own revelation of himself. In Exodus 33, after the golden calf incident, Moses desired to know God rightly in order to teach God's people truly about God (33:13). When Moses further asked to see God's glory (33:18), the Lord's response was, "I will make all of my goodness pass before thee" (v. 19). What the Lord actually showed Moses that day was in the form of a verbal revelation about himself. This is found in the next chapter (Exod. 34).

Exodus 34:6, 7 is God's verbal revelation of himself: his glory and his goodness. It became the basic knowledge of God which his people retained throughout the period of revelation. This description and knowledge of God was later the basis of Moses' own intercession on behalf of Israel at a time when God was angry with Israel (Num. 14:18). It was also the basis of the call of the early writing prophet, Joel, to Israel to repent and return to God (Joel 2:13). It was even the basis of Jonah's reluctance to go and preach to Nineveh—he knew God was like this and he did not desire the salvation of Nineveh (Jonah 4:2). The Psalmist often recalls this verbal revelation of God as the basis for hope (Psa. 103:8, etc.). Finally, in the time of restoration after the Exile, this revelation given to Moses was the basis of the post-exilic call of God's children back to faith (Neh. 9:17).

As we come to the New Testament we read in John 1:1 that the Word was God and that the Word became flesh and dwelt among us (1:14). Thus the verbal revelation of God given to Moses *now*, in Christ, takes on flesh and blood and lives before the eyes of men. Several New Testament Scriptures substantiate the fact that Jesus Christ is the very image of the invisible God (Phil. 2:6; 2 Cor. 4:4; Col. 1:15; Heb. 1:3, etc.). Furthermore, the New Testament calls believers to bear the image of Christ, reflecting his image in themselves (Rom. 8:29; 1 Cor. 15:49; 2 Cor. 3:18; Col. 3:10, etc.).

We can see then why God forbade the making of graven images by the hands of men. God had far greater revelation of himself in store: first verbally, then in the flesh; first in his Son, then in his children who by faith are conformed to the image of his Son.

As we consider this verbal revelation of God in Exodus 34:6, 7, we see in it both the mercy of God toward repentant sinners: merciful, gracious, slow to anger, abundant in lovingkindness and truth, keeping lovingkindness for thousands, forgiving iniquity and transgression and sin; and the severity and judgment of God against sinners. God is not willing to by-pass sin or its consequences. God is holy; his people must be holy too. Sin must be dealt with either by forgiveness, when men acknowledge their sin and believe in the Lord, or by punishment, when they do not. Since this second Commandment and the revelation of Exodus 34 are both given to God's people, we must understand the warning against sin. The God who forgives his children who repent and believe in him will nevertheless visit the consequences of sin upon them. David is a clear example of this, who, while being assured of God's forgiveness for his sins, nevertheless, for the rest of his life, paid the consequence of that sin and the consequences reached to his own children and his children's children.

The third Commandment is closely related to the second (20:7). The words "to take" are better translated "to bear." It means "to carry" or "to bear" God's name before men. The words "in vain" mean "to no purpose" or "carelessly." We often think of this commandment as opposed to cursing and profanity in which

God's name is used. It certainly does oppose this practice but it is much more meaningful than that. We have seen how God's children are to bear the name and image and glory of God in their daily lives by obedience to his Word. God has great respect for his name and the whole nature of God which is revealed to men by it (Exod. 3:15).

God's purpose is that by his children his name may be borne throughout the earth (Exod. 9:16, 17). So the Psalmist expresses this purpose in his life (Psa. 22:22) and he exhorts all of God's children to do so (Psa. 34:1-3). In the Book of Acts the *name* of the Lord is shown to be vital to the salvation of men (Acts 2:21; 2:38; 3:16; 4:12, 18; 5:40; 9:15, 27; 10:43). So every child of God must bear the name of God before men, not vainly or idly or to no purpose, but in such a way that all of his own conduct will glorify God and rightly point men to hope in Christ. So we find Paul exhorting believers to do all that they do in the name of the Lord (Col. 3:17). (Compare 2 Tim. 2:19.) This is bearing God's name before the world in a way pleasing to God. The third Commandment forbids any other way of bearing God's name before men.

The fourth Commandment pertains to the Sabbath. As we have pointed out, the Sabbath ordinance is not new to God's people (Exod. 16:23). The Sabbath principle was established at creation (Gen. 2:1-3). There are two parts to the commandment. The first part is to *remember* the Sabbath day (since it is already established as a special day by God). The second part is to *keep it holy,* separate from the other days of the week which are called profane days, i.e., days when one does his usual work and activity.

Various principles of Sabbath meaning and observance need to be pointed out in connection with this commandment. First, on the Sabbath we are not to have to provide for our needs by work. We see this lesson in Exodus 16:23f., already referred to. God provided enough in the six work days of the week to meet the needs of the people on the seventh. The Sabbath was then, in a way, a reminder of the provision of God as the believer rested and recalled the provisions of God which are sufficient. To work to earn one's living on the Sabbath was a breach of faith in God's provision.

The second principle is that we are to use the day for worship of God. Leviticus 23:3 calls the Sabbath a holy convocation for God's people. Consequently, some (the priests) will find it a very active day of work, tending to various priestly duties (Lev. 24:8, Num. 28:9). It was to be a day of the reverencing of God's sanctuary (Lev. 19:30; 26:2).

The third principle of the Sabbath is that it is a special day in which God delights the believer. First, Isaiah says that the believer in guarding the Sabbath day (Isa. 56:2-5) and then in 58:13f. he shows that it is a day to pursue not one's own pleasures but what pleases God. It is to be a delight, a day of rejoicing in fellowship with God, a kind of sample of heaven itself.

The fourth principle revealed in God's Word is that the Sabbath is a test of the believer's faith. Israel was so tested, according to Jeremiah 17:21-23. The fact that so many loved profane activity instead of fellowship with the Lord was a means of showing the extent of unbelief in Israel.

A fifth principle is given in Ezekiel 20:12. The Sabbath is to be a sign to God's people both of the need of sanctification and the activity of God in sanctifying his people. So on the Sabbath, the thoughts of God's people should be on God's Word and on his purging of sin from them day by day. It is a time of reflection on the continuing work of God in the life of his child to the praise of God's glory.

Finally, we learn one more principle in Isaiah 66:23. The Sabbath Day on earth is to express the ideal of heaven itself. Isaiah expresses the ideal of heaven in terms of God's peoples' worship of him from one Sabbath to another, i.e., continuously. So on the Sabbath, God's people sample that continuing worship in heaven (cf. Rev. 22:3).

As we turn to the New Testament we note first of all how Jesus interprets the proper understanding of the Sabbath as a day made for man and not man for the Sabbath (Mark 2:27). We can trace the examples of Jesus' own use of the Sabbath in various passages: Mark 6:2; Luke 4:31; 13:10; and also that of his disciples: Acts 13:27, 42; 15:21; 16:13; 17:2; 18:4, etc. We see that they were, on the Sabbath, occupied in the reading of Scripture, preaching of the gospel, prayer and study from the Scripture.

Several words of caution are given to believers regarding this observance. Once when Jesus was accused of violation of the Sabbath, together with his disciples, he taught that the Pharisaical use of the Sabbath was without mercy (Matt. 12:7) and forbade the doing of good, i.e., what pleases God (12:11, 12). This is sufficient to warn that the keeping of the Sabbath can never be used as an excuse either for judgment without mercy or for the closing of one's compassions toward another. Jesus healed on the Sabbath as we see here; he was received in the homes as a dinner guest on the Sabbath (Luke 14:1); and he commanded a man to carry his own bed on the Sabbath because to do so glorified God (John 5:10).

Paul also exhorts Christians not to allow others to judge them in respect to their observance of the Sabbath or any other day (Col. 2:16f.). It is wrong to allow others to legislate how or in what ways we can or should observe the Sabbath. Observance is strictly between the believer and his Lord. What we do or do not do on that day must be based on our love of God and desire to enjoy him. As Hebrews 4:1ff. suggests, the Sabbath observance is a type of the eternal rest of God's people with him and ought to be for us a sampling of heaven. Therefore it should be spent in those things which we expect to do in heaven as we dwell with God and his people in love, joy, peace and praise forever.

The New Testament introduces the Lord's Day, the first day of the week, as the Christian Sabbath, not by specific teaching but by example. We find a gradual practice developing of Christians meeting on the first day of the week to worship (Acts 20:7; 1 Cor. 16:2), in honor of the resurrection of Christ on that day. As the last day of the week had marked the end of the first creation, so the first day of the week introduces the new creation in Christ.

The fifth Commandment is seen as a pivotal commandment, like a fulcrum separating the first four and the last five commandments. It fits here because, as we have shown, the home is the beginning place for instruction of children concerning the Lord and one's relationship to his fellow men. God ordained that parents should establish homes where the rudiments of God's truth would be taught (Gen. 1:27; 2:18ff.; 18:19). He taught that salvation itself would come to men through the home (the seed of the woman) (Gen. 3:15).

In Deuteronomy 6:4-9, God insists on a right love for himself and for his Word in the hearts of parents so that they can rightly teach their children God's will. We shall see later that Proverbs as a whole deals with parental instruction to children on how to honor God and how to show love toward others. Ephesians 6:1-4 is the New Testament equivalent of these Old Testament passages. Parents stand at a unique place in the church. Through them we first learn of God, if they are faithful to God. Consequently, the honoring of parents shows love and respect for God and is the means of learning to live with men in the world. Only as Israel obeyed this commandment and only as faithful parents taught God's Word, could Israel expect to endure in the land which God had given her. When parental respect and discipline of children broke down, so did Israel's peace in the land.

The next four commandments shall be considered together. They relate to our love of God as well as to our love of our fellow men. All pertain to violations of God's work. *The sixth Commandment* forbids the taking of life which God has given to man. *The seventh Commandment* forbids violation of the home which God has established. *The eighth Commandment* forbids our taking from one those possessions which God has given to him, since God owns all and merely entrusts it to men as pleases him. *The ninth Commandment* warns against damaging a man's name or reputation which also has come from God. Failure to love God will result in acts of violence against our neighbor instead of deeds of love.

The tenth Commandment teaches us that all of these commandments can be violated in the heart as well as openly by overt acts of evil. The heart does matter to God, and the commandments are to be obeyed in the heart, not simply conformed to outwardly. It is possible to break the Ten Commandments in the heart without actually outwardly doing the visible evils. The sin of covetousness is the sin of the heart. To covet my neighbor's home is to violate the eighth Commandment. To covet his wife is to violate the seventh Commandment. Jesus shows this plainly in Matthew 5:21, 22, 27ff. From the time of the giving of the commandments therefore, the Lord shows us that they are to be obeyed *from the heart.*

Again God taught the people that the object of the giving of the Ten Commandments was in order that the people of God not sin (20:20).

But God did know that they would sin. So along with the Ten Commandments he also gave laws concerning sacrifice (20:24-26). These laws are not here explained. Later, in Leviticus he will expound on the sacrificial system. Suffice it to show here that the sacrificial system is introduced at the time of the giving of the Ten Commandments, so that we may see that God's desire is that we not sin; but when we do, we will need to deal with that sin.

The Law as an Application of Justice (Exodus 21-14). These next few chapters show in a very practical way how God expects his children to relate his will (as expressed in the Ten Commandments) to every facet of their lives.

The whole section is called the ordinances or, better, the *justices.* The word used here is the same word "justice" which is found in Genesis 18:19. It refers to that will of God for his children concerning all their relations to their fellow men. It expresses, in other words, the ways in which God's children are to show their love to one another in terms of all their daily events of life, every circumstance. This is that justice for which God continually looks in the lives of his children.

A quick survey of the matter dealt with in these chapters shows that it pertains to just about any and every kind of circumstance that might occur in one's daily life. Here we see the Lord showing Israel how to apply his Law to all parts of their daily lives.

Many of the specifics in these chapters pertain to customs prevalent in the whole Near Eastern world of that day. God started with his people where they were. We must always remember that he placed these justices between the giving of the Ten Commandments and the revealing of the glory of God (ch. 24), thus laying claim to the devotion of his people and their obedience toward him in all of life.

In principle we learn from this section that in all events and incidents of our life, even the very smallest, we are to seek to apply God's Law to our daily lives.

The Tabernacle (Exodus 25-31, 35-40). The giving of the tabernacle to Israel is according to a heavenly pattern designed by God (25:9). It is reasonable to assume therefore that each part of it is significant to convey to Israel something of the spiritual truth necessary for them to know.

Great detail is given to its structure and to each piece of its furniture. The overall design was a skin-covered structure some 60 feet long by 15 feet wide. This structure or tent was subdivided into two basic parts. One part was called the holy place. The other part was called the holy of holies or the holiest place. This was the smaller section. The priests of the tribe of Levi were to minister in the tent regularly before God according to specific instructions (28:3). But only the high priest could enter the holiest place, and he could do so only once a year, on the day of atonement (Lev. 16:12f.; Exod. 30:10).

The purpose of the whole, including the furniture, was to teach the people what is necessary for their proper approach to the very presence of God. Again we recall God's express will to have a people in fellowship with him, holy and without blemish. It was necessary therefore that the way to the Lord be taught. God determined to do so by means of this visible structure to be set in the midst of the camp of Israel.

On approaching the tabernacle, the first thing we come to is the altar of burnt offering. Here the daily offerings of the people are to be offered at morning and in the evening. This would teach Israel the necessity for the shedding of blood for their sins if they were to come to God (Heb. 9:22). Beyond this, but still outside of the tent, was the laver where the priests must wash before entering the tent. This symbolized the necessity for continual cleansing as one approaches God.

Inside the tent in the holy place are found three pieces of furniture. To the left stands the lamp, giving light to the whole room, signifying the necessity of God's light shown on our path if we are to follow the right way to him (Psa. 27:1; 119:105; Prov. 6:23). On the right is the table of bread which signifies, as bread so often does, God's supply of both our spiritual and physical sustenance for our daily lives. The third thing in this room is the altar of incense which continually burns and gives a sweet smell to the whole room. Incense in Scripture often represents the lifting up of prayers to God (Psa. 141:2; Luke 1:10; Rev. 5:8; 8:3, 4).

A great curtain or veil separates this outer room from the holiest place. Behind the curtain is the ark of the covenant, where the presence of God is among his people. On the ark is the mercy seat. Hovering over the mercy seat are the cherubim.

We last saw the cherubim as guardians of the way of the tree of life (Gen. 3:24). Presumably their presence here is to show that the whole tabernacle structure is designed to show to men the way back to God to eternal life with him.

In Hebrews 8 and 9 we are shown that the pattern of the tabernacle in the Old Testament represented the ministering work of God through Jesus Christ (8:1, 2). The Old Testament tabernacle is called a shadow of the heavenly things (8:5). All of the Old Testament tabernacle structure and furniture therefore pointed to the work to be accomplished in Jesus Christ (9:1-10).

Hebrews 9:11f. shows to us that Jesus Christ has performed all that was symbolically represented by the Old Testament tabernacle, and that he has in reality, for us, approached to the very presence of God. The whole point of the author of Hebrews is that all which was symbolized in the Old Testament tabernacle is fulfilled in Jesus Christ. He came into the actual presence of God for us (9:24).

It is quite reasonable therefore to assume that all of this Old Testament structure was a visible portrayal of the coming work of Christ to accomplish everything necessary for our approach to God.

The *altar of burnt offering* where the lamb was offered daily is in the New Testament seen in Christ, who is called the Lamb of God who takes away the sin of the world (John 1:29).

The laver for continual cleansing points to two passages in the New Testament pertaining to the work of Christ. In the Gospels Jesus tells his disciples that having been once cleansed, there is need only to wash their feet (presumably in reference to the cleansing of sin once and for all by his work of redemption) and then for daily confession of sin in the believer's spiritual life for his own good (John 13:10). Associated with this passage is 1 John 1:7-9, where we read that the blood of Jesus Christ cleanses us from all sin; yet we are to confess our sins continually, assured that the Lord will cleanse us from all unrighteousness.

The *lamp* and the *shewbread* of course remind us of Jesus' words about himself: "I am the light of the world" (John 8:12); and "I am the bread of life" (John 6:35).

The *altar of incense* calls to mind Hebrews 7:25, which says, concerning Christ: "He ever liveth to make intercession for them" (that is, for those who draw near to God through Christ).

Finally, *the ark of the covenant,* the symbol of the very presence of God with His people, behind the veil, surely points to the words of Christ, "I am the way, the truth, and the life. No man cometh unto the Father but by me" (John 14:6). As the high priest once each year entered behind the veil into the very presence of God symbolically, so Christ has once and for all entered into the very presence of God for us (Heb. 8:1f; vv. 24:28; 10:19-23). Therefore on the day of Jesus'death the veil of the Temple was torn in two from top to bottom. The symbolism is not needed anymore. Christ had, in fulfillment, accomplished all to which it pointed (Matt. 27:51, Heb. 10:20).

As the tabernacle stood in the midst of the camp to indicate God's presence with his people, so the children of God learned to seek him by his Temple. In later years reference is often made to his people praying toward the holy Temple, approaching God by the means he has given them (1 Kings 8:29; Jonah 2:4, 7; Psa. 5:5, etc.).

Apostasy and a New Revelation (Exodus 32-34). Two incidents occur in the process of God giving to Moses instructions about the tabernacle and before the tabernacle is actually built. Both relate partially to the second Commandment and the people's knowledge of and worship of God.

Chapter 32 relates the incident concerning the golden calf made by Aaron while Moses was on the mountain top. Aaron's actions were goaded by the people but his own guilt and implication cannot be denied. Reference to the calf being their god (32:4) may have some relationship to an ancient Near Eastern concept of invisible deities which rode on the backs of visible animals. At any rate, it was clearly idolatry in contradiction to God's specific commands.

We see in this incident Moses' work as a mediator. He pleads for the people not because they do not deserve God's punishment but because God's own name and honor are involved (32:11, 12). He recalls too the covenant promised to the fathers, the ground of Moses' own faith (32:13). Moses' own concern for the people is beautifully expressed in his intercessory prayer (32:30-32).

References to *the book* (vv. 32, 33) are made from time to time throughout Scripture (Psa. 69:28; Dan. 12:1; Mal. 3:16, 17; Phil. 4:3; Rev. 3:5; 13:8; 20:15). The Book of Life contains the names of all of God's elect. In Psalm 69:28 we see that "to be blotted out" is parallel or equivalent to "not to be written with the righteous." It is not that God changes his mind, but from our perspective men who may seem to be righteous may be blotted out, i.e., never really included among the righteous.

God's answer here clearly establishes the principle later expounded by Ezekiel, that each man must be accountable to God for his own sins (32:33).

In chapter 33 we find Moses inquiring further about the truth of God. He requests to see the glory of the Lord (v. 18). He was apparently asking for more than could be allowed (v. 20). Nevertheless God did respond by promising to show him his goodness which he associated with his name (v. 19).

We are not really told what Moses *saw* that day other than that he did not see God's face but only his back (v. 23). What is more important is the *verbal* revelation given to Moses that day. In 34:6, 7 the verbal revelation of the goodness of God was recorded just as Moses received it.

We have discussed this revelation already in the study of the second Commandment. This verbal revelation became the knowledge of God, which the faithful always recalled in their need of God or worship of him. We find this passage more frequently quoted or referred to or alluded to in the Old Testament than any other. A few passages are Numbers 14:18; Joel 2:13; Jonah 4:2; Psalms frequently (103:8, for example); Nehemiah 9:17, etc. God's people knew how to pray and what to believe about God in any circumstance because they recalled this verbal revelation. God was always like that. Thus in John 1:14 we are told that the Word became flesh and dwelt among us. Jesus in the flesh was all that God had revealed himself to be (Phil. 2:6; 2 Cor. 4:4; Heb. 1:3).

The Sacrificial System (Leviticus). After the tent had been erected according to the specific commands of God, we read in the book of Leviticus the revelation of God to Israel from that tent (Lev. 1:1). This revelation deals primarily with matters of worship of the holy God.

You recall that at the giving of the Law, God also provided for sacrifices to be made (Exod. 20:24-26). At that time there was no elaboration made of the sacrificial system for Israel. Now this became the primary subject of the revelation of God in the tabernacle. Chapters 1 through 6:7 contain various ordinances for the regulation of the sacrificial system.

We should recall that already God had shown his people the basic significance of the offering, by a sacrifice of a ram instead of Isaac, i.e., substitutionary atonement. The ram died *instead of* Isaac. Again at the Passover the lamb for the family and for the firstborn of Israel taught them that the sacrifice was a substitute for the people (Exod. 12). The shed blood of the substitute would therefore continually remind the believer that one must die for him. As the book of Hebrews expresses it, "All things are cleansed with blood, and apart from shedding of blood there is no remission" (Heb. 9:22).

Here in these early chapters of Leviticus we are given details of the sacrifices required for the sins of the people. We can categorize these sacrifices in various ways. In terms of the *amount* of the sacrifice, there were partial burnt offerings and whole burnt offerings of animals, usually from the herd, a male without blemish.

In terms of the *material* offered, there were animal sacrifices and vegetable sacrifices including grain, oil, and fruit.

The *types* of sacrifices included peace offerings, sin offerings, and trespass offerings. Peace offerings were made for expressions of thanksgiving to God. Sin offerings were apparently for sins later recognized which one might commit unwittingly, and trespass offerings seem to pertain to all kinds of violations of the Law of God; though at times the terminology used does not reflect strict divisions in these two types.

As to the *persons* offering these sacrifices, mention is made of individuals who offer all types of the above sacrifices and who at special times, i.e., times of uncleanness, offer special sacrifices. Some sacrifices are for *whole households*, such as the Passover. Some are *national* sacrifices such as the burnt offering offered twice daily for all Israel. Then there are special sacrifices offered by *the leaders* at certain designated times.

We can see that the extent of the sacrificial system was great. It has been estimated on the basis of the census taken in Numbers that there must have been about two and a half million people in Israel in the wilderness. When we consider such a large number of people and the huge numbers of sacrifices that would be required each day, our minds are overcome. Added to that is the requirement of Deuteronomy 12 that all sacrifices must be made in one place which God chooses.

We see the utter impossibility of the task. God was clearly here requiring what was beyond human accomplishment, beyond human reach. And *that* is the very point! God did not make it easy because of the difficulties associated with bringing so many sacrifices to one place so often. God's intent in the giving of the sacrificial system was to impress on men their own exceeding sinfulness and their total inability to cope with their own predicament. The sense of the enormity of sin and the consequent heartbreak of the people was the result God desired.

Sacrifices were never intended by God to be substitutes for obedience to the Lord but were means of acknowledgment and recognition of sin and the sinner's guilt before God.

The principle is well illustrated in the great contrast between Saul and David at a later time in Israel's history. We shall here only briefly mention it and later look at it more fully. Suffice it here to point out that Saul's attitude was that the sacrifice was a mere ceremony to be performed to appease God (1 Sam. 13:8-13; 15:20-21). Samuel's answer to him at that time (15:22, 23) clearly shows that God never intended sacrifices to substitute for the keeping of the Law. This same truth is reiterated throughout the Old Testament (Psa. 40:6; Isa. 1:11f.; Amos 5:21-24; Mic. 6:6). Sadly, most of Israel seems to have followed Saul in seeing sacrifice as merely a ceremony to be carried out in appeasing an angry God. It became a major Jewish heresy, as subsequent history showed.

By contrast, David quite well understood that when one sinned, what God desired more than sacrifice was a broken and a contrite heart. He so professed on the occasion of his own gross sins and his repentance (Psa. 51:16, 17). The sacrifice should bring one to a broken heart in realization of his own sin and helplessness to do anything about it himself. Sacrifices could not substitute for one's obedience to God. They could only teach one to be humble before the holy God with a broken heart. This is what happened to David, and God was pleased with him.

Of course, the sacrificial system which was inadequate in itself to take away sins but which pointed to the need of God's redemptive work, culminates in the actual work of Jesus Christ, who was the true sacrifice for our sins and whose death did really pay the penalty for the sins of those who believe in him. This is one of the major themes of the book of Hebrews (chapters 7–10).

The rest of the book of Leviticus contains various ordinances related to worship and the sacrificial system. Much attention is given to the consecration of Aaron and his sons for the particular priestly functions related to the sacrificial system (chs. 6, 8-10). The necessity for sacrifice on their behalf underlines the point made by the writer to the Hebrews that the Old Testament system was far inferior to the work of Christ and could only point to it. In the regulations concerning the priests are the ordinances pertaining to their sharing in the portion of the sacrifices set aside for God (7:32f.).

The importance of perfect obedience to all of the ordinances of God is seen in what happened to Nadab and Abihu. We read that they offered strange fire before the Lord. This strange fire is defined as that which the Lord had not commanded (10:1). We need not suppose therefore that what they did was particularly weird. It was apparently simply an innovation, an addition to the prescribed worship. But it perverted God's truth and as such was a threat to the whole purpose which God had established for the service of the priests before him. Again we see how very important God regards his Word that his people may learn to pay proper respect to it.

The laws of cleanliness in chapters 11 to 24 are also designed to teach the people concepts of the distinction which God makes between the clean and the unclean. By this means, God instilled in them a sensitivity to what is holy (set aside for God) as opposed to what is profane. Most particularly, God desired these people to recognize their own holiness as the people of God in contradistinction to the rest of the nations who were not. This is expressly stated in chapter 20, verses 24 and 25.

In the midst of these rather tedious laws which make very difficult reading indeed, we come across a verse like "Thou shalt love thy neighbor as thy self" (19:18), and suddenly we realize that these are not irrelevant laws but that they say much about God and ourselves. God was detailing all of his will toward a sinful people who were inclined to disobey God and harm one another. They were to live in the midst of a pagan culture as the people of God. In the midst of God's myriads of laws, here in just seven words was the essence of the Law as we have noted already. Every ordinance found here was an elaboration on the great commandment as defined by Jesus—love of God with all the heart and love of our neighbor as ourselves.

That the law of love is the spirit that permeates this whole section is well illustrated by the ordinances concerning the year of jubilee (ch. 25). Here was built into the very calendar of God's people a timetable to recall God's love for them in providing them rich inheritances (vs. 23, 24) and to show their love to one another in restoration of all the land each fiftieth year to those to whom God first gave it or to their heirs (vs. 25-28).

The section on vows (ch. 27) includes ways in which special commitments could be made to the Lord. The commitments included persons and possessions and even one's house or land. These commitments were made as special gifts to God and suggest the way of higher stewardship to God. Nothing already claimed by God could be committed in this special way such as the firstlings of the animals which already belong to God (v. 26 with Exod. 13:2); or the tithe (v. 30). The whole section points to the exhortation of Paul to the Roman Christians in Romans 12:1, 2, to wit, our whole bodies ought to be committed to God as living sacrifices, which is our reasonable service.

The Years of Wandering (Numbers 1-20). The basic legislation having been now given, the Lord, still speaking from the tabernacle, instructs Moses to take a census. This numbering, together with a second census at the end of the 40 years (recorded in chapter 26) gives to the book its name.

The census was to include only males 20 years old and older who were able to go to war (1:2, 3). The total number counted was 603,550 (1:46), which did not include the Levites (1:47). Next the marching order of the tribes is given, with Dan and his two associate tribes leading the way. Then came Judah with his two on the right flank, Ephraim and his two on the left flank, and Reuben with his two going as the rearguard.

In Exodus 13:2 God had, on the occasion of saving the first-born of Israel from the judgment on Egypt, claimed the first-born for himself. They were to be particularly his. However, instead of these all rendering special service to God as priests, God chose one tribe, the Levites, for this service. Now tabulation is made of the firstborn of all Israel and of all of the males of the tribe of Levi. The Levites numbered 22,000 (3:39), and the first-born of Israel, 22,273 (3:43). Consequently the Lord took the Levites instead of all the firstborn of Israel. The difference was made up by the redemption of the excess of firstborn, with five shekels for each additional firstborn over the number 22,000 (3:44-51).

In this way, the Lord laid claim to all of Israel to be his own, for in saving the firstborn, as we have shown, he saved all of

Israel; and so in choosing the firstborn (now represented by the Levites for fulltime service to him) he was in reality claiming all of Israel as his own possession for his own service. Chapter 4 contains laws on the various duties of the Levites in service to God.

Chapters 5 and 6 are concerned with varied laws pertaining to the relationship between God and his people as they prepare to move into the land of promise. The law of jealousy in chapter 5 is designed to deal with the problem of adultery which would threaten the home. The method used to test for adultery is similar to other such laws practiced in the various cultures in the ancient Near East. The difference between the law here and in other cultures is in the setting under God's authority, because of God's concern for the family and the blessings on the seed. The Nazarite laws in chapter 6 are a special type of vow belonging to the laws on vows already noted in Leviticus 27. Nazarites were apparently rare in Israel. They serve as an example of the separated holy life to God. Similar to other laws of vows, the purpose here seems to have been to show to the people ideals of service for individuals toward God without requiring such service. It was God's desire that all special commitment to him be from the heart, that is, voluntary.

In final preparation for leaving Sinai, chapters 7 through 9 record the special gifts of the princes of Israel, the lighting of the lamp in the sanctuary, and the reminder of various laws already given, such as the purification of the Levites and laws concerning the Passover.

Chapters 10 through 12 tell of the actual departure from Sinai and constitute the first in-journey testing of the Law of God in the lives of the people.

Unhappily, the faith of the people was weak. Many did not observe God's Law. They quickly became murmurers (11:1) and God began to clean out the dross from Israel (11:1). We are told that the makeup of Israel was a mixed multitude. The exact meaning of this expression is uncertain. Some take this to mean that they were foreigners. However, I rather think that the mixture was the same kind of mixture which we have seen from the beginning, that is, between the seed of the woman and the seed of the serpent, i.e., between God's children and Satan's children. In the visible church in the wilderness, that is, among the Israelites, were true believers in God and those who were not believers. God here, as always throughout his dealings with his people, will not permit this state of affairs. He purges his church always. So here, the slaying of the murmurers was an act of God's purging.

Paul takes this understanding of the incident as we read in 1 Corinthians 10:1-6. Paul speaks of "our fathers" the Israelites, who all were part of the visible church of God. Yet he says that God was not pleased with most and therefore they were overthrown in the wilderness. Jude 5 says virtually the same thing, explaining that when God saved the mass of Israel out of Egypt, he nevertheless destroyed those among them who did not believe. We must never forget that the visible church is not the same as the true people of God. There is always a mixed multitude in the church.

Moses' own faith was tested in those days of journeying from Sinai to Canaan. First, he came to see his own limitations (11:14) and God supplied his needed assistance (11:16ff.). God never tests his own beyond what they are able to do but supplies the needs they have (1 Cor. 10:13).

Again Moses' own family, his brother and sister, tempted him by challenging his leadership (12:1ff). But God sustained him and exalted him over the rest (12:6ff.).

Therefore, before the people even arrived at Canaan, within a few short months they had already demonstrated great weakness and inability to make God's will work in their lives. It is really no surprise when they refused to go into the land of promise. Neither the people nor their leaders were prepared to enjoy the land before the Lord in worship and service to him.

The report of the spies given in 13:27-29, which was one-third favorable and two-thirds filled with warnings and fears, indicates how the leadership lacked faith. One man, Caleb, seems to have demonstrated among these leaders a faith worthy to inherit (v. 30). Note how the "leaders" are led by the thinking of the people and now actually speak against going in (v. 31ff.). This underlines the kind of leadership the church does *not* need, leadership which seeks its cues from the temperament of the people who are to be led.

Again Moses appears as the great mediator between God and God's people. He intercedes for them when God is about to destroy the people (14:11-19). Moses, in his plea for pardon, reaches back to the revelation of God which God had formerly given him at Sinai (Num. 14:19 with Exod. 34:6, 7). God's immediate response indicates that once more he had tested Moses by what he had said, to see whether Moses would hold faithful to the revelation which God had given him.

Because of their refusal to go in and because of their murmuring, God did begin again to purge Israel of all unbelief. He would have only those who believed to enter into the inheritance (14:26-35).

Moses' next trial was the rebellion of Korah (chapters 16 and 17). This second challenge to Moses' leadership showed the extent of rebellion in the hearts of these unbelievers. They claimed to be holy but their spirit and their words spoke to the contrary (16:3). That day God again entered in and stood with Moses, vindicating his leadership and destroying the opposition. The fact that the people did not approve shows how widespread unbelief was among the Israelites (16:41ff.).

After this incident, once more Aaron's authority is reiterated, since Korah and his companions had been of the same tribe (17:1-11). Once more also the Levites are purified for the special service which God has set up for them (ch. 19).

Tragedy after tragedy continued as God proceeded to burn all unbelief from Israel in her years of wandering in the wilderness. Only a few incidents in these years are recorded for us. Chapter 20 records that on one occasion while the people murmured Moses acted inconsistently with his faith and did not honor God before Israel (20:10-13). The result was God's refusal to allow Moses to enter in.

The charge against Moses was that he did not believe in the Lord in what he did. Therefore, he did not glorify God before the people (v. 12). What he did may seem a little thing to you and me. After all, who could blame him for his impatience after so many years? The penalty he had to pay was heavy.

Here the Lord shows to his church once more that in his sight no sin is slight. Even the lawgiver Moses must be at all times subject to God's Law and honor the Lord by it. How important the end of the Law is to God is clearly shown here. Moses that day did not show love to the Lord or to the people. God will never overlook even the seemingly least of our sins. Of course, Moses was forgiven but he had to face the consequences of his sin. He could not enter the land of Canaan.

When rebuked, Moses took the chastisement as a child of God should, showing that he was indeed God's child and not a bastard (Heb. 12:7, 8). We can contrast here Cain's own reaction of bitterness when faced with God's accusation, or later, that of Saul when Samuel faced him with his sin. Moses and David show us well how a child of God must behave in the face of God's discipline.

Chapter 20 records for us the death of Miriam (v. 1) and Aaron (v. 28). Before Aaron's death, his office was given to his son Eleazar (vv. 25ff.).

The End of the Journey (Numbers 21-36). As the people approached
Canaan, nearing the end of their journey, there were evidently
still some who did not believe (Compare Jude 5). In spite of
victory given over the Canaanite enemies while yet outside of
Canaan proper, some murmured and disbelieved (21:1-5). God
sent the fiery serpents as a judgment on the whole camp of
Israel to weed out the rest who did not believe (21:6).

For those who did repent and confess their sin, i.e., who were
of a contrite heart, God provided a way of deliverance, the brazen serpent. To look on that serpent was to live. Here again we
must not fail to note that the particular word used here for "to
look" (v. 9) is not the usual one. It means to look expectantly,
with longing. In this context it no doubt meant to look in faith.
Jesus likened this incident to his own being lifted up. Jesus says
that as men believe in him as he is lifted up, they shall have
eternal life (John 3:14, 15).

That day when Moses lifted up the serpent, all who trusted
God looked on the serpent with faith in God's provision for their
healing and they were healed. The unbelievers that day died. It
is most likely that in some sense the lifting up of this brazen
serpent was similar or related to the incident of God's promise in
Genesis 3:15 to give to those who trust in him victory over our
true enemy, Satan, *the* Serpent.

The next few chapters record the conquest of the land east of
the Jordan. Much attention is given to the incidents concerning
Balak and Balaam. Balaam remains a rather strange personality
in Scripture. The man's reputation was great. Balak in Moab
had heard of him while he yet lived in Mesopotamia (22:5). He
had a reputation for power to bless and curse (22:6).

Balaam seems to have depended on the Lord for his wisdom
(22:8). How he knew the Lord we do not know. Remember,
however, that Laban knew the God of Jacob. Abraham's ancestors had lived there for a long period of time. It is possible that
some real knowledge of God remained in the east after Abraham and Jacob had departed.

God made clear to Balaam that he had blessed Israel, and so
Balaam was not to curse the Israelites (22:12). Balaam obeyed
and refused to go at first but he betrayed his heart's desire for
the rewards of Balak (22:19). God, after showing to him his
displeasure with Balaam's longing to go, permitted him to go but
only to bless Israel.

Four times he blessed Israel according to the will of God,
though Balak protested vehemently (23:7ff.; vv. 18ff., 24:3ff.,
vv. 15ff.). Balaam felt hedged in by God's word though he no
doubt desired the rewards of Balak. Unlike Abraham who re-

fused to be made rich by the rewards of the king of Sodom (Gen. 14:23), Balaam must have lusted for these rewards which were seemingly so out of reach. Scripture tells us here that after his fourth blessing, he returned to his place. I am not sure whether it means back to Mesopotamia or merely back to his dwelling place there in Moab. Scripture later tells us more of Balaam.

In 25:1ff., we read of the children of Israel playing the harlot with the daughters of Moab. Evidently they had sexual union with them and even worshipped their gods. They broke their covenant with God and angered the Lord. Because of this, 24,000 died (25:9). In 31:16 we read that the intermingling of these Midianites of Moab with Israel was according to Balaam's counsel. Here we have to reconstruct what must have happened. Evidently Balaam, frustrated for not getting his reward and seeing that God would not allow him to curse Israel, gave advice to Moab to seduce the Israelites and cause them to sin against their God.

Whether Balaam was rewarded for this advice or not, we do not know. At any rate, he did not live to enjoy it. He was killed in war against the Midianites (31:8). For further insight into the evil counsel of Balaam see also Jude 11 and Revelation 2:14, which comment on this incident. Jude in fact uses the name of Balaam as one of the examples of faithless and ungodly men who may even appear in the church.

The second census, at the end of the forty years of wandering, shows that the size of Israel now was not greatly different from its size earlier. In the forty years of purging, the Lord blessed Israel with more seed, a more disciplined, and more obedient seed who were now ready to go in. The first generation, who had refused to go in, were now all dead (26:64).

The noble nature of Moses is shown in his concern for the people after his death. He continues to act as a true mediator as he pleads for a successor for their sake (27:16). The Lord comforted Moses that day by the appointing of Joshua (27:18).

The land of Canaan was to be given these survivors of the wilderness experience (26:52). It would be Joshua's task to conquer and distribute the land. The land given was to be perpetually in the same family (26:55). Herein lay a problem when the daughters of one man who had died sought their rightful share (27:1). The Lord established that all women as well as men had a right to their family's portion. Yet, as developed later, no heiress could marry outside of her tribe so as to carry land away from one tribe to another (see chapter 36).

As the conquest of the land east of the Jordan began, two and one-half tribes desired to have the conquered land because of their large amounts of cattle (32:1ff.). It was given to them on condition that they would not enjoy their inheritance before the other tribes had received theirs.

In these instances concerning the inheritance, we see God's concern for all and the bond of love and sense of responsibility which he was building in the hearts of his people toward one another. The land was really the Lord's and was usable by Israel so long as the people were faithful. This was the old covenant of blessings in the land provided they obeyed God. Their obedience was in essence an indication of their continuing to love God and one another. So long as they were concerned for one another's rights and privileges, they would show love. When they became self-seeking and unconcerned to love and meet the needs of others, then God would take all from them. Here we see God establishing a principle to instill in them the responsibility for one another as together they entered into the Lord's land.

The Second Legislation (Deuteronomy). The name Deuteronomy means the second Law. It refers to the messages of Moses to Israel at the end of their long wilderness journey. It was no new law but an interpretation of the Law and of the experiences of Israel in the wilderness years. The place of the deliverance of these messages is on the east side of the Jordan, just before Jericho. The Arabah refers to the Jordan valley (1:1).

The first address (1:4-4:40) is primarily an historical review of God's dealings with Israel. Stress here is given to the uniqueness of the God who has dealt with Israel (3:24; 4:39). This uniqueness is brought out in the ways in which God has blessed and punished Israel in accord with her relationships to the Lord. In the light of the Lord's uniqueness before Israel, he calls Israel to be his people and to give complete obedience to God (4:1). What God has taught must be obeyed if Israel is to please the Lord. Nothing of God's revelation may be tampered with (4:2). Obedience to God's Word constitutes the uniqueness of his people and sets them off from all around them (4:6, 7).

As we saw in the giving of the Ten Commandments, God is not asking for mere outward conformity to the Law but for heartfelt obedience. Therefore here again the problem of the heart is stressed. It is in the heart that God must be obeyed if he is to be obeyed at all (4:9).

The theme of the heart is one of the major themes of Deuteronomy. We can trace it in a few verses to see its import here. In 4:9 he teaches that the obedience must be from the heart. Since the heart of man is prone to wander from God, the Lord expresses how very much a new heart is needed in these people so that they will obey God and love and fear him (5:29). In 10:16, that need is expressed in terms of a circumcised heart. Here we see that the sacrament of circumcision was intended as a sacrament or sign of the inward cleansing needed for the salvation of his people.

Tracing the theme of the heart further, in 29:4, Moses recognizes that God has not yet given them a heart capable of obedience, i.e., a new heart. They are still unbelieving. But in 30:6, he tells of the promise of a heart that will do God's will. It is a circumcised heart, cleansed, reborn. In this treatise on the heart, interwoven into the text of Deuteronomy, God is showing that what he demands and Israel cannot produce on her own, God will provide.

In addition to the introduction of the theme of the heart in chapter 4, Moses also warns again against idolatry (v. 15) because they are to be uniquely God's own people (v. 20).

Noticeable throughout Deuteronomy is the predictive element concerning Israel's future spiritual state. We see this first in chapter 4. Moses foretells the day when Israel will fail God and be punished (4:25ff.). He also points the way to her return to God (v. 29). Moses' assurance of God's readiness to forgive Israel's sin when she repents is no doubt based on that revelation which God had given to Moses earlier (Exod. 34:6, 7).

The first message, which dwells on the uniqueness of God toward Israel and the uniqueness of Israel among the nations, appropriately closes on the note of the uniqueness of Israel's God. There is no other (4:39).

Between the first and second addresses is a brief historical interlude (4:41-43). Moses, having assured them of their entrance into Canaan, now set up three cities of refuge in Canaan even before they crossed the Jordan.

The second address (4:44—26:19) is in the same setting as the first. It begins with a review of the Law of God which distinguishes the people of God from the world. The Law is reviewed in 5:6-21 and varies only slightly from the original given at Sinai and recorded in Exodus. It is plain that God recognizes their inability in themselves to keep the Law as he calls for what is needed: a heart that will obey God. Verse 29 may be compared to Genesis 18:19. Thus we see the continuity of God's dealing with his people. God never alters his purpose for his people.

Now we turn to chapter 6. Here a right heart is defined as one that loves God totally. There can be no room in the heart of the righteous person to love any other besides God (6:4). Yet contained within our love of God is love for one another. As John later points out, if we do not love one another we do not have the love of God in our hearts (1 John 4:20). This passage beginning with Deuteronomy 6:4 is called "the Shema" because it begins with the Hebrew word *Shema*, which means "hear."

This passage contains specific instructions pertaining to parental duty. It cannot be isolated but should be taken in context with such passages as Genesis 18:19 and the fifth Commandment. God's church is built by the families which God calls to himself. Therefore Moses calls the parents to believe and love God and to teach their children to believe and love him.

God has ordained that church instruction should begin in the home. The Sunday school or vacation Bible school will never be able to do what is required here. Not even the Christian day school can be a substitute for parental instruction in the home. It is a parental duty that is imperative and incumbent upon all Christian parents. When this command is taken seriously, God's people prosper as the fifth Commandment promises.

In chapter 7 Moses dwells on the reason God chose Israel. He chose them to be holy (set aside for God). This makes them unique in all the earth. The reason given for God's choosing them as his own people is always and only, love. Beyond this we cannot go (vv. 7, 8).

Moses now, forty years after the first abortive attempt to enter Canaan had failed because of their unbelief, seeks to build the faith of the people in God and not in themselves (7:17, 18, 23). He exhorts them to learn from the lessons of the past forty years of wandering (8:2-5). Particularly, they are to have confidence in the Word of the Lord (v. 3).

Though once the problem of the people was fear of their enemies, now another problem has developed. The people are threatened with spiritual pride. They are not to suppose that God is giving them the land because they deserved it for their righteousness. It is because of the wickedness of the Canaanites that God is expelling them (9:4, 5). Here once more we see the doctrine of the sovereignty of God over all the earth. All belongs to God, who gives it to whomsoever he pleases. All are accountable to God.

In 10:12, once more Moses stresses heart obedience and summarizes the whole Law as love of God with the whole heart while serving the Lord from the heart. It is here that the heart problem once more is noted. It must be circumcised (cleansed) if the people are ever to obey God (10:16).

In 11:26, alternatives are placed before Israel: the blessing or the curse. She will be blessed if she obeys God; and if she does not, she will be cursed. Blessings bring unique responsibility to these privileged people. This is to stress the truth that God's people, who have the unique privilege of God's blessings above all other people, must also meet the responsibility of that privilege or suffer greatly for their faithlessness. Later history in Israel will illustrate the relationship between blessing and obedience on the one hand, and cursing and disobedience on the other.

Chapter 12 demands that all offerings be made on one altar (vv. 11, 14). In studying the sacrificial system as given in Leviticus we noted how difficult it would be to do this because of the many offerings required daily for the sins of so many people. And this is precisely the point. God was teaching them that only one place of sacrifice was acceptable to him, no matter how difficult it was for them to comply. No doubt this one place, which God would designate, points to the real one place of the true offering—Calvary.

Chapter 13 speaks of certain threats to the continued blessings of God on Israel. These threats are in the form of false prophets or teachers that may arise in Israel. Even though they may work impressive signs or predict things that come to pass to persuade the people, they are not to be followed if they teach what is contrary to God's revealed Word. This makes the Law of Moses the standard for all following revelations and teachings. God's infallible Word is the sole authority for God's people. No one can be allowed to lead us from the Word, neither prophets (13:1), nor members of one's own family (13:6), not even a whole city (13:12, 13).

God's concern for the poor of his people is expressed in chapter 15. Here God warns through Moses that we must never use the Law as a means of hurting people or taking advantage of them. Later, the Lord accused the Pharisees of just that kind of sin (Mark 7:10-13).

An interesting warning against future kings over the people is found in chapter 17. The amazing detail of similarity between these warnings and the actual conduct of Solomon, long after, shows the great spiritual insight given to Moses as he prepared the people for the best and the worst that could happen to them depending on their obedience or disobedience (17:14-17).

Because God would reveal further truth through other prophets to come, just as formerly he had warned against the false (13:1ff), so now he prepares the way for the true prophets (18:15-19). The true prophet will be like Moses, i.e., in harmony with God's Word through Moses. He too will speak God's Word, not man's thoughts. As with Moses, so with him, what he says is authoritative because it is God's Word (v. 19). The test for the true prophet given here is the secondary test. It is always subject to the first test, which is agreement with the revelations given through Moses. We know this because God had earlier said that one might predict what does come to pass and yet be false (13:1, 2). But only the true prophet will be in harmony with God's Word. (Compare Acts 17:11 for a New Testament example of this principle).

In chapter 20 we note two different instructions given to Israel in regard to her enemies. Those in lands not promised to Israel are to be approached in peace and attacked only if they refuse peace (20:10-12). In contrast, cities close at hand, i.e., in Canaan, which is promised to Israel, are to be totally destroyed because God will not have his people living in the midst of a sinful people (10:16-18). It was in a vain attempt to observe this law that Joshua later got into serious trouble which would prove to be detrimental to Israel's whole history (Josh. 9:3-15).

Chapter 22 contains passages reflecting God's concern not only for Israel and for humans in general, but even for the little creatures of the earth (22:6, 7). This shows how God is concerned for all of his creatures and knows the need of each, protecting them from their enemies and feeding them as they have need. This doctrine is of great comfort to God's people as well, as we see in Job 38-41 and in Matthew 6:25-34.

The remaining chapters of this address (chapters 24-26) contain various laws pertaining to relationships among the citizens of God's Kingdom. Among them we note in 24:1-4 the law relating to divorce. It is well to keep in mind here that divorce is permitted because of the sins in men's hearts, as Jesus himself taught later (Matt. 19:7, 8). The occasion for divorce as Moses allowed it here is that the wife is no longer loved by her husband. He has found fault with her (24:1). Lest by cruelty he cause her to suffer greatly or be injured, divorce is permitted. But as the Lord taught in Matthew, from the beginning it was not so. God never purposes divorce as good or desirable.

God's concern for the weak and helpless is quite evident in these chapters. In addition to his concern for the mistreated wife, in 24:14, he expresses his concern for the poor hired servant; and in 24:17, 19, for the stranger and fatherless or widow. Even an ox must be treated fairly (25:4). This latter law was applied by Paul as a principle for ministers of the Word. They too are to be paid by those to whom they minister the Word (See 1 Cor. 9:9).

We note also the principle of individual guilt as it is taught here (24:16). In later years evidently the people believed that this principle was not so. They complained that they were being punished for their fathers' sins (Jeremiah 31:30; Ezek. 18:2-4).

The address closed with a final statement of God's goal for his people. They are to be, above all the nations, a unique and holy people of God (26:19).

Chapters 27-30 contain the record of the renewal of the covenant of God with his people. First he states what God expects: keep all the commandments (27:1). There follow instructions which serve to remind the people of God's will. The Law is to be written in plaster in the heart of the land so that all may see and be reminded (27:2-8).

The ceremony at Mount Gerizim and Mount Ebal, described in 27:11ff., was again to serve as a sober reminder to the people of the seriousness of their covenant with God. The two mountains which stand in the heart of the land near Shechem are separated by a narrow valley. People standing at the foot or on the lower sides of the two mountains and facing one another could easily be heard by each other.

Most of the curses noted here pertain to secret sins which might not be detected by the people if committed. This made them particularly dangerous sins, thus the terrible curses attached to them. We see later, in the time of Joshua, how a secret sin nearly destroyed these people (Josh. 7:1ff.).

The heart of God's covenant with Israel is clearly set forth here in chapter 28. So long as the people were faithful to God, they would continue in the land of Canaan and prosper (28:1-14). But should they fail to live as God's children, then God would bring judgment on them and terminate their stay and their prosperity in the land (28:15-68). Included in the judgment are cursings (vv. 20ff.); smitings (vv. 25ff.); capture (vv. 36ff.); suffering (vv. 47ff.); and dispersion (vv. 64ff.).

In the subsequent history of Israel we see how completely these judgments did fall on a disobedient Israel. This was the old covenant, based on the ability of Israel to obey God and keep his commandments. It promised prosperity in the land of Canaan so long as they were faithful.

No wonder the writer to the Hebrews speaks of the new covenant based on the obedience and work of Christ as more sure and with greater promises, i.e., an inheritance forever in a heavenly home (Heb. 8:6-13). The old covenant served to show God's people their need of the new. The new was not dependent on men's works but on God's grace and work through Jesus Christ. By the failure of the old, the land was lost. By the success

of the new through Jesus Christ, eternal inheritance is assured
for those who believe in Christ. It is an inheritance that will not
fade away as did the land of Canaan (1 Pet. 1:3-5).

Even here in the context of the old covenant, Moses speaks of
the necessity and sure coming of the new covenant (ch. 30). Basic
in the hope of the new covenant to come is the changing of the
hearts of the people (the circumcision of the heart—v. 6). This is
no doubt the same as the new birth which Jesus speaks of in
John 3.

Paul saw these promises in the context of the gospel he was
preaching. He quoted from this passage (30:11ff) in Romans
10:6-8. We see then that while Moses is the human mediator of
the old covenant, yet even he is permitted to see and point to the
greater covenant mediated by the greater person, Jesus Christ,
which holds better promises for God's people.

Chapters 31-33 contain the last words of Moses to the people
whom he had led so faithfully for forty years. He sought in his final
words to lead the people to complete trust and dependence on
the Lord (31:6). The Lord gave to Moses insight to see that
Israel would be faithless in years to come. The long poem in
chapter 32 tells of the failures of Israel to come. It is a poetic
expression of the future dismal history of Israel. Its purpose too
was to lead the people to trust in the Lord and not in themselves.
The poem or song was to be memorized by all the people and
taught to their children in order to prepare the faithful for what
was to come (31:19).

The poem itself traces God's good deeds for Israel and her
own subsequent rebellion and punishment. It ends on the note
of hope in the work of expiation which God shall perform for
his people (32:43).

At the end of the poem Moses once more states succinctly the
terms of the covenant (32:46-47). Note how this passage ties in
both with those earlier words of God with Abraham (Gen. 18:19)
and with the fifth Commandment as well as Deuteronomy 6:4ff.
This old covenant was based on the continuance of the people in
faithfulness to God.

Chapter 33 is a final blessing of Moses on the people, tribe by
tribe, somewhat reminiscent of Jacob's earlier blessing recorded
in Genesis, chapter 49.

Deuteronomy closes with a record of the death of Moses and a
high tribute to the man. It is not necessary to insist on the Mosaic
authorship of this one chapter. The style here is very like that of
the opening words of Joshua and it is most reasonable to assume
that Joshua wrote this concluding chapter as an epilogue to the

whole writings of Moses and also as a connector with his own writing which follows, the book of Joshua.

In review of the Pentateuch we note that the first two chapters of Genesis gave to us the account of God's creation and his purpose for man whom he made in his own image. When in Genesis 3 we read of man's failure to carry out God's purpose for him, we also find here immediately God's plan of redemption to save a people for himself. Chapters 4-11 show how, over a long period of time, God did preserve a line of faithful people by his grace until, in chapter 12, he introduces Abraham who is to be the father of the faithful people of God. The rest of Genesis traces the line of faithful men who became the family of God through Abraham, Isaac and Jacob.

The first 19 chapters of Exodus tell how the Lord redeemed from their enemies this people of God who by now had grown into a large nation in Egypt. The rest of the Pentateuch is concerned with teaching the people how to live as the people of God.

From Exodus 20 through Numbers, we see recorded the giving of God's Law to Israel together with certain means of learning what God requires if the people are to please God. Here, as we have noted before, the tabernacle and the sacrificial system point ultimately to Christ as the fulfillment of all that God requires in obedience and in worship. The book of Deuteronomy, reflecting on the forty years of Israel's wandering in the wilderness, interprets the Law, predicts the future failure of the people to keep it, and finally points to the hope of God's redemption of his people from their sins.

The Pentateuch is certainly the foundation for our understanding of the rest of God's verbal revelation. We shall constantly refer to it as we progress in our study of the rest of the Old Testament and also the New Testament.

THE PEOPLE
INHERIT THE LAND
Joshua

THE BOOK OF JOSHUA falls easily into two nearly equal parts of 12 chapters each. The first 12 chapters tell of the conquest of the land of Canaan. The second 12 chapters relate the dividing of the land among the tribes of Israel.

We have seen in the Pentateuch how the Lord established and called a family through Abraham and made that family into a nation in Egypt; how he called Israel out of bondage, established her as a nation for God and gave her the Law at Sinai.

Now as Israel is matured in the wilderness and ready to enter into Canaan, the book of Joshua records the account of God's kept promise to Abraham, that he would give to his seed the land of Canaan as an inheritance.

The book of Joshua is a kind of Old Testament eschatology. It tells of the people coming into the inheritance which God has prepared for them. Canaan is therefore a type of that eternal dwelling place which God has prepared for all his children. Though through the Old Covenant, for a time they held Canaan, yet, as the writer of the epistle to the Hebrews shows us, even Abraham understood that the real fulfillment of God's promises reached far beyond the land of Canaan, to an eternal city not made with hands, whose Maker is God (Heb. 11:10, 16). This is what both the Old and New Testaments call the new heavens and the new earth (Isa. 65:17; 66:22; 2 Pet. 3:13; Rev. 21:1) or the new Jerusalem (Rev. 21:2).

Inasmuch as the book of Joshua is the record of the dispossession of Canaan from the Canaanites, we need first of all to observe God's own declaration of his right to do just the thing regarding any kingdom or nation of people on earth. We saw earlier in Deuteronomy the reason why the Canaanites were expelled from Canaan (Deut. 9:4, 5). In Jeremiah 27:5, God further declares that he has made earth and all in it and has given it to whomsoever it seems right to him.

In chapter one of Joshua we have the commissioning of Joshua, after Moses' death, to lead the people into the inheritance.

We see here the predominance of the personal pronoun "I" in reference to God. It is God who makes the promises of success and God who will see the people through to success with Joshua as leader. The promise here is reminiscent of God's earlier words to Moses. It is the familiar "I will be with you," by which the Lord is known to his people in every generation (1:5).

Since the people now have the Word of God written as the standard for their lives and the authority for their whole service to God, they are here reminded to observe it as the basis for their success (1:7). This passage reminds us of Genesis 18:19 and Deuteronomy 6:4ff. which also insisted upon the observance of God's Word as the way to success in God's eyes. That principle is still true today and always will be.

After Joshua's commissioning the leadership of the people, they are then prepared for the conquest (1:11). The two and one-half tribes which had already received their inheritance east of the Jordan are reminded of their solemn commitment not to settle in their own lands until their brothers have received their inheritance (1:12ff.).

The readiness of these people to do all that Joshua commands is a pleasant contrast to the earlier refusal of their fathers under Moses to go in and possess the land (1:16—see Num. 14). This is a new generation, no more numerous than the Israel of forty years before, but they are of greater faith.

As a prelude to their entry into the land, certain spies are sent to Jericho, the first stronghold of Canaan across the Jordan (2:1ff.). Just what their purpose was, we are not told. Presumably they were to bring back encouraging reports of the preparation which the Lord had made for the conquest.

They came to the house of a harlot, Rahab. At the risk of her own life, Rahab hid them when the king of Jericho sought to catch them. In verse 9 she tells why she did this. She is herself a convert to faith in the God of Israel from what she already knows of him and his people (2:11, 12, 13). The book of Hebrews tells us that in receiving the spies she acted in faith (Heb. 11:31). James too uses Rahab as one of two Old Testament examples of faith (Jas. 2:25).

It is rare in the Old Testament to find Gentiles who believe and are included among the people of God. The period of the Old Testament was not the period of the extension of the gospel to the Gentiles, but incidents like this one do occur and give promise of that later inclusiveness of the Gentiles of the world in God's Kingdom. This inclusiveness was hinted at in Noah's prophecy (Gen. 9:27). Other notable examples of Gentile inclusion in the Old Testament era are Tamar, the wife of Judah, Ruth the Moabitess, and possibly Bathsheba, the wife of Uriah the Hittite, together with Naaman the Syrian in Elisha's day. The four women noted above all appear in Jesus' genealogy as recorded by Matthew in the first chapter of his Gospel.

Some find a moral dilemma here in that Rahab did not tell the truth to the men of Jericho but deceived them. Yet Scripture knows no such dilemma. Rahab's act is approved by the New Testament testimony to her great faith, as we just noted. Suffice it to say that this was war; and in war, frequently in Scripture, deceit is practiced by God's people without any apparent impunity. An example can be seen in this very book later on (Josh. 8:15). Nevertheless, one should never justify lies from such cases. To develop the principle that lying is sometimes right or to advocate the pernicious doctrine of situation ethics so-called which is so popular today from such incidents in Scripture is to misuse the Scriptures. The case seems to be very much as Christ expressed in relationship to divorce. It is permitted under certain circumstances because of the hardness of the hearts of men, but from the beginning it was not so (Matt. 19:8). God did not purpose lies or deceit as a proper part of man's conduct but at times it was permitted with apparent impunity.

The report of these spies was quite optimistic (2:24). There followed, therefore, the actual crossing of the Jordan river by Israel in the way prescribed by God to bring all glory to God (chapters 3, 4). God's stated purpose in performing this miracle of the drying up of the river is given in 3:7, to magnify Joshua, i.e., to build up the people's confidence in him. The river is small and shallow. Even at flood time it is not much of a river. It could easily have been crossed without a miracle. But a miracle showed that as God had been with Moses, so he was with Joshua.

A further instance of making a memorial in stone of this event is given in chapter 4. The results of the crossing in the manner prescribed by the Lord are told us in 4:14. We are told plainly that the stones were a memorial to glorify God (4:20-24). It is possible, however, that later these stones were worshipped or otherwise misused in Israel as Amos 4:4 suggests. We know for sure that Israel did later misuse and worship the brass serpent Moses had made in the wilderness (2 Kgs. 18:4).

No sooner had the people crossed the Jordan than the two sacraments which had been established by the Lord through Moses were observed in the new land (chapter 5). By this the people were reconsecrated to the Lord as his people.

We are not told why the sacrament of circumcision had been neglected in the wilderness; but though the people may have taken the sacrament lightly, God would not. Once Moses had almost been killed for neglecting circumcision with his own son (Exod. 4:24-26). Remember that with God the outward sign indicates the inner need of cleansing of their hearts. This is no light matter.

The passover was also kept at this time, when the manna ceased (v. 12), no doubt because, at last, they had arrived in a land whose fruits could sustain them.

The interesting event recorded at the end of chapter 5 no doubt was intended to recall the beginnings of God's deliverance of his people when God had confronted Moses at the bush. In both cases the holiness of God is emphasized to stress the truth that none can approach God except by God's will. Our overfamiliarity with God, which is related to human pride, is never allowed by God.

Chapter 6 records the actual fall of Jericho. The manner of its capture was designed to show that the city was delivered over by God. And since it was the first Canaanite city to fall, like the firstborn of Israel, God lay claim to the city altogether (v. 17). The term "devoted" means that every living creature was to be

killed, none spared, and that all of its treasures were to be given
to God (v. 19).

After the fall of the city Joshua lay a curse on the one who
would build its walls again, since God had willed it destroyed.
The effect of this solemn curse would be felt centuries later in an
age of unbelief when one would dare to rebuild the city (1 Kgs.
16:34).

A most important lesson for people of God is taught in chapter 7. Achan, of the tribe of Judah, disobeyed God's command
and took for himself some of the city's treasures. He no doubt
felt that it was little enough and would go undetected. But he did
not reckon with God. God knew, and when Israel attempted to
take the next town, much smaller than Jericho, she was badly
beaten.

The reason for her defeat is stated in verse 11. Israel sinned.
Note that the whole people were liable for what the one man
did, and all were affected. When one in Christ's church fails, all
are hurt. Hypocrisy above all else can destroy God's people and
their effectiveness. A hypocritical people could not stand against
their enemies (v. 12). The punishment of the sin may seem
severe (v. 25), yet the welfare of the whole people was at stake. In
the New Testament we see Ananias and Sapphira in the same
problem and the same severe punishment (Acts 5:1-11). The
fact that God does not strike down every hypocrite in the church
today by no means indicates that it no longer matters to God.
The Word of God shows plainly how God feels about it and
shows how dangerous it is when the church tolerates it.

The conquest of Ai is recorded in chapter 8 together with the
account of the recording of the Law at Ebal. The ceremony
described in verses 30-35 is related to the specific instructions
given in Deuteronomy 27:11-14.

Chapter 9 records a second threat to Israel's well-being in
addition to the hypocrisy ferreted out in chapter 7. This time the
danger was compromise with unbelievers. God had soberly
warned against such compromise as we see in Exodus 23:32 and
Deuteronomy 7:2. Yet Joshua and those with him, perhaps because of flattery, made a pact of peace with the Canaanites of the
land. The important thing here is that they did so without seeking God's will (14, 15). Though they later did punish these
people by making them servants at hard labor, yet even this was
to turn out for bad. The idea of having Canaanites to do their
dirty work and hard labor caught on quickly and later others, no
doubt appealing to Joshua's example, did the same thing, to the
detriment of Israel (Judg. 1:35).

These two major threats to Israel's well-being: hypocrisy and compromise with unbelievers would over and again threaten Israel as they continue to this day to threaten the strength of Christ's church.

Chapters 10 to 12 relate the conquest of the rest of the land in rapid succession, led by Joshua. Of considerable interest in this section is the prayer of Joshua recorded in 10:12, 13. He prayed for the sun to stand still while in battle. This miracle, we are told, was unique in all history. Attempts by many to explain this away as some natural phenomenon cannot be supported by the plain Scripture recorded here. Certainly the Sovereign God of the universe could do this if he so desired, and we are told that he was pleased to answer Joshua's prayer because the Lord fought for Israel.

Chapter 10 tells of the conquest of the south. Chapter 11 traces the northern conquests. Chapter 12 summarizes the whole record of conquest. This ends the first major section of the book.

The second section of Joshua is given over primarily to the record of the dividing up of the land among the nine and a half tribes which were to settle on the west side of the Jordan. In addition to the ordinary inheritances of the tribes we are told of the designation of cities of refuge and cities for the Levites whose inheritance was scattered among the tribes (chapters 20, 21).

The incident noted in chapter 22 when the eastern tribes began to return to their lands shows the seriousness with which Israel took God's Word at this time. These were indeed people of faith. The problem was the danger of the setting up of another altar besides the one designated by the Lord in the light of the warnings of Deuteronomy 12. When it was explained that the altar built by these eastern tribes was not for sacrifice but simply a memorial like the stones taken from the Jordan earlier, then the threat disappeared (22:28).

The farewell address of Joshua concludes the book. He exhorts the people as God has exhorted him (23:6 cf. chapter 1). Their continued prosperity depended on their continued obedience to the will of God, as the Old Covenant stated (23:12, 13, 16).

In 24:2, Joshua tells of the ancestry of Abraham from which we know of Abraham's pagan background. Joshua reviews here the history of God's grace toward Israel and then concludes by leaving them something very precious, his own personal testimony of faith and commitment to the Lord (24:14, 15).

In spite of the people's enthusiasm for commitment to the Lord (24:16ff.), Joshua sternly warns them of the danger and difficulty of living faithfully, perhaps recalling that Moses in his final song had warned of bitter times to come (see Deut. 32).

The challenging testimony and exhortation of Joshua recorded in verse 15, lays out the choice which always faces God's people. Christ later would, as Joshua does here, declare that "no man can serve two masters" (Matt. 6:24). Later too, Elijah at Carmel would place the same choice before a sinful and vacillating Israel (1 Kgs. 18). In the messages to the seven churches that are recorded in the book of Revelation, the most stern rebuke falls on the church at Laodicea, which was neither hot nor cold but lukewarm (Rev. 3:15, 16). Evidently, in spite of God's clear teaching of the necessity of total commitment to him, the church has always had many in it who do not take God seriously but seek to serve two masters, i.e., to please God and at the same time the world; to enjoy citizenship in heaven and a worldly life. It simply cannot be done.

The record of Joshua's death was written by one who succeeded as a prophet of God's Word, perhaps the author of Judges, whose name is not given.

The effect of this man's life and its force in Israel is summarized in Joshua 24:31.

5

THE SPIRITUAL
DECLINE OF ISRAEL
Judges, Ruth, 1 Samuel 1, 2

WE ARE NOW MOVING chronolog-
ically into one of the darkest periods of Israel's history. It is
impossible to know exactly how many years are involved in this
period of the judges. There is uncertainty about the time of the
Exodus itself. Some hold to an earlier date in the fifteenth century, while others point to considerable evidence of a later date,
sometime in the thirteenth century. At one time conservatives
generally held to the earlier date and liberals to the later date,
but today this cannot be said. Many conservatives with good
arguments, now insist on a thirteenth century exodus. Scripture
is not at all clear on this matter, and we have no reason to be
greatly concerned about the exact date.

Similarly the duration of the period of the judges cannot be finally ascertained. It seems apparent that the years of the individual judges of the period cannot be consecutive, since this would require more years than we have to work with between the Exodus and the time of David, which is rather certainly about the year 1000 B.C. We can therefore assume that in the times of the individual judges we have overlapping by various judges in different parts of the land.

We would err to spend too much effort attempting to work out the chronology which Scripture has not made clear to us. Better to see the lessons taught by this dark period of Israel's history.

THE BOOK OF JUDGES

Like the book of Joshua, the book of Judges falls into two basic parts. The first part (chapters 1-16) deals with the cycles of Israelite history in this period. The last part (chapters 17-21) gives us some examples of the spiritual state of Israel at that time.

The aftermath of the period of Joshua is covered in chapter one of Judges. We find at first after Joshua's death a willingness on the part of Israel to seek out and follow the Lord's will (1:1-3). The various tribes were busy in finishing up the conquests, as chapter one indicates. This shows that Joshua had not completed the job of conquest but that there were numerous pockets of resistance left throughout the land (1:22, 27, 29-34).

In addition, we learn that many of the tribes, apparently following the example of Joshua as recorded in Joshua 9, were putting the vanquished Canaanites to task work, making slaves of them rather than destroying them as the Lord had commanded (1:28, 30, 33, 35).

This state of affairs provoked the Lord to send an angel to warn Israel that her disobedience to God's command would bring sorrow to the land (2:2, 3). The fact that the people reacted to this word from God by repentance is in itself a good indication that at this point the people were still spiritually conscious. They could be sorry for their sins (2:45).

So long as those who remembered Joshua still lived, the people were generally faithful to the Lord (2:7). But even that generation failed in one very important respect. They failed to follow the instructions of Deuteronomy 6:4ff. to teach their children what they had learned from God. There arose a whole generation after them who knew nothing of God or the Law of Moses (2:10).

The parents' neglect to instruct their children strikes at the very heart of God's purpose in calling a people and establishing his covenant with them to be their God and they to be his people. What God had first expressed to Abraham concerning parental duty (Gen. 18:19) and later said specifically to all the families of Israel (Deut. 6:4ff.) was ignored, with the very worst results. A whole unbelieving generation arose.

In the later history of God's people the same sin and its consequences can be traced right on down to our own day. Most of the ills of the church today spring from the neglect of Christian parents to teach God's Law and live it before their own children.

The rise of an unbelieving generation, described in Judges 2, gave entrance to the series of cycles developed in the remaining chapters of the book.

The pattern of that cycle is given to us in 2:11-23 and is as follows: 1) the people did evil, forsaking their worship of the Lord (vv. 11-13); 2) God in anger punished them by raising up enemies to harass them (vv. 14, 15); 3) the people in distress called on the Lord (v. 15); 4) and the Lord raised up judges to save them from the hand of their enemies (v. 16). Then the cycle would start all over as they quickly forgot their Lord and returned to evil (vv. 17ff.). The purpose in the Lord's raising up nations to punish Israel is given in 3:1-6. They were left in the land to test Israel's faithfulness and to build up the strength of the faithful.

In 3:7, we begin the record of the cycles which carries through to the 16th chapter. There are at least seven separate cycles such as was described above in this period of Israel's history.

The first cycle (3:7-11) tells of the sinfulness of Israel that provoked God to send Mesopotamian kings against her. Then after Israel's cry to God in distress, the Lord raised up Othniel, a kinsman of Caleb, to rescue Israel. In this case as in many others we are told that the Spirit of the Lord came on the judge giving to him wisdom and special power for his task (v. 10).

The exact function of the Holy Spirit in the Old Testament era is not altogether clear. He certainly is active in creation and in guiding Israel, particularly by endowing certain individuals with the ability to do special tasks. He did so to some in the wilderness, enabling them to do skillful work in making the tabernacle which God had commanded to be built (Exod. 31:1-4—see also 1 Samuel 10:6). We know too that the Holy Spirit guided the recording of the written Word of God by those prophets called to that task (2 Pet. 1:21). There does not seem however to be a constant indwelling of the Spirit of God with

God's children in the Old Testament time as we see in the New Testament after Pentecost. The Spirit in this time, the period of the judges, seems to have come upon certain people for periods of time and then later to have left them. This evidently is the case with Othniel (v. 10).

The second cycle (3:12-30), relates the rather gory episode of the killing of the enemy of Israel, Eglon, king of Moab. Some complain of such bloody scenes in the Bible and seek to fault the Bible as written on a sub-Christian standard. However, no scenes are bloodier than the ones we find in the book of Revelation. They all underline the fact that sin has brought on the necessity of the shedding of blood. If the Old or New Testament is too gory for some, such people are naively ignoring the real issues of life and death and the terrible threat of hell that hangs over every individual entering into the world.

The third cycle (3:31) is mentioned only briefly here, and without elaboration.

The fourth cycle (4:1—5:31), tells us that when men failed to fulfill their responsibility in the church in leadership, the Lord could and did at times raise up women to fill that office. But we are not to conclude from this that God has given to women, as to men, the usual place of leadership in the church. As Christ said about divorce, so here too, from the beginning it was not so (5:7—cf. Matt. 19:7, 8; 1 Tim. 2:9-15). It is clear from 4:8, that the reason Deborah was chosen was that men who ought to have led were not willing.

The poetic expression of Deborah's victory given in chapter 5 makes clear that not Deborah but the Lord was the victor that day. Even the stars of heaven fought against Sisera, Israel's enemy (5:20). This is no reference to astrology but as Joshua 10:12, 13 shows, the sovereignty of God controlling even the heavenly bodies can reach down and affect the lives and destinies of men at will.

The fifth cycle (6:1—10:5) covers the delivering of Israel from the hand of Midian, her enemy, by the judge, Gideon. This was a particularly low period spiritually in Israel. God sent an unnamed prophet to rebuke the people for their unfaithfulness (6:7-10).

The call of Gideon reminds us somewhat of the calls of Moses and Joshua. Again God promises to be with the one he has called and sent to do his work (6:15, 16).

Gideon's request for a sign recorded in 6:17, and the subsequent episode with the fleece, 6:36-40, is by no means to Gideon's credit. Gideon's insistence upon a sign is not an indication of his spiritual strength but of his spiritual weakness. Though he is called a man of faith (Heb. 11:32, 33) yet his faith here is weak, as the request for signs clearly indicates.

Gideon's obedience to God was the better evidence of his faith, as he tore down the Baal altar and built one for the Lord (6:26, 27—cf. the same kind of obedience of faith in Abraham, Gen. 12:4 and in Noah, Gen. 6:22). We see here an example of the child leading the father as the father of Gideon evidently displays faith in God, following his sons' lead (6:30-32).

The fleece episode recorded in verses 36ff., displays, as we said above, not the strength of the faith of Gideon, but its weakness. God had promised to be with him and prosper him, yet Gideon required a sign, not once but twice (vv. 36, 37, 39). The practice of some today to discern God's will by "laying out the fleece" needs to be answered in the context of one whose faith is so weak that without a visible sign he is unwilling to obey God.

The method of choosing the ones who were to fight with Gideon as we read of it in chapter 7, is not the primary point, I believe. Many have made much of the significance of the way some drank with their hands while others dropped to their knees to drink, trying to prove that one way was preferable to the other. I am not so sure that this is the point. The point is, God sought to eliminate most of the men in order to show that the victory was by God and not men. The ones he chose may have been the least able of the 10,000.

The dream of the Midianite which Gideon was allowed to know was a further assurance of God's promise to give the victory to Gideon (7:9-14). The latter part of chapter 7 relates the routing of the Midianites as God struck confusion and fear into their hearts.

We see something of the wisdom and diplomacy of Gideon as he allays the wrath of the Ephraimites. In essence he flattered them by saying that what he and his small band of men had done was nothing in comparison with what Ephraim had done.

When the people of Israel offered to Gideon the kingship (8:22ff.), Gideon showed his great humility before men and God by refusing to be king and at the same time affirming the kingship of the Lord (8:23). Truly the Lord was the only rightful king, as Moses had proclaimed long before (Exod. 5:18).

It is hard to understand how this same Gideon could immediately turn away the hearts of the people from the God he had just proclaimed. But he did (8:24-28). The end of the story of Gideon and his family is sad, no doubt because of his folly in making the ephod (a priestly garment) which caused the people to stumble (v. 27).

Of Gideon's seventy sons (he had many wives) only one, Jotham, survived the slaughter by Abimilech. Jotham too was forced to flee after pronouncing a curse on Abimilech (9:7ff.). The curse was that the men of Shechem and Abimilech, all of whom had mistreated Gideon and his sons, would mutually destroy one another (9:19, 20). The balance of chapter 9 tells how the curse came to pass.

The sixth cycle (10:6—12:15) is the story of Jephthah and how he led Israel to victory over the Ammonites. Jephthah was despised by his own people until they needed him (11:1ff.). In the meantime the Ammonites threatened Israel and, as before, the people called on God for help (10:10). This time, however, the Lord did not quickly respond to their pleas for help but rebuked them for their faithlessness (10:13). Only after they showed real evidence of sincere repentance did God raise up a deliverer, Jephthah.

The success of Jephthah is that by God's help he subdued Israel's enemy, the Ammonites (11:33). The tragedy of the story of Jephthah is that in seeking insurance for himself against defeat he made a hasty and needless vow which cost him dearly (11:30, 31). In a way Jephthah was willing to bribe God to give him victory. He already had every indication that God was with him (v. 29). What he expected to come from the door of his house on his return I cannot imagine except some member of his own family.

Here it must be said that God never so bargained with Jephthah or any man. God never agreed to honor such a vow. God had already indicated his presence with Jephthah, thus assuring victory. The whole idea was Jephthah's. Furthermore God did not ever condone what Jephthah did. It is recorded in God's Word not as an example of what God's children ought to do. Just the opposite, the thing which Jephthah did was a crime against God's Law. Neither do we read that God required it of Jephthah even though he had vowed as he did. Never is it necessary to carry out a vow that is against God's Law in the first place. Once more, we do not see here an act of great faith but a sin that is no example to God's people. Jephthah himself is numbered among the faithful but was by no means exemplary in this deed of his life (Heb. 11:32).

The seventh and final cycle (chapters 13—16) is the well known cycle of Samson and the Philistines. From birth, Samson was dedicated by his parents to be a Nazarite at God's instruction (13:3-5). Like the other judges, Samson was endowed with God's Holy Spirit (13:25).

Like Jephthah and Gideon, Samson, though numbered with the faithful in Hebrews chapter 11, is nevertheless not a good example of what God's child ought to be. For one thing he desired to marry a Philistine girl (14:2) which was out of accord with the will of God.

The following episodes of his dealings with the Philistines and from time to time slaughtering great multitudes of them was all, no doubt, part of God's purpose for delivering Israel from the hands of her enemies (14:5—chapter 15).

In chapter 16 we read of the end of Samson's life. Apparently learning nothing from the unpleasant experiences in marrying one Philistine girl, he became involved with another from Gaza, a Philistine city, and she was a harlot (16:1ff.). This sin nearly cost him his life.

Then to add sin to sin he loved still another girl, Delilah, who was probably a Philistine also since she knew the Philistine lords quite well (16:4, 5). From the beginning she loved money and her own self more than Samson (16:5), and sought to betray him into the hands of his enemies. She finally succeeded (16:18-21).

His last act was perhaps Samson's greatest and most unselfish. He waited patiently for his hair to grow back, i.e., to return to the state of a Nazarite so that he could do what God had raised him up to do. He endured great suffering to accomplish this one last act of deliverance of his people. Yet even this act may well have been one of personal vengeance more than a sense of service to God and his people (16:28).

All in all, the series of judges raised up to deliver Israel from time to time are a dismal lot. We see in the whole period many heroes but few real spiritual leaders who walked with the Lord. They were for the most part not examples of faithful living. We find no one like Moses or Joshua or Samuel to come. The leadership was weak mainly because the whole people were weak and the spiritual climate of those days was poor.

The fact that the period of the judges is justifiably called the Dark Ages spiritually in Israel is well illustrated by the two stories coming out of that era as recorded in chapters 17—21.

The first story, in chapters 17, 18, tells of a man named Micah who apparently stole from his mother some silver (17:2). For some reason he returned the silver to his mother and she decided it should be dedicated to the Lord by *making a graven image* (v. 3). Thus the second and eighth commandments were violated and also the fifth, for he had not honored his mother. This leads the author of the book to comment, "In those days there was no king in Israel: every man did that which was right in his own eyes" (17:6). This sentence can well be called the refrain of the book of Judges (cf. 18:1; 19:1; 21:25).

Whether the author was writing from the perspective of a time when there were or would be human kings in Israel, we cannot say for sure. One meaning of this statement is surely that the people had rejected the Lord and his Word. In their hearts the Lord did not reign as king. But God has been declared their king (Exod. 5:18; Judg. 8:23). It was a sin-filled age.

The sin of Micah was compounded when he made a Levite his own personal priest (17:10-13). God had never allowed for such a thing. It was an abuse of the office of the Levites.

In those days apparently some tribes sere still unsettled. Some from Dan came across Micah and his private priest (ch. 18). They ultimately stole the priest for the whole tribe (18:19, 20). Neither was this allowed by God. Micah's attempt to get his priest and idols back was thwarted by their threats against him (18:25). Thus the sin of one man became the sin of a whole tribe (18:30). Here then is one example of the kind of lawlessness that prevailed in Israel in those days. This is the kind of people the judges were trying to lead. Humanly it appeared a hopeless task.

Perhaps the saddest part of this whole account is that when the priest is finally named in 18:30, it turns out that he is a direct descendant of Moses. This speaks of the power of Satan to move so quickly among the children of God, working havoc. Even the family of the godly man Moses was not immune to Satan's wiles. This grandson of Moses dropped to a very low state spiritually, becoming rebellious against the Laws of Moses, his grandfather.

The second example is recorded in chapters 19—21. This story also involves a Levite and also the city of Bethlehem (19:1, cf. 17:7). It is a horror story and quite sordid. This Levite took a concubine from Bethlehem who later fled from him back to her father in Bethlehem (19:2). The Levite returned to Bethlehem to get her and after being detained by the father-in-law for several days, finally, with his concubine, he began his return to Ephraim.

Note the condemnation of Israel in these days as he by-passed a pagan city, Jebus (Jerusalem), in order to spend the night among Hebrews, only to find the Hebrew city, Gibeah, of Benjamin, filled with hostility and inhospitality (19:12-15). The city of Gibeah proved to have many of the characteristics of Sodom and Gomorrah. (Here we might compare the words of Isaiah much later—Isa. 1:9.) There was in the city a stranger (sojourner) who did show hospitality to the Levite much as Lot, a stranger in Sodom, had shown hospitality to the angels, thinking them to be men in need of help (19:16ff.). Also, much as at Sodom, so the Benjamites railed at the sojourner and his Levite guest and desired to "know" (have sexual relations, i.e., sodomy) with the Levite (19:22). The sojourner who had asked the Levite into his house, even as Lot earlier had done to the angels, offered his daughter and also the concubine of the Levite to the men (vv. 23-24).

The evil men of Benjamin abused the concubine all night exhausting her physically so that she died (vv. 27, 28). The Levite's reaction seems horrible to us, yet it was effective (19:29) in that it rallied all Israel, for once, to punish the entire tribe of Benjamin (ch. 20).

Only a few of Benjamin were left when the battles were over. Thus one tribe was nearly exterminated. That tribe would never be strong again, and would ultimately unite with Judah. The ingenious ways in which the Israelites solved the problem of obtaining wives for those remaining Benjamites illustrates how sin was compounded upon sin until nothing could be done without some violation of God's Law (ch. 21).

In conclusion of the lessons drawn from this book we have seen that the period of the judges was basically a period of spiritual chaos. We have seen illustrations of the breaking of nearly all of the Ten Commandments: dishonor to parents, stealing, making graven images, worshipping other gods, covetousness, lying, killing and adultery. It was a way of life then.

What brought about this spiritual chaos? In the opening chapters of Judges we find the answer. The parents who knew Joshua and God's deliverance of Israel from the Canaanites, were apparently too busy to take the time to teach God's Word to their children, in disobedience to God's specific commands in Deuteronomy 6:4ff. This brought on a whole generation which did not know the Lord nor the work he did for Israel (2:10). This in turn brought about spiritual ignorance and chaos as we see here in the book. It underlines the necessity of godly parents to teach their children faithfully God's Word. Otherwise they will not know the Word of the Lord.

THE OTHER SIDE
OF THE STORY—
ELIMELECH AND ELKANAH
AND THEIR FAMILIES
Ruth, 1 Samuel 1, 2

While the book of Judges gives us the prevailing spiritual picture of the era of the judges, yet it is not the total picture. There were some godly parents in Israel who did not follow the faithless trends of the times. We can see this exemplified in the families of Elimelech and Elkanah. The Lord, as we saw from creation onward, has put great emphasis on the importance of the family. The books of Ruth and Samuel well illustrate how God blessed the faithful families.

The book of Ruth records the experiences of the family of Elimelech, who married Naomi. Interestingly, the two were from Bethlehem (1:1) as were some of the more sordid characters we read of in the book of Judges. Because of a famine in the land they went to live for a while in the land of Moab. While there, the two sons of Elimelech and Naomi married pagan wives of Moab. Perhaps this is the reason why those two sons died. Yet godly Naomi desired to return to her home.

Naomi did not expect her daughters-in-law to leave their home in Moab, but one of them, Ruth, did prefer Naomi and Naomi's God to her own people and their gods (1:16, 17). Verse 16 has been often quoted as illustrative of Ruth's great faith and devotion; and so it is, but we cannot overlook the fact that it also commends the spiritual stature of Naomi whose own devotion to the Lord and love of her daughter-in-law so moved Ruth to leave her own people and go with this old woman to a strange home.

Back in Bethlehem, Ruth, in God's providence which the book shows, met another godly person, Boaz, and by God's blessings the two ultimately married, thus establishing another godly home (chapters 2—4). From that home of faith was ultimately to come the great King David (4:22) and the even greater Lord Jesus Christ (Matt. 1:1).

Here again we see a pagan, Ruth, brought into the line of the faithful. Once more God gave a token of the day when people from the nations of the world will be included among the people of God.

Thus God blessed the faithful Naomi who so showed the presence of God in her life that a pagan girl was drawn to that God by Naomi's life. God provided for Ruth a godly husband and together they raised a godly family which culminated in the person of Jesus Christ. All was not lost in this sinful godless age because God is gracious and would not let the light go out in Israel.

The family of Elkanah and his wife Hannah also well illustrates the presence of devout people in Israel in the time of the judges. He was of the hill country of Ephraim from which Micah in Judges 17 came (Judg. 17:8) and from which also the Levite of Judges 19 came (Judg. 19:1). His spiritual life is illustrated by his regular worship of the Lord with his family at Shiloh, where the tabernacle then was (1 Sam. 1:3—cf. Josh. 18:1). Note the contrast between his obedience to God's command regarding the worship at one place which God should choose (Deut. 2) and the disobedience of the Danites who set up their own sanctuary separate from the House of God.

Hannah, wife of Elkanah, had a rival in the other wife of Elkanah, Peninnah (1 Sam. 1:6, 7). Hannah, who was barren, desired a son very much and prayed to God earnestly for one. Contrast her commitment of her son to the Lord as a living sacrifice to God with the foolish commitment and vow of Jephthah (1 Sam. 1:11—cf. Judg. 11:30, 31). Eli's failure to recognize that Hannah was praying in itself is quite a commentary on the spiritual debauchery of the age (1:12-13). Prayer was so rare then that even a priest of Israel could not recognize it.

When God gave Hannah a son, she named him Samuel. The name means "His name is God," and was a tribute to the God who had given her this son. Samuel was nurtured in a godly home (1:21ff.) and finally given over to the Lord (1:22, 25, 28). Thus Hannah and her husband proved to be parents faithful to the Lord and loving God. They showed that love in the commitment of their son to serve the Lord forever.

The prayer of Hannah in chapter 2 is one of the most beautiful prayers recorded in Scripture. It reveals the great depth of her faith and her spiritual insight into God's Word. Above all, it shows the great work of God in the hearts of some in those days of spiritual darkness.

In this prayer she reveals an understanding of how the Lord humbles the proud but exalts the lowly (2:1, 3, 4, 6, 7). Thus she comprehends the true purpose of the sacrifices to bring God's people to a broken and contrite heart in order that God may lift them up. She speaks of God's holiness and sovereignty over all the affairs of men (2:6, 7, 8). She particularly expresses confidence in God to keep his own while judging the wicked (2:9), very similar to Psalm 1. Her spiritual depth no doubt reflects much of what she had been taught by her parents and or

perhaps by her husband. The prayer shows that she knew God's
Law and understood its meaning for the child of God.

We shall end this chapter here. We see that the period of
darkness in Israel was not able to overcome the light of God's
truth and good purposes. Though the majority were evil in
Israel, there were those who did not live as the majority but who
took God seriously. In times of spiritual darkness in the church,
God still raises up some to be faithful. We may ask, "What can I
do?" Naomi and Boaz, Elkanah and Hannah show us the answer
as they remain faithful to do what God had told them in his
Word they must do as parents and as children of God. From
them God raised up Samuel and David, two of the greatest Old
Testament children of God whose lives were effective in bringing Israel as a nation back to the Lord.

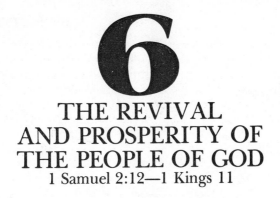

THE REVIVAL
AND PROSPERITY OF
THE PEOPLE OF GOD
1 Samuel 2:12—1 Kings 11

THE DAWN
BREAKS—SAMUEL
1 Samuel 2:12—7

WE HAVE NOW been introduced to both sides of the period of the judges: the prevailing evil of those days and the persistent good shown in the lives of some. Matters became worse and worse in Israel until God intervened. As before, we see the Lord intervening by raising up godly people to serve him and be faithful, through whom he changes the direction of the people of Israel.

In the lives of Eli's two sons we see once more the personification of the worst that was in Israel. These two sons of Eli did not

know the Lord. They were therefore a product of their age
(2:12). An example of their evil is given here. Evidently these
priests not only neglected their duty to God but even coveted for
themselves those offerings which belonged to God. They were
apparently without conscience, forcing people to surrender their
offerings to them rather than give them in the prescribed way of
the Law of Moses (2:15—cf. Lev. 3:3-5, 16). Their sin did not go
unnoticed by God (2:17).

In contrast, Samuel ministered to the Lord (2:18). Here we
see indication of things to come. God's eye was also on Samuel to
prepare him for a great and faithful work (2:21).

Eli the priest was not innocent in all that his sons did. He knew
their sin, not only in the matter of sacrifices but also in the evil of
lying with women who did service at the tent (2:22). There was
no impropriety, as such, in the women being there. The Law of
Moses had provided for women to render service at the tabernacle (Exod. 38:8). But what happened between the sons of Eli and
those women was outrageous. It was apparently an act in imitation of the Canaanites' practice of their religion. We know from
archaeological evidence that a part of the Canaanite religious
worship was to perform sexual orgies such as are here described.

Though Eli knew the sins of his sons, he only verbally rebuked
them and evidently made no effort to stop them (2:22ff.). The
point of verse 25 seems to be that the sons of Eli were guilty of
the unpardonable sin of refusal to repent toward God. For such
a sin there is no forgiveness and no escape. This was their sin.
The phrase, "The Lord was minded to slay them," simply means
that God chose not to intervene in grace to spare them. They
became hardened in the hearts and would not repent, much as
Pharaoh had done in Egypt in the days of Moses.

Once more we see Samuel in stark contrast to these two (v. 26).
Here was the grace of God, working in Samuel to prepare him
to be the means of turning Israel back to God.

The Lord warned Eli who was evidently guilty of profiting
from his sons' sins though he had rebuked them (2:29). The
solemn "therefore" of verse 30 introduces the pronouncement
of God's judgment against Eli and his house. The priesthood of
Eli, a descendant of Aaron, had failed. Eli and his sons would be
removed from office by death (2:34).

In verse 35, we have God's promise of a better priesthood
than that of Eli and Aaron. The promise here may apply immediately to the raising of Samuel to take his place. But there is
far greater meaning here. Samuel would only point to the ultimate, greater priest. God did not build a priesthood on Samuel.
The priesthood of Aaron had failed. Therefore, ultimately the

Lord was pointing to and promising that a greater priesthood would be established, one that would not fail. The writer to the Hebrews in 7:11ff, tells us that the greater priesthood belonged to Jesus Christ, the perfect priest who would offer the perfect sacrifice, himself, for our sins.

Against the background of the sinfulness of Eli's sons and his own failure in the priesthood we have the continuing theme of the spiritual growth and awareness of Samuel, destined to be the one who would lead Israel out of the morass in which she had been caught (3:1).

The state of affairs spiritually is again described for us in the statement in verse 1 that the Word of the Lord was precious or rare in those days. God was not revealing, and the revelation which God had already made was not being circulated among the people. Few knew of it or cared.

But God was not giving up. The lamp of God referred to in verse 3 is representative of God's Truth and Light (2 Sam. 21:17; 22:29; 1 Kings 11:36; 15:4, Psa. 119:105, etc.). The meaning is that God's grace continued in this time in spite of man's sins. Evidence of that continuing grace is given in this chapter when Samuel is called by God and raised up to be a prophet of the Lord (3:19—4:1).

Since Israel's trust had ceased to be in the Lord in those days, God humbled Israel by giving her defeat at the hands of her enemy, the Philistines, as was the pattern of the period of the judges (4:1, 2).

The people put their confidence not in God but in the ark as their means of manipulating God. They felt they had their God in a box and could compel him to help by taking the ark to battle (4:3-5). Later Israel would put her confidence in the Temple and not in God, believing falsely that God would not let Jerusalem fall to her enemies because the Temple was there. In both cases the foolish Israelites were proven wrong.

This time, the ark was captured, the sons of Eli were killed and the army was beaten. All Israel was filled with grief (4:21).

In is interesting to see how God, who gave the ark into Philistine hands, nevertheless would not allow them to boast or suppose their gods were greater than the God of Israel. By himself, the Lord punished the Philistines and brought them low (chs. 5, 6). The Lord would not even allow Israelites to treat the ark carelessly or with disrespect (6:19-21). Even David later would have to learn that lesson (2 Sam. 6:1-11).

The people of God had finally been humbled to the point of lamentation before the Lord. God had prepared his man for that hour, and when the hearts of the people were contrite before God (7:2) then Samuel, the man of the hour, prepared by God, stepped forward to show the people how to return to fellowship with God.

Samuel described for Israel the way of return in three steps. This description of repentance given here (7:3, 4) is an excellent guide for all, whether individuals or churches, which are brokenhearted and desire to return to God.

First, the conditions of repentance must be right. It must be from the heart, i.e., with a broken and contrite heart. This being so, the *first step* is to cease from the evil previously done. For Israel this meant putting away her foreign gods. All true repentance must be shown by works worthy of repentance, the ceasing to do evil. One cannot expect to be restored to right fellowship with God if he insists on continuing headlong in those sins that broke the fellowship. One must confess that he is a sinner and has sinned against God and be sorry for it.

As the *second step* Israel had to direct her heart to the Lord, serving only him. It was not enough simply to cease from evil, there must be a pursuit of what was good, what was right in the eyes of the Lord. Later Elijah would call on the people to stop vacillating between the Lord and Baal and serve only the Lord (1 Kings 18:21), even as Jesus still later warned the disciples that one cannot serve two masters (Matt. 6:24—cf. Matt. 4:10 and Deut. 6:13).

The *third step* in Israel's return would be God's step. When they had done these things from the heart, then the Lord would deliver them from their enemies, the Philistines.

What followed after Samuel had taught the way of return was that the people faithfully obeyed Samuel, first putting away the false gods (7:4). Then, confessing their sins, they recommitted themselves to the Lord (7:5-8). Finally, the Lord did respond by giving them victory over the Philistines (7:9-11).

The stone erected at Ebenezer in memory of what God did that day was similar to the stone at Gilgal, when Israel crossed the Jordan, a visible reminder of God's help. The name Ebenezer means "stone of help." It marked, as it were, the trail of God's blessings on Israel to this point.

After this, Samuel judged Israel for several years. He was the last of the judges and doubtless the greatest. Presumably as he made his yearly circuits he judged the people and dealt with their spiritual problems no doubt also teaching them the Law of Moses so that the people's spiritual condition could be improved.

THE MAKING OF A
KING—SAUL
1 Samuel 8—15

In the early verses of chapter 8 we read that Samuel's sons were sinners, similar to the sons of Eli. However, we note one big difference. When Scripture mentions Eli's sons, much of the blame for their sin rests on Eli's failure. Later, the same can be said of David. His sons reflected much of David's failure. But on Samuel no blame is put. In fact Samuel is one of the very few personalities in Scripture about whom not one critical or negative thing is said. It does not mean that Samuel was sinless. It is a high tribute to the man however.

The sins of Samuel's sons are to be seen in their own failure to walk in Samuel's way, though they had been faithfully taught by their father (v. 3). This enables us to see that at times parents can do all they ought to do and yet their children will not obey. Parents are not always to blame for their children's failures. This particular sin was one which Paul and Peter would later warn ministers against (1 Tim. 3:3, 6:10; Tit. 1:11; 1 Pet. 5:2). The perversion of justice was a frequent sin of later rulers in Israel which the prophets often condemned.

The reaction of the people which is recorded in the first part of chapter 8 reminds us of Moses' words in Deuteronomy 17:14, 15. Israel had been warned that one day she would ask for a king and now that had happened. Surely the people, God's unique people, were ready to sell their birthright to be like other nations. Samuel was disheartened but God showed him that it was not his personal failure. After all, they were rejecting not Samuel but God from being their king (8:6, 7). The Lord showed however that he was in control (8:9). The Lord still reigned (Exod. 15:18).

The description of their future miseries with their desired king are in stark contrast to God's own blessings on his people in the past. The Lord gave them sons, daughters, fields, vineyards and olive yards. But the king will take all these things from them (8:11ff.). The end would be that they would lose not only all which God had given to them but also their very fellowship with God (8:18).

They wanted a king to judge them and go out before them and fight for them (8:20). God had done all of these things for them and never deserted them, but in the end their kings would desert them as indeed the last king of Judah surely did just before the fall of Jerusalem.

What Samuel foretold that day did happen exactly as he had forewarned. The people in essence were saying, "we do not wish to walk by faith before an invisible king but we want to walk by sight before a visible king."

God permitted a king to reign in Israel but it is clear that God was in control of all things. The way in which young Saul came into contact with Samuel at just this time and on the occasion of his father having lost his asses shows that God was going to be in charge of the selecting of the king of Israel. The statement in 9:2 that there was no better prospect in Israel than Saul indicates that God led them to the choice of the very best man for the job. The fact that this best prospect failed simply underlines the truth that the best of men is not sufficient to lead God's people. Only One can truly lead the people of God, that is the Lord himself.

It is interesting that God seems to avoid the use of the term king when speaking of Saul. He is called a prince but not a king. The terminology found in 9:16 is reminiscent of the period of the judges as though God viewed Saul more as a judge than as a king.

Saul's humility commends him to us in the beginning, much like Moses himself (9:21). In chapter 10, when he is anointed king, he is given three signs of his new calling. They are note-worthy because they seem to relate to the general way in which God has set aside any for special service in his kingdom, even ministers of the gospel today.

The first sign relieves him of his former responsibility. The asses are found, so he need not concern himself any longer for that problem (10:2). Second, his physical needs are now to be met. Remember he was broke (9:7). Now food is provided (10:3). Finally, the Holy Spirit would come on him enabling him to serve the Lord and do God's will (10:6). All of this would mean that God was with him (10:7. Compare Exod. 3:12 and Josh. 1:9). Thus the servant of God, called into special service in God's kingdom is relieved of his former duties and obligations. He is promised the necessities for his living, and endowed with whatever gifts of the Holy Spirit which would enable him to do that work to which he had been called.

The command in 10:8 seems to have been a custom to be followed by Saul before undertaking any new project for God. By this custom Saul would always be reminded that his success depended on God's blessing and guidance. Its performance would always remind Saul and the people that God is still king.

When Samuel made the announcement concerning Saul being their new king, he was careful to remind them that the very asking for a king had been sinful (10:19). He further pointed out that the one chosen was God's choice (10:24). The majority favored God's choice (10:24, 27).

Again we stress that the Lord, complying with the people's request for a king, led them to choose the very best man available for the position. The fact that he failed does not indicate God's bad choice but declares that, in reality, no man is sufficient in himself to be the king of God's people, not even the best of men.

In chapter 11 we read of Saul's first act as king. He shows himself well here. By the end of the battle when he had rescued the people of Jabesh-Gilead from their enemy he was the hero of Israel and had seemingly united all Israel behind him. His wisdom in not seeking vengeance on those who had opposed him is also commendable (11:12, 13).

Samuel's farewell address is very moving as we read of it in chapter 12. The integrity of the man is obvious since no one can lay a charge against Samuel (12:4). After a review of Israel's history as the people of God, Samuel gave a final exhortation (12:14, 15). We see that it related clearly to the covenant which God had made with Israel to bless them in the land so long as they obeyed God.

For the first time the people of Israel acknowledged their sin in asking for a king (12:19). Perhaps as they contemplated the death of Samuel and realized that Saul was a poor substitute for such a godly man they repented. Nevertheless Samuel sought to comfort them (12:20ff.). The formula for their continued blessing is here outlined by Samuel. They are to be faithful to God and will be upheld by Samuel's prayers. Israel at this moment had a lot going for her.

It is a sad thing to come to the 13th chapter and to the decision that this promising young man Saul had feet of clay after all. The occasion of the beginning of Saul's downfall was another battle with the Philistines. Saul grew impatient waiting for Samuel to come and offer sacrifices according to the formula we noted in 10:8. So, on seeing that the people were beginning to scatter, he offered the sacrifice himself. In this act he betrayed a woeful lack of spiritual depth.

When confronted by Samuel with his sin he sought to make excuses. It was difficult for Saul to admit a sin as a mistake.

Samuel's charge in verse 13, "thou hast done foolishly" demands comment. In our English language we usually think of a foolish act as synonymous with a ridiculous or stupid act. However in Hebrew it means something quite different. The fool in the Bible is one who lives and acts as though there is no God. He may be quite respectable in the eyes of men and even greatly admired. The world would not call him a fool, but in God's sight he, whose activities and life run counter to God and who lives as though he has nothing to account for before God, is a fool.

From this point on we see the rapid decline of Saul. Already David, God's new choice for king, is on the horizon. Here he is identified only as "a man after his (God's) own heart" (13:14). But he has already been chosen by God though unknown to man.

In the very next chapter, 14, we see how Saul began to crumble before the people. His foolish demands in regard to the fighting men not eating until the battle was won that day, hurt the army and curtailed the victory (14:24). It was not the act of a wise military leader.

Nevertheless Saul continued to lead Israel to victory in spite of his weaknesses and Scripture continues to commend his military ability (14:48).

In the matter of Agag, king of the Amalekites, we have a second example of Saul's spiritual depravity (v. 15). God had specifically ordered the destruction of the Amalekites and all which they possessed, as he had done regarding Jericho in Joshua's day. Saul's act of disobedience (15:8, 9) was the occasion of a second encounter between Saul and Samuel.

The words "it repented the Lord" (v. 11) trouble some. It does not mean that God changes his mind or errs as men do. This interpretation is ruled out in the same chapter (15:29). It expresses the complete failure of Saul to do God's will as though God had made a mistake. The real point is that no man, not even the best, is good enough to rule God's people in and of himself.

In the second encounter, Saul again protests his innocence while Samuel points out to him his acts of disobedience (15:13, 14). Saul's insistence on the fact that his intentions were good (and his effort to put the blame on the people rather than on himself) did not turn away Samuel (15:20, 21).

In verses 22 and 23, we have been given great insight into God's purpose in the institution of the sacrificial system. It was clearly never intended to be a substitute for obedience to God's Law. As we noted in discussion of the sacrificial system in Leviticus, the purpose of the sacrifices was to bring the people to an awareness of their sin and an expression by the sacrifices of their need of help from God. For Saul, the sacrifice was clearly a substitute for obedience, i.e., "Since I did not strictly keep God's Law, here are these fine animals for sacrifice to pacify God."

The contrast between Saul's defensive attitude here and David's own acknowledgment of his sin when confronted by God's prophet at a later time is very important. In Psalm 51 David exposed his own heartfelt sorrow for his sin and expressed a right understanding of the sacrificial system; namely, that it was to bring the sinner to a broken and contrite heart (Psa. 51:16, 17).

Even the verbal admission of guilt on Saul's part is apparently not genuine. He seems to be saying "O.K., so I sinned, let's get on with the worship" (15:25).

The tragedy of Saul's failure is but a forewarning of Israel's later failure. From Isaiah 1:11ff. and numerous other passages in the prophets we ascertain that Israel as a whole failed to grasp the true intent of the sacrificial system, and their worship was not acceptable to God. In their proud hearts they came with the sacrifices but not in humility.

The tragedy of Saul is therefore the tragedy of Israel. The people desired a king like the other nations, a man, an arm of flesh. He could not succeed in the eyes of God, and he pressed the cause of expediency over obedience with the result that he and the people lost greatly.

In all of this, Samuel was exemplary. He was personally hurt by their rejection of the God whom he had sought to live for, yet he continued to pray for them and never deserted them. Even after Saul's second failure, Samuel sought to carry on as well as possible for the good and for the sake of Israel and for the glory of his Lord (15:31).

THE RISE OF DAVID
1 Samuel 16—31

In these chapters we learn of God's choice of David to be king instead of Saul. Remember that David has already been described by the Lord as "a man after his own heart" (13:14. Compare Acts 13:22). Plainly here God had rejected Saul and set up his choice now to be the king (16:1).

Note how the Lord still deals with families, again stressing the place of the family and responsibility of parents in God's kingdom (16:1). The choice is designated as Jesse's son until verse 12. The Lord designates the new choice as king unhesitatingly (v. 1).

An important lesson here is the difference between man's

choosing and God's choosing. Man looks on the outward appearance as men did toward Saul. Saul commended himself to men, but God looks on the heart, i.e., what a man really is underneath his outward appearance (16:7).

We are told that the Holy Spirit came that day to *abide* on David unlike his coming and departing in reference to Saul (16:13). David was to have the Holy Spirit in great measure since he was God's choice to lead his people and was to be himself a figure of the Christ who was to come from his descent.

Mention of the evil spirit on Saul (16:14) need not trouble us if we remember that the word "evil" has two senses in Scripture. It can mean "moral evil," which is never associated with God, or it can mean the judgment from God on sinful men which always comes from God. The latter sense is to be understood here in that the spirit sent from God to Saul was a spirit of judgment.

It was certainly no coincidence that one was on hand to recommend David as a gifted harpist to soothe Saul (16:18). God introduced his servant to be trained in the affairs of the kingdom and in warfare just as earlier he had prepared Moses in the courts of Pharaoh. Again it was no coincidence that David found favor just as Joseph had with Pharaoh much earlier. The sovereign God is always in charge and works all for his own glory and for the good of those who trust in him.

In chapter 17 the account of David's fight with Goliath is quite familiar. We should note that when David was given occasion to fight Goliath, he rested his confidence not on himself but on the Lord. He gained this confidence not suddenly but over the years of seeing God's protection in his own life (17:34-37). He not only expressed his faith in words but in acts, giving to the Lord all the glory for the victory that day (17:45-47).

David's victory resulted in two things: his close friendship with Jonathan (18:2, 3), and the unending jealousy of Saul (18:9). Again Saul showed his real self by his determination to destroy this one who was a threat to his throne (18:11, 17). In spite of Saul's efforts, however, it was evident that the Lord was with and was prospering David. Thus the enmity between God's child and Satan's seems evident here (18:29).

Chapters 19—26 tell of the relentless pursuit of David by Saul. Jonathan's intercession on David's behalf availed little (19:1-10). When David was forced to flee from Saul, Jonathan and David parted with tears. The moving scene recorded in 20:14ff. is perhaps a pointer to events that would come later. We cannot overlook the fact that the tribe of Benjamin in later history survived just because it came under the shelter of the tribe of

Judah. Later still, a descendant of Saul, also called Saul, would commit himself to serve the greater Son of David, Jesus Christ (Acts 9).

There is much to be said for Jonathan because of his humility and meekness, and because of his desire to glorify God and do God's will, even at the cost of glory and power to himself. He is truly one of the noble personalities of Scripture.

In David's escape from Saul, Michal his wife seems to be for David but her words betray a lack of love for David even at this time (19:13-17). Saul could not succeed in capturing David because it was against God's will (19:20).

On a second flight recorded in chapters 21—24, David in flight endangered the priests at Nob. Later David would take the blame for Ahimelech's death (22:22). We cannot know how Ahimelech would have reacted to David had he known that David was fleeing from Saul. Thinking that David was on a mission for Saul, he gave him holy bread and the sword of Goliath. This, from Saul's point of view, was aiding and abetting the enemy.

David's entrustment of his parents to the king of Moab reminds us that David's great grandmother was a Moabitess, Ruth (Ruth 4:17).

Ahimelech's death, as we just noted, comes as a result of David's lie (22:11ff.). David's invitation to Abiathar, the son of Ahimelech, to be allied with David may not have altogether satisfied Abiathar. We see that at the time of David's death Abiathar joins the revolution against David's son Solomon, David's choice for king (1 Kings 1:7).

At En-gedi (chapter 24) and at Ziph (chapter 26) David showed his trust in the Lord by not killing Saul when Saul was put into his hands. Saul could never understand such things and never respected the Lord's anointed as David had done even though the title "the Lord's anointed" was more appropriate for David at this time than it was for Saul.

In chapters 27—31 we have the last days of Saul, which also prove to be the last days of David's persecution by Saul. By now, Samuel had died (25:1). Saul was on his last legs, but David did not yet feel safe (27:1).

In desperation as the enemy Philistines began to close in on Saul, he sought once again to get advice from Samuel who was now dead (28:1ff.). The reason for his desperate attempt to communicate with Samuel in death through a medium was doubtlessly because all communication with the Lord had been cut off (28:6).

No doubt the woman was as surprised as Saul when Samuel actually appeared and spoke to Saul (28:12). We are not to suppose that Scripture gives credence to witchcraft. God allowed Samuel to appear because it suited God's purpose once more through Samuel to tell Saul of his judgment. Just as God had allowed the magicians to turn staffs into serpents in Egypt, so here he allowed this witch to call forth Samuel; not because she had the power in herself to do so, but to teach both her and Saul a lesson.

The death of Saul in battle is covered in the last chapter of 1 Samuel. The discrepancies between the account of Saul's death in 1 Samuel 31 and the report of his death as given by the Amalekite in 2 Samuel 1 are explained by the desire of the Amalekite to get reward for having slain David's enemy. His lie brought his own death.

In assessing the reign of Saul, we conclude that the tragedy of his life is that though he was the best of men humanly speaking, for the task of being king of the people, yet his whole reign shows that the best of men is simply not good enough to lead God's people. Only God is the true king. He alone is able to be their king. That is why eventually God himself would have to come through David's line, the leader who recognized his limitations and trusted in the Lord. The greatness of David is not seen in his superiority to Saul humanly speaking but in his humble and contrite heart which recognized that true greatness lies in humility before God and total dependence upon God. David always understood that God was king and not he.

THE REIGN OF DAVID
2 Samuel 1—24

David was informed concerning the defeat and death of Saul by an unnamed Amalekite who took credit for slaying Saul, perhaps expecting some reward. Whatever his motivation, his story varied from the biblical account of Saul's death given in 1 Samuel 31 (2 Samuel 1:10). Apparently he expected some reward for his efforts but instead he was put to death by David who was true to Saul as long as Saul lived (1:14-16).

David's own feelings are expressed beautifully in the song he wrote as recorded in verses 19—27. We may wonder how David could say of Saul that he was "lovely and pleasant in his life" (v. 23). Actually, he couples Jonathan and Saul here and perhaps sees Saul through his own love for Jonathan. It says something about David too. There is never any evidence of animosity on David's part toward Saul, though Saul persecuted him through many years. He seemed to understand why Saul was jealous and angry and showed only the greatest patience toward Saul. Perhaps before the days of hostility there were some lovely experiences with Saul.

David was very careful to be guided by the Lord in every step of his taking over the kingdom of Israel (2:1). As soon as he was made king over Judah, he acted like a king, rewarding those who had been faithful to the former king (2:4).

When Abner, the captain of Saul's army, sought to establish a surviving son of Saul as king, David did not regard the act as treason since the issue of who ruled had, as yet, not been settled. David expressed great patience toward these loyal to Saul which again demonstrates his meekness and willingness for God to establish his throne as the Lord had promised.

In chapter 2 for the first time Joab, the nephew of David, is mentioned. Compare 1 Chronicles 2:16. At this time or earlier, he emerged as the leader of David's men and showed his skill in putting Abner to flight (2:17). He also showed his sinful inclination and his hostility toward Abner who had killed Joab's brother in battle fairly (2:18-32).

Abner championed the cause of Ish-bosheth, the son of Saul, for a long time (3:1). The name Ish-bosheth is itself interesting. In his lifetime he had apparently been called Ish-baal (compare 1 Chron. 8:33 and 9:39) which literally means, "man of the Lord," using a common Semitic name for the Lord, Baal. Later however, by the time of Hosea the name Baal had become so associated with the Phoenician god of fertility that God would not allow himself to be called by that name anymore (see Hosea 2:16 and compare 1 Kings 18:21ff.). In later days therefore it was the custom, whenever the name Baal appeared among Hebrew names, to change the Baal to Bosheth, which means "shame." Therefore Ish-bosheth really means "man of shame." If Elijah wrote this portion of God's Word in 2 Samuel, as some suppose, then it is understandable how he, the great opponent of Baal worship, would have been unwilling to use the real name Ish-baal.

While David awaited the throne of all Israel in Hebron, six sons were born to him, three of whom would bring great grief to David later on: Amnon, Absalom, and Adonijah.

When Abner increased in strength, Ish-bosheth accused him of taking his concubine (3:7). This was tantamount to accusing him of treason as we have noted already in an earlier incident.

For this accusation, whether true or false, Ish-bosheth paid dearly because Abner then desired to go over to David.

David, who was now gaining superiority over Saul's house very rapidly, demanded what may be considered a petty thing. He wanted his wife back, the daughter of Saul who had married another man by this time (1 Sam. 25:44). The parting of Michal and her second husband is sad but we must remember that the marriage contract was violated when she married this second man. David was certainly within his rights to take her back but the two never again lived together happily, it would seem (6:16). Whenever the bonds of marriage are violated for whatever cause, there is no truly happy solution.

Abner's agreement with David and the ensuing peace they planned, was marred by the murder of Abner by Joab. Perhaps it was partly vengeance because Abner had killed his brother in battle, a tragedy but certainly not Abner's fault (2:19-23). But surely Joab also feared that Abner who was much more to David's liking would be put over Joab. Again David showed how he felt as he praised Abner and condemned Joab (3:31-34). David never forgave Joab, but neither did he ever punish Joab. It is not clear why. David's neglect to discipline was one of his greatest flaws as his later life shows.

The people of Israel now came to David and subjected themselves to him (5:1ff.). From this time on for several years David had one triumph after another (chapters 5 to 10). In the process David brought the Ark from the house of Abinadab where it had been for many years from the time of Samuel (1 Sam. 7:1). The judgment on Uzzah which displeased David was like all of God's judgments, designed to glorify God and humble men before him. Even David in his entourage must respect and be subject to the Law of God. No man was above that Law, not even David, not even Moses, the giver of the Law, as we saw earlier (Exod. 4:24-26).

David had in mind in bringing the Ark to Jerusalem, the city which he had captured (5:6-9), the building of a permanent place for God to be worshipped (ch. 7).

The Lord was pleased with David's desire to build a house for God. But in responding to David's desire, the Lord gave him a promise which overwhelmed David. He spoke of David's seed to come (7:12) and the kingdom to be set up (7:13) and the house of God he would build (7:13). In a sense, the Lord was talking about Solomon, through whom the kingdom begun in David would continue. But ultimately the Lord was speaking of David's greater Son and the greater kingdom he would establish and the greater house of his own body which Jesus Christ would some day offer for the sins of God's people and for their salvation. It was, in the end, not in Solomon but in Jesus Christ that the kingdom of David would be established forever (7:16).

David was overcome with amazement at God's grace and decision that all be done that God might be glorified (7:20ff.). Yet David himself would be reminded of his own frailty and continual need for dependence on God lest he become too proud and self-confident.

In chapter 11 begins one of the saddest episodes in Scripture. The writer indicates that David himself opened the door to trouble by failing to go to war to lead his troops. Instead he sent Joab, whom he knew to be an unworthy man. In his idle hours he saw a woman bathing. She was beautiful. There was no sin in his temptation; but when he learned she was married, he should have put her out of his mind. Instead he let his lust take over and sent for her to have sexual intercourse with her. Having gratified his lust, he sent her home (11:4).

But she became pregnant and this meant trouble. To cover up his own sin, he sought to get her husband to come home and lie with his wife so as to fool him into thinking her pregnancy was due to him. But the husband showed himself more willing to do his duty than David was to do his duty. It disturbed his conscience to enjoy his wife while his companions were at war out in the field.

David tried again, this time getting Uriah drunk, but to no avail. In the end, he had Uriah murdered by the enemy's hand to cover up his own sin. Joab, a scoundrel himself, must have relished the task of getting Uriah killed, and perhaps he knew about David's sin. Besides committing two terrible sins, David was even willing to sacrifice several soldiers' lives to carry out his evil desires (11:17).

David took Uriah's widow to be his wife, but though he may have thought that that was the end of the problem, the Lord did not forget (11:27).

Nathan's approach to David is a classic example of the prophet as God's servant commissioned to rebuke even kings when necessary. As Samuel had on several occasions confronted Saul, now Nathan, the prophet of the Lord, confronted David with his sin.

Here the real integrity of David was tested, not in the fact that he had sinned but in that now when he was faced with his sin he would show what sort of person he really was; just as Saul had revealed his heart of unbelief by denying his sin, or as Cain showed himself by his anger toward God and murder of his brother Abel.

The greatness of David is revealed here and shows that he *was* a man after God's own heart. His simple confession was "I have sinned" (12:13). Just as simply he was assured, "the Lord has put away thy sin; thou shalt not die" (12:13). This simple confession of his sin was undoubtedly sincere because the Lord who searches the heart could by Nathan so quickly assure David of forgiveness. David spoke his words from the depths of his heart and showed that he had a heart which was humble and contrite before God. This is always what the Lord desires in his servants.

We see David's heart more fully revealed in Psalm 51, which appears to have been David's fuller confession and prayer on the occasion of his sin in regard to Bathsheba and Uriah the Hittite. While we shall look at this and other Psalms in a later section, it is important to point out here a few things respecting this Psalm.

First, David approaches God with assurance that the Lord is truly the one he has revealed himself to be in his written Word. He speaks of God's mercy and loving kindness, no doubt looking back to that revelation of God which had been given at Sinai (Psa. 51:1—compare Exod. 34:6, 7). He knows also that God will not overlook sin by that same revelation in Exodus 34 and so also asks God to wash it away (Psa. 51:2).

David knew also that his sin was primarily against the Lord (51:4). True, he had sinned against Uriah and Bathsheba and indeed against the whole army of Israel but primarily against the Lord. All sin is primarily against the Lord and therefore cannot be dealt with until one has confessed it to the Lord.

David knew the privilege of God's children to confess their sins to the Lord. He knew too that as God's child he could not cover his sin or ignore it but only bring it to the light (Psa. 32:3-5). He felt the loss of the joy of his salvation, not the loss of that salvation itself. He was still God's child (51:12) and still longed to be able again to do what God's children ought to be doing—leading others to serve God (51:13).

In 51:16, 17 David comes to the heart of his confession. It is not God's will that he merely offer sacrifices to appease God as Saul had thought. He understands that the real purpose of sacrifice was to bring the sinner to a contrite and broken heart. This is now David's state and it is why God is pleased with him.

Every child of God must understand this. God desires us to feel about sin as he does. He has not taken the possibility of sin from us in this world but when we do sin he desires in us a broken heart. He wants us to be contrite before the Lord. God, as Samuel's mother had seen, exalts the humble but casts down the proud (1 Sam. 2:5-10).

From this point on, the life of David is filled with tragedy after tragedy, many of these tragedies emanating from his own home. Herein lies another important point. Forgiveness of sin is not equivalent to being freed from the consequences of sin in this life. While David was assured that in respect to his position before the Lord he was forgiven, nevertheless he was warned of sad consequences of that sin which would affect the rest of his life (12:10-12).

Many believers do not understand this, but it is important to understand. I may lie to someone and afterwards repent and thereby be forgiven, but the consequences of that lie are not removed. Because I lied, someone may have been wronged, someone may have been denied what was due to him, someone's reputation may have been hurt. That cannot be undone. I may drive carelessly and exceed the speed limit and kill a child. God will forgive me if I am a believer and I confess my sin to him; yet the child is still dead and its parents' hearts are broken. I may have to go to jail and my own family may well suffer for my carelessness. These consequences are not escapable. Forgiveness and the deliverance from the consequences of sin in this world are not the same thing.

The difference between Saul and David is seen not in that one sinned and the other did not, not even in that one had a tragic life after his sin and the other did not. Both lives were, after their sins, filled with tragedy. The difference is that one had no broken heart and no forgiveness and therefore no fellowship with God to sustain him, while the other had all of these things and actually grew spiritually in the midst of his tragedies.

The tragedies of David's life are mirrored in his own sons. First, the child born of illegitimate conception died. David, not the child, was punished (12:23). Why was this and the subsequent tragedy necessary? Because David had despised the Word of the Lord in his sin and had despised therefore the Lord himself (12:9, 10). This brought great dishonor to the Lord whom David trusted. If there had been no evil consequences, the world would have felt justified in sinning. In a similar way, we have seen how Moses' act of impatience toward God brought on dire consequences for him. He was not permitted to lead the people in though he had done so well up to that point. The Lord will not excuse anyone, even his most faithful servants, and will not allow them to despise his Word, no, not for a minute.

Chapter 13 tells of the rape of David's daughter by his son, Amnon. Here is mirrored the ugliness of David's own taking away Uriah's wife to gratify his own lust. The chapter also tells of

Absalom, the son of David, in revenge killing Amnon for having raped his sister. Here is mirrored David's murder of Uriah. The loss of Absalom by flight from David again reminds David of the loss of that son born by Bathsheba.

Absalom's succeeding acts of treachery against his father David related in chapters 15 to 18, reflect also David's treacherous act against one of the families in Israel, that of Uriah. The conspiracy of Absalom also gives to us some of the most beautiful scenes in David's life in spite of the tragedy of it all.

We see in David's flight great examples of love expressed by his true friends (15:21). We see also David's awareness that all of these things are in God's hands and that he is to seek God's help and endure whatever punishment is necessary. He honors God through it all (15:25; 16:10-12). He trusts in the Lord and his trust is not in vain. All was indeed in the hands of God who bent the purposes of men to serve his own ends and his own good will (17:14).

We see too the love David still had even for the rebellious child. No wonder he had a heart after God's own heart (18:5). Joab, the impetuous, proud and vain kinsman of David, could not understand such a heart and cruelly murdered Absalom, having no regard for the feelings of David (18:9-15). Even Joab's counsel, though perhaps wise for the occasion, was for a cruel and evil purpose. It was designed not to comfort David but to hurt him (19:1-6).

David's troubles were not ended here. Chapter 20 tells of another rebellion in Israel led by Sheba of the tribe of Saul. This rebellion served no particular end, and was quickly put down. However, it did show once more the evil of Joab who murdered David's new choice for captain of the host, Amasa (20:4-10). As he had killed Abner, a threat to his own position, so Joab now murdered Amasa. David's failure to discipline this man long before, continued to haunt him.

The rest of David's life is quickly recorded in the Word of God. Chapters 22 and 23 record some of the Psalms of David in praise of God. In chapter 22 he relates how God has delivered him from all who sought his life. He praises God as his deliverer (v. 1, etc.) and God's Word as tried and sure (v. 31, etc.). In the end he reflected on the promised seed and no doubt looked to the Messiah to come of the Seed of David (v. 51; compare Matt. 1:1).

In chapter 23 David clearly claims that what he has written is from God's Holy Spirit (23:1, 2). He reflects on the promise of God to him and his seed, the everlasting covenant as he calls it here. Compare 2 Samuel 7:9ff. As clearly as the Psalmist expressed it in Psalm 1, so David here sees clearly that there are only two kinds of people in the world, the righteous and the unrighteous, the godly and the ungodly, the saved and the lost, the sinners forgiven and the sinners unrepentant (23:5-7).

In the closing chapters of 2 Samuel we are told of one more sin of David which brought sadness to him and to Israel. David's sin, as all sin, began in his pride. He delighted to count the population under his control. In doing so, he showed pride and vanity (24:3, 9). As soon as he had done it, he was convicted (24:10) and again had to see the consequences of his sin. Again we see David look to the mercies of God as a solution (24:14). In all fairness to David, it appears that he was not alone in this sin. The whole people had provoked the Lord, as we are told in 24:1 and therefore the whole people had to endure the punishment. Once more, David's great heart, after God's own heart, is seen. He was more concerned for the people than for himself (v. 17).

The place which David bought as the site for the altar is called in 2 Chronicles 3:1, Moriah, and is presumably the same site at which Abraham had once, long before, prepared an altar to offer up his own son Isaac. See Genesis 22.

This brings us to the close of David's active rule. Interwoven with the life of David are the lives of several others. The two books of Samuel give us some very interesting character studies or studies in contrast.

There is first the contrasting character of Eli and Samuel. *Eli* was a failure in God's sight because he was willing to live in sin with his sons and compromise with their evil, though he knew the truth himself. He was weak in his own house. *Samuel* was a success in God's sight because of his integrity and great devotion to the Lord. He always saw himself as God's servant rather than as a pleaser of men.

There is also the contrast between Saul and David. *Saul* was promising at the beginning but his heart was far from God. He was not a spiritual man but lived for what was expedient. Vain pride filled his life and was in the last analysis his undoing. *David* also showed great hope for Israel in his beginning. He pleased God because he had a heart that was right in God's sight. He did sin, as Saul had sinned, and his sins were not slight, but he knew how to deal with sin, a thing which Saul never learned and it is here that David's greatness stands out. Even when he suffered terrible consequences for his sins he nevertheless grew spiritually in the midst of his sorrow.

Finally, there is a contrast between Jonathan and Joab. *Joab* was a failure because in his subordinate role he sought to please himself and not the Lord. As he served David, he was always looking out for himself more than for David and in the end proved not to be faithful to David at all. *Jonathan* also served in a subordinate role. Though he was the prince in Israel, he humbled himself because he would please the Lord. In the end he was highly exalted and shines forth as one of the purest characters in all the Old Testament.

THE REIGN OF SOLOMON
1 Kings 1—11

The opening chapters of 1 Kings give to us the transition from the rule of David to the rule of Solomon, David's choice to be his successor.

Not even in his last days on earth was David to know peace on earth. As he was near death, one of his sons, Adonijah, sought to secure for himself the kingdom of David (1:5). Here we find a most interesting comment on the failure of David to discipline his own sons. David had never called Adonijah to account for his wrongdoing (1:6), therefore in a way, this act of rebellion on Adonijah's part reflected a failure in the father again.

This time two who had always been with David before were now found on the wrong side: Joab and Abiathar the priest.

Those with David were concerned about the turn of events and reported the danger to Bathsheba, the mother of Solomon, David's choice for successor. The Shimei who is mentioned here as on David's side may have been the same one who once had cursed David. (Compare 2 Sam. 16:5ff. and 19:18-21).

When David received news of what was happening he hurriedly called together those he could trust and had Solomon anointed king in a place close enough to the followers of Adonijah, so that they could hear the celebration of the crowning of the new king and know that their cause was hopeless (1:41-43).

Adonijah was quickly left alone and pleaded for mercy to Solomon. Solomon was surprisingly lenient toward his half-brother (1:52, 53).

David's charge to Solomon before his death is reminiscent of the last words of Jacob or other patriarchs of old (2:1-4). In this charge he makes specific mention of the Law of Moses as the foundation for faithful living for the king and for all his people. The charge is not unlike the words spoken by God to Joshua after the death of Moses (Josh. 1).

David went on to give another charge concerning many who had sinned in his reign and had not been disciplined. He mentioned first Joab (2:5) and all the evil he had done. He also mentioned Shimei who had cursed him (2:8). He called for the death of both of these men (2:6, 9).

It is sad in a way to see such bitterness in David's heart at the end. But David was righteous and knew God would not overlook sin and would surely punish the one who does not discipline when God calls for discipline. In short, David did not wish for Solomon to suffer because he had failed to punish these two men for their sins against the Lord's anointed. He was also concerned that those who had honored the Lord's anointed be rewarded (2:7).

The beginning of the reign of Solomon is recorded in 1 Kings 2:12. The first acts of the new king were in carrying out the dying wishes of his father. The first problem arose in the kingdom when Adonijah made it quite evident that he had not learned a thing from his recent defeat. In his heart he still resented the fact that Solomon reigned instead of him and he did not seem to grasp the fact that his brother had been quite lenient toward him (2:15).

In asking for Abishag, the girl who had last lain with David (2:17), he was doing more than asking for a wife. He was committing treason. As we have shown before, to lie with one's father's concubine was tantamount to claiming the inheritance for one's self. This is the way Solomon interpreted it and why he ordered Adonijah to be killed (2:22-25).

Though Abiathar had favored Adonijah over Solomon, Solomon was also quite lenient toward him. His removal from the office of priest is here related to the curse put on Eli's house by the Lord much earlier (2:27—compare 1 Samuel 2:27-36).

Now Joab saw that his time had come and we see him run like a coward (2:28). But Solomon was determined and the judgment on Joab long overdue finally came for this ruthless man, who, though ostensibly on the right side, was unworthy of David and his true friends. Whenever one is not in heart a child of God and yet nevertheless manages to be identified with God's people, he always does much harm to the good name of the Lord and his people. God always hates the hypocrite (Josh. 7:25; Acts 5:1-11).

Now only Shimei was left. Solomon's gentle treatment of Shimei was probably due to the fact that Shimei had sided with Solomon in the controversy between Solomon and Adonijah (2:36-38). The fact, however, that he had cursed David, the Lord's anointed, was still displeasing to the Lord so that Shimei forgot the warning not to leave Jerusalem, and forced Solomon to punish him. Solomon expressed this judgment as the Lord's judgment on him and he had Shimei killed. The words to Abraham so long before held true: those who cursed the true seed of Abraham would be cursed (Gen. 12:3).

Chapter 3 begins the strange account of the very complex character of the man Solomon. The contrast in his own character remains one of the great mysteries in Scripture. On the one hand, he appeared to be one of the most devout and godly of men. But on the other hand, he proved in the end to be one of the most reprobate of the people of Israel.

I believe that the best way to see the complexity of Solomon is to trace each of three distinct traits of the man from chapter 3 through chapter 11. We will talk first about his merits, then about his weaknesses (his excessiveness) and finally about his sins. 1) *His merits.* The principal one of his merits has to be his love of God (3:3). We shall see this love wax cold before the end but here Scripture plainly teaches that he did, at least for a time, love the Lord.

We see another commendable trait in Solomon in his humility (3:7) and his keen sense of responsibility (3:9).

Chapter 3 goes on to tell of his commendable and marvelous great wisdom (3:28). He had also great talents and gifts so as to excel all before and after him in Jerusalem (4:32). He amassed a great amount of knowledge in his lifetime and amazed all who met him (4:33, 34).

When we come to his prayer at the time of the dedication of the Temple we read one of the most beautiful prayers recorded anywhere (8:22ff.). He was certainly a man of deep religious feelings.

The prayer itself shows a great love for God and for his fellowmen. He anticipates trials to come to Israel later and seeks from God assurance that he will see them through their difficulties. He even anticipates the time when they will be carried away captive (8:46ff.).

Even the queen of Sheba had nothing but praise for Solomon (10:1ff.). Surely this man would be a success. Yet even in the midst of these commendable traits there emerges a considerable flaw in his character. 2) *His weaknesses (excessiveness).* I use the term "excessiveness" to describe what appears to be a recurring weakness in the man Solomon.

We see this excessive nature in the man even in his worship. When he worshipped God he could not be satisfied with a simple offering of sacrifice but offered a thousand sacrifices on the altar (3:4). Perhaps he did not understand the whole meaning of the sacrificial system as David his father had (Psa. 40:6 and Psa. 51:16, 17).

Solomon's excess is also to be seen in his way of living. This excess is described in 4:22-26. He could seemingly do nothing in a simple way but liked to live always thinking big and vainly.

Again in the building of the house of the Lord, he used excess far beyond what the Lord desired. He overlaid all with gold, even the floor (6:21, 22, 30). He seems to have thought of the glory of the Temple in proportion to the gold that was in it. It is noteworthy that later the Lord spoke disparagingly of the temple Solomon had built and considered the glory of the much less pretentious temple built after the captivity to be more glorious (Haggai 2:7, 8). Perhaps too Jesus alluded to Solomon's obsession with gold when he spoke to the Pharisees (Matt. 23:16, 17) who put such great importance on the gold of the Temple. In the end, the gold did not glorify God but men.

Solomon's own obsession with gold continues to show his vanity as he even made shields of gold (10:17), an utterly useless thing; and even overlaid beautiful ivory with gold (10:18).

I am suggesting that in these marked excesses in Solomon's life probably lies the clue to his own spiritual depravity. There is no doubt that he was spiritually depraved, despite all the formerly mentioned merits. 3) *His sins.* The sins of Solomon are apparent and the sad thing is that there is not a shred of evidence that he repented of them. First, he married a foreign woman, an unbeliever, and even used the marriage to make an alliance with a pagan power (3:1).

Another sin of Solomon connected with his own ambitious nature, was that he made a levy in Israel, thus making Israelites into slaves (5:13). This later precipitated the rebellion which brought the dividing of the kingdom in his son's day.

His own pride and love of self cannot be ignored when we read how he spent more time on and built bigger the house for himself than the Lord's House. Compare 6:2, 38; 7:1, 2. He spent seven years in the Temple but thirteen on his own. The Temple of the Lord was about half the size of his own house.

It must be said that Solomon's heart was not right before God as was David's. His sins and excesses lead us to chapter 11, where we see Solomon described as a reprobate. His excess of wives and concubines, many of them foreigners, led him into idolatry as the Lord had warned (11:1-4). In the end, his epitaph is like that of the wicked kings who followed: "He did evil in the sight of the Lord" (11:6).

The passage in Deuteronomy 17:14-17 sounds almost like a

catalog of Solomon's failures. It is interesting that God mentioned so long before by Moses the exact things that would spell the undoing of the kingdom of Israel; and how true the prophecy of Samuel proved to be also, in the end (1 Sam. 8:10-17).

It is important to note that the New Testament is singularly unimpressed with the glory of Solomon. He is mentioned rarely in the New Testament, and that in a none-too-flattering way (Matt. 6:29). Solomon in all of his glory could not match a simple flower of the field. This seems to indicate that most of Solomon's glory was not from God but pseudo-glory from men.

We search to find the lesson from Solomon's life. One thing we note. Solomon lived a life without any trials or testing of his faith. His life was too easy, too free of hardship and trial, in great contrast to his father or other great men of God such as Abraham, Jacob, Joseph, Moses, and Samuel. These men grew in faith as they faced trial after trial. Solomon knew none of this. We learn therefore the lesson that in this life it is important that our faith be tested by trials. So the New Testament also teaches (John 16:33; 1 Pet. 1:6-9, Heb. 12:4-11).

The rest of the life of Solomon tells of God's displeasure with him and the consequent punishment which came against him and his kingdom (11:9-13). The primary punishment was a division of the kingdom. But God also raised up enemies to harass him for the rest of the days of his life (11:14ff.). Some of these enemies would later cause much trouble for his successors (11:26).

The offer of God through Ahijah the prophet to give ten tribes to Jeroboam was certainly a legitimate offer on which God made good (11:37-39). However, Jeroboam sadly did not take seriously the conditions and responsibility of taking over the leadership of so many people of God and therefore he began the rapid decline of the northern kingdom.

Solomon spent his latter years in fighting enemies and fearing competitors. His life ended not gloriously but ingloriously (11:40ff.). It is not for us to make judgment about the eternal destiny of the soul of Solomon. I cannot forget the words spoken in the early part of his life that he loved the Lord. It is hard to see how this could still be true of him in the latter days of his life, but again I say it is not up to us to make judgment about the eternal destiny of Solomon. That lies solely in the hands of God.

THE AGE OF
THE PROPHETS
1 Kings 12—2 Kings 25

AS WE BEGIN to study the age of the great Old Testament prophets, it will be helpful to give a brief chronology of the times. These dates are approximate and others will differ in giving the chronology of this period. It is not the dates which are so important but the events and lives lived in these times. This chronology will however help to tie together the events and personalities not only in the kingdoms of Israel and Judah but also in foreign lands.

The chronology on page 00 will take us as far as the fall of Jerusalem and the Babylonian captivity.

As we begin to study the period of history which has been designated as the Age of the Prophets, it is well to explain why we give it this name. We are speaking of the period in which the

writing prophets take such a prominent part. Of course, in a
sense the Age of the Prophets began at least as early as the time
of Abraham, who is the first man to be called a prophet (Gen.
20:7). But the era of the great writing prophets is introduced
about the time of Elijah and Elisha, who, though they might not
have written anything that has been preserved (though we cannot be certain of this) nevertheless were the forerunners of the
writing prophets who began to prophesy in the ninth century at
about the time of Elisha's death. We shall say more of this later.

1 Kings chapters 12—14 cover the rule of Rehoboam, the son
of Solomon, the last king of the united Israel. We see the folly of
Rehoboam and learn immediately that he was not a wise king as
his father and grandfather had been in their best years. He
rejected sound counsel, which is always a sign of weakness in any
ruler. Part of Rehoboam's failing lay in his desire to rule with an
iron hand, perhaps an imitation of his father (12:10, 11).

The rebellion led by Jeroboam was of the Lord as chapter 11
has shown (12:15). The only remnants left to David's kingdom
are Judah and Benjamin (12:21). God would not even permit
Rehoboam to go to war to try to win them back (12:24).

Jeroboam soon proved however that he was no better than
those he parted from. His rebellion against Rehoboam may have
been of the Lord but his further rebellion against the Lord was
to bring continued sorrow to the northern kingdom of Israel.
He did not trust the Lord. He attempted by his own cleverness
to hold the northern tribes to himself (12:26, 27). Ignoring
God's promise to bless him if he obeyed God, he wilfully disobeyed in making other centers of worship than the one at the
place which God had chosen where his Name should be (compare Deut. 12). He presented to the people alternative places to
worship which God had not chosen. Bethel and Dan became
causes of sin among the Israelites as later prophets would remind them (12:30).

Jeroboam set up not only illegitimate places to worship but
also illegitimate priests (v. 31) and illegitimate feasts (v. 32). Thus
the division in the Old Testament church proved to be tragic for
all concerned. But perhaps it left for us some lessons to be
learned about church division when the people of God can no
longer walk together. We can therefore make four observations
about this church division.

First, it was the Lord who brought on the division, as a judgment against a faithless church and in particular, against faithless leaders. Here God was plainly seeking a better foundation
on which to build his church. A comparison of 11:11 and 31 and
12:15 makes it clear that God did it. So we can conclude that

when God is not pleased with his church because it is failing to glorify him, division may follow.

Second, sin caused the church to divide. This does not contradict the first observation. God often uses the sins of evil men to carry out his good purpose, as we see in the case of Joseph and his brothers and or in the case of those who crucified Christ. 1 Kings 11:9-11 makes this clear as do other portions of Scripture (11:33; 12:8-14).

Third, we are taught that God had concern for both sides. It could not be said that God was on one side but not the other. He was for Judah (11:13, 36, 39) if she would obey him, and he was for Israel if she would obey (11:37, 38; compare 2 Kings 17:13). The long list of prophets whom he sent to the north are testimony to God's concern for her: Elijah, Elisha, Hosea, Amos, etc.

Fourth, it has to be said that there was wrong on both sides. Both sinned, Jeroboam and Rehoboam (12:25, 26; 13:33; 14:22; 15:3). There was sin in both: rebellion and turning from God (14:30 and 15:6).

Through it all we learn that God was concerned for integrity and faithfulness to his Word above all. That is what he looked for on each side (9:4; 14:8; 15:4, 5).

In the end, the side that seemed to be the more in the right at the beginning turned out to be the greatest failure. Israel produced no good leaders though she had many faithful prophets and believers. Judah, which seemed to be least justified at the beginning of the division, in the end proved more faithful for a longer period of time, producing several good kings among whom were Asa, Jehoshaphat, Uzziah, Hezekiah and Josiah.

In conclusion we must say that right is not to be determined by counting noses but by whether any church stands faithful in relation to the Word of God. Nothing therefore was actually settled by the division but only much later when one side proved to be more faithful than the other.

The next two chapters, 13 and 14, show that God would not overlook Jeroboam's sins. The remarkable prophecy concerning the coming of Josiah to destroy the altar built by Jeroboam was fulfilled in just the way it was foretold by the nameless prophet (13:1, 2—compare 2 Kings 23).

The tragic end of this prophet whose name we are never given, once more stresses God's clear lesson that his Word must be taken seriously at all times by all, especially by those whom he calls to be his spokesmen. (Compare the tragic judgment on Moses, etc.)

Because of Jeroboam's faithlessness, God predicted his over-

Dates	Rulers of Israel	Rulers of Judah	Foreign Rulers	Prophets	Special Events
		David/Solomon			
1000-950					
950-900	Jeroboam I Nadab Baasha Elah Zimri Tibni Omri Ahab Ahaziah Joram (Jehoram)	Rehoboam Abijam Asa Jehoshaphat	Hiram—(Phoenicia) Shishak—(Egypt) Ben Hadad—(Syria)	Nathan Ahijah Jehu	966—Temple begun 930—Kingdom divided
900-850			Shalmaneser III (Assyria)	Elijah Elisha	878—Omri builds Samaria
850-800	Jehu Jehoahaz	Jehoram (Joram) Ahaziah (Athaliah) Joash (Jehoash)	Hazael—(Syria)	Joel	
800-750	Jehoash (Joash) Jeroboam II Zechariah Shallum Menahem Pekahiah	Amaziah Uzziah (Azariah)	Tiglath-Pileser III (Pul)—(Assyria)	Jonah Amos Hosea	
750-700	Pekah Hoshea (End)	Jotham Ahaz Hezekiah	Rezin—(Syria) (Shalmaneser)— (Assyria) Sargon II—(Assyria) Sennacherib—(Assyria) Assurbanipal—(Assyria)	Isaiah Micah	732—Fall of Damascus 722—Fall of Samaria 701—Siege of Jerusalem
650-600		Manasseh Amon Josiah	Pharaoh-Necho II (Egypt)	Zephaniah Nahum Jeremiah Habakkuk	621—Josiah's discovery of the law 612—Fall of Nineveh 605—Daniel to Babylon
600-550		Jehoahaz Jehoiakim Jehoiachin Zedekiah (End)	Nebuchadnezzar— (Babylon) Nabonidus Belshazzar (Babylon)	Daniel Obadiah	597—First capture of Jerusalem 586—Fall of Jerusalem

throw and downfall as he had foretold to Jeroboam once the downfall of Solomon's kingdom (14:13, 14). The remainder of chapter 14 tells of the reign of Rehoboam which is here characterized as evil (vv. 22ff.). At this time the glory of Solomon began to fade as his shields of gold and his treasures of gold were carted off to Egypt by the powerful king Shishak of Egypt (vv. 25ff.).

Perhaps the best survey of these times is given in verse 30. There was continual war between the two divisions of the Old Testament church in the days of these two kings who both disobeyed the Lord.

With chapter 15 we begin to trace now one, then the other of the two kingdoms until Israel, the northern kingdom, fell in 722 B.C. From chapter 15 to the end of 1 Kings, we learn of the reigns of Abijam, Asa, and Jehoshaphat of Judah and of Nadab, Baasha, Elah, Zimri, Omri, and Ahab of Israel. This covers approximately one hundred years from around 950 to 850 B.C.

THE PERIOD OF STABILIZATION
(950 to 850 B.C., approx.)

In both the north and the south, this was a period of stabilization. First, in Judah we note that *Abijam,* the third successive disobedient king of Judah, ruled only three years (15:2). Then God intervened to save Judah from going in the same deteriorating path Israel was following. This is the meaning of the statement, "For David's sake did the Lord his God give him a lamp in Jerusalem" (v. 4). You recall that in 1 Samuel 3:3 we saw a similar phrase. (Compare also 2 Samuel 21:17; 1 Kings 11:36.) In all of these the meaning is similar. God's light was the life of man spiritually and God never let it go out. Before his people sank hopelessly into sin, God always intervened. We see this throughout Scripture and throughout the history of the Christian church since the close of Scripture.

In *Asa,* the son of Abijam, we see a revival of faithfulness on the part of the kings of Judah (15:12, 13). Much of his reign was spent in undoing the evil his predecessors had done. The writer of the book of Kings faults him in only one area: he did not remove the high places or popular places of worship which were contradictory to God's Law (15:14—See Deut. 12, one altar). The phrase "the heart of Asa was perfect with the Lord" is a way of expressing his sincere desire to walk in God's ways and do

God's will. See 1 Kings 8:61. In short, it declares him a true child of God, in God's judgment, which is the only judgment that truly counts.

However, like David and Solomon, Asa had his weaknesses. The hiring of Ben-Hadad of Syria to fight against the northern kingdom was an act similar to that of other kings later, such as Jehoash (2 Kings 12:17ff.) and Ahaz, in the days of Isaiah the prophet (2 Kgs. 16:7ff.—cf. Isaiah 7). It always indicated a lack of faith on the part of the king to trust more in human alliances than in the protective power of God.

As for Israel, we find a quick succession of kings leading up to the period of Omri and Ahab. *Nadab,* Jeroboam's son, was no better than his father and so the end of Jeroboam's dynasty came swiftly, as God had forewarned through his prophet, Ahijah (15:29—cf. 14:9-16).

Baasha, the instrument for the overthrow of Jeroboam's dynasty, proved to be no better (15:34). Another prophet of God, Jehu, was therefore raised up to foretell the overthrow of Baasha's house also (16:1-3), which happened in the reign of his son *Elah* at the hand of his captain, Zimri (16:8-10). *Zimri* in turn lived one week before he too was overthrown by Omri (16:17, 18).

In quick succession Israel had four unstable kings while Judah enjoyed the stability of Asa's rule. Finally, *Omri* emerged as supreme and succeeded in giving to Israel its first stable reign from the time of its inception (16:23).

When we speak of Omri's greatness we are speaking politically and not religiously. There never was a good king in Israel from God's point of view. All bear the same epitaph. They walked in the way of Jeroboam who made Israel to sin. Yet in the political world Omri accomplished much. First, he established Samaria as the capital, an excellent choice (16:24). Samaria was in an excellent position to guard all the routes north and south, and was also quite defensible, being high above the plain with natural high walls which could not be easily taken. So great was Omri's reputation among other nations that in the Assyrian annals Israel is always called "Omriland" hereafter. Even Jehu who later overthrew the house of Omri was known in Assyrian records as "the son of Omri."

On Omri's death we come to the most wicked reign in Israel's history, that of *Ahab* (16:29, 30). He added sin to sin in marrying the wicked Jezebel, a Phoenician pagan who worshipped Baal. Following Solomon's example, Ahab built in Samaria a place for her to worship her god against all that God had warned through Moses (Deut. 7:1-5).

Illustrative of the exceeding wickedness of the people in that day is the act of a certain Hiel of Bethel who so disregarded the Word of God that he dared to rebuild Jericho in open rebellion against the words of Joshua, God's servant (16:34—cf. Josh. 6:26). Thus we see in Ahab's day an utter disregard for the things of God and for God's will.

It was time for God to intervene as he had done before when man's wickedness reached a certain point. Now God sent the great prophet Elijah to confront Ahab and the iniquity of his realm.

Chapters 17 to 19 tell of the great confrontation between Elijah and Ahab and the great lesson which the Lord taught through this experience. There is no warning of Elijah's appearance. This great man suddenly appeared before Ahab and declared that it would not rain again except by Elijah's word (17:1). We can imagine how Ahab and his court must have laughed at this strange man in strange clothing (see 2 Kings 1:8). They laughed even more when he spoke with the authority of a god. Who did he think he was?

But then it did not rain and it did not rain and it did not rain. Meanwhile, Elijah was taken care of by the Lord, as the rest of chapter 17 tells us.

In his stay with the widow of Zarephath in Phoenicia near the home of Jezebel, Elijah through many signs proved to be God's prophet and spokesman as had Moses long before. Once more we see through the words of this widow, when Elijah brought her son back to life, that the biblical miracles primarily were to give authority to those whom God had chosen as his spokesmen (17:24—cf. Exod. 4:1-5).

Elijah introduces us to the second great era of miracles, the first being in the days of Moses. We see numerous miraculous signs in the days of Elijah and his successor Elisha, thus introducing the second great period of revelation, that of the writing prophets who would follow Elijah and Elisha.

In chapter 18 we see once more a confrontation between Elijah and Ahab. This time Ahab is much more respectful if more hostile toward Elijah. He calls Elijah the troubler of Israel (18:17). Elijah's answer is the classic answer of God's people in any era who are accused of troubling the church because they stand for the truth of God and rebuke the sins of the church. His words: "I have not troubled Israel; but thou, and thy father's house, in that you have forsaken the commandment of the Lord, and thou hast followed the Baalim," point to the heart of all trouble in the church of God and among the people of God.

The source of trouble is always the departure of some from the Word of God.

The contest on Carmel exposed the false claims of the Baal prophets and priests. After they had failed to show any evidence that their god was a living reality, Elijah took over (18:30ff.).

All that Elijah did was designed to give glory to God. What he did was a lesson to Israel, to return to the old foundations of her faith, to the God of her fathers. The twelve stones for the sons of Jacob recalled God's former blessings to the patriarchs who trusted in the Lord. In his prayer, too, Elijah called back to the days of the patriarchs and the era of Israel's young faith (18:36).

In declaring that all he did was according to God's Word (18:36), Elijah was again seeking God's glory and not his own. The word to which he refers might just as well have been the written Word through Moses as any specific new command which God may have given to him in that day.

Elijah's own theology was solid and clear. He knew that only as the hearts of the people were turned would they believe (v. 37). Later, this would become the heart of the prophetic message, that the Lord must turn their hearts to him if they are to believe in him. So also in the New Testament Christ similarly says that we must be born again, i.e., have hearts which are turned by God to himself, if we are to see God's kingdom (John 3).

We see then that in a way similar to Samuel at an earlier time, so Elijah calls the people to repentance and to return to the old ways, the same and sure paths of God. Compare 1 Samuel 7:3. God responded by sending the fire for which Elijah had prayed; and the people, seeing the evidence, cried out in approval of the Lord over Baal (v. 39).

The act of slaying the Baal prophets may seem to us quite severe, yet we must remember that these false prophets threatened the whole people of God, and the Baal prophets' very presence in Israel was against God's clear command. God had long ago declared the proper punishment for such people (Deut. 13:5).

We might have hoped for a sweeping revival in Israel at this time, but such was not the case. Jezebel's ire at hearing of the defeat of the Baal cult sent Elijah fleeing from the land (19:2ff.). Where were the crowds who had so recently declared that the Lord is God? Apparently theirs had not been a true conversion. Elijah felt all alone now and defeated (19:10).

God had allowed Elijah to reach this spiritual state in life so that he could teach Elijah and all succeeding believers a vital lesson. First, he led Elijah back to Sinai (Horeb) where God had given the first of his Word through his servant Moses (19:8).

Then he caused Elijah to see many mighty external signs or powers similar to the sign of the all-consuming fire at Carmel (19:11ff.). But after each external sign of power the phrase is repeated: "But the Lord was not in the wind (earthquake, fire)." Then after these signs, we hear the words "a still small voice" (19:12).

What was God teaching Elijah? Simply that hearts are not turned (18:36) by mighty signs and powers, but by the Word of God speaking to the hearts of men, as a "still small voice." Similarly, we see the words of Zechariah 4:6, "not by might, nor by power, but by my spirit, saith the Lord of Hosts." Hence we shall hear the Word of God spoken through the great succession of God's prophets, each with his own mighty "thus saith the Lord . . ." It is this written Word of God which Peter later declares as "more sure" than all the signs and wonders and even the audible voice of God from heaven (2 Pet. 1:18-21). This too is what is meant in Deuteronomy 30:11-14 when God declares that the Word of God in you is the real power to salvation. Compare Romans 10:6ff.

From this time on then, God prepared through Elijah and Elisha, his successor, the coming of the good news through the prophets. It was this and not mighty signs that would turn the hearts of the people to God.

The rest of the nineteenth chapter relates certain specific tasks given to Elijah before he was to be taken from the earth. He was to anoint Hazael over Syria, Jehu over Israel, and Elisha to be his successor (19:15, 16).

As evil as Ahab was, nevertheless, God had mercy on Israel in the days of Ahab and delivered them out of the hand of their enemy, Syria. Some unnamed prophets and men of God are involved in the communication between the Lord and Ahab, assuring him of victory (20:13, 22, 28). In verse 35 we have the first mention of "the sons of the prophets" who are also elsewhere called "the company of the prophets" (1 Sam. 10:10) and are supposedly a school where prophets were trained and developed in their knowledge of God and his Word. Here the term "son" would mean disciple or pupil.

Ahab, in a way similar to Saul, the first king of Israel, was lenient on his enemy beyond what God had permitted (20:34— cf. 1 Sam. 15:9). As a result, Ahab was rebuked (v. 42).

The incident in chapter 21 of Naboth's vineyard again shows the viciousness of Jezebel and the weak character of Ahab. Naboth was seeking to obey God's Word in refusing what the king demanded (cf. Lev. 25:23; Num. 36:7). Ahab, brought up on at least the rudiments of God's Word, knew that Naboth was right. However, Jezebel, reflecting the Phoenician concept of a king, thought quite differently and seeing the kingship as absolute and under no authority, not even the Law of God, proceeded to do what Samuel long ago warned the kings of Israel would do (see 1 Sam. 8:11-17). Yet Jezebel went even farther, and her lies had Naboth put to death (21:13).

In a way similar to his dealing with David after he had sinned against God, God once more sent his prophet to rebuke king Ahab for his grievous sin. Only this time there was no shred of hope but only a severe punishment (21:17ff.). Ahab's only act of decency in his entire reign was his apparent penance on hearing this news (21:27). He was spared seeing all the terrible things happen to his house which Elijah foretold (21:29) but in essence all that this meant was that Ahab would very soon die, a source of little comfort.

The final chapter in 1 Kings contains the strange account of Jehoshaphat's unhappy alliance with Ahab. The reign of *Jehoshaphat* is not given until the latter part of this chapter. It begins in verse 41, though Jehoshaphat himself is introduced at the beginning of the chapter. Let us look first at verse 43. Here we learn that Jehoshaphat was like his father Asa, a king who sought to serve the Lord. Yet he made a serious error in making peace with the ungodly Ahab (v. 44).

This set up the strange alliance between Ahab and Jehoshaphat that the first part of chapter 22 relates. The sad and erroneous judgment of Jehoshaphat that there was no distinction between the people of Israel and the people of Judah indicates a serious blind spot in Jehoshaphat's spiritual life (22:4). For the people of God to ally with those who live contrary to God's will is always condemned in Scripture. From the time of the patriarchs when Abraham avoided any intermarriage with the Canaanites, to the warnings of Paul for Christians not to be unequally yoked with unbelievers (2 Cor. 6:14), we see that God has placed enmity between the believer and the unbeliever (Gen. 3:15). Whenever the believer ignores this distinction set up by God, he compromises his life and that of those who follow him.

When Jehoshaphat sought to have a word from the prophet of God about the pending battle (v. 5), he was guilty of doing what Christ later warned against, "casting our pearls before swine" (Matt. 7:6). This man Ahab, an unbeliever, had no desire to know God's will. To entrust to him one's religious inquiry or one's life was sheer folly. First, Ahab sought to persuade him by bringing in false prophets (v. 6). He later sought for Jehoshaphat to be killed in his stead (v. 30). This act nearly resulted in

Jehoshaphat's death (v. 32). So we see the truth of Jesus' words that they will turn and rend you (Matt. 7:6) i.e., Ahab with whom Jehoshaphat sought to deal religiously, in the end sought to destroy Jehoshaphat to save himself, perhaps hoping to be rid of two enemies at once, Syria and Judah.

The fact that Ahab was killed in spite of his own efforts, and the particular way in which that death occurred, speak to the sovereignty of God to control all events according to his own good purpose in spite of all human effort to the contrary. God's Word did prevail (v. 38—compare 21:19).

Apparently Jehoshaphat learned his lesson because we see later that he refused to be allied with Ahab's son in a commercial venture (22:49).

The beginning of Ahaziah's reign in Israel after his father Ahab, introduces us to the second period of the kings covered in the first 11 chapters of 2 Kings.

THE PERIOD OF TREACHERY
(850-800 B.C. approx.— 2 Kings 1—11)

The first 11 chapters of 2 Kings tell of the tragic period leading up to and including the reign of Jehu, who exterminated the seed of Ahab in Israel. It also tells of the debauchment in Judah due to the intermarriage between the house of Ahab and the house of Jehoram of Judah, Jehoshaphat's son.

Since the narratives about Elijah and Elisha are interwoven into this period, it is easy to lose the continuity of the kings that ruled in those days.

Jehoshaphat's reign overlaps several kings of Israel including Ahab, Ahaziah and Jehoram or Joram as he is also called. Another confusion of the times is that the names of the kings in both Judah and Israel were identical in those days probably because of the close relationship between the two families which was established in the days of Jehoshaphat and Ahab, as we have seen. Again the danger between unholy alliances such as this is seen in that it terminated in an actual marriage between the houses of Israel and Judah. Jehoshaphat's son took the daughter of Ahab (Jezebel's daughter too) as his wife and introduced the wickedness of Jezebel into the house of Judah (2 Kgs. 8:16-18).

Ahaziah, the son and successor to Ahab in Israel, did not live long. He reigned only two years and continued the evil of his father (1 Kgs. 22:15-53). His mother Jezebel continued to live and to spew out her evil venom that polluted Israel and Judah.

So wicked was Ahaziah that when he fell in an accident and was sick, he did not look to God for help but to Baal-Zebub, the god of Ekron (2 Kgs. 1:2). Thus, although before when any wicked people in Israel became distressed, they had looked to God for help (1 Kgs. 21:27-29), so low had the spiritual state in Israel dropped by now that the king in trouble looked to pagan gods. Hereafter the name Baal-Zebub would become synonymous with Satan himself (Matt. 10:25).

Ahaziah was strongly rebuked by God and told that he would never recover from his illness (2 Kgs. 1:3, 4). The episode recorded in 1:9-16 is the last view we have of Elijah, God's servant, before he is taken up to heaven. In it we see both the wrath of God toward the arrogant and his mercy toward the humble.

Jehoram, the son of Ahaziah, succeeded his father in Israel and so at this time the names of the kings in Judah and Israel are the same (1:17). It is Jehoram the son of Jehoshaphat who married Ahab's daughter. Presumably the Jehoram of Judah was for a time a co-ruler with his father Jehoshaphat, since in 1:17 we are told that the Jehoram of Israel began to reign in the second year of the Jehoram of Judah while in 3:1 he is said to have begun his reign in the 18th year of Jehoshaphat.

The most positive thing said about Jehoram of Israel is that he did not sin like his father or mother (3:2). It was in his days that Elijah was taken to heaven and Elisha became his successor among the prophets. The reason for so much attention to the reign of Jehoram of Israel is that the primary activity of Elisha is during his days. This explains the nine chapters that are given to the reign of Jehoram who is a comparatively unimportant king of Israel.

The instigation of Elisha's career is at the time of Elijah's ascension recorded in 2 Kgs. 2. It must have been apparent to all of the prophets that Elijah was about to ascend. Elisha was careful to stay by his side. Apparently Elijah's frequent commands to Elisha to stay behind (2:2, 4, 6) were intended to test the commitment of Elisha to his calling.

When Elijah ascended to heaven, he joined a small and exclusive group who ascended to heaven without dying. Only Enoch, the godly pre-Flood man besides Elijah, had done this. Only Jesus would do it again, after his resurrection. At the end of time when Christ returns, many more presumably will rise to meet Christ in the air without dying (1 Cor. 15:51). Elijah's mantle fell on Elisha at this time and he continued the ministry of Elijah.

Long afterwards Malachi prophesied that Elijah would return

before the day of the Lord (Mal. 4:5). Jesus interpreted this passage to be fulfilled in the coming of John the Baptist (Matt. 11:14). Elijah together with Moses appeared with Jesus on the mount of transfiguration also (Matt. 17:3).

The cry of Elisha calling Elijah "the chariots of Israel and the horsemen thereof" is a tribute to his greatness, greater and more important to Israel than all her armies (2 Kgs. 2:12). Later the same tribute was paid to Elisha by Joash the king of Israel (2 Kgs. 13:14).

A series of some fifteen miracles are recorded by the man Elisha as he lived for a long time in Israel, in fact, up until the time of the earliest of the writing prophets.

The *first* miracle was an imitation of one just before done by Elijah (2:14—compare 2:8). The *second* was in healing the bad water (2:19ff.). The *third*, the destruction of forty-two children by two bears, may not have been a miracle, but has caused difficulty to some who would accuse Elisha of cruelty to young children (2:23-24). Two things however need to be remembered in connection with this act: first, not Elisha but God sent the bears; second, their words probably reflected parental mocking of God's servant. Certainly they had never been taught to respect their elders. Failure to obey God's Law always has as its penalty death. In God's judgment these children and/or their parents were due the punishment which he meted out that day.

The *fourth* miracle was in connection with the rebellion of Mesha king of Moab (3:4-27). We know of this king Mesha from another source also, the Moabite Stone. On that stone which has been discovered by archaeologists, is Mesha's own record of his rebellion against Israel. In that record Mesha boasted that by the help of his god he overthrew Ahab's son. Once more Jehoshaphat joined with Israel at Jehoram's insistence. Again Jehoshaphat insisted on hearing from the Lord's prophet (3:11). This time, none other than Elisha appeared and directed by God, foretold how the allies could gain victory over Moab. By God's working the Moabites saw trenches of water as though they were filled with blood (3:22, 23). And the Moabites erroneously assumed that the allies had fallen out with one another and destroyed each other (3:23). It was a fatal error which ended Moab's rebellion.

The *fifth* great sign was the increase of the widow's oil miraculously (4:1ff.). The *sixth* sign was the promise of a child to a woman grown too old to bear. She was from Shunem (4:8ff.).

Later that same woman bore a child and then years later the child took ill and died (4:17ff.). The woman found Elisha at Mt.

Carmel and led him to her home. The *seventh* miracle was the raising of that child from the dead (4:35).

The *eighth* and *ninth* miracles have to do with food. In one, Elisha made pure food that had been accidentally poisoned (4:41). In the other, he worked a miracle similar to the two done by Jesus, feeding a large number with a small amount of food (4:42).

Chapter 5 tells of a most interesting miracle (the *tenth* one) in connection with the leprosy of Naaman. Naaman, captain of the armies of Syria, was the enemy of Israel. Yet when he learned that a prophet in Israel could work miracles, he went to find him. On being told to go wash in the Jordan seven times by Elisha, Naaman was indignant, supposing that he had wasted his time. But a wise servant of his counseled him to obey, and as he did obey, his leprosy left him (5:14).

The event convinced Naaman and he became an apparent believer in the Lord (5:15). His conversion seems to have been genuine (5:17ff.). But the deceitful act of Gehazi, Elisha's servant, gained for him not the riches he desired but the leprosy of Naaman (v. 27). This was the *eleventh* miracle. The next miracle, the *twelfth*, was the floating of an iron axe head (6:6).

Miracle number *thirteen* was the vision of the armies of God that was shown to the servant of Elisha (6:17). The king of Syria had become angry because Israel always seemed to know what was being planned. When he learned that Elisha the prophet was informing the king of Israel of all that Syria planned (6:12), he sought Elisha's arrest. When the armies came to take him they were hit with blindness and led as captives to Samaria (6:19).

The *final* miracle of Elisha's life was the sudden defeat of the Syrians who were besieging Samaria and the abundance of food it left for Samaria when the city was on the brink of starvation (chapter 7). Before Elijah had ascended, God had given to him three tasks to do: anoint Hazael as king over Syria, anoint Jehu as king over Israel and anoint Elisha to be his successor (1 Kgs. 19:16). In this lifetime Elijah accomplished the last of these, but in doing so he must have considered Elisha to be the one to accomplish the other two tasks for him.

In 2 Kgs. 8 we read of Elisha's anointing of Hazael to be king instead of Ben-Hadad. This chapter also records the marriage between Jehoram of Judah, Jehoshaphat's son and the daughter of Ahab and Jezebel (8:18). As we remarked earlier, this marked a new low for Judah and threatened, before it was through, the entire line of David. Again however the mercy of God shows through, and God preserved the line for David's sake (8:19—compare 1 Kgs. 11:36). It was a revolting age as God showed his displeasure with Jehoram of Judah (vv. 20, 22). After a relatively short reign of eight years, Jehoram died and his son Ahaziah ruled. In his days, his mother, Athaliah, was prominent and she was the daughter of Ahab and the granddaughter of Omri (8:26).

As could be expected, Ahaziah of Judah allied with Jehoram (Joram) of Israel and the two, being kin, were very close (8:29).

Now the Lord began to intervene. Elisha set about to carry out the third of God's commands to Elijah long before. He sent one of the prophets to anoint Jehu to be king of Israel. Jehu had been chosen by God to destroy the line of Omri and to eradicate Baal worship in Israel (9:8).

While Ahaziah was visiting Jehoram of Israel, Jehu led a revolt against the king. In the end Jehu killed Jehoram (9:24) and Ahaziah of Judah (9:27). Jehu then went to Jezreel and there destroyed the proud and vain Jezebel (9:30ff.) and later all the sons and descendants of Ahab (10:11). He even killed all of the brothers of Ahaziah of Judah for he too was now descended from the line of Ahab.

In the process of wreaking havoc on the houses of Israel and Judah, Jehu encountered Jehonadab, the son of Rechab (10:15). He showed respect for this honored family in Israel which is also mentioned later in the prophecy of Jeremiah (35:6-19) as a model family of faithfulness.

The extermination of Baal worship in Israel was most effective and Baal worship never rose again in Israel though it did continue in Judah (10:18ff.). With Jehonadab, Jehu killed all of the Baal worshippers in Israel (10:28).

He followed God's will in all he did so far, yet sadly Jehu did not honor God, thus making his own mass slayings evil rather than having done what he did to please God. For this reason, Hosea later describes and condemns the sin of Jezreel (compare 9:30ff. and Hosea 1:4). Jehu's crime was not in killing all the house of Ahab but in doing it out of personal gain instead of as a service to God (10:31).

This marked in reality the end of Israel as the people of God. Indeed, Hosea would declare that they are not God's people. Compare 2 Kings 10:32; Hosea 1:4, 9, etc.

The slaughter of so many of Ahab's kin left his daughter in Jerusalem in an interesting situation. She was now the apparent successor to the throne and she sought to destroy all of her competitors, the seed of David (11:1). Yet in God's providence one was saved and hidden away until the proper time (11:2, 3).

One son of Ahaziah, Jehoash, a year old, was hidden away in the Temple for six years while Athaliah thought that she had successfully secured the throne for herself (11:3). When Jehoash the priest who had protected Jehoash revealed to Judah his existence, all Judah was apparently ready for the change (11:12, 14).

THE LAST GREAT PERIOD
OF ISRAEL
(800-750 B.C.—2 Kings 12—15:7)

Jehoash of Judah had a long and mixed reign so far as his spiritual capabilities were concerned. His faithfulness to the Lord was dependent on the presence of Jehoiada, the priest, his protector and counselor (12:2). He did show concern for the repair of the Temple probably under the influence of Jehoiada (12:4ff.). It was generally an era of good will and mutual trust so long as Jehoiada lived (12:15).

Once more, however, the king when threatened by enemies resorted to the worldly bribe instead of trusting in the Lord (12:17, 18). He bought off Hazael of Syria who had threatened him.

We are not told here why Jehoash was assassinated, but in Chronicles we shall learn more of his days as king after the death of Jehoiada the priest. In those days his own life fell apart spiritually and he proved to be both wicked and vengeful.

Returning now to the northern kingdom, we read of the evil reign of *Jehoahaz*, the son of Jehu, the exterminator of Baal worship from Israel. Jehu had proven to be unfaithful to the Lord and his son followed his wicked way, being no better than the family of Ahab which God had destroyed (13:1ff.).

As God had done in the days of the judges, so again he raised up adversaries, this time in Syria, who plagued Israel in those days by many raids. Involved in the raids were Hazael and Ben-Hadad of Syria, both known from secular historical records of the times (13:3).

During the time of Syrian oppression, this son of Jehu showed some integrity before the Lord in that he called on the Lord for help. The situation reminds us of the period of the judges very much. God heard his cry and delivered Israel from her oppressors (13:4-6).

Succeeding Jehoahaz of Israel was his son, *Jehoash*, who was also evil (13:11). At this time Elisha was old and about to die but still revered in Israel. Jehoash of Israel acknowledged his greatness by calling him the chariots and horsemen of Israel as Elisha had once titled Elijah (13:14—cf. 2:12). Jehoash's lack of enthusiasm for Elisha's final command resulted in an indecisive victory over the Syrians. Perhaps he was not as much of an admirer of Elisha as he pretended to be.

One final miracle is associated with Elisha, this one after his death, when his bones gave life to a corpse that had been cast into Elisha's tomb. Thus God's continuing testimony of the greatness and authority of his prophets is seen (13:21).

We marvel as we see the summation of God's continuing grace to Israel in those days in spite of her continuous sin. The long-suffering of the Lord is beyond doubt, just as he had declared to Moses so long before (13:23, compare Exod. 34:6).

In Judah at this time, *Amaziah,* son of Jehoash of Judah reigned. He seemed to be sensitive to the will of the Lord and desirous of obeying the Law of Moses (14:5-6).

For the first time since the days of Asa of Judah and Baasha of Israel (1 Kgs. 15:32), Israel and Judah were at odds with one another and met in battle (14:8ff.). This marked the end of the alliance which had been between the two nations from the days of Jehoshaphat and Ahab. The result of this battle was the defeat of Judah at the hands of Israel (14:12). Israel took the battle to the very gates of Jerusalem and raided the Temple (14:14).

So foolish had Amaziah proven to be as king of Judah that he too was assassinated and his son, *Azariah (Uzziah)* became ruler at sixteen years of age (14:21). This introduced the longest single reign of any king of Judah, some fifty years, right up to the time of the call of the prophet Isaiah (Isa. 6:1).

At about midway through the reign of Amaziah of Judah, Israel's last powerful king began to rule. His name is ominous, Jeroboam. He is known as *Jeroboam II* of Israel. He too had a long reign, though not quite as long as that of Uzziah. He ruled some forty-one years in Israel.

The name he adopted is significant and indicative of the rebellious attitude against God in those days. He chose to take the name of the king who had in the first instance made Israel to sin, Jeroboam I, in the days of the division of the kingdom after Solomon's death.

Though he is dealt with only briefly in Scripture, presumably he had what, in the eyes of men, would be judged to be a successful rule (14:25, 27, 28). It was in his days that we have mention of the first of the writing prophets whose names appear in the historical sections of Scripture. That prophet was Jonah, son of Amittai of Gath-hepher (14:25).

The long reign of Azariah of Judah who was also known as Uzziah and of Jeroboam II of Israel, marks the end of Israel's power. While Jeroboam did wickedly in God's sight, Uzziah sought to please the Lord (15:3). Thus the continuing special grace of God toward Judah sustained her for many years after the fall of Israel.

THE LAST DAYS OF ISRAEL
(750-722 B.C.—2 Kings 15:8—17:41)

In quick succession the last kings of Israel ruled in the midst of conspiracy and the even greater threat of destruction by Assyria. *Zechariah,* the son of Jeroboam II, lasted only six months. He was succeeded by Shallum who killed him. *Shallum* lasted only one month and was killed by *Menahem,* who ruled for ten years (15:17ff.).

In those days at last the power of Assyria reached into the land of Canaan and touched Israel. The great Assyrian king who threatened Israel in those days was Tiglath-Pileser III, known in Scripture as Pul (15:19).

While Uzziah still ruled in Judah, *Pekahiah,* son of Menahem succeeded his father for two years before being killed by Pekah, his army captain in Samaria (15:25).

Pekah succeeded in ruling Israel some twenty years. He began to reign about the time of Uzziah's death, in the days when Isaiah first began to preach in Judah (15:27). Tiglath-Pileser began to increase his activity against Israel and Syria. He actually captured portions of the Israel kingdom in the northern part (15:29).

In those days, *Hoshea,* the last king of Israel, killed Pekah and ruled nine years until the fall of Samaria in 722 B.C.

But before coming to that time, still in the days of Pekah and Rezin king of Syria, these two allied against Judah and threatened to take Jerusalem (15:37). At this time *Jotham* was ruling in Judah instead of his father Uzziah. Before the siege was lifted, Jotham died and *Ahaz,* one of the most evil kings of Judah, succeeded his father (16:1-4).

In Isaiah 7 we are told how when Syria and Israel were threatening Ahaz of Judah, Isaiah came to reassure Ahaz that God would not let them take Jerusalem. However, as we read in 2 Kings 16:7ff., Ahaz, not trusting in God, put his trust in human alliances and looked to Assyria for help against his enemies. Again he showed his faithlessness toward God.

The evil act of Ahaz did succeed in bringing the downfall of Damascus at the hands of the Assyrians in 732 B.C. (16:9). Then ten years later Samaria, capital of Israel, would fall in 722 B.C. (17:6). But the Assyrians would not stop there. By 701 they were at the gates of Jerusalem in the days of Hezekiah of Judah as we shall study later. Thus Ahaz' plot resulted in the near destruction of his own kingdom in the days of his son, Hezekiah. But this is ahead of the present study.

Returning now to the rule of the last king of Israel, Hoshea (2 Kgs. 17:1ff.), we learn that Shalmaneser V, as he is known in secular history, brought Hoshea under his control, forcing him to pay tribute (17:3). When Hoshea attempted to bribe the king of Egypt to help him, the king of Assyria set siege to Samaria. Scripture only tells us that the king of Assyria took Samaria in the ninth year of Hoshea (17:6). From extra-Biblical sources we learn that by this time the Assyrian nation was ruled by Sargon II, who is actually credited with taking the city in 722 B.C. (17:6). As was Assyrian policy, the citizens of Israel were carried away into other lands to live (17:6) and people from other lands were brought in to populate Samaria (17:24).

So ends the history of the northern kingdom of Israel. Its people were scattered throughout the empire of Assyria and were lost sight of forever.

At this point, the book of Kings summarizes God's dealings with the people of Israel over a long period of history. The charges against Israel, the sins which brought her downfall, are enumerated here, but in essence, she sinned against the Lord in spite of God's continuing care for her and his sending prophet after prophet to call her back to him (17:7, 13). The only proper response to God's Word as delivered by his prophets, was faith in God. This Israel refused to show (17:14). And so God removed Israel out of his sight as no more being the people of God.

In judging Israel, the Lord spared a remnant, Judah, which continued to live before the Lord as a nation for another 136 years before going into Babylonian captivity. Judah too was disobedient, however, and ultimately only a remnant of Judah would be saved as prophet after prophet would declare.

The origin of the Samaritans of later history is given in the latter half of the 17th chapter. We learn that people were brought in to populate Samaria from various places as we have noted above (17:24). Because these strangers did not honor the Lord, the Lord punished them by wild beasts (17:25). In order to learn how to please or appease the gods of the place, the Samaritans were given a teacher, a priest of the Israelites, who

taught them how to worship in the Israelite manner. The amalgamation of religion which resulted is summarized in 17:33,
"they feared the Lord, and served their own gods." The impropriety of the new religion which developed in Samaria and resulted in the Samaritan religion is clearly stated in the final
verses of the chapter.

The Samaritans are particularly significant in Scripture in the
days of the return of the Jews from Babylonian captivity and
then later in the time of Jesus. There are still Samaritans living
today who worship at Mt. Gerizim and have their own version of
Moses' writings but who reject the rest of Scripture. They are
today in Israel very few in number but still identifiable. Yet their
religion, being a mixture of fearing the Lord and serving their
own gods, has much in common with much of the "religious
world" today, even among churchgoers.

We shall study more thoroughly the age just passed through
when we study the writing prophets of Israel in the next few
chapters.

THE LAST DAYS OF JUDAH
(725-586 B.C.—2 Kings
18:1—25:30)

Returning now to Judah, we have learned of Ahaz' wicked reign
in chapter 16. He was king for sixteen years in Jerusalem and
one of the most evil. But after his death his son *Hezekiah* began to
rule (18:1). Hezekiah, in stark contrast to his father, was one of
Judah's finest kings. He was like his ancestor David (18:3). His
greatness is seen in his faith in the Lord (18:5).

As the Lord had been with Moses, Joshua and David, so he
was with Hezekiah (18:7).

In his days Shalmaneser came to besiege Samaria and the
Assyrians took Samaria in 722 as we saw above (18:9). You remember that Ahaz, who did not believe in the Lord as his son
later did, had first employed the Assyrians to attack Damascus
and Samaria. As a result, the Assyrians took Damascus in 732
B.C., Samaria in 722 B.C. and were now knocking at the doors of
Jerusalem in about 701 B.C. (18:13ff.).

Hezekiah at first sought by his own resources to appease the
Assyrians (18:14-16) but this was to no avail, the Assyrians desired the unconditional surrender of Jerusalem and Hezekiah
her king (18:19-35).

The king of Assyria, through his messenger, demanded their

surrender. In his long speech before the people of Jerusalem, Rabshakeh, the one sent by Sennacherib who was then king of Assyria, expressed contempt and contradictory views of Judah's God. At first, he implied that their God was displeased with Jerusalem and was therefore punishing them by the Assyrians (18:22, 25). Yet later he ridiculed that same God as insufficient to save Jerusalem from the hands of the Assyrians (18:32).

From the Assyrian annals of those days, we read that Sennacherib boasted of having Hezekiah the Jew locked up like a bird in a cage so that the idle boasting of the king in Scripture is also reflected in the Assyrian annals or historical records.

The faith of the good king Hezekiah was now tested greatly. His own resources had failed. He was indeed like a bird in a cage and helpless but he had faith and turned toward the Lord in this dark hour (19:1). We see his greatness now as he put his whole faith in the Lord his God. His courage was like that of his forefather, David (19:4—cf. 1 Sam. 17:36).

He sent for Isaiah, God's prophet of the hour. Remember that Isaiah had earlier been sent to his father Ahaz, in a similar situation to assure him that Jerusalem would not fall to Syria and Israel (16:5, 6—compare Isaiah chapter 7. Ahaz had not believed in the Lord and had hired instead Assyria to protect him. Now as a result of Ahaz' faithlessness at that time, the Assyrians were threatening to take Jerusalem as well.

Hezekiah though, trusted in the Lord. He looked to God's messenger, Isaiah, who assured him that Jerusalem would not fall to the Assyrians (19:6, 7). The same record is found in Isaiah chapters 36 through 38.

Again the Assyrians defied the God of Hezekiah (19:10ff.) and once again Hezekiah trusted in the Lord and delivered a beautiful prayer of faith to the Lord (19:14ff.).

Isaiah once more came with reassuring words to show that the sovereign God would put down this great enemy Assyria (19:20ff.—cf. Psa. 2). In Isaiah's message to Hezekiah, he declared God's complete control of the situation and God's absolute ability to overthrow all of his and Judah's enemies (19:23-28).

Again the remnant is mentioned (19:31). This is one of the primary themes of the writing prophets and defines the true believers in Judah who are God's children and who shall be saved.

We are not told just what kind of plague hit the camp of the Assyrians by the will of God but it was effective to remove them from besieging Jerusalem (19:35). After this, Assyrian strength faded rapidly until the Babylonians finally overthrew Assyria and became the dominant power in the ancient Near Eastern world.

Chapter 20 records Hezekiah's sickness and near death and the act of weakness on his part when he responded to the flattery of the Babylonian visitors and showed them all of his treasures (20:15). His sin was one of pride, a response to the flattery of the king of Babylon who sent men to inquire of his health. His sin was similar to that of Joshua and the men of Israel in their own response to the men of Gibeon (Josh. 9:14, 15).

One other event of Hezekiah's day ought to be mentioned. In 20:20, note is made of a conduit built in the days of Hezekiah to bring water into the city. This was evidently done to bring in water during the siege. Jerusalem had no water within its ancient walls. All of the springs were outside the walls. Since in the time of siege this put Jerusalem in a bad position, Hezekiah undertook a tremendous engineering feat to bring in water from the spring to a pool or reservoir inside the city walls where it could be safely reached.

The conduit or tunnel which he dug is still visible today. In the late 1800's some boys while swimming in the pool of Siloam, found the record written in Hezekiah's day of how the tunnel had been dug. Today one can walk through the length of that tunnel and actually see marks of the pickaxes which were used to dig the tunnel. It still brings water from the spring underground to the pool below, known as the pool of Siloam.

After Hezekiah, his son *Manasseh* ruled. He proved to be as bad as his grandfather Ahaz and not at all like his father Hezekiah (21:2-6). He is rated in Scripture as among the very worst of Judah's kings (21:9). In fact, the evil of Manasseh brought about the final fall of Jerusalem, though not in his day (21:11, 12). The reference to the line of Samaria and the plummet of the house of Ahab (21:13) refers to God's righteous judgment against Israel earlier. The verse may be compared to Amos 7:8.

After Manasseh, *Amon* his son, who was just as evil, reigned for two brief years (21:19-22). As a result of his evil he was assassinated (21:23) and his son, Josiah, began to rule Judah at the very tender age of eight.

Josiah proved to be the most faithful and the last faithful king of Judah and was like his great grandfather Hezekiah. The record of his accomplishments is recorded in chapters 22 and 23. At first he instigated a cleaning up of the House of the Lord (22:3ff.). In the process of cleaning out the Temple, the Book of the Law was found which apparently had been lost for some time (22:8).

Much has been written about this find. Some who doubt the reliability of Scripture suggest that it was not the Law of Moses at all but a much later writing. They view the book of Deuteronomy to have been written in these days. The book does seem to have been mainly the book of Deuteronomy, but there is no reason to doubt that it was Moses' book that was found. The resulting reforms established by Josiah seem to have been guided by the content of the book of Deuteronomy.

The Lord was pleased with Josiah's own contrition of heart because of the words of judgment found in the book (22:19).

Josiah truly sought to bring Judah back to God by great reform in the people (23:1ff.). He even went to Bethel, the place of worship established by Jeroboam long before, and destroyed that place as the unnamed prophet had foretold in Jeroboam's day (23:15, 16—cf. 1 Kgs. 13:2).

The Passover feast celebrated at this time was according to the rules of Deuteronomy 16:2-8; 23:21. He also put away all sinful practices in Judah in accord with Deuteronomy 18:10-12. Yet all he did did not really change Judah. It seems apparent that though Josiah tried hard and sincerely to bring Judah back to the Lord, he failed in the end. Jeremiah, commenting on these times, said that the people turned to God feignedly, but not with their whole heart (Jer. 3:10).

The Lord determined to punish Judah in spite of Josiah's reforms (23:26ff.). Perhaps to spare Josiah those awful days to come, Josiah was killed in battle against Pharaoh Necoh at Megiddo (23:29). After Josiah's death in quick succession four kings ruled briefly before the final fall of Jerusalem in 586 B.C.

The first of the final four kings of Judah was *Jehoahaz.* He was evil and lasted only a short time before he was taken captive to Egypt (23:31ff.). He was Josiah's son.

The king of Egypt, after deposing Jehoahaz, made his brother, also Josiah's son, king in his place. His brother's name was Eliakim, but was changed to *Jehoiakim* when he was made king (23:34).

In the days of Jehoiakim who was also evil, Nebuchadnezzar of Babylon came and laid siege to Jerusalem (24:1ff.). This was the beginning of the end for Jerusalem. The Babylonians were very powerful and extended their empire from the Euphrates River to Egypt (24:7). They took some of Judah's best sons to Babylon at this time (Dan. 1:1ff.).

After Jehoiakim's death his son, *Jehoiachin,* ruled briefly (24:8). In his days again Nebuchadnezzar besieged Jerusalem

and took many of the best of Judah to Babylon including
Jehoiachin (24:10-16). In those days, most probably men like
Ezekiel were carried to Babylon where they later served the
Lord in the days of captivity (24:14; Ezek. 1:2).

Now Jerusalem was under Babylonian control although still
having her own puppet king. Nebuchadnezzar made Mattaniah
king and gave him the name Zedekiah (24:17).

Zedekiah's reign was quite stormy and on one occasion he rebelled against Nebuchadnezzar (25:1ff.). In Zedekiah's 11th
year, 586 B.C., the city fell and two sons of Zedekiah were killed
before his eyes, after which Zedekiah's eyes were put out and he
was led blind and captive to Babylon (25:7). The end of the
kingdom of Judah had come. It would be the task of the exilic
and post-exilic prophets to show that this did not mean the end
of God's kingdom.

In Jeremiah we find a contemporary report of the last kings
who ruled Judah and of the spiritual state in those days. Later as
we study Jeremiah in some detail we shall note this.

Nebuchadnezzar took all of the treasures of Jerusalem and of
the Temple to Babylon where they remained until God raised
up Cyrus to overthrow Babylon and restore these things to Jerusalem (25:9-11). The Temple and its furniture were all destroyed at this time.

The account of the brief rule of Gedaliah and of his murder
by Ishmael (25:22-26) is more fully described in Jeremiah chapters 40 to 45.

As a sign of God's grace in these last years, the Lord did lead
the king of Babylon to be gracious unto Jehoiachin who, as you
remember, surrendered to Nebuchadnezzar and was therefore
carried captive to Babylon. Apparently Ezekiel was taken at
about this same time (25:27-30—cf. Ezek. 1:1-3).

I have not mentioned for the most part the parallel record of
Judah's history which is found in the books of Chronicles since
the books of Chronicles were written after the return from exile
and served a different purpose from the history of Judah
recorded in the books of Kings. However, when we do look at
the Chronicles later we shall note that they give some informa-
tion not given in Kings.

Having dealt now with the age of the prophets, and using this
as historical background, we shall turn to a study of each of the
prophets in their proper chronological order.

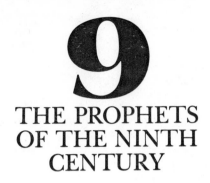

THE PROPHETS
OF THE NINTH
CENTURY

JOEL, ABOUT 850 B.C.

WE COME NOW to a study of the writing prophets of Israel and Judah who began to minister the Word in the ninth century B.C. Our study of all the prophets is of course against the historical background we have just covered in chapter 7, the age of the prophets.

We have seen already several prophets mentioned whose writings we do not have or at least cannot identify as such. I name only a few: Nathan, Ahijah, Jehu, Elijah, and Elisha. Now we shall study those prophets whose writings are preserved in Scripture.

The first of these is Joel, but this early dating of Joel is not

without problems and there are many who would place Joel
much later, even among the last of the prophets. The problem is
that in the content of the book itself there is no definite evidence
of the time of the prophet Joel.

However, it seems to me that there is much to commend the
early date of Joel among the first of the writing prophets. The
content of Joel reveals that it is written in a period when the
priests are quite influential and among the spiritual leaders of
the people. This was not often the case in Israel's history after
the time of Solomon. In the mid-800s to the end of that century,
however, priests did occupy an influential, even powerful place.
It was the time of the rule of Joash of Judah, the young man
reared in secret for many years by Jehoiada the priest. Athaliah
had sought to kill all of the seed of David as you recall (see our
discussion of the rule of Athaliah and Joash of Judah).

Elisha himself, the successor to Elijah, had reached down to
the same period, thus giving divine approval to the message
brought in that period from one of God's prophets such as Joel
may have been.

So long as Jehoiada lived, Joash was a good king and no doubt
in that time the prestige of the priesthood rose. There is other
evidence for the early date which we will note later in our discussion of the book.

The book of Joel itself is divided into four logical parts. The
first part deals with a terrible event that had just occurred in the
land, a plague of locusts. This section is from 1:2 to 2:11.

The second section contains the call of God to the people to
repent, lest worse things come to pass. They must return to God
in terms of the revelation which God had given to his people
through Moses in the wilderness. Joel calls them to true worship
and promises greater blessings to come if they repent. This section includes 2:12 to 32.

Section 3, *3:1-13*, tells of sure judgment to come on all of the
nations of the world. The Lord is God not only of Israel but also
of all nations and rules over all. In this section he emphasizes
certain themes which are to be seen in most of the prophets: the
sureness of judgment to come on all nations and the certainty
that God's people who put their trust in him will be saved while
the wicked perish.

The book closes on the note that the hour of decision is now
(vv. 14–21). It will not be delayed, men must be reconciled to
God or be judged.

Returning now to look at each section more closely, we look
first at the opening verse. The prophecy of Joel begins as do
many others, "the Word of the Lord" (compare Jeremiah 1:2;

Ezekiel 1:3; Hosea 1:1). These words remind us that what is written here is certainly God's Word and not merely the thoughts of men about God. Here is one raised up after Moses, like Moses, authorized to speak and record the very Word of God. His message like that of all of the other prophets will be fully in accord with what is written in the Pentateuch and fully as authoritative for God's people.

The man himself is simply identified as Joel, the son of Pethuel. We know nothing further from his writing and from the rest of Scripture about Joel or his father.

The *first section, 1:2 to 2:11,* calls attention to a devastating plague of locusts which has recently swept through the land and shows how this plague points to an even worse plague that threatens the people of God.

The locusts are described here in such an impressive way that it implies that the people cannot forget it quickly. It cannot be ignored. Perhaps rather than four different kinds of locusts we have only four different stages of the same kind of locust. This is not certain (1:4). What is certain is that it was such a devastating event that it will be remembered for several generations (1:3).

It is interesting to note the irony of verse 3. Earlier the Lord had shown through Moses that parents ought to tell God's wonders and teach God's truth to their children (Deut. 6:4ff.). But as you remember, according to Judges 2, parents evidently failed to do this so that as a result a whole generation grew up who did not know the Lord or the things which he had done (Judg. 2:10).

Now there has occurred an event that will be told for generations to come; as if to say, since you did not tell of God's wonders on your behalf, you will have to tell of God's judgments against you.

Verses 5-7 describe the extreme devastation of the locust plague. It is enough to awaken drunkards out of their stupor (1:5). The locusts are here described in terms of an invading army to prepare the way for what Joel shall say later. They chew up everything in their path. It is intended to strike fear in the hearts of the people as they recall the terror of this most recent experience.

Now the people lament the awful event (vv. 8-12). There is a shortage of everything. The priests mourn because the sacrifices from which they are to be sustained are stopped. The farmers lament because the fields have produced nothing, neither the vineyards nor the orchards. All of this the people know. For all of this the people are very grieved. But now Joel introduces something even more terrible that has happened in the land, something worse than the loss of food because of the locusts. It is the loss of joy among the people of God (1:12).

It is as if to say, "You see the terrible physical devastation that has happened to you; well, God sees an even worse spiritual devastation that has come on Israel—joy has passed from among the people."

Spiritual joy between God and his people has always been an essential relationship. It is a sign of the bond of love between God and his people. When the people's relationship to God is no more in joy, then this is the first sign that the religion is decaying just as the white branches of the trees and vines indicate that a terrible locust plague has passed through the land.

Joel is calling the people to return to their joy in the Lord before it is too late. While the people have been concerned for the loss of their physical fruit, God is concerned for the loss of their spiritual fruit, joy in his people.

In Psalm 51, David, lamenting his own spiritual joy which had been lost because of his sin, asked the Lord to restore it (51:12). Now on a larger scale, joy has been lost from God's people and unless it is restored, worse will come. Consequently, Joel now calls on the spiritual leaders to lead the people to repentance (1:13, 14). He still speaks of the sacrifices as meaningful if done in a right spirit of repentance. This would also point to an earlier period of Israel's history when sacrifices could be meaningful if done rightly. Later prophets would declare that sacrifices in the whole worship of Israel had reached a stage of being altogether unacceptable to God because the hearts of the people were far from the Lord (compare Isaiah chapter 1; Amos 5:21-23).

The repeated call to cry unto the Lord (1:14) is understandably and undoubtedly a call to repentance before God after the manner of the cry of Nineveh in the face of her sins before God and her realization of God's impending judgment (Jonah 3:8) or even after the manner of the cry of Jonah himself in his distress (Jonah 2:1ff.). We shall compare Joel and Jonah more fully when we have looked at the message of Jonah also.

Beginning in 1:15, Joel compares what has just happened in the land, the locust plague, to the coming day of the Lord, the great day of reckoning between God and men. Once more he compares the resultant lack of food because of the plague of locusts to the far worse scarcity of joy and gladness among God's people in the House of God, the place of worship (1:16). When all is right between God and his people there should be seen joy and gladness at the place of worship. It is not found, however, in the house of God in Jerusalem. Therefore the prophet warns of the spiritual plague which has hit the land, a far worse plague than the lack of physical food. Where is the joy and gladness in the Lord which bubbles over so obviously in the Psalms of David and songs of triumph of an earlier generation? It is absent. Here the Lord clearly shows what he later emphasizes, that God is concerned for the heart of the worshippers and not just the ritual and the worship itself.

In verse 19, he likens the plague that has hit the land to fire. The judgment of God is hereafter quite often compared to fire as all consuming and relentless.

It is but a step now to the warning of later prophets of God's judgment on the people by pagan armies. Joel introduces this concept here in the opening words of chapter 2, "Blow ye the trumpet in Zion, and sound an alarm in my holy mountain" (2:1). The people are called to get ready for "the day of the Lord." Once more we see this term which occurs frequently in Joel and later prophets (2:1, 11, 31; 3:14; Zeph. 1:14-16; Mal. 4:1-5). While it no doubt points ultimately to the final judgment and consummation of all things between God and man, it points also to lesser confrontations and lesser judgments of God on nations and individuals before the end of time. Here, it is pointing to God's reckoning with Israel unless she repents. Verses 2-11 compare the coming confrontation to that of an invading army. Sometimes the terminology here seems to better fit the locust plague that has just swept through the land, but sometimes it seems to point to an actual army of men that shall invade the land. Once more we see the analogy of consuming fire (2:3). Most important, we note that the judgment is God's judgment. The army, whether of locusts which have swept the land, or of people such as the Assyrians and Babylonians who would later sweep the land, is God's army, under his control and doing his will (2:11).

It would be helpful to compare this message to Israel with a similar message of the Lord to Ephesus in the New Testament. In Revelation 2:1-7, the Lord through John the Apostle, delivers a similar warning to the Christians at Ephesus. Although they are still quite orthodox in their faith and zealous for the gospel, yet the love of God which is required from his people (the first fruit of the Spirit) is lacking in them and unless they repent and return to it (as Israel to her joy in the Lord) the Lord will judge the Ephesian Church and remove it from his sight.

In both cases we see God's concern for hearts that love the Lord and rejoice in him. All outward conformity to the Law or ritual or gospel is of no value if the hearts of the people are not right with God. Here then is an eternal principle between the

Lord and all bodies of believers in all of the church's history. It
applies equally to us today. We must examine ourselves to know
whether or not our orthodoxy and worship ritual are from the
heart or not. It does matter to God.

In *2:12*, we begin the *second main section* of Joel. It goes to the
end of chapter 2. Having attracted the attention of the people to
their real spiritual problem, Joel now introduces a solution, the
alternative to invasion and judgment, the way the impending
disaster can be averted. It is not by alliances with men, as was
tried often in Israel, but rather, by true repentance toward God
and faith in him. Spiritual problems have spiritual solutions, a
lesson which is very hard for many to learn.

Joel calls here for true repentance of the kind Samuel had
earlier called for in a similar time of spiritual depravity (compare
1 Sam. 7:3). He uses terms such as "all your heart," "rend your
heart," and "turn unto the Lord your God." By these terms he
stresses the necessity for soul searching of the kind that can only
be done by the Word of God in our hearts. God requires a
broken heart in his children because of their sins. True repentance and confession of sin demand this, as David well knew
(Psa. 51:17). All the sacrificial system was to lead the people to
that kind of true repentance, as we discussed in our study of
Leviticus. Inner repentance is here emphasized by contrasting it
to the rending of one's garments which was an outward sign of
the inner broken heart that God requires. This kind of open
acknowledgment of sin before God is always required for a right
relationship to be restored between the Lord and his children.
(Compare 1 John 1:8-10 and Romans 7, where Paul shows his
own spiritual struggle against sin.)

Here the basis for such repentance is, as always, the written
Word of God. God's Word is the sword of God which pierces to
the inner heart and reveals what we are in the inner man (Heb.
4:12, 13). The word quoted in Joel is from Exodus 34:6, God's
revelation to Moses of His own nature (Joel 2:13). Since God is
that kind of God, we have reason to hope for forgiveness if we
repent. Time and again we shall see that great passage from
Exodus 34, quoted and referred to by prophets of Israel and the
Psalmist. It was the verbal revelation of the nature of God. It
would be well to note what we observed when we studied that
passage.

Verses 5 to 17 are then a call to worship as an alternative to a
call to war. Compare 2:1. It is to be a true worship led by truly
repentant priests who act as true mediators and intercessors in
their prayers on behalf of the people.

If this is done, then certain inevitable blessings shall follow in accord with the word of our Lord in Matthew 5:4, the first Beatitude: "Blessed are they that mourn for they shall be comforted" (see Joel 2:14).

Instead of invaders and plagues that strip the land, there shall be abundance (vv. 18-20). The word "then" in verse 18 indicates that when there is a true return to the Lord the following things will occur. When they repent, God will show his pity. Grain and abundance of food shall come (v. 19). The northern army shall be removed (the army threatened in 2:4-11). Incidentally, the judgment of God by armies is usually spoken of as from the north, i.e., Assyria and Babylon of later years.

Instead of fear and terror, joy (2:21-27). That joy which is now missing will return as God proves to be able to restore all of our losses when we repent and trust in him (vv. 23, 25). The lost fellowship with God will then be restored. They will know (have fellowship with) the Lord.

Instead of judgment, the gift of God's Spirit (2:28-32). God promises to pour out his Holy Spirit upon them, to make all of the people prophets much in the same way Moses had once expressed his own desire for Israel (Num. 11:29).

God had promised blessings on Israel in that time if they repented in truly broken hearts and turned to him. He would restore the land and make them prosper again both materially and spiritually. But sad to say, Israel did not repent. She did not come to God with a broken and contrite heart, at least not as a nation. She went on from evil to evil, as we have seen in our historical survey, until the Lord brought against her the northern nations that he had warned of through prophet after prophet beginning with Joel (2:20).

We know that for God's church the promises given here were not fulfilled until Pentecost, as Peter himself declared (Acts 2:16-21). The wonderful promises given here in Joel could not be fulfilled until Jesus Christ came. They did not happen until he died on the cross and his shed blood truly changed the hearts of men.

Our Lord came to impart to his people that joy which sin had destroyed (John 15:11). He came to make his people truly fruitful (John 15:1ff.). What the Lord here demanded as the condition for God's blessings on Israel his church, the people could never attain, so he came himself and in the person of Jesus Christ accomplished all that he had demanded of his people, thus making it possible for the fullness of God's blessings to fall on Israel in Christ Jesus. Then Peter could justly proclaim at

Pentecost that those promises of God so long withheld from the church were now poured out and fulfilled.

But in the meantime, God was, out of Israel, calling a people who would, of God's grace, repent and call on the name of the Lord (2:32). These people, as the writer of Hebrews teaches us, died not having received the promises but having seen them from afar (Heb. 11:13, 39, 40). These were the Old Testament remnant, whom God called to himself and saved before Christ came, even when Israel and Judah as a whole were disobedient and were judged.

The promise given here, "whosoever shall call on the name of the Lord shall be delivered (or saved)" (2:23) reaches all the way back to man's earliest history on earth (Gen. 4:26; 12:8; 26:25) and distinguishes the true remnant, the true church in all ages, as opposed to the false. It also reaches ahead to the great era of evangelization after Pentecost and shows the continuing work of God to call a people to himself not only out of Israel but out of all of the nations (Rom. 10:13).

Joel 3:1-13, contains the *third main section of the book.* In this section, the Lord shows that God's reckoning with all nations and all peoples is sure. First, he will surely save his people out of all the nations (3:1). Second, he will execute judgment on all the rest of mankind (3:2). We remember that in the very beginning God made a clear distinction between his people, the seed of the woman and between Satan's children, the seed of the serpent. Ultimately the Lord recognizes only these two categories among mankind. Now here in Joel he proclaims that all these children of Satan and all the nations who have, over history, opposed his people, will be judged by God and destroyed.

The nations mentioned here are Tyre, Sidon, Philistia, Greece and Sheba, but these nations doubtlessly represent all the nations of history (3:4-9). The judgment scene described in 3:12, 13 is very similar to the last judgment on the nations recorded in Revelation 14:17-20. It is symbolized by the call to beat their plowshares into swords and their pruning hooks into spears (3:10). It indicates that just when the nations think they are prospering and have attained peace without God, God will make war with them. Indeed as Christ promised, there shall be wars and rumors of wars until the end comes (Matt. 24:6-8). Later the symbol was reversed in the context of the good news of God to those who believed in him and the reverse figure became symbolic of the everlasting peace promised by God to those who trusted in him (Isa. 2:4, Mic. 4:3).

The *final section of Joel (3:14-21)*, makes clear that for every man, now is the hour of decision (3:14). The Lord shall be known to all men, all men will have to face the Lord, either as a roaring, devouring lion (3:16a) or as a refuge and stronghold (3:16b). God will have a people who are holy and without blemish before him in love as he purposed before creation (Eph. 1:4—compare Joel 3:17). But the rest who resist him will know him as the devouring lion. There is no room in God's dwelling (the holy and new Jerusalem) for strangers (the unreconciled to God—compare Isa. 52:1 and Rev. 21:27).

The last verses, 3:18-21, once more in terms of physical prosperity, describe the blessings of God on his people, the called ones, the remnant, the faithful in contrast to the nations who reject the Lord.

Much of Joel then is indicative of what is to come in the following prophets: the warnings of judgment to come on the church if the people do not repent; the prediction of nations raised up by God to judge Israel; the call to repentance; the promises of blessings if the people repent; the hope held out to a remnant who do call on the Lord; the sure judgment of God on all the nations of history; and the final destiny of all men, either to peace and safety in the Lord (for the remnant) or judgment and destruction without God (for the nations, i.e., Satan's children).

This message says much to us in Christ's church today. God is still concerned to see the evidence that we are the children of God that we might glorify him in the world. It is easy to fall into the snare in which Israel and Judah fell by going through all of the outward demands of our religion without contrite hearts before God. This the Lord will not accept, either in the ninth century B.C. Judah or in the twentieth century church today. In his message to the church at Ephesus, the Lord showed that orthodoxy is not enough, there must be joy and love in the heart toward God and toward one another if the church is to be acceptable to the Lord (Rev. 2:1-7).

We need, therefore, to examine ourselves in respect to our own hearts. If the joy of being in worship before the Lord is absent, then the situation calls for broken and contrite hearts repentant over the sins that stand between us and our Lord, lest we too be removed.

JONAH, ABOUT 800 B.C.

We are placing Jonah in the ninth century though he may well be placed near the beginning of the eighth century B.C. He is one of the few prophets to be specifically mentioned in the historical section of the Old Testament (2 Kgs. 14:25). From that context we assume that his ministry began either prior to or during the reign of Jeroboam II who ruled in the eighth century. Both in the book he wrote and in the book of Kings, he is identified as the son of Amittai (Jonah 1:1). In Kings, he is further identified as from Gath-Hepher, a village near Nazareth.

The historicity of Jonah the prophet is verified in the historical sections of the Old Testament and also in the New Testament by the very words of Jesus Christ. Jesus compares his own death and resurrection to the experiences of Jonah (Matt. 12:39-41). Jesus clearly teaches the historical accuracy of the content of Jonah's book since he compares that content with his own historical death and resurrection, events which must be historical for Christianity to be valid. It is unthinkable that Jesus would have compared such momentous historical events as his own death and resurrection, to an Old Testament parable. We say this because many have doubted the historicity of Jonah and the events that occurred at Nineveh. It is as though the Lord, in anticipation of these doubts, particularly stressed the history of Jonah and all that happened to him.

The book must be understood against the historical background of the ninth and eighth centuries. It was a time when Assyria was on the rise as a great power in the world. The Assyrians were a people living in the area of Mesopotamia, and though they are not mentioned by name, presumably they were the people from the north who were already a threat in the days of Joel (Joel 2:20). Assyria began its great rise to power around 900 B.C. in the days of Shalmaneser III, as our chart indicates.

The capital of this vast empire was Nineveh. Since Nineveh posed a threat to God's people ultimately, we can understand Jonah's reluctance to go and warn those people of God's wrath. Jonah could actually want nothing more than their destruction. Jonah doubtlessly knew that because of the wickedness of the kings of Israel and the people of Israel, God's judgment would fall, Joel had actually made such a warning. We can see why, when Jonah heard the command to go and preach to Nineveh (1:2), he could want nothing more than that God would wipe Nineveh off the map and so remove a very real threat to Israel (1:3). Jonah wanted to go in the opposite direction from the express will of God.

In fact, Jonah later tells us exactly why he wanted to disobey God at this time. In Jonah 4:2, he answers God by saying, "I knew that thou art a gracious God, and merciful, slow to anger, and abundant in loving kindness, and repentest thee of the evil." How did Jonah know that God was this kind of God? As we see in Joel (Joel 2:13), God had long before revealed himself in just these terms to Moses (Exod. 34:6, 7). Since Jonah knew God was this way and that therefore he would probably show that mercy to Nineveh, Jonah, who desired Nineveh's destruction, fled from God (1:3).

The first section of Jonah (1:1-16), records the commission of God and Jonah's disobedience. When Jonah does disobey the express will of God (God's Word revealed to him), then God intervenes, showing that no one can go counter to the purpose of God. The *secret* will of God to save Nineveh from destruction will not be thwarted by Jonah's refusal to obey God's revealed will. It is important to distinguish between the two categories of God's will and not to confuse them. God's revealed will may be disobeyed by men but no one can alter God's secret will or purpose.

The method of God's intervention is indicative of God's sovereignty in all of the affairs of men. We read in 1:4 that God sent a great wind. There is here an interesting chain of events by which God accomplishes his purpose in respect to Jonah. God desired for Jonah to be in the midst of the sea in a state of helplessness. This was in order to humble Jonah and make him face his own complete dependence on the God he sought to flee (1:15). Between verses 4 and 15 the chain of events unfolds by God's hurling the wind upon the sea. The Hebrew word "hurl" is found three times in this section. First, God *hurls* the wind. Then the sailors *hurl* out the baggage in response to the wind in order to seek to save the ship and their lives (v. 5). Finally, the men *hurl* Jonah into the sea (v. 15). English translations use various words in these three verses but in the Hebrew they are all the same word, stressing God's sovereignty in his dealings with men. God wanted Jonah in the water and this is what occurred by the agency of the sailors.

In the process of putting Jonah into a helpless state, the Lord showed mercy to that handful of sailors on the unhappy voyage with him. God worked all things together for good to them.

Note first of all that the sailors were put in great fear (1:5). At this point, they were clearly pagans, calling on their own pagan gods. These sailors, caught up in God's judgment against Jonah, were first terrified and then were taught the truth of God.

Once again the sovereignty of God is seen in that when the lot was cast, it fell on Jonah, and it was certainly no accident. God intended it so (1:7). At this point Jonah became the reluctant witness of the God of Israel, his people's God, the God whom he had sought to flee. Certainly it had not been Jonah's intent to bear witness to these pagans, but God intended it so and God was in control. He preached to them the truth about his God (1:9). When he mentioned the dry land, we can be sure that the sailors became interested. No words sounded better to them at this point. He pointed them to trust in his God who controlled both sea and land.

The sailors tried to save Jonah (1:13). But God determined that Jonah should be in the sea. Finally, they submitted to God's will but we note how knowledgeable they had become of the Lord in the process. They acknowledged his complete sovereignty to do as he pleased (1:14). They now addressed him by the Hebrew name "Lord," the covenant name of God. When they had hurled Jonah into the sea and saw the immediate calm, they feared the Lord even more (1:16). Note that the focus of their fear of the storm has now changed to be upon the Lord of the storm. They appear to have had genuine conversion experiences. They offered sacrifices and vowed vows (1:16). We have no right to reject the genuineness of this experience. What happened to them afterward we do not know. The Scripture leaves them at this point at the mercy of God. The focus of attention is on Jonah.

And where was Jonah? Just where God wanted him, in the midst of the sea, also at the mercy of God (1:15).

The second section of the book really begins with the last verse of chapter 1. It tells of Jonah's salvation from the sea and his own confession to God (1:17—2:10). This section is divided into three unequal but distinct parts.

First, we are told of *God's preparation* for Jonah's rescue. While Jonah was in the midst of a raging sea and sinking fast, God had already prepared a great fish, a means of his salvation from the sea (1:17). Presumably the Lord had prepared the fish even before Jonah was hurled into the sea. This leads us into the great debate about the nature of the fish that swallowed Jonah. Many have argued that no man could live in the belly of any fish or whale known today for three days. Others equally vehemently have sought to cite cases where men did survive in a way similar to Jonah. Both miss the point. God prepared or ordained this fish for this purpose. It does not matter whether we can find a fish equal to the fish that swallowed Jonah. The Lord *prepared that fish* for *that purpose!*

Jonah could not live in the water. He was sinking and as he sank he thought he was dying. Then the great fish saved him out of the raging sea.

The *second* part of this section records Jonah's prayer and testimony while he waited in the belly of the fish for God's next move. We see *his own personal faith* come through clearly here (2:1-9).

Jonah in his prayer reflects on what has happened to him. In his affliction (his being cast into the sea), Jonah prayed to God and the Lord had answered him (2:2). This really tells the whole story but Jonah expands upon it. He felt that his descent into the water was just like going into hell itself. Yet as he sank he cried to God and God heard (v. 2).

In verses 3 to 6 he expands upon the experience he had while in the water. Note that he believed that the Lord had cast him into the water. The Bible says that the sailors threw Jonah in. Yet Jonah knew that God's purpose was being worked out by these sailors.

The feelings of a drowning man are recorded in these verses. The flood of water, the waves and billows, made him sink into the deep waters. Note that he viewed all as God's doing—"thy waves . . . thy billows . . ."

More important, he felt rejected spiritually by God (2:4a). Yet at that moment of deepest spiritual despair he remembered the Lord his hope. He looked toward God's Holy Temple in faith (2:4b). The Temple, as God's Word teaches, is the way we approach to God. We recall that the Tabernacle with all of its structure and furniture was so designed as to teach God's people about the proper approach. Compare 1 Kings 8:30. Jonah's prayer in this time of helplessness and distress was an act in faith, a looking to God to help him. The word used here for "to look" is the same word we have mentioned before, as for example in the case of Lot's wife who looked toward Sodom and in the case of the children in the wilderness who were commanded to look toward the serpent upon the staff. In all uses of this word in the Hebrew, it has the sense of "to look longingly toward" or "hopefully," not merely "to look with the eyes." Thus Jonah looked in trust and in hope toward the Holy Temple.

His own strength was exhausted so that he continued to sink (2:5, 6). God was his only hope now. Only the God he sought to escape could help him now. As Jonah afterward sat in the belly of the great fish, he reflected on how God did indeed save him (2:6b). Verse 7 is a summary of the whole experience.

In conclusion, therefore, Jonah drew a lesson from all of his experiences with God (2:8). The meaning of this verse appar-

ently is that he, in regarding the lying vanity that he could escape
God's will for him, was only fleeing from his own mercy. How
foolish he had been. The idea that we can go it on our own
without God is indeed folly. It is the vanity of vanities.

The whole prayer is concluded with a commitment to the
Lord (2:9). Jonah is now thankful and intends to obey God from
now on. His conclusion that salvation is of the Lord echoes what
Joel had declared earlier (Joel 2:32).

The last part of this second section is the record of God's
response to Jonah's confession and prayer (2:10). The Lord
directed the fish to toss Jonah back on dry land. Jonah was now
back where God wanted him in the first place, in a position to be
able to carry out God's will.

The *third* section of Jonah includes the third chapter and part of
chapter 4. It tells of *the commission of God to Jonah* and his subsequent obedience to God's command. This time when commanded, Jonah obeyed (3:1-3). The description of Nineveh as a
city of three day's journey has provoked many different in-
terpretations. It is doubtful if it could mean that it was a city so
vast that it took three days to go through it or even around it. In
the context of the command to Jonah, it seems more likely that
the meaning is that it would take Jonah three days to pass
through its streets, declaring the message which God had given
him.

The message was brief and whether we have only a part of the
message we cannot know (3:4). Considering Jonah's reluctance
to be in Nineveh at all, he probably was very brief. He was still
not happy about the prospects of Nineveh's salvation.

The response of the people is given in 3:5-9. They believed
God (v. 5) and proclaimed a fast as a sign of true repentance.
Even the king was moved by the message to a contrite heart (v.
6). As the leader of his people, the king called them to repentance before God (vv. 7, 8). Moreover, he led the people in a true
reform from their evil ways.

In verse 9 we have something reminiscent of Joel's words
found in Joel 2:14. These people looked to God in hope that his
fierce anger would be turned away. In verse 10 we see God's
response to their repentance. God repented of the evil he had
said he would do and did not do it.

As in other similar contexts, we should not suppose that this
means that God repents in the same way men repent, correcting
their former errors. God is not wishy-washy. This is a means of
expressing in human terms God's readiness to forgive. It implies
change, but not change in God. God effects the change in men

so that it is not necessary for him to carry out the former pronouncement of judgment. This is one way of expressing what is elsewhere called God's mercy. Often when God warns of judgment to come, he is telling what man deserves. However, by his mercy he often changes men so that the judgment they deserve does not actually come upon them.

There is a most interesting parallel between chapters 2 and 3 of Jonah. In chapter 2 we read of Jonah's distress and how God prepared a way of deliverance from that distress by the great fish. Next we read of Jonah's repentance and prayer in his distress, and then how God responded by delivering him out of the sea to the safety of dry land. Similarly in chapter 3 we read of the distress of the people of Nineveh as they were under the judgment of God. We read too of how God prepared Jonah to be the means of their escape from judgment. Then we read of the repentance of the Ninevites and their cry to God as Jonah had cried from the sea. Finally, we see God's response at their repentance by saving them from the impending judgment as he saved Jonah from the sea.

The parallel between the experiences of Jonah and that of Nineveh is obvious. The Lord put Jonah through this experience in order to teach him how God deals mercifully with sinners. It should have been an obvious lesson to Jonah, but Jonah was slow to learn.

Chapter 4 shows us that though Jonah obeyed God's command the second time, he was reluctant to do so. He was in fact displeased with the outcome. He was angry. He had anticipated God's mercy to be shown on Nineveh and he had not wanted that (4:2). In verse 3, he is perhaps comparing his distress now with that of Elijah (1 Kings 19:4). But Jonah was no Elijah, not at this time anyway. How could Jonah forget so quickly the lesson the Lord had taught him in showing mercy to Jonah?

God asked the question—do you do well in being angry? (4:4) But Jonah did not answer. He simply went out of the city and sat out in the field to see what would happen to Nineveh. Perhaps he still hoped that the people would be destroyed (4:5).

With verse 6 we begin *the last section of Jonah* (4:6-11). In this section the Lord once more teaches Jonah the lesson of God's merciful dealing with men. In a way, parts of this section are ludicrous, purposefully so, in order to point out the great weakness in the character of Jonah.

The vocabulary of these verses is humorous in the light of the context. God prepares a vine to cover Jonah's booth to protect him from the sun. The Bible says, to deliver him from his evil case (4:6).

It is as though God were saying, "All right, Jonah, you are stubborn and hard-headed and have missed altogether the point I sought to teach you in rescuing you from the sea. Let's try again. You're sitting out in the sun and the sun is making you very uncomfortable. But I will come to deliver you from your *evil case.*"

Now the words "evil case" are usually reserved for some very serious distress such as Jonah's former distress in the sea had been. To use these words to describe the situation of a stubborn man sitting out in the sun, too stupid or too hard-headed to get out of the sun is, to say the least, ludicrous. No one had told Jonah to sit out in the hot sun; he did it on his own. No doubt God's choice of these words was intended to put Jonah to shame.

Jonah's reaction to the growing of the plant was equally ridiculous. He was exceedingly glad (4:6). God had just saved a whole city from destruction and Jonah had been angry with that, but now he was "exceedingly glad" because he had his comfort from the sun. How greatly Jonah's own sense of values had been perverted.

This time, however, God altered his dealing with Jonah and took away his mercy in order to teach Jonah what it is like to live without the mercy of God. God prepared a worm to destroy the vine (4:7).

As with the fish, so with the vine and the worm, it does not matter whether we can find such plants or know just what kind of worm destroyed the plant. The point is that all of these things were specially prepared for God's dealing with Jonah.

Jonah's reaction is by now expected. He is angry again over the loss of the vine. As the wind becomes oppressive to him, he desires to die (4:8). Still no one had told Jonah he must remain out there. He was free to go, but he preferred to die.

At this point (v. 9ff.) God applies the lesson to Jonah. He points out that Jonah was angry at the loss of a little vine that lasted only 24 hours but had no cared at all for the great threat of the loss of the lives of all of the people of Nineveh (4:10). The Lord here compared his own sense of values, concern for the lives of the citizens of Nineveh, to that of Jonah's sense of values, concern for the little plant. In reality, Jonah's concern was for himself. He had been inconvenienced and that was what made him angry.

The Lord's description of the people as not knowing their right hand from their left is probably figurative of their spiritual ignorance.

Many applications can be made of the lessons of the book of Jonah. We may perhaps see much of ourselves in Jonah. We may wag our heads over his spiritual obtuseness but are we any better? Consider how much God has done for us, yet how slow we are to apply God's mercy shown to us to others. We are thankful for what God has done for us. How we rejoice in his dealings with us! But we do not show the same enthusiasm for those who are still lost as we once were.

Like Jonah, we fail to glorify God in our lives because though we know what he is like, we do not reflect his image in ourselves. We cannot show the same mercy and long-suffering toward others which the Lord has shown to us. Yet this is just what God desires in us.

There is a consequent failure in our missionary zeal. We remain unconcerned for those who remain under the wrath of God as we once were under his wrath. See Ephesians 2:3. The message of Jonah clearly comes through—as I have been merciful to you, go out and become my messenger of mercy to others. It is a great missionary book.

One final thing is implied in this book which we must not overlook. What brought the ultimate fall of Israel in the Old Testament was not external enemies such as Nineveh and Babylon. They were merely God's instruments of wrath. The fall came because the people, filled with pride, refused and failed to reflect the glory of God in their lives as Jonah failed. Israel fell because of internal selfishness, not because of external enemies.

At the summation of Israel's history which we have studied in that section of 2 Kings, we are told that the people were judged because they refused to hear God's Word. As we shall see in our study of later prophets, the people refused to show God's love toward one another, so selfish was their daily motivation. While living in the lap of luxury themselves, the rich oppressed the poor believers and took from them whatever they owned.

We may ask why the book of Jonah is among the prophets since it is quite unlike the other prophets. Yet as we analyze the message and see the experiences of Jonah, we see that the prophetic message of Scripture comes through quite clearly. It was a timely warning to Israel and to God's people to become subject to God's will and purpose lest they suffer great judgment.

In many ways, the message of Jonah is comparable to the message to the Ephesians in the New Testament. In Christ's words to the church at Ephesus, he warns them lest they leave their first love and be removed from Christ's sight (Rev. 2:1-7). In Paul's epistle to the Ephesians, he had called them to be imitators of God as beloved children and to walk in love (Eph.

5:1, 2). Now several decades later the Ephesians were in danger of judgment because they had apparently failed to do this, though they had put great emphasis on the teaching of sound doctrine.

Like Jonah, they knew the truth about God, what he is like, yet they refused to reflect his glory in their daily lives and in their dealings with one another.

In this sense too, we see a clear relationship between the messages of Jonah and Joel. Joel too was calling the people back to a joyous fellowship with God which could not be compensated for by mere outward conformity. God always judges the motivations of the heart. We stand or fall there.

THE WRITINGS
TO COUNTER
SOLOMON'S FOLLY
Ecclesiastes and the Song of Songs

BEFORE CONTINUING our survey of the prophets, we shall introduce here two writings which seem to belong generally to the age which we are studying. While not books of prophecy, they contain a message which is not unlike the messages of the prophets.

I believe that in these two works, Ecclesiastes and the Song of Songs, we have writings from a period sometime after Solomon—writings which were given to counter the evil influence of Solomon and those of his ilk. Remember that Solomon, in the minds of the people, had represented all that was the finest. He was David's choice, rich, wise and powerful. The conduct, therefore, of his latter days would have great influence on the young people of that era and on such succeeding eras if something were not done to show that God was displeased with Solomon.

Of course, in the history we have studied, we read of God's displeasure with Solomon but no doubt many who lived so close to his age could not see this. At any rate, the successive kings of Judah, Rehoboam and Abijam, followed in their father's footsteps and may well have led Judah down the same path that Israel followed when Israel proved never ever to have a king faithful to the Lord.

I submit that Ecclesiastes and the Song of Songs (which is sometimes called the Song of Solomon) are both written to counter the evil influence of Solomon and his ilk, and are addressed to God's true people in those days to instruct them in the will of God in contrast to the example of Solomon.

We shall now proceed to look at each of these two books and the message which they had for God's people in a time of predominantly bad spiritual influence and see also their relevance for believers today.

ECCLESIASTES

The word "Ecclesiastes" means that which pertains to the church or to the preaching, i.e., the message. The book of Ecclesiastes is then to be considered as something like a sermon.

The introductory sentence (1:1) contains the word "preacher" or, if transliterated from the Hebrew, "Kohelet." This word basically means one who presides at a gathering. "Preacher" is a good translation, but "moderator" might be more accurate.

The identity of the preacher is never given, though the description in verse 1 would seem to point to Solomon. Properly all of the kings of Judah could be called sons of David. Even Jesus later bore this title (Matt. 1:1).

The opening sentence does not mean that the preacher, whoever he is, is the author of the book. He is actually quoted in the book, sometimes at length, but the author clearly holds a position which is opposite to the words of the preacher introduced in verses 1 and 2.

In essence, the outline of the book gives us first a statement by the preacher which is then expanded upon in 1:2 to 2:23. There follows a rebuttal of the preacher's theme in 2:24—12:8. Finally, there is a conclusion to the whole.

Looking now at the first part of the book, we see that the primary theme of the preacher is "vanity of vanities ... all is vanity" (1:2). The phrase also occurs at the end of the book (12:8), thus showing that the debate is ended.

This theme or outlook on life is further expounded upon in the section 1:2 to 2:23. In addition to the phrase "vanity of vanities," another phrase is used both by the preacher and the writer of this book. It is the phrase "under the sun" and refers to life as men see it, life as viewed by man whose vision is limited and who is confined to the place under the sun, not as God who sees differently and from a greater perspective.

Let us now see the point of view of the preacher who probably is intended to represent Solomon but perhaps also others of his ilk, such as Solomon's son Rehoboam and the other kings of Judah whose lives were not pleasing to the Lord.

Certainly the devastating effect of faithless kings in Judah was great in all the land. Messages from God's prophets in those days and later indicate that all the leaders—kings, priests and prophets—were sinful. And "like priests, like people."

The statement of the preacher, "all is vanity," summarizes his point of view and well summarizes what must have been Solomon's point of view in his later life when his life seemed to be a shambles (1 Kgs. 11). As the preacher looked over his own life, he could see that he had tried everything and yet found no meaning of life in anything.

He saw God's creation and providence but all he could conclude was that it was tiresome and monotonous (1:4-11). The rising and setting of the sun, the blowing of the wind, the flow of rain into the rivers and the rivers in turn into the sea, was weariness to him. It was no blessing to him (1:8). Contrast this view with that of the Psalmist who proclaimed that "the heavens declare the glory of God; and the firmament showeth his handiwork" (Psa. 19:1). The Psalmist sees natural revelation as preaching a sermon to all the world of the glory of God (19:4-6).

In order to find some meaning to life, the preacher sought to use all the resources at his disposal. His resources were vast. He had great wisdom so he sought by his wisdom to find a meaningful life (1:12-18). Yet he concluded after the exercise of that wisdom which God had given him, that wisdom brought only grief and sorrow (1:18).

Next, he pursued mirth and pleasure as only one with great wealth could do (2:1-3). Again he was disappointed and empty (v. 2).

Then he determined to build great structures and to do great works (2:4-7). With his resources he structured all kinds of things and filled his land with innumerable servants and great herds of cattle. This not satisfying, he amassed wealth and bought the best entertainment for himself (2:8-11). Nothing was too much for him to undertake. Whatever he wanted of material things, he had (2:10). Yet all of this could not gain for him what he wanted to find, namely, some meaning to life (2:11).

His conclusion was sad but predictable. He hated life (2:17). He hated all of his labor (2:18, 19). Therefore he despaired of life (2:20).

At this point we should pause and reflect on the life of Solomon. Why was it this way with him? As we consider the life of Solomon given in 1 Kings, chapters 1 through 11, and particularly as we see the end of his life in chapter 11, we note that he violated God's first commandment: "Thou shalt have no other gods besides me." His riches, his wisdom, his power, and his wives were all put before God. His life was devoted instead to these things. In violating this commandment, he was guilty of what Jesus later warned against when he said, "Ye cannot serve two masters" (Matt. 6:24). Similarly, James warns against the doubleminded person (Jas. 1:5-8). See also Jesus' words to the church that was neither hot nor cold but lukewarm (Rev. 3:15-17).

God continually calls his people to a total commitment to him. When their hearts or minds are divided between God and other masters or gods, then their lives, like Solomon's life, end up in disaster and they can never find or know the full life of God's children.

Evidently, the influence of Solomon had great effect on Israel in later years. In the time of Elijah we find that great prophet accusing the people of vacillating between the Lord and Baal. He rebukes them and calls them to take their stand (1 Kgs. 18:21). Even in the days of Jesus, this was still a problem with God's children. So Jesus related the parable of the unrighteous steward in order to teach that the sons of this world (who consistently serve their own interest) are wiser than the sons of God (Luke 16:8, 9). In that parable Jesus was certainly not teaching that God is pleased with the evil life of evil men. He was rather showing that while the evil ones are consistently and predictably evil, God's children, alas, to their own shame, are neither consistent nor predictable in what they do.

Returning now to Ecclesiastes, in 2:24 we pick up a new and different point of view from that introduced in the first chapter. This viewpoint is that of the writer of the book of Ecclesiastes and not Solomon's view. It is written to counter Solomon's desperate conclusion and deplorable example.

The counter theme, God's message, is that there is joy and meaning in work and life that is seen as from God and done in fear of God, i.e., in faith. Note in 2:24-26 that the writer affirms that the truly good life, in contrast to the vanity of Solomon's life, is joy in one's labor (daily task), seeing it as from God's hand and therefore to be done to please God.

This concept is most basic to all the life of God's children. Remember that when God created man, he gave him work and responsibility to fulfill.

In succeeding verses, the writer of Ecclesiastes develops this theme of joy in labor done for the glory of God. In 3:14 he calls this work the gift of God. It is indeed a working together with God. In verse 22 of the same chapter he calls this joy the proper portion of a man.

Note the great contrast between the earlier conclusions on vanity on the part of the preacher and the grand conclusion of 5:18-20. It is very much like Paul's great conclusion at the end of Romans 8.

We cannot help noting the contrast between joy in work and the meaningful life described by the writer in these chapters and the repeated allusions to Solomon's own vain life. Compare 6:1-3.

Again in 7:18 the note of fear of God is struck. It is not merely in work, therefore, that joy is to be found, but in work done in the fear of the Lord. The fearer of the Lord is contrasted to the wicked (8:12, 13).

Joy in labor has abiding values which Solomon never found in spite of all his wisdom and riches and power. God's child who does what work he has to do as unto the Lord and to please the Lord, has already the assurance that his work is accepted (9:7).

This great theme, woven throughout the book of Ecclesiastes, is one of the most overlooked themes in the Christian's life today. It needs renewed emphasis. Ecclesiastes teaches us that which Paul dealt with extensively in his epistles. God's child is to see that his labor, i.e., all of his life, is for the Lord and not for men. No matter how irksome or tiring that labor may seem to be, it can be a joy and it can fill life with true meaning if it is done as unto the Lord. Note that Paul could say this even to those who labored under the most trying circumstances we can imagine, as bondslaves of Roman pagans (Eph. 6:5-8, Col. 3:22-24).

If we today could see as the writer of Ecclesiastes shows us and as Paul echoes, that we are all full-time laborers for the Lord, whatever our daily job may be, then we could do that work not to please the boss or to get a raise or to get to the top of the heap but rather to please our Lord. Thus in every job we Christians would so outshine the world in commitment and faithfulness to our task that our good works would shine forth for the glory of

God and open many doors of witness never opened before. One ought to be able to see us work and know that we are different.

Ecclesiastes concludes the section on the true meaning of life by a picture of old age, the time when the opportunity for labor is over. It is addressed primarily to the young who still have opportunity to set the course of their lives according to God's Word.

Young men tend toward vanity, supposing that they have a whole life to be lived as they please. Therefore they are warned that if they seek to live as they please and not as unto the Lord, then they shall fail in life in God's sight (11:9, 10).

There follows a beautiful but pathetic portrayal of old age in chapter 12:1-7. Old age for the vain life is a time of evil (v. 1). There is no longer any pleasure in life (v. 1). Light begins to fail and the eyes are darkened (v. 2). The arms (keepers) and legs (strong men) begin to fail and tremble weakly, no longer able to carry one where he wishes to go (v. 3). The teeth (grinders) are few and the eyes fade (v. 3). One can only hear with great difficulty and yet at the same time every little noise startles (v. 4). As darkness and death close in, so does fear (v. 5). Grasshoppers and other delicacies of that era and that area of the world, are no longer desired; nothing tastes good anymore (v. 5). Verses 5 to 7 are a beautifully poetic description of death and the end of all hope and meaning for him that is not right with God.

The whole section is a powerful elaboration on Genesis 3:19.

Verse 9 begins the conclusion of the book. How could one so wise as Solomon have a meaningless life? It was not altogether meaningless. His great wisdom was able to teach many. He was used of the Lord to write many of the Proverbs which we shall study later (12:9, 10).

We shall note that the "words of the wise" mentioned here (v. 11) are recorded for us in Proverbs 22:17—24:22 and also in Proverbs 24:23, 24. We shall later see just how they are goads. Note that it is understood that all the words of Proverbs, whether from Solomon or others, are in reality, from the one shepherd, i.e., the Lord (v. 11).

The conclusion to the book of Ecclesiastes, given in verses 13 and 14, again calls us to a fear of the Lord and a life of labor according to his will. God is the final Judge of all men and of all their works. They stand or fall in accord with whether or not they have pleased the Lord.

As Paul says in Ephesians 2:1-10, we are saved by grace, not by our works, but, we have been saved in Christ *for* good works "which God afore prepared that we should walk in them."

THE SONG OF SONGS

The background for the Song of Songs (or Song of Solomon as it is also called) is similar to that of Ecclesiastes. The lives of Solomon and his successors on the throne of Judah were a great stumbling-block to God's people. While on the one hand these men lived in the splendor of the kingship of Judah, yet at the same time they openly defied the will of God by their lives. Solomon in his later life showed himself to be excessive, carnal, vain, lustful and indeed an example of what God's child should *not* be.

Yet Solomon and his children could not be easily challenged by the righteous in the land. How could the message of God reach the people in such times? One way was by such writings as Ecclesiastes and the Song of Songs, which were messages to God's true people in the midst of such apostasy, showing them the greater will of God in contrast to the evil influence of the faithless rulers.

The book before us is written in the form of a drama. This is not to suggest that it was ever intended to be acted out on a stage. There is no suggestion in Scripture that this was done. However its form is that of a drama inasmuch as it contains certain characters who have spoken parts over the main body of the book. The book is a record of the exchange of words between the characters involved without any introduction of the speakers at all being given to us.

The way I interpret the Song of Songs, it presents three primary characters—the Shulammite girl, who is the heroine of the story; the Shepherd, who is the hero; and Solomon, who is the villain. In addition there are the daughters of Jerusalem who speak occasionally. The first verse, which gives the title, tells us that the writing is entitled "The Song of Songs" and is about Solomon; for the phrase in Hebrew simply says that it pertains to Solomon. It by no means teaches that Solomon is the author.

The setting for the story is to be seen from three separate but similar verses: 2:7; 3:5; and 8:4. These verses also serve to divide the drama into four separate parts or scenes. The word suggests that the Shepherd and his Shulammite are together and at peace and safely in the fields, his home. The last pronoun, translated in some texts "until *he* please" is better translated "until *she* pleases" according to the Hebrew.

The whole point of the drama is that the Shulammite ought to be with her Shepherd out in the fields rather than in the harem of Solomon to which she had wandered for a time. Therefore

through the eyes of the Shulammite we look back in retrospect
on what has recently happened in her own life. Now, when she is
safely with her Shepherd again, she recalls what had happened
in her earlier life. The drama reflects on her having left her
Shepherd to live with Solomon for a time until she came to her
senses.

The first three scenes tell the same story but with increasing
detail. The first scene introduces the story and gives it in broad
outline. The second scene gives us more detail and the third
scene goes into the greatest detail.

Scene one (1:2 to 2:7) describes the Shulammite girl in Solomon's
house. Throughout the drama we can identify the speakers only
by the use of the masculine and feminine pronouns used in
address, i.e., when the Shepherd or Solomon speaks to her, he
addresses her using the feminine pronoun "you." When the
Shulammite addresses either Solomon or the Shepherd or
others, she uses the appropriate masculine or feminine pronoun
"you." Inasmuch as in English we make no distinction between
masculine and feminine of the pronoun "you," English translations do not make clear who is speaking to whom. Only the
Hebrew can help us here. Some more recent English translations have sought to make these distinctions by notes in the
margin.

Another distinguishing mark which helps us to identify the
male speakers, is that the Shepherd when he is speaking to the
Shulammite, consistently uses rural terminology, outdoors terminology, while Solomon uses terminology of the palace and
relates to his own excessive preference for that which is rich and
lavish. We shall note this as we progress.

In scene one we find the Shulammite girl in Solomon's house,
where she reflects on her own unfaithfulness and longs for her
Shepherd.

The first part of the scene (vv. 2-7) contains her own words
reflecting on her unfaithfulness and her desire for her
Shepherd and her inquiry after him. Verse 4 gives us the clue
that she is now in Solomon's house. She is therefore out of her
rightful place. She is an outdoors or country girl, not used to the
dainty life of the palace (vv. 5, 6). The allusion to her own
vineyard which she has not kept gives us a clue to her problem.
Later we shall see her body likened to a vineyard which is to be
protected from intruders. Here she confesses that she has not
kept her body from the intrusions of Solomon as she ought to
have done. In the first part of verse 7, she inquires after her
Shepherd. She wants to go with him. The last part of the verse

again implies that she does not belong in Solomon's harem "as one that is veiled."

The next part of scene one, verse 8, is a refrain by the daughters of Jerusalem addressed to the Shulammite girl. The daughters of Jerusalem seem to give the girl direction and encouragement in her quest. Later they rebuke Solomon for his lustful desires after her. In essence they say here—"Where would you expect to find a Shepherd if not out among the flocks?"

The third part of scene one, verses 9 to 11, represents the allurements of Solomon addressed to her to keep her with him. The Hebrew clearly shows that she is being addressed. The terminology used in the address is not that of the Shepherd but of Solomon. Note the rich terminology: jewelry, gold, silver. Who but Solomon would compare her to a steed in Pharaoh's chariots? Had he not married an Egyptian princess? He is here offering to her the riches of his kingdom to stay with him.

The next part of scene one, verses 12-14, clearly shows that while at Solomon's table, her heart went out to her Shepherd. She thinks of him in rural terminology. Note particularly verse 14. Thus in the rest of the scene, 1:15 to 2:6, we see the true lovers in conversation, the Shulammite and the Shepherd. Note again the rural terminology throughout. In verse 15 he speaks of his love to her. In verses 1:16 to 2:1 she speaks of her love for her Shepherd. All is in the terminology of the outdoors, where she belongs. In verses 3 to 6, she concludes by telling how the Shepherd has brought her back to his rural home where they now dwell together in peace and love.

The divider between scene one and scene two, as we have already noted, is 2:7, a refrain addressed to the daughters of Jerusalem.

Scene two (2:8 to 3:5) contains an elaboration on some of the matters introduced in scene one. It is basically an elaboration on her experience with her Shepherd. The first part of the scene, 2:8, 9, recounts the Shepherd's call to her while she was in the house of Solomon, to come with him back to the peaceful rural life, away from the lures of the city. He is likened to a roe or a gazelle and comes seeking her, peering through the window looking for her.

Verses 10 to 14 are a long quotation by the Shepherd, inviting her to come back to him. Note again his use of rural peaceful terminology to call her away from this city life of Solomon which has lured her from her shepherd.

Verses 15 to 17 are her affirmation to the Shepherd. Note

again the rural terminology. She gives her heart to her shepherd once more.

The remainder of scene two (3:1-4) tell how she sought her lover until she found him. She looked first in the city (v. 2). She inquired of the watchmen (v. 3). She finally found him and the two were married, which is evidently the meaning of the words "I brought him into my mother's house" (v. 4). Compare 8:2 and also Genesis 24:67.

Scene two is divided from scene three by the same refrain (v. 5) which we saw in 2:7.

The third scene (3:6–8:3) gives the greatest detail of the story which has already now been introduced in scenes 1 and 2. It begins by telling how she was lured away from her Shepherd in the first place by the seduction of Solomon. The first part of the scene, 3:6-11, describes Solomon in all of his glory as he passes by her way and sees her and seduces her. Note the description of Solomon, emphasizing his excesses and his perfumes.

He came up from the wilderness, apparently having been on some mission of state. He is heavily perfumed and powdered as only the rich could be (v. 6). He is accompanied by sixty soldiers who are expert swordsmen but fearful of attack (v. 8). Next, in verses 9 and 10, his car (palanquin) on which he is carried is described in the most ornate way, reminiscent of his excessiveness in building the Temple and his own house as we saw in 1 Kings. The reference in verse 11 to his being crowned by his mother may in some sense be a slap at Solomon.

The next part of scene three, 4:1-15, is a long speech by Solomon in which he seduces the Shulammite girl. It is an elaboration on his seduction of her which has already been introduced in scene one (1:9-11). Solomon gives great attention to her bodily beauties, her physical features, which he describes with great passion (vv. 1-5). He suggests in verse 6 that he wishes to know her carnally.

In verses 7 and 8 he invites her to come from her rural home in Lebanon to live with him in the city. He likes all he sees about her and is ravished by her beauty (v. 9). He considers her beauty to be wasted in the rural Lebanon, like a garden which is shut up or a fountain which is sealed. He wants to open her to his own desires (vv. 12-15).

In verse 16 we have the record of her yielding herself to Solomon's allurements. She gives her garden (body) to him. She did not keep (guard) her own vineyard. Compare 1:6. Solomon had pictured her as a beautiful garden and had desired that she open her garden to him. She therefore says to him in essence "Here I am, indulge yourself."

In 5:1 we read of Solomon's indulgence in the Shulammite girl. Then shamefully he invites his friends to indulge also, reminiscent of the king of Persia who offered his wife Vashti to his friends to adore her beauty (Esther 1:10-11).

The next part of scene three, 5:2-8, pictures the Shulammite in Solomon's house. In the night she hears her Shepherd call her (compare 2:8-14). She hesitates and when she does finally open the door he is gone. She has to look for him. Note the Shepherd's rural terminology once again as he calls through the door for her to open the door and come away with him back where she belongs (v. 2). But she makes excuses that she is prepared for bed and cannot get up again (v. 3). The Shepherd however is persistent and seeks to enter her room (v. 4). When she finally gets up and opens the door for him, he has gone (v. 6), perhaps because she smelled too much of Solomon's perfumes (v. 5).

Now she desperately wanted her Shepherd (v. 6—cf. 3:2). She inquired of the watchmen (v. 7—cf. 3:3). Note that here we are told that the watchmen show her no sympathy but instead beat her. She appealed to the daughters of Jerusalem (v. 8). Their response in verse 9 is in essence "What is so special about your Shepherd that you seek our help in finding him?" This gives her occasion to describe the Shepherd in beautiful detail (vv. 10-16).

In this description we note the use of both Solomonic terminology and rural terminology as if to say that her Shepherd is all that Solomon is and much more. But the terminology is predominately rural as she describes her Shepherd whom she truly loves and to whom she now truly desires to return.

The daughters of Jerusalem are convinced and desire to help her find her shepherd (6:1). The Shepherd is of course where he ought to be, out in the field with his flocks (6:2,3). Cf. 1:8.

But now Solomon again enters the picture. The next part of scene three is a second prolonged speech by Solomon in which he seeks to lure her back to himself (6:4-13a). He tells of how she has captivated him by her beauty (v. 5). She is the choicest in his large harem (vv. 8, 9).

He wants to enter her garden (body) again, i.e., indulge himself (v. 11). There is no doubt that it is Solomon who is talking here (v. 12). He calls her to return to him and wants to continue to share her beauty with his friends (v. 13a).

Now the daughters of Jerusalem rebuke Solomon for his lust (v. 13b).

Solomon, ignoring the daughters of Jerusalem, goes on to describe in lustful terminology her beauty once more (7:1-9) as he seeks to seduce her.

This time, however, she refuses to yield to Solomon's charms (7:10—8:3). She is determined to go with her Shepherd back to the fields (v. 11). She recites the rural life where she belongs. She longs to marry her Shepherd (8:2—cf. 3:4) and live with him (8:3—cf. 2:6).

The next scene divider occurs in 8:4 and separates the fourth and final scene from the rest. The final scene is 8:5-14. In this scene we see the triumph of true love as she turns her back on Solomon in his glory and returns to her Shepherd. Verses 5 to 7 tell of the enduring quality of true love which can withstand such trials as the ones which the Shulammite and her Shepherd have been through. Verse 7 is a stern rebuke to Solomon who has attempted to buy her love.

The next part of the last scene, verses 8 to 12, reflects on the past life of the Shulammite girl and the meaning of her whole experience. As a child, it was uncertain what her life would be. Her brothers, when she was young, before she had developed into a beautiful young girl, determined to try to help her (v. 8). If she turned out to be a wall (cold and standoffish), they would seek to make her attractive. If she was a door (readily opening herself to any man), they would build a wall of protection around her (v. 9).

She realizes that she must be a wall, not open to all men, certainly not to the likes of Solomon (vv. 10-12). Solomon had tried to claim her but in the end she belonged only to her true love, her Shepherd (vv. 11, 12). In verse 12 she is saying in essence, "Solomon, you keep your money and riches, I want only the Shepherd."

The whole drama draws to a close with a loving exchange of words between the Shepherd (v. 13) and the Shulammite girl (v. 14).

In conclusion, what can we say about the purpose of the book? Some have suggested that it shows the contrast between true and false love. That is, the love as seen in the Shepherd's persistent love for the Shulammite in spite of her faithless lapse in contrast to Solomon's love which is only skin deep and base in nature.

However, this work is not just a thesis on love. It tells the story of God's faithfulness and love toward his people even when they themselves are faithless to God and lured away from the Lord to other gods. It is similar in its message to the book of Hosea, portrayed particularly in the first three chapters of Hosea which speaks of Israel as like a faithless wife in spite of God's love for her.

I believe that Solomon and his ilk had done much to lure God's people away from the Lord to pagan gods. The Lord, the Good Shepherd, who never abandons his people, seeks them out and calls them back to himself. Just as Ecclesiastes had done, so the Song of Songs shows that the right relationship between the Lord and his people, not the vain life as exemplified by Solomon, is what God desires.

The message of the book would be understood by God's people as one and the same with the message of the prophets beginning to be heard in those days. It would be a great encouragement to them even as the book of Revelation was to God's people in the midst of the first century persecutions.

This Song, like the book of Revelation, continues to be an encouragement to the people of God to be faithful to him and not to be lured away, even by so-called religious leaders who would seek to lead the people of God away from God. Christ in his earthly ministry warned against the hirelings and the false shepherds who would have places of leadership in the church but who were not truly God's shepherds. So God warns here against false shepherds such as Solomon and his sons who sought to lead Israel away from God. The book warns us not to follow the vain and false promises of men who themselves are not faithful to God but rather to look to the God who loves us and gave himself for us and to be faithful to him.

10

THE EIGHTH CENTURY PROPHETS

AMOS

WITH AMOS we come to the prophets who preached in the eighth century B.C., a time of rapid spiritual decline for both Israel and Judah. Before the century was over Israel would be no more and Judah would be badly beaten and her chief city, Jerusalem, under siege.

Amos preached in the time of Jeroboam II and his message was primarily addressed to the Northern Kingdom of Israel. To the north, Tiglath Pileser III was on the rise in Assyria, that northern nation which Jonah feared so greatly. In the south Uzziah was on the throne over a long period of time in Judah.

In Israel the people for the most part were oblivious to the danger and living higher than they had for a long time. Jeroboam II had a prosperous reign in the eyes of his subjects, at least in the eyes of the rich and prosperous of that day. Yet his reign was evil in the eyes of the Lord. He followed the path of all the kings of the north in doing evil. The people lived in luxury and sin, in imitation of the sins of Solomon.

The book of Amos is primarily one of judgment, judgment against the nations and against God's people, Israel. The first chapter and one-half, through 2:8 contains a long introduction dealing with God's judgment against pagan nations and Israel alike. The rest of the book deals strictly with Israel.

In the remainder of chapter 2 Israel's sin is shown to be particularly inexcusable in the light of God's kindness to her.

Chapters 3 through 5:15 expand upon the sins of Israel. This is followed by about a chapter (5:16—6:14) laying out certain woes to come upon Israel for her sins. The balance of the judgment passages contain a series of visions given to Amos, all pertaining to the inevitable judgment of the Northern Kingdom.

Then, in 9:8, suddenly there is a change from a message of judgment to one of hope. The book closes with this hopeful message for the remnant who are truly God's people.

Returning now to view the message of Amos in more detail, we learn in 1:1 of Amos' origin and occupation. He is from Tekoa, south of Jerusalem, and he labors there as a herdsman. Later he also tells us that he was a dresser of sycamore figs.

Amos' ministry occurred in the time of Jeroboam II as noted above. It was a most unlikely time for a message of judgment and woe, since the people were enjoying unparalleled good times. The fact that it was also a time unparalleled in sin did not bother the rich or the leaders in Israel.

The first part of the message of Amos (1:1—2:8) introduces the message of God's judgment against sinners. The message occurred two years before the earthquake (1:1). We do not know when this was, but it was so impressive that it was remembered centuries later in the time of Zechariah (Zech. 14:5). Perhaps it is mentioned here because it served to impress the people with the urgency of Amos' message.

Amos' text for the whole message is given in verse 2. He is apparently quoting from Joel 3:16. Joel had declared that when the Lord roared from Zion it would be a day of terror for God's enemies but God would be a refuge to his people. We see that this is exactly the essence of Amos' message, for Amos deals with the sureness of God's judgment on his enemies both in the pagan world and in the church. He also offers hope to those who put their trust in the Lord.

The style of Amos' first unit is to introduce God's judgment on the nations in two clusters of three nations. Verses 3-10, the first cluster, describe nations which have been traditional enemies of Israel, pagan nations with no real kin to Israel: Syria (Damascus), Philistia (Gaza) and Phoenicia (Tyre).

The second cluster, 1:11—2:3, deals with nations also in Israel's history, but which were in some way kin to Israel, brotherly nations. These include Edom (for Esau, Jacob's brother); Ammon and Moab (sons of Lot, the nephew of Abraham) (Gen. 19:37, 38).

In each cluster, indeed in dealing with each nation, the style is similar. First, he gives an opening formula. "For three transgressions . . . ," which is a Hebrew style for saying "for sin after sin." Then he states the particular act of cruelty the people (naming the capital or chief city in the first cluster and the nation in the second cluster) are guilty of. Finally, the judgment is pronounced and it is always fire, which will destroy the land. The figure of fire as a means of judgment was introduced by Joel earlier (Joel 1:19).

It should be noted that in all cases the particular acts against God which are cited are cruelties of men to men. Sometimes the victims are Israelites (1:3, 13). At other times the victim is not named but presumably are the Israelites (1:6, 9, 11). At other times, the victim is also a pagan people (2:1).

In all of these cases, we can be sure that the Israelites would be pleased to hear that their traditional enemies were displeasing God and would feel God's wrath.

But then, Amos turns to the south, to his own land, and condemns Judah in the same style (2:4, 5). Here the sin is Judah's rejection of the Law of God (v. 4). This too would be pleasing news to Israel, since by now Israel and Judah are no longer allies but enemies.

Finally, Amos turns the focus on Israel itself. He is now stepping on toes. The style of the charges leveled against Israel is the same as those above. Here however, the sins cited are sins against God's commandments to love the Lord and love one's neighbor.

In violation of God's commands regarding the treatment of the poor among God's people, given specifically in Deuteronomy 15:7ff, two things need to be noted here. First, the poor referred to in Deuteronomy are not the poor of the world but "of thy brethren," i.e., among God's children. Second, the synonyms used here for poor are "righteous," "needy," "meek."

We can conclude then that their sin was not against society in general but against God's people in particular.

The Psalmists in particular use the terms "poor," "needy," "righteous" and "meek" to refer to God's true children. Therefore, to take this out of its context and make it teach that the will of God is that believers should seek to redeem society by aiding the poor and underprivileged of the world today, is to twist Scripture. Essentially Amos here is dealing with inner-church sins in which those who have more of the riches of this world have wronged those in the church who have less. Indeed, they have their gain by wronging God's true children.

Not only that but they have profaned God's name by shameful conduct in the sanctuary (vv. 7, 8).

The introduction of Amos ends at 2:8. There follows a very brief resume of why Israel's action is particularly inexcusable (1:9-16). God had in Israel's history shown his goodness and mercy to Israel time and time again. He defeated all of her enemies in giving to Israel rich blessings. But the people showed little respect for their God (2:12).

When the judgment of the Lord comes, therefore, all of the human strength and pride on which Israel has leaned will collapse (2:13-16).

The next part of Amos (3:1—5:15) is an expansion upon the subject of Israel's sin and God's consequent judgment. The section begins by God's restating the heinous quality of Israel's sin: she sinned in spite of God's special love shown to her (3:2). Then in a series of cause and effect examples (3:3-6) Amos shows why he is presently bringing this message to the northern people of Israel. He is compelled to do so because God has spoken and he cannot be silent (3:8 cf. Jer. 20:9; 1 Cor. 9:16).

The scene described in 3:9-12 is a lesson in geography. Samaria, set upon a high hill, rises above the plain. But surrounding that plain are still higher mountains. The nations are called to sit upon these mountains as if in a gigantic amphitheater and look at the stage (Samaria), where the Lord will execute terrible judgment upon Israel as an example to all nations of God's judgment. The adversary is doubtlessly the northern power referred to by Joel (Joel 2:20). Judgment would come from the north. It is from the north that ultimately Assyria, the conqueror of Samaria, and Babylon, the conqueror of Jerusalem, did come.

Evidently there were some sinners in Israel who kept saying that even if Israel fell they would be rescued. The picture in 3:12 shows in a vivid manner that from the rebellious in Israel and

Samaria there would be no remnant. A piece of an ear or a leg will do the lamb no good when he is devoured by the lion. This verse does not teach that a remnant shall be saved, just the opposite. The sinners of God's church who are not his people will not be saved!

Once the judgment of the Lord gets started, it will seek out all the vain luxuries of Samaria and destroy them all (3:13—4:3). The reference to houses of ivory has been clarified by archaeological discoveries of remains of Israelite houses of that era which were panelled with ivory. In 4:1-3, the target is particularly the fat women of Samaria called here kine (cows) of Bashan, a particularly luxuriant area where the cows are fat. Now they wallow in their wealth but in the end they will be carried away into captivity.

The futility of their trust in their man-made embellishments of worship is pointed out in 4:4-5. Remember, all of their ritual was invented by Jeroboam I as a substitute for the true worship which the Lord had commanded (1 Kgs. 12:26-33).

The long-suffering of the Lord is beautifully exemplified in 4:6-11. Likewise we see here an example of the stubbornness of Israel over a long period of her history. The plagues promised in Deuteronomy 28:20-25 had already fallen on Israel to bring her to repentance but Israel refused.

In a very dramatic way, after citing the numerous times the Lord had sought to bring Israel to return to him, in verse 12 he states that the judgment on Israel will be so terrible that it cannot even be mentioned. In that verse he never does say just what the Lord will do, but he says that because he *will* do it, Israel had better get ready to meet her God.

It is quite proper at this point that the Lord, through Amos, calls the people who are hearing him to repentance and mourning, just as Joel had done (Joel 2:12, 13; Amos 5:1-3).

Along with repentance, he calls them to seek the Lord, not in their places of worship which are not in accord with God's will, but where the Lord is, i.e., in accord with God's revealed will, in the doing of righteousness and justice which they have perverted (5:7).

Yet, instead of seeking the Lord through obedience to his will, they have opposed both God and those God has sent (5:10). They mistreat God's children and therefore violate the justice God demands (5:11-13).

In essence, here, Amos is calling the people to cease from their habits of evil and to begin living as God's children ought to live (vv. 14, 15). Reference to the remnant here makes clear that there is hope only for those who will repent and obey the Lord.

The next major part of Amos (5:16—6:14), contains chiefly a series of woes against the land because the people persist in their sins. Some probably desire the day of the Lord while continuing in their sins. They suppose that the day of the Lord will be good news for Israel (a day when the Lord will destroy all her enemies), but in reality, it is a day when most of Israel will be destroyed too, because Israel has become the enemy of the Lord. That is why here the day of the Lord is described in the darkest terms, not a happy day at all for sinners. (5:18-20 cf. Joel 1:15; 2:1, 2, 22). Judgment must begin at God's house, in the church itself (1 Pet. 4:17).

Lest there be yet any doubt in the mind of anyone as to whether their religious exercises have any merit before the Lord, God makes it quite clear in 5:21-24. Again we see the Lord lift up his standards of righteousness and call for a veritable flood of these to come upon the land (5:24). But the man-made substitutes for true worship and service deserve only to be carted away into captivity (vv. 26, 27).

How is Israel reacting to such a message as this? By the words of 6:1-6, the word is "business as usual." The people remain at ease, satisfied with their luxuries and shameful lives. They refuse to believe what God's servants are saying (6:3). They pursue their old habits and show no concern that the church is corrupting from within (6:5). Reference here to instruments of music "like David" apparently indicates an attitude of mockery as they try to implicate the godly Psalmist in their debauchery, likening their idleness to his moments of inspiration when with a harp he would compose one of the many Psalms of Scripture.

In verses 6:7-14 the Lord plainly spells out Israel's end. The land will go into captivity (6:7), thus ending all of the reveling. God will raise up that nation he had warned of in Joel (6:14).

The last part of Amos pertaining to the subject of Israel's impending doom is a series of visions shown to Amos to help him and Israel to visualize the significance of the judgment (7:1—9:8a).

The *first vision* is locusts, reminiscent of Joel's message (7:1-3—see Joel 1:2-4). When Amos sees this visualized he is so overcome that he pleads for God to spare Israel such a fate.

The *second vision* is a picture of judgment by fire. It too is unbearable for Amos, who once again intercedes for Israel much as Moses did in the wilderness (7:4-6).

A *third vision* however puts Amos to silence much as Abraham was put to silence after pleading for Sodom (7:7-9). Here, the Lord showed Amos how he sees Israel by holding a plumb line up against the people of Israel. It is implied that when this is done there is no more room for doubt that Israel deserves her judgment. The sword threatened in 7:9 is the same as the fire judgment of earlier chapters. It points to ravages of war by nations too powerful for Israel.

At this point an historical interlude tells of the opposition to Amos (7:10-17). The false priest of Bethel sends word to Jeroboam in Samaria that Amos is stirring up trouble in Bethel. It is interesting how his words to Amos show how right Amos is. He calls the sanctuary the king's house. It certainly is not God's! (7:13). Amaziah, in telling Amos to leave, implies that Amos is preaching for profit (7:12).

Amos' reply is not a denial of his prophetic office but he disassociates himself from those false prophets, abundant in his day, who did preach for money and who were professionals (7:14, 15). For the first time the words of Amos are directed to an individual, Amaziah, who shall feel the hand of God in a very special and personal way, but in the judgment which shall fall on all Israel (7:17).

The entire eighth chapter is taken up by the *fourth vision* which comes in the form of a play on words. In the English this is missed. The Lord shows to Amos a basket of summer fruit which in Hebrew is pronounced "keets." Then the Lord declares that the end (in Hebrew, "kates") has come on Israel. Once more the sins of the people against the children of God are enumerated (8:4-6). By their lust for money and power they cheat and wrong the poor and are ever impatient to have the Sabbath to pass so that they may cheat some more (vv. 5, 6). God says, "I will never forget" (v. 7).

Among the terrible things that will happen to these people who were once the blessed of the Lord, nothing is so awful as the thing mentioned in 8:11, a famine of God's Word. No longer, where they are going, will they ever again hear God's prophets or the Word preached. Saul had known such a day in the latter part of his life (1 Sam. 28:6). Now it would happen to all Israel. These people who in Israel continue to rebel and refuse to obey God are offered no hope here (v. 14).

The *last vision* (9:1ff.) takes away any hope that might be left. Not only must the houses of luxury be destroyed but also now the very altars they have erected to worship God will be smitten and their own heads smashed by the stones of the altars (9:1). There will be no escape (9:2-3), not even in the land of their captivity (9:4). The first part of verse 8 is quite final with respect to the unrighteous in Israel.

It is at this point that Amos turns to give *hope to the righteous* who do remain in the land (9:8b-15). The Lord will have a people and will preserve that people in the midst of judgment. Here the Lord clearly distinguishes between his people and the sinners or unrighteous ones in Israel. The latter will perish but the remnant will be saved (9:9, 10).

Reference to David in verse 11 points to the continuing plan to save his people through the house and seed of David.

The book closes on a note of joy and expectation based on God's continuing purpose to have a people holy, without blemish, before him, in a relationship of love (9:13-15; cf. Eph. 1:4). The blessings are put in terms of agricultural abundance because throughout the Old Testament this was the way God described his blessings on his people and the way he showed his favor to them. However, we must remember that from Abraham on, those blessings were indicative of something far beyond temporal blessings of the world (Heb. 11:8-10; 12:22; 13:14).

In conclusion we can say that the book of Amos was addressed to the pseudo-religious who separate their religion from their daily lives, ignoring the principle regarding religion which James so clearly expressed much later, that "pure religion and undefiled . . . is to visit the fatherless and widows in their affliction, and to keep oneself unspotted from the world" (Jas. 1:27).

What Amos said to these people was that God will not overlook their sins but punish them. Such people have no place among God's people. They shall not stand. But God would spare the faithful ones, those who are righteous in Israel (2:6, 7), i.e., the righteous, the meek, the poor and the needy of his flock.

Why does God destroy Israel? Because he loves the church too much to let it die, which is what was happening. He would clean it and plant it again, not this once but over and over when the people of God failed him. We can take great comfort in the truth that God will never stand by and let his church perish from the face of the earth but will shake it and prune it and give it new life.

HOSEA

Like the book of Amos the book of Hosea is set in the time of Uzziah of Judah and Jeroboam II of Israel. Hosea too addresses his message primarily to the Northern Kingdom of Israel shortly before the fall of Samaria, the chief city of Israel.

The message of Hosea is divided into five parts. The *first* part (1:2—3:5) deals with Hosea's sad experience with his wife

Gomer and what God taught Hosea and Israel through this event. The *second* part (4:1-14) is a brief summary of God's indictment against Israel. The *third* part (4:15-19) is a brief personal message to Judah. The *fourth* part (5:1—10:15) develops God's case against Israel to its conclusion. The fifth and final part (11:1—14:9) is a presentation of God's grace which triumphs over man's sin and failure.

The name of Hosea's father is Beeri (1:1), but we know nothing more about him. Hosea's name means "salvation" and is borne by four others including Joshua, the successor of Moses. Our only other source of knowledge about Hosea is found in the personal experiences of the prophet as recorded in the book itself.

The main body of the message begins in 1:2. We shall call the first part, *Lessons found in Hosea's experience with Gomer* (1:2—3:5).

As with the other prophets so with Hosea, what he writes are not his own words but God's (1:1, 2). The command of God in 1:2 raises a problem of interpretation. At first it seems that God commanded Hosea to do something which is everywhere in Scripture forbidden, to marry an unrighteous person, a practicer of evil. Since God is never inconsistent with himself we must assume that God did not command Hosea to do evil. Some argue that the whole thing never happened but was symbolic. However, specific names are given for his wife and for her father. Furthermore, the whole point of this first section is the comparison between Hosea's experience with Gomer and that of God with Israel. It would lose significance if it never really happened.

The most likely explanation is that Hosea, looking back on his marriage, saw that God had guided him through this experience so that he could teach Israel how like a faithless wife Israel had proven to be. At some point Hosea came to realize that the woman he had married was a whore, perhaps when she became pregnant with the first child after their marriage.

Instead of being bitter he sees this experience as under the control of his sovereign God and therefore for a good purpose. The key to the whole section is at the end of verse 2 where the whole land of Israel commits whoredom against the Lord. It would have been difficult if not impossible for Hosea to marry a righteous person at this time.

The name Jezreel (1:4) recalls the deed of Jehu, the king of Israel appointed by the Lord to destroy the house of Ahab. It was at Jezreel that he killed Jezebel (2 Kgs. 9:30-37) and from that city he ordered the death of the seventy sons of Ahab

(2 Kgs. 10:1-11). In all of this he was doing what the Lord had commanded (2 Kgs. 9:7-10). So what was the sin which God was now condemning? It was that Jehu did all of this out of an evil heart, an evil motivation so that Israel was no better off after the slaughter (2 Kgs. 10:29ff.).

The significance of the name of the second child, Lo-ruhamah (1:6) is that the name means "no mercy" and pronounces God's judgment on a people who have refused to respond to God. Significantly, the Lord does hold out hope for any in Israel who may repent by declaring that in Judah his mercy is still to be found (1:7).

The name of the last child is Lo-ammi, meaning "not my people" (1:9).

We see then in the three children something of the descent of the people of Israel who refused to honor God in their hearts as Jezreel reminds them, and who therefore ceased to know God's mercy and finally now have come to be cut off from God, no longer his people. Thus with them the covenant of Exodus 19 is revoked.

But the Lord, whose purpose to have a people will not be thwarted, determines to have a people in spite of Israel's failures (1:10—2:1). Paul, later, sees this verse as a prophecy of the ultimate inclusion of the Gentiles into the people of God (Rom. 9:26). The concept of God's people all being united ultimately under one head (1:11) certainly points back to God's covenant with David to establish his throne forever (cf. 3:5) and also ahead to David's Greater Son, Jesus Christ (Matt. 1:1; 1 Cor. 8:6).

The Lord develops his controversy with Israel in 2:2-7. The word "controversy" used in 2:2 is a legal or forensic term. It speaks of God's case against Israel. She has acted like a whore and gone after her lovers but God has determined to hinder her departure (2:6). God does this in love, not willing that she should perish (2:3).

However it is necessary to discipline Israel for her faithlessness. He does so by stripping her (2:8-13). God had given to Israel all that she had in the first place (2:8). Now that she has refused to use God's gifts rightly, i.e., to serve the Lord, God will take it all from her. All of her blessings will be denied her now, all that she took for granted: her food and clothing (2:9); her joy (2:10—cf. Joel 1:12 and Amos 5:21; 8:10); and her good crops (2:12). All of this the Lord describes as the stripping naked of a vile woman, to bring her to shame.

Baal worship is mentioned here (2:13) because from the time of Ahab the people had followed after Baal worship and turned from God (cf. 1 Kings 16:29-32).

God's hedging Israel in as mentioned in 2:6 is shown to be for the good purpose of bringing Israel to repentance and to return to the Lord (2:14-20). God, who has spoken of Israel's guilt, now speaks to her comfortably (2:14). Thus the Lord does here as he does also through Isaiah: after speaking of Judah's sin in Isaiah for some thirty-nine chapters, in chapter 40 he begins to speak words of comfort (Isa. 40:1ff.).

We see how God intends to bring back his people to himself, as a man might seek to bring back his faithless wife to himself. To do this he takes her back to the wilderness experience to that situation in which she depended totally on the Lord as in the days of Moses (2:14, 15).

In verse 16 we have a play on words. The Lord will no longer allow his people to speak of him as "my baal"—though the word "baal" was actually a perfectly good Semitic word meaning "Lord." But the name had become so associated with the name of the Phoenician god, Baal, that God would no longer be called by that name (2:17). The name by which he will be called by his people is "Ishi," meaning "my husband."

In verse 19 God speaks of the renewal of his covenant with his people in sure and certain terms, not like the old covenant that Israel could not keep, but in the certain terms of God's own work of love. The promise that the people shall *know* the Lord speaks of a transformed heart to know him truly, i.e., from the heart (2:20). Israel's failure was that she had not known the Lord in her heart, i.e., *really* (2:8; 4:6; 5:4; 11:3). Later Hosea will call the people to know the Lord (6:3, 6). In all cases, the term "to know" means to have that certain faith in God which God requires of all his children (see Gen. 15:6).

Verses 21-23 again point to the future hope of God's people to be in God's presence in a fellowship of love as God himself has purposed from before creation (Eph. 1:4). Again it envisions the whole people of God, including the Gentiles who are to be brought in (cf. 1:11).

The very brief third chapter shows how the Lord helps Hosea apply the lessons he has learned about God's dealing with faithless Israel to his own personal tragedy (3:1-3). Thus Hosea was enabled through his own personal suffering to be God's spokesman to Israel at this time.

The second part of Hosea deals briefly with the indictment against Israel (4:1-14). Again God uses the term "controversy" (4:1). In short, the people have substituted a life of sinfulness for the justice and holiness God had expected (4:1, 2). They therefore proved not to be God's people. Their leaders, the prophets and priests themselves were no better (4:4, 5).

They had rejected the knowledge which God had taught them through his Word (4:6-10). Since they refused to live by God's standard of righteousness and justice, the Law of God, their lives were filled with sin (4:7, 8). Therefore the Lord warns that they will surely be punished (4:9, 10).

Not only have they refused to do God's will but they sin so much that they do not even realize their predicament (4:11-14). Like drunken persons they stagger after false gods, looking in all of the wrong places for the right answers. Their minds are dulled to reality.

At this point, Hosea inserts a brief interlude, *a personal message to Judah* (4:15-19). Judah must see that Israel is under condemnation and is in no way to be allied with Israel or her sins. This is said, no doubt, because often in Judah's history she had allied with Israel—and always to her own hurt (cf. 1 Kgs. 22:1-4).

We begin the main body of Hosea's message in 5:1, where Hosea begins to develop *The case against Israel* (5:1—10:15).

The first point is that Israel cannot turn to God, so extensive and deep-seated is her sin (5:4). The problem of Israel is the problem of an evil heart and the sinful heart keeps them from ever finding the Lord (5:6). The strange children born to them, mentioned in verse 7, of course refers to the first three chapters where Israel was described as like a faithless wife bearing illegitimate children. It indicates the broken covenant. Israel is rearing a whole generation of children who do not know the Lord, much as happened in the days after Joshua's death (Judg. 2:10).

The only solution therefore is for God to bring some to repentance after great afflictions (5:8-15) as he had indicated in 2:6ff.

Hosea therefore speaks of Ephraim's (Israel's) oppression and affliction to come at the hands of the Lord (5:11-14). The mention of God as like a lion recalls Joel 3:16 and Amos 1:2. There can be no help for Israel until she repents and returns to look to the Lord for help (5:15). This is in accord with Amos' words (Amos 5:6; 9:8ff.). All of the sacrificial system instituted in the wilderness had been just for this purpose to bring the people to a broken heart. It is that for which God calls here.

It is proper then that Hosea should at this point call for the people to return to the Lord (6:1-3). It is a strong evangelistic appeal to get right with God. God has judged. God can also heal (6:1). The picture here suggests not only a lion who tears but also a physician who can heal. Isaiah later also uses the imagery of the physician (Isa. 1).

Reference to the raising up on the third day (6:2) may point to Christ's resurrection on the third day since in Christ's resurrection is our own also if we believe in him. Actually the people did not repent in large numbers until the coming of John the Baptist and it was soon after that that the Lord *did* triumph over sin and death for us through Jesus Christ. Paul says in 1 Corinthians 15:4 that Christ was raised from the dead on the third day *according to the Scriptures.* Perhaps he is referring to Hosea's words in 6:2.

Once more, however, Israel must be reminded that her return to the Lord cannot be based on her goodness (6:4-11). The Lord alone is the standard of true goodness. Therefore, the "goodness" of men is far from God's standard. It has no real substance but is like a cloud that quickly disappears (6:4). This is true of Judah as well as Ephraim (Israel). By prophet after prophet the Lord has shown Israel that her works are not right before God (6:5). Israel's reliance on ritual and the sacrificial system as works which earn her salvation continues to keep her from God. The words in verse 6 which sum up what the Lord really desires are in keeping with what we have seen earlier (see 1 Sam. 15:22; Psa. 51; Amos 5:21ff.).

The reference to Adam in verse 7 probably refers to the sin of Adam in failing to keep the covenant of works established between God and Adam in Eden by which Adam should live so long as he obeyed God perfectly but would die on the day he sinned (Gen. 2:16, 17). This verse then simply teaches us that we are all spiritually dead, unable to do any good work in our natural state. As Paul puts it later, "All have sinned, and fall short of the glory of God" (Rom. 3:23).

As God had said earlier, the evil of Israel must be stripped bare to expose her sin (7:1-7, cf. 2:10). There can be no healing until the full extent of her spiritual disease is exposed (7:1). Here Israel's sin is likened to an overheated oven which consumes everything and everybody (7:4-7). God knows the full extent of Israel's sin and he will not overlook it (7:2).

In a series of graphic imageries Hosea next describes Israel's complete inability to help herself (7:8-16). In the first place the people are like a half-baked cake (7:8-10). They may look good but on closer investigation they are seen to be unacceptable. They simply do not know their own lacks and so do not return to the Lord.

Again, they are like a silly dove, not able to make up their mind to whom to look for help (7:11, 12). They fly back and forth between alliances with Egypt and alliances with Assyria when they ought to fly to the Lord.

Finally, they are like a deceitful bow, looking strong but breaking under pressure (7:13-16). Evidently there was some show of reform in Israel at this time, as later there was in the time of Josiah of Judah. But the reform was not from the heart (7:14). The return, whatever it was, was not to the Lord, but perhaps only to some ritualistic religious appearance (7:16). It was certainly hypocritical and not genuine for they went right on transgressing and plotting evil (7:13, 15).

All of this means that judgment from the Lord is inevitable (8:1-14). The call here for trumpets is to sound the alarm, a forewarning of God's impending judgment (8:1 cf. 5:8 and Joel 2:1).

The people claim to know the Lord (8:2) but all they have known is their own idols made with their own hands, and this God will not accept as true worship (8:4-7). They have also made alliances with the pagan nations rather than trust in the Lord (8:4-7). They have substituted their own sacrifices and set their own goals and standards (8:13, 14).

Consequently, the Lord will not accept their sacrifices (8:13) but send them back into slavery to the nations. (Egypt reminds them of their former 400 years of bondage.) They may build and make their plans but God will destroy it all (8:14).

The final part of God's development of his case against Israel lays out the consequences of Israel's having broken the covenant with God (9:1—10:15). Remember, the old covenant had stipulated that in order to enjoy the continued blessings of God in the land of Canaan, Israel must continue to honor God and keep his commandments. God had in much patience and long-suffering sought to keep Israel faithful but it is now evident that Israel had failed. Therefore, the consequences of her faithlessness must follow.

First, there will be an end of true worship in Israel (9:1-9). Here he points out that in the captivity into which they go there will be no opportunity to serve the God whom they had refused to serve when they could (9:3-5). Second, there will be no enduring fruit in Israel (9:10-17). This means that there is no future for Israel when they go into captivity. God had called Israel to be a fruitful vine, to have children and be his people, but since they disobeyed, they will dry up and have no future (9:11, 12, 14, 16).

Third, their kingdom and therefore their history will come to an end (10:1-15). Since they rejected God as their king they will be denied any king (10:3). Instead they and all they possess will be carted off to Assyria (10:6ff.). The line of kings in Samaria will be cut off (10:7).

Ephraim (Israel) is here described as a stubborn heifer that will not learn from discipline (10:9-11). Yet the Lord calls for obedience once more even as he concludes his case against the people (10:12). The people, unable to help themselves, must look to God for help.

But for the grace of God, the message might well have ended here. However, the Lord, rich in his mercy and love, shows in the concluding chapters how *his grace triumphs over our sins* (11:1—14:8).

He begins by speaking of God's love for Israel, even when the people were slaves in Egypt (11:1). He called them from there to be his children. The later use of this passage by Matthew to show that God had purposed Jesus to be called back into Palestine from Egypt when he was a babe, simply shows how Jesus, our substitute, is identified with his people whom he came to save (Matt. 2:15).

The Lord went right on calling to his people by prophet after prophet. Note how his dealing with them had to change from dealing as with sons to dealing as with stubborn animals (11:3, 4).

Israel deserved punishment because she refused, in spite of all of God's patience and love, to return to God (11:5-7).

Yet this pitiful plight of Israel provoked God's great compassion (11:8-11). God will have a people holy and without blemish. He will not give Israel up (11:8). He will not treat them as he did Admah and Zeboiim (lesser known sister cities of Sodom and Gomorrah) (Gen. 14:8).

The imagery of God as a roaring lion is used again, this time to show that God will roar and his people from all parts of the world will come trembling to him (11:10, 11). This must have reference to God's determination to have a people drawn from all the nations, much as we saw in 1:10—2:1.

God makes clear that Ephraim, the Northern Kingdom, is rejected but that God will continue to work in Judah to have a faithful people (11:12). The only answer for God's children in Israel is to *wait* for the Lord (12:6). This very important word "wait" is a key word in the later prophets, calling the people to despair of any hope in themselves and to look to God for the answers.

The next section, 12:7—14:3, is like the deliberations of a judge who ponders the pros and cons of a case until he makes his final verdict. On the one hand Israel is vain and filled with pride, living in deceit (12:7, 8). But on the other hand God has had a purpose for Israel from the days of Egypt (12:9, 10).

On the one hand Israel is full of iniquity (12:11). His land is full of altars symbolizing his rejection of God. But on the other hand God has faithfully preserved Israel from the days he called Jacob and led him (12:12).

On the one hand Israel has consistently provoked God to anger with her idolatry. The people are like smoke with no substance (12:14—13:3). But on the other hand God is their only hope, their only real God (13:4, 5).

On the one hand the people deserve to be punished. They have brought it all upon themselves. Their leaders in whom they trusted have all failed them (13:6-13). But on the other hand God has the power over hell and death and he can rescue them (13:14).

In conclusion, the Lord makes clear that the sinners who have not repented must be destroyed (13:15, 16). But, those who look at God, acknowledging their sins and looking to God's mercy will be spared (14:1-3).

The final verdict of the Judge, who is the Lord, is given in 14:4-8. He will heal. He will love them freely for it is only by his free grace that they can survive. He calls them therefore to take refuge in him (14:7).

We see then that in Hosea, Israel is made to see first of all her great sin against God and to see that she cannot do anything to correct herself. She must cast herself on the mercy of God and take refuge in him.

If this is so for Israel, it is also true for all men. Hosea closes with a general application of the lessons learned here (14:9). God will save and bless those who walk by trust in the Lord. They are the justified ones even as was Abraham (Gen. 15:6) and even as Habakkuk also reaffirms (Hab. 2:4). But the transgressors, those who refuse to repent and turn to the Lord for help will fall.

ISAIAH

The prophet Isaiah directed his message to Judah, the Southern Kingdom, in the last days of Israel and Syria to the north. He was called in the last year of Uzziah and continued to prophesy well into the reign of Hezekiah (1:1).

A brief survey of the contents will be helpful before we look more closely at the development of his message.

Isaiah's book in its earliest chapters is developed by a recurring cycle: 1) God's purpose; 2) Judah's sin; 3) consequent judgment; 4) prevailing hope for the remnant. We can see this cycle in chapters 1 through 12 in particular.

The next section of Isaiah (chapters 13 to 27) deals with God's judgment on the nations which God has used to discipline and punish his people. This section also closes with an expression of hope for the remnant who believe.

The third section, chapters 28 to 35, makes application of the above two sections by pronouncing the woes to come upon all evildoers whether in the nations or in Judah and by offering hope to those who put their trust in the Lord.

A brief historical section illustrating the principles of judgment and hope (chapters 36 to 39) separates the first three sections of Isaiah from the final section.

The final section of the book begins with chapter 40 and develops the hope theme of the earlier chapters. It is addressed to the remnant, God's true people, who trust in the Lord.

Let us now look more closely at each major section, beginning with the development of the recurring cycle of God's purpose, man's sin, consequent judgment and prevailing hope.

A Recurring Cycle (Isaiah 1-12). Chapter 1 serves as an introduction to the whole book and at the same time gives to us the first examples of the cycles so characteristic of the first 12 chapters. Chapter 1 also summarizes the message of the whole book. It closes in a way similar to the conclusion of the entire message in chapter 66.

God's purpose is stated briefly in the first part of verse 2. It speaks of God's purpose to have children, without any elaboration. However, we know from all of the former revelation of God that he purposed these children to be holy and without blemish in his presence, in a relationship of love toward God and toward one another. It was necessary here therefore only to imply that purpose by the use of the word "nourished."

Judah's sin, the second part of the cycle, is introduced next (vv. 2b-5). Israel has rebelled, she does not know the Lord (v. 3). Therefore Israel is addressed as a sinful nation and a seed of evildoers (v. 4). Thus the people have despised the Lord who is called here the Holy One.

The holiness of God is one of the major subjects of Isaiah. By that term we understand the perfect harmony of God in character, person and purpose. God is holy and therefore there is no room for any flaw in him or in anyone or anything having to do with the Lord. Thus here in verse 4 God's holiness is placed over against the sinfulness of the people of Israel who were supposed to be the people of God. The extent of the sin is emphasized in verse 5 by the words whole head and whole heart.

The *consequent judgment* follows (vv. 6-8). As Joel and Amos had already taught, Israel has been wounded and bruised in order to bring her to her knees. Judgment by fire, first introduced by Joel and then developed by Amos (Joel 1:19; Amos 1:4, etc.) is noted here also (v. 7).

Yet here too is seen the *prevailing hope* based on God's determination to have a people in spite of man's own frailty and failures. Verse 9 holds out hope, making clear that there is a remnant that shall survive, unlike Sodom and Gomorrah from which no remnant emerged. Furthermore, it is God who is the cause of this remnant, *God* has chosen to leave a remnant, which is different from a remnant surviving on its own merit or strength.

Here then in the first 9 verses of Isaiah we see the recurring cycle for the first time in Isaiah: God's purpose; Judah's sin; the consequent judgment and prevailing hope.

This is followed by a brief section dealing with the only solution to Israel's sin (vv. 10-20). Here the people are called "Sodom and Gomorrah" (v. 10) to remind them of the seriousness of their sin. All hope in the ritualistic sacrificial system is dashed by God's total rejection of all of her religious life including her practice of prayer (vv. 11-15). All of the sacrificial system and prayer had been instituted by the Lord through Moses long before. However, the people had conformed only outwardly and not in their hearts, so that God now makes clear that such worship, no matter what its form or appearance, is unacceptable to him.

This is no new thing. Long before, God had rejected Cain's offering because his heart was far from God. He was of the evil one (1 John 3:12) while on the other hand his brother Abel's sacrifice was accepted because he brought it to the Lord in faith (Heb. 11:4).

There can be, therefore, no pleasing of God by Israel until the people are clean in heart, living lives which come from right hearts (1:16, 17). What God calls for here we have seen him demand elsewhere (compare Amos 5:14; Hos. 6:4-6). The point is, because the hearts of the people are sinful, they are never going to be able to meet God's requirement on their own.

Verses 18 to 20 anticipate the 53rd chapter of Isaiah and therefore offer to those willing in heart, the hope of clean hearts, a work which only God can do. The bloody hands of sin noted in verse 15 above are due to bloody hearts of sin and can only be cleansed by God's cleansing.

Once again and in order to stress Israel's need of God's help, the prophet returns to the subject of Israel's stubborn sinfulness (1:21-23). The picture here of evil in the land is typical of other prophets already studied (compare Amos 2:6ff.).

The concluding part of chapter 1 shows how the Lord will, on the one hand punish and purge out all of his enemies and on the other hand, save a remnant (1:24-31). Those who do not look to God for cleansing shall be purged out. They are God's enemies (vv. 24, 25). They are the transgressors who refuse to repent and turn to trust in God (vv. 28-31). They shall in the end be cast into the fire of God's judgment (compare Amos 9:10).

The rest, the remaining ones, who are truly God's people, who are converts to God, having turned to trust in him, shall be redeemed by God's justice and righteousness applied to them (vv. 26, 27). Here Zion, as elsewhere in Scripture, is viewed as the true people of God. Thus only two alternatives are open to men: repent and be saved by trusting in the Lord, or refuse and perish.

Chapters 2 to 4 trace that cycle introduced in 1:2-9. The cycle is in these chapters more fully developed.

First, he describes *God's good purpose* in 2:1-4. Here the latter days refer to that time when God's purpose to have a people shall reach out to the nations to the ends of the earth and draw God's elect from all peoples of the earth (2:2). God's people shall be distinguished on the earth as those who love God's Word and desire to know it and obey it (2:3—cf. Psa. 1). Joel 3:10 will be reversed and God's people shall win not by the weapons of war but by the sword of the Spirit, the Word of God (cf. Matt. 26:52, Eph. 6:17). These verses no doubt refer to the days of the proclamation of the gospel to the ends of the earth, that is, the time after Christ's great commission and the coming of the Holy Spirit to enable God's people to do what in their own strength they could never do.

Following this, we see the *second phase* of the cycle, the present *sin of the people* (2:5-8). In contrast to God's good purpose, the people in reality at the time the prophet wrote were filled with the world's customs and with sin (2:6-8).

This leads to the *third phase* of the cycle, the *inevitable judgment* of God on this sinful people (2:9—4:1). Here the theme of God's judgment is greatly expanded. In a way similar to Joel, Isaiah speaks of the day of judgment as the day of the Lord (2:12).

Compare also Joel 1:15ff. Proud men shall be brought low so that only the Lord will be exalted (2:12, 17). Considerable attention is given to the significance of this for Jerusalem itself (3:1-12). Everything upon which the people had vainly depended shall fail (3:1-3). The city will fall into ruin (3:8). The rulers (3:13-15) and the women who love luxuries (3:16-24) are singled out for special rebuke (compare Amos 4:1-3; 6:1-6). The judgment shall come in the form of nations which shall war against the city and take the people captive (3:25, 26—cf. Amos 6:7ff.).

But God who is rich in grace and will not abandon his good purpose, here once again in the *final phase* of the cycle, gives *hope to the remnant* (4:2-6).

There will be some left, a remnant, purged of all evil, God's holy people (4:3). They are the *true* citizens of God's *true* Jerusalem. Here we must recall how the Book of Hebrews shows us that God's true children have always, by faith, looked beyond the earthly city to the New Jerusalem, the true Jerusalem as their real home (Heb. 11:9, 10; 12:22-24; 13:14. Compare Gal. 4:25, 26; Rev. 3:12; 21:2, 10).

Chapters 5 and 6 present the cycle still another time in the form of a parable and a call to Isaiah from God.

The cycle begins with the now familiar *first phase,* God's good purpose. The Lord planted a vineyard. He did everything necessary in order that that vineyard should produce good fruit (5:1, 2). Here Israel, as we shall see, is represented by the vineyard. They are the people from which the Lord expected good fruit. We can compare this with chapter 1, verse 2a.

But Israel did not meet God's expectations. Instead, the people sinned against God and produced bad fruit (5:2, last part, to verse 4). Here again we find the *second phase* of the cycle, the people's sin and failure (Compare 1:2b-5).

There follows *phase three* which is the consequent judgment (5:5, 6). Again we see God's purging.

Verse 7 summarizes the sin of Israel and her failure for emphasis. In the English translation much is lost, for we have here a most interesting play on words. God looked for justice (Hebrew: *mishpat*) but instead oppression (Hebrew: *mispach*). God looked for righteousness (Hebrew: *sedaka*) but instead a cry (Hebrew: *seaka*). The double pun is impressive and memorable. Note again that the will of God is expressed in these same terms, justice and righteousness. Compare Genesis 18:19.

In the remainder of chapter 5, God's judgment against Israel is expanded. There is much that reminds us of other prophets we have studied already: 5:8 (1 Kgs. 21:17-21. Also, later, Jer.

22:13-17; Mic. 2:2; Hab. 2:9-12; 5:11, 12; Amos 6:3ff.; 5:13; Hos. 4:6; 5:23; Amos 2:6ff.; 5:26-30; Joel 2). The judgment will come in the form of warring nations which shall ravage by wars against Jerusalem (5:26-30).

Finally, with chapter 6 we come to the *fourth phase* of the cycle, *hope for the remnant*. This phase here includes the call and ministry of Isaiah and explains why he records his call not at the beginning but at the proper point, as a part of the hope of God's remnant. This is in accord with what the Lord had shown Elijah long before—that the hope for a faithful people of God is connected with God's call of the prophets to proclaim God's Word so that the Word might take hold in their hearts. (See our comments on 1 Kgs. 9.)

The call of Isaiah is indeed an occasion for hope. It begins with Isaiah seeing a vision of the Lord in his glory and holiness. Isaiah is overcome as is any sinner when standing in the presence of the Holy God (6:5).

The Lord immediately assures Isaiah that he is purified by the Lord (6:6, 7). Thus because Isaiah recognizes his sinfulness and need of God's cleansing, the Lord assures him that his sins are forgiven (v. 7). For Isaiah, then, the conditions expressed in 1:18 are a reality. Isaiah therefore is an example of what must happen to every true child of God: he must come to an awareness of his own sinfulness and cry to God for help, receiving the cleansing power which only God can provide.

Now, Isaiah is called to bear witness and be God's messenger to the church (6:8-13). This will be a difficult ministry and most will not believe his message, but a remnant will. Those who do are the holy seed (6:13). Once again we see that real hope is offered only to the remnant.

Chapter 7 give us still another opportunity to see the cycle, this time in an historical event of the period. The historical situation is described in verses 1 and 2. Ahaz was now on the throne of Judah. He was threatened by Syria and Israel the northern kingdoms.

At this point Isaiah, the prophet, came to assure Ahaz the king that there was nothing to fear, for God would defeat Ahaz' enemies and save Jerusalem from capture (7:4). What was required of Ahaz was to trust the Lord and believe in him (7:9). This constitutes God's good *purpose* to *have a people*, the first part of the cycle. Significantly, Isaiah's son is named Shear-iashub which means, "a remnant shall return." Thus, as with Hosea's children, bearing a message to Israel in the very name.

The second part of the cycle is seen in Ahaz' refusal to believe

and thus his *sin against God* (7:10-16). Ahaz' sin may not be so
evident here, since he pretends not to want to tempt God (7:12).
However, in 2 Kings 16:7-9, we learn that instead of trusting to
the Lord to defeat his enemies, Ahaz bribed the king of Assyria
to fight and defeat them. Of course, Tiglath-Pileser was glad to
oblige since he had intended to do this anyway. This way he got
paid by Ahaz for doing it. He took Damascus, capital of Syria in
732 B.C. and ten years later he captured Samaria in 722 B.C.

Significant in this historical event is that it is the occasion for
the beginning prophecies about a babe to be born who will rise
to be the Savior of God's people.

The birth of the child is foretold here in 7:14. He shall be
born of a virgin. Noteworthy is the fact that this promise was
made not to Ahaz but to God's people, the house of David, from
which the child should come.

In recent years there have been those who claim that the 14th
verse does not promise a virgin birth but only the birth by a
young woman. However, the word used here for virgin is
elsewhere used in contexts where it may always mean virgin.
Besides this, the earliest translation of the Old Testament, the
Septuagint Greek, uses the Greek word which can *only* mean
virgin. In addition, the very point of this being a sign of hope to
God's people is that it is a miracle, evidence of God's supernatural working. Finally, and more important, the New Testament understands the verse to be predicting the virgin birth of
Jesus Christ (Matt. 1:23—compare Luke 1:27, 31-35). The birth
of this child would be the hope of God's people and the sign of
God's coming in the flesh (Luke 2:10, 11).

The name given here, Immanuel, means "God with us." This
name points to the coming of the Lord in the flesh to be with his
people to save them from their sins. When the Lord first called
Moses he promised to be with him. He established his own name
as a reminder of that promise. (See our comments on Exodus 3.)
God, after that, continually demonstrated his presence with his
people. Now, he is promising through Isaiah to be with them in
a new and special way, in the flesh, when the virgin appointed
has a son.

Because of Ahaz' unbelief, the *judgment phase* of the cycle follows (7:17-20). Now God names the pagan nation which he will
bring up against the land. It is Assyria (v. 17). Assyria is described here as a hired razor, controlled by God but having the
nature of a destroyer, cutting wherever it is placed (v. 20).

Finally, the historical incident closes with a promised *hope* for
the *remnant* (7:21-25). The butter and honey in abundance

suggest a blessing for those left after God's judgment (the remnant) (v. 22).

Chapters 8 to 12, the concluding part of the first section of Isaiah, is an interweaving of the four themes already introduced. The whole climaxes with the triumph of God's grace and great hope for all believers in the Lord.

First, Isaiah's own son is shown to be a token of the son yet to be born of a virgin. His name suggests the defeat of Judah's enemies, Syria and Israel, as God had promised Ahaz (8:1-4).

Israel, the Northern Kingdom, is destroyed because she refused God's gentle discipline (the waters of Shiloah—verse 6). She will therefore be destroyed by the strong river, Assyria. But Assyria will not stop at the borders of Judah (v. 8). The king of Assyria will sweep down like a flood into Judah.

Now there is given a word of encouragement to Judah. Because of Immanuel, God with us, Judah shall stand (vv. 8, 10). We see then how Immanuel is given as a promise in Ahaz' generation, of deliverance from Judah's immediate enemies: Syria, Israel, and Assyria. But in the fuller sense, Immanuel is the hope of the deliverance of all of God's people from their great enemies: Satan and sin (compare Matt. 1:21).

Isaiah personally responds to this hope in the words of 8:16-22. In the affirmation "I will wait for the Lord" (v. 17), Isaiah joins testimony with all of God's people of the Old Testament era who waited (looked for) God's deliverance as their only hope. The writer of Hebrews affirms this interpretation by quoting from this passage (Isa. 8:18) and making application to the work of Jesus Christ in defeating our enemy, the devil (Heb. 2:13-15).

The concluding words of chapter 8, verses 19-22, contain a warning to all who reject this word of hope (8:20). At the end of the chapter, Isaiah multiplies the words connoting gloom and darkness (v. 22), to stress the truth above, that for those who reject God's Word of hope, there shall be no morning.

Chapter 9 is a continuation of the thought of chapter 8. In contrast to the gloom for unbelievers, there shall be the shining of a great light for God's people in the latter time (9:1). Matthew 4:15, 16 quotes these verses as fulfilled in the coming of Jesus into the area of Capernaum. Thus again we see that the term "latter time" has reference to the time of Jesus' coming in the flesh.

Once more the theme of the hope that centers upon the birth of the child is developed (9:6, 7). This time he is declared to be not only the son of man but also to be God himself (v. 6). He shall be heir to David's throne on the one hand but also by his faithfulness in righteousness and justice prove to be the true seed of Abraham (v. 7—compare Gen. 18:19).

This good news for those who put their trust in the Lord will prove to be bad news for the proud and arrogant who have refused God as exemplified in the Northern Kingdom of Israel (vv. 8-21). Then, in 10:1-4, in a way which calls to mind the words of Amos, Isaiah pronounces solemn woe on the wicked in the land who oppress God's children.

As a preview of the second part of Isaiah (chapters 13-27), the prophet turns aside briefly to deal with Assyria, the rod of God's anger (10:5-19). God had said that he would use Assyria to punish Israel and Judah (8:4-8). However, Assyria has not done God's will out of a proper motivation, to serve or please the Lord, but out of pride (10:7-11).

This section gives to us an excellent picture of the work of the sovereign God in history. He takes evil men and evil nations to use them to accomplish his purpose. Yet they are to be punished themselves because they have done what they did out of an evil heart (10:12-14). Such evil nations and people are likened to an axe or a saw (10:15). Their nature is destructive. They exist to cut and rip and tear. But in the hands of the Master Craftsman they accomplish God's purpose just as a saw in the hands of a carpenter does his bidding. The prime example of this is of course the crucifixion of Jesus, at one and the same time the most heinous of crimes and also the accomplishment of God's sovereign purpose (Acts 2:23).

The remainder of the first part of Isaiah, 10:20 to 12:6, deals with the hope theme and brings it to a triumphant climax.

He speaks of the remnant once more (10:20-22). They are the saved, those who lean upon the Lord (trust in him). They are not the whole of Israel (v. 22) but they are the true Israel, God's true children.

In chapter 11, he returns to point the people again to hope in that son to be born. He is here called the shoot out of the stock of Jesse (11:1). He, in contrast to faithless Israel, shall bear fruit pleasing to God (11:1—cf. 5:1ff.). His ministry is described in verses 2 to 5 in terms later applied to the ministry of Jesus Christ (Matt. 3:16; John 1:32). Note again that he will accomplish for the believer what the believer could not accomplish for himself. Here the believer, God's child, the one benefited by the Savior's work, is called the poor and the meek (v. 4) in a way similar to Amos 2:6-8.

We see then a chain of revelation pertaining to that seed first promised in Eden, the seed of the woman (Gen. 3:15). Later he is declared to be the seed of Abraham (22:18) and then the seed of David (Isa. 9:7). He is to be born of a virgin (Isa. 7:14) and be also very God (Isa. 9:6). All of this, of course, culminates in the person of Jesus Christ. This is the great point of Matthew chapter 1.

The scene of peace described in 11:6-10 reminds us of 2:2ff. and points to the ultimate peace of God that shall prevail when God's children are gathered to him forever. The remnant theme is dominant in the rest of chapter 11 (11:12, 16).

The clearest concept of who the remnant are is found in chapter 12, a kind of testimony of the remnant. They are those who have known both God's anger at their sin and his loving comfort and forgiveness (v. 1). They trust in the Lord, seeing him as their strength, (the one who can and does do something about their plight—v. 2). Consequently, when others are terrified at God's wrath and run to hide from God, they who are at peace with the Lord through repentance of their sin and faith in him, rejoice and give God the thanks and glory (vv. 3, 4, 5). He is truly with them, his people (v. 6).

This completes the first major section of Isaiah, chapters 1-12. We see that it has dealt with four major themes: God's good purpose; Israel's sin; consequent judgment; and finally, triumphant hope for the remnant. Furthermore this hope for the remnant is centered in the person and work of the Man-God who shall come to accomplish all of God's will on behalf of God's children who have believed in him.

God's Judgment on Nations (Isaiah 13-27). The *next major section of Isaiah* (chapters 13 to 27) expands upon the idea introduced in 10:5-19, that the Lord will judge the pagan nations also who have been used by God to punish his people because they are evil and have done what they did, not out of a desire to obey God, but out of sinful pride and arrogance.

We shall not study this section in detail, though it is an important part of the entire message, for it shows clearly that God knows the sins of all of the nations and holds all accountable to the Lord.

The Lord therefore declares that he shall judge sinful Babylon by the Medes whom he shall raise up (13:1—14:23). In this section is a passage often interpreted as having reference to the fall of Satan himself (14:12-15).

While the passage may have a secondary reference to Satan, it is clear from the context that it primarily speaks of the proud and ambitious rulers of Babylon. New Testament passages such as Luke 10:18 and Revelation 9:1 are pointed to as arguments for this passage being also in reference to Satan's fall. Certainly, the attitude of Satan and his pride are seen here. The ambition to be like God (v. 14) is exactly the suggestion Satan planted in the minds of Adam and Eve in Eden.

In 14:24-27, Isaiah returns to Assyria, mentioned earlier (10:5ff.), and shows that that nation will also be overthrown. Then in successive sections, other nations which have played a part in Israel's history and have often been used by God to measure out punishment to Israel, are dealt with one by one: Philistia (14:28-32); Moab (15:1—16:14); Damascus (17:1-14); Ethiopia (18:1-7); and Egypt (19:1—20:6).

Two things in particular we need to note in these passages. First, the passages of judgment on the nations are interspersed with messages of hope for the remnant of Israel (14:1-3, 32; 16:5). Secondly, there is even to be found here eventual hope for some in the pagan nations who will also be included in God's kingdom just as Noah had prophesied (Gen. 9:27), and just as the Lord had promised Abraham (Gen. 12:3). See now Isaiah 19:19-25 and compare Isaiah 2:2-4.

In chapter 20 we see an historical illustration of the principle of God using one evil nation to punish another as the Assyrians go up against Philistia and take Ashdod, a forewarning of their attack against Egypt and Ethiopia also.

In chapter 21, the fall of Babylon is again brought into focus (21:9) and the cry "fallen, fallen is Babylon" becomes the cry of God's Word for the sure overthrow of all the nations of this world and of Satan's kingdom itself (see Rev. 14:8 and 18:2).

Before returning to judgment on the nations, in chapter 22, special warning is directed toward Jerusalem which is exposed to the threat of invasion and capture (22:9). The people of Jerusalem are endangered because they have not learned from history (22:11). They have refused to repent when God called them to repentance and to mourning through his prophets (22:12-14). Compare Joel 1:8-14.

In this section Shebna (v. 15) the scribe in Hezekiah's day (2 Kgs. 18:18), is replaced by Eliakim (v. 20) in the office of overseer of the house of the Lord, apparently because Shebna proved to be faithless. Then Eliakim, who replaces Shebna, is described as one entrusted with the keys of the house of David (v. 22). In this sense Eliakim becomes a type of Christ as we see in Revelation 3:7.

In chapter 23, Isaiah returns to the judgments pronounced against the nations, specifically, against Phoenicia. In this chapter he states specifically the great purpose for all such judgments—namely, to profane the pride of all glory and to bring into contempt all those on earth who are proud (23:9).

Finally, in reference to the nations, he includes in chapter 24 a general, summary statement on the sovereignty of God as he deals with all nations and even with Israel and Judah who are sinful like the nations (24:2). The picture of the chaos which shall come to the earth after judgment is similar to that of the earth before God brought order at creation (see Gen. 1:2 and compare Isa. 24:1, 3). The picture of a polluted earth because of the violation of God's established laws suggests one of the greatest problems of our present time (24:5). A sweeping finale to God's judgment is seen in the words of verse 21, the spiritual powers of ungodliness in the heavenly places and on earth shall be punished. Compare Ephesians 6:12.

As a conclusion to the whole section on the judgments on the nations, Isaiah once more points us to the great hope of the remnant (chapters 25-27). He frames these chapters in the form of a personal testimony to God. He is thankful that God is sovereign over the mighty nations (25:2) and protector of the weak who trust in him (25:4—cf. 4:5). Above all, he praises God who triumphs over death for his people (25:8). Verse 9 expresses that true hope and faith in the Lord as expressed in the concept "wait on the Lord." Compare 8:17 and also chapter 12.

Chapter 26 is a hymn for God's people (26:1). In the hymn he rejoices in the peace that shall come to those whose faith is in the Lord (vv. 3, 4, 12). He also testifies to his own desire in seeking after the Lord (vv. 8, 9). He celebrates the good effects of God's chastening on his people to bring them back to God (vv. 16-18). There is even expressed here hope for the bodily resurrection (v. 19—compare later writings, Ezek. 36, 37 and Dan. 12:1, 2).

The defeat of the enemy promised in Genesis 3:15 and completed at the final judgment (Rev. 20) is here anticipated (27:1). As a result, God's people can be assured of being fruitful in the end (27:6—cf. ch. 5, where that fruit had failed under the old covenant).

Finally, it must be noted that the chastening by the nations to purge the people and preserve the remnant has as its good purpose the preserving and calling of a people from all the nations to be God's holy people (27:7-9, 12, 13).

Isaiah has now established that God will judge all sinners, those in Judah and those in the nations, who have refused to be subject to his will. He will also save out of Judah and ultimately out of all the nations those who recognize their sinfulness and turn in repentance and trust to the Lord, waiting on him to accomplish their salvation.

Woes upon Evildoers (Isaiah 28-35). Now in a sweeping crescendo he solemnly pronounces *woe on the wicked* and declares *hope for the remnant who trust* (chs. 28—35). There is a weaving of these two themes all through this section. Here, as at the end of chapter 1, there are just two alternatives: God's judgment or God's blessing, woe or hope, death or life.

Woe to the proud (28:1-8). They are described as drunkards, staggering in their pride (vv. 1, 3, 7, 8). Their pursuit of strong drink destroys their ability to function in the leadership of Israel (v. 7). Verses 7 and 8 are a clear denunciation of strong drink. Yet even these verses offer hope for the remnant (v. 5).

Hope for those instructed by God's Word (28:9-13). Who then will understand? Who are the remnant? Those who learn the truth as a little child learns, line upon line, here a little, there a little; for the people are slow to learn (v. 10). Because of the prevalence of unbelief in Judah, God will speak to them by those using strange tongues and even then most will not believe (vv. 11-13). This is perhaps what happened at Pentecost (Acts 2:1-21—cf. 1 Cor. 14:22).

Woe to the scoffers who lead Judah (28:14, 15). These are those who have rejected God's Word and are substituting for it their own lies. They are in league with the devil and seek his protection instead (v. 15). We might compare here Peter's description of the last days (2 Pet. 3:3). Contrast their refuge in lies with the cover of the remnant (Isa. 4:5, 6).

Hope by the stone in Zion (28:16-29). This passage is clearly Messianic. It points to the coming Savior and likens him to a stone, i.e., the foundation of God's people (v. 16—see Rom. 9:33; 10:11; 1 Pet. 2:6). The only right relationship to the coming Savior is belief (v. 16). Only in him are the righteousness and justice which God expects in his children possible (v. 17; Gen. 18:19, Isa. 5:7). To escape the judgment of God against all sinners, it is imperative that the people cease to be scoffers of God's Word and believe (v. 22).

Woe to the false worshipers (29:1-21). Jerusalem is here called Ariel, which means "the lion of God" (v. 1). The symbolism probably comes from the words of Joel and Amos, who portray the Lord as a lion roaring from Zion (Joel 3:16, cf. Amos 1:2). The lion is also associated with David's throne (Rev. 5:5—cf. Gen. 49:9).

Here the problem is that the people go on through the ritual of worship (v. 1) but though their lips speak words honoring God, their hearts are far from him (v. 13). The heart of the people is wrong and, as God had established from the beginning, those not worshiping God from the heart in belief are not acceptable to him (Gen. 4:4, 5—cf. Heb. 11:4; 1 John 3:12). Woe comes to them because they think that in their hearts they can think as they please and not be known by God (v. 15).

Hope for the remnant who stand in awe of the Lord—29:22-24. These, like Abraham, respect God's Word and seek to honor him. They may err and even murmur, but God, in patience, leads them to the truth (v. 24).

Woe to the rebellious children (30:1-14). The imagery here is from the wilderness experience. It recalls the rebellion of many in the wilderness who in the end were cut off because of their unbelief (vv. 1, 2—cf. 1 Cor. 10:1-5; Heb. 3:17; Jude 5). They refused to hear God's Law (v. 9) in contrast to the remnant who hold God in awe and reverence (29:23). Their opposition to true prophets (v. 10) is similar to what Amos said (Amos 2:12; 7:13). As despisers of the Word, they are therefore to be punished (vv. 12, 13).

Hope by returning and waiting (30:15-33). The call here to returning and rest is one and the same as the call to wait on the Lord (v. 15). We shall see later how Habakkuk had to learn to wait for the day of chastisement to come, and how he learned to rest in faith. This passage is therefore addressed to the believers in the land who, with the unrighteous, must now face the hardship to come on Jerusalem because of her sin (vv. 18-20). God, by his still small voice will continue to guide and bless his people (v. 21—cf. 1 Kgs. 19:12). The description of God's latter-day blessings on his faithful ones is in terms of agricultural bliss in accord with God's practice of teaching spiritual truths through physical figures.

Woe to those who look to men rather than to God for help (31:1-9). Here the practice of many kings of Israel and Judah to seek alliances with men rather than to trust in God is denounced (31:1, 3, 6, 8). Compare also Hosea 7:11. In the Book of Isaiah itself in two historical sections we have the sharp contrast between a king who seeks human alliances, Ahaz (ch. 7), and a king who puts his trust in the Lord, Hezekiah (chs. 36-38).

Hope in the righteous king to come (32:1-8). The king mentioned earlier and his kingdom shall triumph in the end (v. 1—cf. 9:6, 7; 11:4, 5). God's grace shall be active in that kingdom and enable those who cannot see to see and who cannot hear to hear (vv. 3, 4—cf. 6:9, 10). God has his eye upon his children who are mistreated and will avenge them (vv. 5-8). By this we see that the miracles of Jesus' day pointed to God's power to heal the spiritually blind and deaf as well.

Woe to the women at ease (32:9-15). Again Isaiah directs particular rebuke to women who are at fault. Compare 3:16ff. and Amos 4:1ff. Verse 11 reminds us of Hosea's words in the opening chapters of his book. The picture in this section is that things will get worse until God intervenes in man's history and changes hearts. Isaiah, in verse 15, looks back to that promise through Joel (Joel 2:28).

Hope for those who look for God's righteousness and justice (32:16-20). The preceding verse speaks of the coming of God's Spirit and the resultant fruitful field (32:15). Building on that the prophet now declares that the fruit of the Spirit to be expected is righteousness and justice which God demands of his children (Gen. 18:19; Isa. 5:7—cf. Gal. 5:22, 23). Only by the gift of God's Spirit and his work can the people ever come to peace with God (v. 17) and live in true safety (v. 18).

Woe to the treacherous sinners in Zion (33:1-16). Once more the alternatives are laid out. God will punish and purge out those in Zion, his city, who are evil and are clearly not his children (33:1, 14). But God will be gracious to those whose trust is in the Lord, who wait for him and whose lives show that God's righteousness and justice are in them (vv. 2, 5, 15, 16). We see clearly here the principle that judgment must begin at the house of God as God purges out sinners from among his people (v. 14). Amos also taught the same thing. See Amos 3:2. Habakkuk later builds upon this theme particularly (compare also 1 Peter 4:17).

Hope in the Lord our King (33:17-24). We have seen how the hope more and more centers upon the one person, the Lord, our King to come. God will indeed keep his promise to be with his people as he first promised Moses (Exod. 3:12). Now it is clear that he will come in the flesh as the King of his people to rule over them and to save them (vv. 21, 22). (Compare Isaiah 7:14; 9:6, 7; 11:1-5.) As the Lord is declared to be the only true King of his people, the events of 1 Samuel 8 are seen to have been most futile. The declaration of Moses and the people at the crossing of the Red Sea is upheld, the Lord *is* King (Exod. 15:18). He never abdicates his throne.

We come now to the final stage of this series of woes and hope. As if in a summary of all that has been said in this section, Isaiah concludes that there shall be *woe to those who receive God's indignation* (34:1-17). Nations and people who displease God and rebel against him shall be punished forever (vv. 2, 3, 8, 10). The rest of the verses disclose the total destruction of the nations of the world and the resultant prosperity of the little creatures where men once built their cities of rebellion (vv. 4, 11-15).

At the same time, there shall be *hope for those who receive God's compassion* (35:1-10). God can make of that wilderness and desert, described above, a blessed place. In verses 1 and 2 he is speaking of the devastation described in 34:11-15. It shall be turned into a place of blessing for his people. Those who shall be privileged to share in the future blessings of the Lord are the weak, the feeble, the fearful who have put their trust in the Lord (vv. 3, 4). As was said before, God will open eyes to see and ears to hear (vv. 5, 6). Again we point out that when Jesus came opening eyes and ears, he was pointing to the fact that the time of God's grace to turn men to himself had indeed come (Matt. 11:5).

The great highway to Zion, the way for God's people to come to him, earlier noted in 2:2, 3, shall be provided (v. 8). This way of holiness is the only way man can come to God. Surely, this is therefore the way of salvation which the New Testament declares to be in Jesus Christ alone (John 14:1-6). No enemy of God, no sinner in unbelief will be able to come by Jesus to God (vv. 8, 9—cf. Rev. 21:26, 27).

Historical Illustrations (Isaiah 36-39). The next major section of Isaiah, chapters 36 to 39, are an historical illustration of the doctrine of trust in the Lord. We have already dealt with the events of this section in the study of 2 Kings 18-20. Here we shall only note that these chapters of Isaiah ought to be studied in contrast to chapter 7. In chapter 7 we have the case of Ahaz, Hezekiah's father, who did not believe and did not rely on God but on human strength rather than on God. As a result of his alliance with Assyria to defeat his enemies, Syria and Israel, he instigated the invasion not only of Syria and Israel but even of Judah itself, for the king of Assyria was not satisfied to stop at Judah's borders, as Ahaz had thought, but kept coming until, in 701 B.C., he reached the very gates of Jerusalem. Meantime, Ahaz had died but this left his son Hezekiah faced with a formidable enemy all because Ahaz had not trusted in the Lord.

In Isaiah 36 to 39 we note how Hezekiah, in contrast to his father, did look to the Lord, encouraged by the faithful prophet Isaiah. And God delivered Jerusalem out of the hands of Assyria because Hezekiah had put his trust in God and not in men.

Hope For God's People (Isaiah 40-66). We come finally to *the last major section of Isaiah, chapters 40 to 66.* We have seen how, in the preceding chapters, Isaiah has interwoven the themes of God's purpose, Israel's sin, their punishment and the hope for the remnant. This final section is a development of the hope theme, before introduced, and is therefore addressed to the remnant. It is they to whom the words "comfort ye, comfort ye my people" apply. God's remnant are the believers who are in the church in that day and always.

The entire section is divided into three parts, all of these having to do with the message or Word of God, as follows: 1) God's Word, the promise (chs. 40-55); 2) God's Word, the commandment (chs. 56-62); 3) God's Word, the judgment (chs. 63 to 66).

Remember that God had said that he would accomplish his great work of changing hearts through the hearing of his Word. This, as we have noted, was implied in the experience of Elijah at Sinai (refer to our comments in 1 Kings 19). In this first part of the final section of Isaiah 40 to 55, God develops this truth. The whole section, 40 to 55, is embraced by two strong affirmations about God's Word. *First, God's Word shall stand forever* (40:8). *Second, God's Word will not return to God void* (55:11), but accomplish what God pleases and prosper in what God has sent it to do. Therefore we see here the affirmation that God's promise as expressed in his Word and revealed by the prophets will never fail. Men have indeed failed.

The word "comfort" used to open this entire section (40:1, 2) recalls the words of 12:1. God has a word of comfort for his remnant, those who have believed in him. It tells us that the entire section is a message of comfort to God's children; and then it proceeds to enumerate the bases of this comfort.

There is *comfort because God exalts the lowly* (40:3-5). In accord with what God has often said, he lifts the humble and puts down the proud (v. 4—cf. 1 Sam. 2; Isa. 2:11, etc.). The Gospel writers applied this passage to John the Baptist and his duty as Christ's forerunner (Matt. 3:3; Luke 3:4-6). In the end, God will raise those who have been humbled by their own failure and who sense their need of God's strength.

There is *comfort because when all else fails, God's Word will not fail* (40:6-8). Salvation cannot come by flesh and blood (human strength), it must come by God's strength, declared by his Word.

There is *comfort because God is the Shepherd of his flock* (49:9-11). Here the Lord is portrayed as the Great Shepherd. At one and the same time, his arm is mighty to save and protect (v. 10) and also gentle to gather God's sheep, the remnant who believe (v. 11) (compare Psalm 23; John 10:1-18).

There is *comfort because God is sovereign* (40:12-31). This passage gives us an awesome picture of God's greatness. God is great in his creative power (v. 12), great in his knowledge (vv. 13, 14), great in his dealings with nations in history (vv. 15-17—cf. chapters 13 to 24). God is so great that men appear as insignificant before him (vv. 22-24). God is great in his power (v. 26).

Because God is so great, he knows all things and nothing escapes his sight. He knows the needs of his own and in his sovereign power he can give power to those who wait upon him (vv. 28, 29). The only answer therefore for the remnant who trust in the Lord is to wait on him, that is, to look to God and await his answers to their needs and his action on their behalf (v. 31).

The word "wait" found here is a key word of the prophets. It denotes not idleness but living on in the expectation of God's doing what he has promised to do for his children.

Isaiah has already used the word several times beginning in 8:17. A survey of Isaiah's use of this word "wait" gives us clear understanding of its importance. In 8:17, Isaiah expresses his own intention to wait for the Lord, until the Lord reveals his face (favor) to his people. In 25:9, he shows that his own intent to wait is the proper attitude for all of God's children. All wait for God's salvation. In 26:8, 9, he shows that this waiting is in the form of a soul-felt desire for God. In 30:18, Isaiah shows that God's children must wait because God is waiting for the acceptable time of redemption. And all who wait on him are counted among the blessed (cf. Matt. 5:3-12). Finally, in 33:2, he shows that the confidence of God's child is in God's arm of salvation which is able to save to the uttermost all who look to and wait upon him.

There is also *comfort because God's covenant with Abraham will not fail* (41:1-16). The certainty of God's plan of salvation rests solely upon the eternal power and presence of the Lord. There was none before the Lord who could control God nor is there any who comes after God and who can alter God's intention or plan (41:4).

Verses 8 to 14 express beautifully God's good purpose as it embraces his whole people including those whom he will call from the ends of the earth. Based on his friendship for Abraham and his having chosen him and his seed (v. 8—cf. Gen. 18:19) God will call a people from all the nations of the earth (v. 9). His promise to all is just as it was to Moses when he first called him (Exod. 3). "I will be with you" (v. 10). Note the three words of encouragement here to God's children: I will strengthen thee . . . I will help thee . . . I will uphold thee . . ." (v. 10). As he promised Abraham in Genesis 12:3, so he applies that promise to all believers now (v. 11).

In verse 14 he uses that terminology which he had used in Exodus, calling himself their redeemer. The whole concept of the seed of Abraham coming from all nations is further expounded upon by Paul in Romans 4:16-18; 9:6-8.

There is *comfort because God is a God of compassion* (41:17-29). In the prophets, synonyms for the believers include "the poor," "the needy," and similar terms (v. 17). God sees the needs of the helpless who recognize their plight and he will respond to their cry. Men have to be brought low in order that they may know that it is God alone who can help them (v. 20). It is certain that no help can be found among men (vv. 28, 29).

There is *comfort because God has a chosen servant* who shall come among men and who is able to do all that God has willed (42:1-25). Here the term "servant" surely applies to the Messiah, the Christ. He is that child to be born of a virgin (7:14), who is truly God in the flesh (9:6, 7). God declares his complete pleasure in the Christ (v. 1—cf. Matt. 3:17). Joined to the promise of his bringing the gospel to Gentiles as well, is the forewarning of his suffering (vv. 2, 3). He will accomplish that justice (perfect obedience to all of God's law) (v. 4) which God has demanded of his children from the beginning (Gen. 18:19). He makes clear in this passage that the redeemer, the Christ, is no less than God himself (vv. 6-8).

God's people are in darkness and need God's light. They are blind and deaf to God's gospel. They need Gos's power to see and to hear. Compare Isaiah 6:9-13.

The Law perfectly expresses God's will for his people, but left to themselves, the people cannot keep that Law nor please God (v. 22). This is why they need a servant of God to come who can perfectly do all of God's righteousness and justice.

There is *comfort because God has purposed to redeem his people* (43:1-21). Here the Lord shows clearly that he is the only Savior. They should expect no other. In the words of Exodus 3:15, he promises to be with his own, having loved them (v. 4). Note again how he shows that he will call his own from all nations (vv. 5, 6, 7).

In words reminiscent of Acts 1:8, the Lord calls his own whom he has redeemed to be his witnesses. He shows that the very purpose for which he has saved them is that they may know him (believe in him) and declare him to be the only Savior (vv. 10, 11). We are all called to be to the praise of his glory (v. 21—cf. Eph. 1:6, 12, 14).

There is *comfort because God truly forgives the sins of his children* (43:22-28). Left to themselves, men will not call on the Lord (v. 22). Men will not rightly even fulfill the ceremonial law given by God to teach them repentance and humility (v. 23). As Isaiah had said in the opening verses of his Book, the people's sins are ever a burden and weariness to God (v. 24—cf. 1:13, 14). We have seen this also through the writings of Joel, Amos and Hosea.

But God will deal with the sin of his children once and for all in order that they may be no more a burden to God or to us (v. 25). All hope in human strength is vain, it cannot get rid of sin (v. 27). Only in God is there hope therefore.

There is *comfort because God will revive, give life to his own* (44:1-23). The personal relationship of each of God's children begins not when he first believes in the Lord, but long before. God made and formed his children in the womb, even before they were born (v. 2) and Paul tells us that we were chosen in Christ before God even created the world (Eph. 1:4).

Like rain from heaven on dry unproductive ground, so will be the outpouring of God's Holy Spirit on his children whom he has chosen, when the proper time comes (v. 3). This reminds us of Joel's words earlier (Joel 2:28) and even Isaiah in 32:15. Verse 5 of Isaiah 44 shows how God's children all come to the consciousness that they are his children after the Holy Spirit comes on them and regenerates them to eternal life.

This wonderful hope by the mighty God is in awesome contrast to the ignorant men who hope in images which they have carved (vv. 6-20). Only the redemption purposed by God brings the response of believers in praise to God (vv. 21-23).

There is comfort because God is central in all history and will work all things for the good of his people according to his purpose (44:24—46:13). Here the Lord begins with an affirmation of his control over all things, as seen in creation (v. 24) and demonstrated in all history and events of men (v. 25), culminating in his determination to carry out his good purpose on behalf of his children as he has spoken through his servant (v. 26).

Immediately following the Lord speaks a name not yet heard by the ears of men and names a future ruler of a great empire not yet on the horizon of history, the name is Cyrus (44:28; 45:1). He declares that he has foretold Cyrus' coming to serve God's purposes in order that his own people may be assured that God is indeed the sovereign of all history and of the life of man, not only in the present but in the future as well (45:4).

This section expands upon the greatness of Israel's God as the unique, only true God (v. 5). That greatness is particularly seen in his power to create light and darkness (a reminder of the beginning of creation—Gen. 1) and to create peace and evil (45:7). Here we need to remember that the term "evil" can refer either to man's illegal deeds against God's will or the resultant punishment which God sends on those who have done evil. The same Hebrew word is used in both senses and of course here the latter meaning is obvious. God can either bring to men peace if they trust in him or evil (judgment) if they do not (compare 9:6; 26:12; 32:17; 48:22; 53:5; 57:21 and also 26:3).

God is the only God with whom men have to do. Therefore, those who do not make peace with God are in great danger (45:9). This of course leads to an invitation to all to look to this sovereign God who alone has the answer to our needs (45:22-24).

God who is the Lord of the universe, is the Redeemer who presents himself here, able to control all nature and all history (46:10, 11). He will therefore call Cyrus out of the future history of man to do his will and liberate his people from captivity in Babylon. This is the God of Israel!

There is *comfort because God surely judges the evil ones who will not repent* (ch. 47). Babylon, as we have seen in Scripture, represents the worldly kingdoms on earth which stand against God's kingdom. They too are under God's control. Just as the Lord had said to Israel long before, so now he says again that he will overthrow the enemies of God and of God's people (47:1).

The reason for God's wrath against Babylon here is seen in the way they will deal with his people (47:5, 6). True, God shall deliver Israel into the hands of Babylon. But the Babylonians will not deal with Israel out of a sense of service to God, but rather as a proud and boastful people (47:7, 10). Note that God speaks of Babylon's activities as already past. This is frequently done so that we may see that with God the future is as certain as the past.

We note too that the final judgment on Babylon shall have no appeal. It will be final (v. 11). All of their magic and confidence in the flesh will fail (vv. 12, 13).

There is *comfort because God will surely call his own to himself* (ch. 48—50). God by no means overlooks the sinfulness of Israel. He sees there are many hypocrites (48:1, 2). He has told them of the future deliverance from Babylon so that they cannot at that time say that their idols have saved them (v. 56). God will deliver his own children but will not spare them the affliction of war and captivity (vv. 9, 10). God will allow his children to be carried off with the rest of Israel who are not his believers. But all of this could have been avoided. It came only because the people would not keep God's commandments and have respect to his will (48:18). Now God will purge Israel in the furnace of affliction (Babylon) and the wicked will not know peace there (48:22).

Chapter 49 gives us a picture of Israel personified. The true Israel was chosen by God from the womb (49:1). Later the same thing will be said about one of his children, Jeremiah (see Jer. 1:5). God intended to be glorified in his people when he called them out of the womb of Egypt (49:3) and made his covenant with them in the wilderness. But Israel learned through painful experience both in the wilderness and afterwards in all of her history that she could not do God's will. Her labor was in vain (v. 4). This became apparent in the days of the judges and nothing later changed the fact that Israel was too weak to save herself and too faithless to serve God.

But God does not give up. He will bring Israel again to himself (v. 5). God has great plans for his people. They are not only to be to his glory but shall also glorify him among the nations (v. 6). What God promised to Abraham must surely come to pass. The seed of Abraham will be a blessing to the nations (see Gen. 22:18).

At the present time, even as Isaiah brought this message, it seemed that Judah was forsaken. Later, at the fall of Jerusalem, it would seem even more so, but God has not forsaken nor forgotten them even as he did not forget Israel in Egypt long before (49:14, 15).

The lesson here is clear. God's true people must expect to suffer greatly when the visible church (in this case Israel) has disobeyed God. Nevertheless, God does not forget his people who trust in him. He will preserve them to be his witnesses to the nations. Note that Paul uses verse 6 to show that when the Jews had rejected the Gospel, then the apostles had to turn to the Gentiles (cf. Acts 13:47 and Matt. 28:20).

Returning to the motif given by Hosea earlier, Isaiah now shows that though God puts away his people, as a man may put away his wife by a bill of divorcement; nevertheless, God can redeem or buy her back (50:1, 2). In the rest of this chapter (ch. 50) Isaiah speaks as representative of the true believers. God has intervened and made them obedient (v. 5). Therefore they can take whatever comes and know that God will not forsake them (v. 5). This is very similar to the conclusion that Habakkuk came to in his third chapter after God had shown him the necessity of the Babylonian captivity. Much of what is said here reminds us of the suffering of Christ. Surely Christ did suffer for us, taking our place and was himself spat upon (Matt. 26:67; 27:30). Nevertheless, Isaiah is here speaking of the affliction of every believer who suffers when God has to judge his church and purge it.

As we said before, the one thing that distinguishes God's children from the hypocrites is their trust in the Lord (50:10—cf. Isa. 12:2).

There is *comfort because God will reaffirm constantly his covenant with Abraham* (51:1—52:2). Much as Paul later does, so Isaiah here appeals to the institution of God's covenant with his people back in the time of Abraham. He sees all of God's children (those

who follow after righteousness) as the children of Abraham,
springing from the same covenant established on faith in God
(cf. Rom. 4:1-18). This is the comfort God offers to his children
(51:3).

God again makes clear that what he requires of his children
(righteousness and justice—Gen. 18:19), he will provide himself
on their behalf (Isa. 51:4, 5). Therefore he calls their salvation *his*
salvation. The evidence that we are God's children is the evidence that God has worked in our hearts his work of salvation.
We *know* righteousness (God's righteousness reckoned to us as to
Abraham—Gen. 15:6) and therefore guard God's Law in our
hearts (v. 7).

That joy and gladness so evidently missing in Joel's day (Joel
1) shall be seen in those whom God ransoms from sin and death
(51:11). Thus it is God who is the ground of our comfort, God
and his work (51:12).

The particular distinction of those who are God's people in
that day is that they have his Word entrusted to them, the message of God to men. All of God's people then become as
prophets of God, spokesmen for God on earth. They have God's
Word in their hearts by God's direct action of saving them and
making them his children (cf. Deut. 18:18; 30:14 and Rom.
10:8).

The spiritual stupor into which Israel had fallen is like unto a
drunk person (51:17ff.). God will now sober up his people who
have gone through affliction so that they may walk straight before God. God no doubt looks to the final state of his people
when he promises the day to come when all unbelievers will be
purged out of his church (52:1, 2).

We must see then that God constantly reassures his people
who live in a sinful world and even in a church visible which is
replete with unbelievers and hypocrites, that it will not always be
so. The church of the future, of eternity, will be without blemish.
It will be filled with holy people who shall be able to dwell before
God in a relationship of love (see Eph. 1:4). God will never
abandon his purpose and present situations to the contrary, God
will have such a church. It is necessary therefore for God from
time to time to remind his people of this because the church in
the present age (until Christ returns) is going to be imperfect.

There is *hope because God has declared his plan of redemption*
(52:3—55:13). At such an early stage it might have been asking
too much to hope for God to lay out vividly that plan of salvation
which he would work out some 800 years later. Yet God in his
graciousness does just that. We get therefore in these chapters a
preview of the work of Christ written so vividly that one might

think that Isaiah was an eyewitness of God's work of redemption through Jesus Christ.

In 52:3-12, Isaiah introduces God's plan of salvation which is about to be revealed. First he tells Isaiah that God's plan will cost Israel nothing. They have nothing of value to pay God. They are broke spiritually and have nothing to offer God. Therefore God's plan will not involve their bringing anything to him. In fact, they can be ready to receive his salvation only when they are willing to acknowledge their spiritual poverty (52:3, 4).

He calls this plan which he is about to unfold "good tidings," as he had done earlier in 40:9 (52:7). The good news in essence is that God still rules (v. 7). This tells the people that in spite of all of the unstable and uncertain history of Israel's past, her God, who is steadfast, is still in charge of all. Nothing that has happened is too difficult for Israel's God to handle.

In 52:13 to 53:12, we have the heart of God's plan of salvation declared. Returning to the servant motif which is seen all through this section (Isa. 41:8, 9; 42:1, 19; 43:10; 44:1, 2, 21, 26; 45:4; 48:20; 49:3, 5, 6), the Lord presents the servant here as one individual. He is characterized by his wise dealing (52:13). By this we recognize that he, unlike Israel, will consistently not only know God's Word but obey it. This is the biblical meaning of wise living. He will therefore succeed where Israel, the servant of God, has failed.

Here there is inserted in the midst of the prediction of his success a sober warning—he will not look the part of a victor! (v. 14). This verse will have to await the next chapter for any explanation; nevertheless, we must take note of it here.

The next verse, 15, goes on to tell of his success. He shall sprinkle many nations. The reference to his sprinkling perhaps refers to Numbers 19:18-21. In that passage we are told of the clean person who shall purify what is unclean as he sprinkles the purifying water on the unclean. Later, Ezekiel would also make reference to this sprinkling that is to be done by God in purifying all of his children. In that latter context the sprinkling is clearly identified with the saving work of the Holy Spirit (Ezek. 36:24-27).

In the New Testament this cleansing work applied by the Holy Spirit is called the work of regeneration and renewing of the Holy Spirit poured out on believers through the work of Christ (Tit. 3:3-7). The writer to the Hebrews therefore sees the Old Testament ceremonial sprinkling as figurative of the sprinkling by the Holy Spirit, i.e., the work of regeneration (Heb. 9:13, 19; 10:22).

The words in Isaiah 52 indicate that as the nations are sprinkled they shall see and understand (v. 15). This points to the miraculous work of rebirth or regeneration by which men who were blind and ignorant of spiritual things are made alive and able to respond to God's invitation to come. This is nothing less than Jesus told Nicodemus later: "except one be born anew, he cannot *see* the kingdom of God" (John 3:3).

Thus the blindness and ignorance of the hearers, of which the Lord warned Isaiah in calling him, will be dealt with by God, giving them new eyes to see and minds to comprehend the truth of God. This is the significance of rebirth itself and why it is that in any sound doctrine, rebirth must precede the expression of repentance and faith on the part of the believer.

Chapter 53, which is frequently attested to in the New Testament as a prophecy concerning Christ (see for example Acts 8:32, 33), begins by asking a question (53:1). The question is in the Hebrew form of parallelism, that is, the second line is to be taken as a parallel thought to the first line and states the same thing in different words. This is the normal mark of Hebrew poetry. In this case therefore the question "Who has believed our message?" is answered in the second line "To whom has the arm of the Lord been revealed?"

As we said earlier, none can believe except it be first revealed to him by the Lord through the Holy Spirit. So, those who will believe are those to whom God's salvation has been revealed. The description of salvation as represented by God's arm is in accord with what we have seen in 40:10, 11 of the arm of God as both ruler and tender shepherd.

Already, in 52:14, we are warned that God's salvation and God's servant sent to save would not look the part. Beginning in 53:2, 3, he elaborates on this fact.

He is like a plant rooted in dry, unproductive land (v. 2). This indicates that he is not a product of the soil. Thus the servant will not succeed because of his background or environment.

His virgin birth, already mentioned earlier (see Isa. 7:14), would also indicate that his birth is by an act of God, not of man. He is of the stem of Jesse (11:1) but not a product of David's line.

As a man, there is nothing about him to attract men to him (v. 2). This by no means means that he was ugly. But neither was he the handsome rugged "man's man." His success would not depend on his looks.

Indeed, his would be a hard life. He was despised (v. 3), meaning simply that men saw no great value in him (such would be the case with the carpenter's son). He was a man of sorrows, acquainted with grief. Sorrow was around him. Hard life did not escape him. He would not be what the world called successful in his business, therefore he was despised (counted of little worth, counted for little with men).

This is why the prophet warned earlier that his visage was marred so that he did not look the part of the Savior.

But now, verses 4-6, Isaiah explains that his deceptive appearance was for a very good reason. The grief and sorrow he bore was for ourselves, what we ought to have borne (v. 4). What appeared to be affliction for his own sin was in reality his suffering on our behalf. It was because we were sinners and he suffered our punishment. Thus, in judging him afflicted and smitten of God, men were in reality judging themselves. What they saw fall upon him really was what ought to have fallen upon *them*.

Here the concept of substitutionary atonement (one suffering on behalf of others to bring peace between the sinner and God), which was first seen in Genesis 22:8, 13 and then reenacted at the Passover event (Exod. 12:3-7; 12:13) and later instituted into the entire sacrificial system, here comes to its full meaning and development in the concept of one faithful servant of God being the substitute for all of those servants who were in themselves not able to be faithful because of their sinfulness.

The festers and sores with which Israel was inflicted according to chapter 1:6, are dealt with by the stripes of punishment which God's servant would take on our behalf (v. 5).

Natural man, like a wandering sheep, goes astray, turning to what pleases him as opposed to God's way (v. 6—cf. Gen. 18:19). The Hebrew expression "laid on him" really reads, "caused to come to rest on him." He is the focal point of all of our sin.

Verses 7-9 detail the events surrounding his death, how he suffered without complaint (compare Matt. 26:63; 27:12, 14). His being likened to a lamb for slaughter recalls Abraham's words in Genesis 22:8 as well as the later words of John the Baptist in John 1:36.

Again, as indicated in 52:14 and 53:3, all of his suffering, though for the sake of God's children, was hardly so recognized when it occurred. His own generation was not able to see the significance of his suffering (v. 8).

Though it was the intent of those who killed him to shame him in the process by having him die with the wicked (v. 9), Isaiah foretells that nevertheless, his death would be with a rich man (v. 9). It is as though the Lord would say after his death, "That is enough. Now let him be honored." We do know that Jesus, in accord with this verse, was intentionally crucified between two known thieves, thus identifying him with sinners (Matt. 27:38). Yet so did God ordain that he was buried in the grave of a nobleman who was rich (Matt. 27:57-60).

This later honor done to his body after his death would be because in reality he had done no violence or deceit (Isa. 53:9). Thus God overruled whatever intention there might have been to disgrace or perhaps desecrate the body of his servant by his enemies. Once he had died, he had paid the full penalty. He had done his work. It was finished. Compare John 19:30.

The final verses of Isaiah 53, give us the theological import of these events of the suffering and death of God's perfect servant. From the time of the Exodus, the Lord had been teaching the people that there was only one place where true sacrifice was to be offered, the place of God's choosing (Deut. 12:5-11, 13, 14). This place, symbolically represented in the Old Testament by the altar at the sanctuary which was first at Shiloh and later at Jerusalem, no doubt pointed to the one place where God would meet man, at the place of his perfect servant's death, that is, in Christ, where men can worship God in spirit and in truth. Compare John 4:23-24.

The words which declare that it pleases the Lord to bruise him seem harsh until we realize that this statement is to be taken in the context of his being an offering for sin (53:10). We must remember that God had said earlier that he was not pleased with the works and efforts of sinful men (Isa. 1:11). Therefore a better and more perfect sacrifice was needed. This, we are taught here, was provided by God's servant with whom God was well pleased (compare Matt. 3:17; 12:18; 17:5). God was not pleased with the act of sinful men who put his servant to death but he was pleased to ordain Christ's death as a substitute for our own death which we deserved (compare Acts 2:23, 24). Here we see in one act both God's judgment on sin and his grace toward his children whom he spared through the death of his servant.

The reward of the servant who so suffered on our behalf is that his work will succeed. He will see his seed (53:10), all whom the Father has given to him (compare John 6:37, 39). He will make long (eternal) not only his days but those of the rest of God's children. God will be satisfied with the servant's suffering and accept it on our behalf (v. 11). The key to this satisfaction is in the fact of the servant of God being all that God required us to be, righteous (v. 11).

Verse 12, in summary, states again that his death was beneficial to the blessing of a whole multitude (all who trust on the Lord, as God's Word throughout Scripture teaches). He saved God's children not only because he died but also because he died a transgressor's death (v. 12). He saved God's children not only because the sin of the many centered upon him but also because he would make intercession for the transgressors (v. 12—cf. John 17:2, 9:17, 20, 24).

In Isaiah 54, God's plan of salvation just revealed is applied to the chosen recipients of the benefits of Christ's death and triumph over sin and death. The recipients are numerous. They are like children of a barren woman, adopted (54:1). In apparent reference to the prophecy of Noah long ago, God shows that the tent of dwelling of God's people must be enlarged to take in the large number that shall be added to the people of God (54:2, 3). Reread Genesis 9:25-27 where Noah foretells that Japheth (representative of the Gentiles) shall live in the tents of Shem.

In the Old Testament era, few Gentiles entered into Israel to become children of God, but that would change. After the Savior's death and accomplished work of redemption, room will be made for Jew and Gentile. Believers shall join God's family from all of the nations (54:3—Isaiah 2:3, 4; Matt. 28:19, 20).

In verses 4-8, another analogy is used. This time God is seen as the husband and his people are seen as his bride. This motif is similar to that of Hosea. The wife had been faithless and forsaken, but God takes her back. In all, the time of discipline seemed short compared to the time of God's mercy, which is everlasting (vv. 7, 8). This means that the suffering and hardship of this world endured by God's children both before and after their conversion, is nothing to be compared with eternal blessings stored up for them. Compare Romans 8:18. Verses 7 and 8 summarize the simultaneous judgment of sin by God in Christ and the determined purpose of God to have a people.

In verse 9, the Lord shows that his general covenant with all mankind established at the time of the flood was indicative of the special covenant of God with his own children whom he now promises are at peace with God, not to be punished for sin since God is satisfied with Christ as our substitute (53:11). This is here called the covenant of peace—peace between God and believers (v. 10—cf. Rom. 5:1).

The remainder of the chapter assures us of that comfort so long awaited (v. 11). It also teaches that the application of the work of Christ to us shall come by our being taught of God, i.e., regenerated by his Holy Spirit so that we have eyes to see and ears to hear and hearts to understand what God in Christ has done for us (compare 50:5; 51:7). Jesus later shows that Isaiah 54:13 does have reference to regeneration (John 6:44, 45—compare 1 Thes. 4:9; 1 John 2:27).

This, Isaiah calls the heritage of all of the servants of the Lord (54:17). We receive all of the benefits of the death of the perfect servant of God, the Christ, described in chapter 53. We are reckoned as righteous, just as was Abraham, because the righteousness of God is applied to us in Christ. Thus God provides for us what he has demanded of us.

Finally, the gracious invitation of God to men *to come* and partake of this plan is offered (Isa. 55:1-7).

God had said that he would freely provide water for the poor and needy (Isa. 41:17). Now, this water of life is freely offered to all who are thirsty (55:1—cf. John 4:10-14). Note that the invitation is to everyone who is thirsty (v. 1). Consistently, God's gracious invitation goes out to all (compare 45:22; Matt. 11:28; Rev. 22:17). None of God's children therefore has the right to restrict the free invitation. We know of course that only as God works in the hearts of men to make them know their poverty and thirst, their need of him, will they respond. They must be taught of God in order to know their need of him (54:13). But when it comes to the offer of salvation, it must be made to all, without distinction.

The offer is a free gift, not purchased by the things men value (55:1, 2). The sure mercies of David, mentioned in verse 3, refer to the kind of mercy which David himself knew and expressed in his 51st Psalm. On that same basis of a contrite and broken heart for sin, God will show his mercy to all who confess their sin and their need of him (compare 54:7). That mercy is here beautifully described (55:6, 7). It is sure because it is dependent upon God and not upon man.

This plan of salvation which God has now presented is shown to be not according to man's thoughts, because man would always see his "good works" as a part of any plan he helped to devise. Caution is therefore given lest we reject God's plan simply because we do not think as God thinks (55:7-9). God sees our so-called "righteousness" as filthy rags (see 64:6). As the writer of the Proverbs has said, "there is a way which seemeth right unto a man; but the end thereof are the ways of death" (Prov. 14:12).

In conclusion of this whole first part of the last main section of Isaiah once more the Lord returns to the certainty of his Word accomplishing all that he has purposed it to do (v. 11—cf. 40:6-8). We see therefore that the certainty of the word depends on the speaker of the word, the Lord, the provider to all men of their daily bread (v. 10). He has always proved trustworthy and dependable in the natural provisions he has made, and his Word is sure as it speaks of the provision for our salvation.

Verses 12 and 13 conclude the whole first part of the final major section of Isaiah (chs. 40 to 55) with a typical agricultural representation of the blessings of God on his people. The first part of the final major section of Isaiah has dealt with *God's*

Word, the promise. Next, we shall look at the second part of the final section, *God's Word, the commandment* (ch. 56—62).

The second part of the last division of Isaiah's prophecy begins in chapter 56 and goes through chapter 62. This section could be titled *God's Word, the commandment,* because it is still dealing with God's Word but now particularly as it serves as a guide for believers. God is showing here that he expects something of those who are redeemed. As Paul states in Ephesians 2:10, we are saved for good works, to walk in God's will.

Here God once more lifts up the standard he expects in all believers: righteousness and justice (56:1). This is that same standard which he originally set before Abraham (Gen. 18:19) and which he has never altered.

Thus, God's children, redeemed as God has shown already in the earlier chapters, are now to live in a manner demonstrating that they are indeed the children of God (v. 2). The Sabbath commandment is possibly mentioned here (vv. 2-5) because it was the original purpose of God to set aside that day as symbolic of the eternal fellowship of God with his people. It was established at creation. At the time of the giving of the Law it was treated as a commandment already known and practiced.

I believe that the Sabbath commandment can test the believer's spiritual state. God's child is therefore marked as one who enjoys the Sabbath. It is like that eternal rest with God. If the Sabbath is for him irksome and tiresome, then either he is misusing it or he is not yet ready for eternity.

Later, in 58:13, 14, God elaborates on Sabbath observance. We shall therefore at that point consider the subject in more detail.

Included here in chapter 56 among the children of God are those who were traditionally despised by most of Israel: the foreigner (vv. 3, 6, 7); the eunuch (vv. 3-5) and the other outcasts of Israel (v. 8). God's grace and love are thus extended to all, no matter their past or present predicament, who trust in the Lord (v. 8). To them will be given the power to be called the sons of God (v. 5). They are among those who will ultimately come to God's holy mountain, i.e., to salvation and heaven (v. 7—cf. Isa. 2:2-4).

Such people will not only be joyful but their works and worship will be acceptable because they have trusted in the Lord and not in themselves (v. 7). We contrast this with the former state of Israel without faith in God (Isa. 1:11-15). We compare this with David's contrition after sin and his complete trust in God which would once more make his worship acceptable to God (Psa.

51:19). We see then here a return to the significance of the very
first sacrifice offered by men: Cain's being unacceptable because
he trusted in himself and not in God while Abel's was accepted
because he offered it in faith (Gen. 4:3-8 compare 1 John 3:12;
Heb. 11:4).

In the rest of the chapter 56 (56:9-12) and on into a portion of
chapter 57, he returns to speak to those who still do not trust and
are therefore unchanged from the former state of Israel which
was declared in chapter 1. In the unbelieving church men still
turn to their own way for selfish reasons (56:11). They make the
righteous believer suffer and even put him out (57:1).

Such people are called the seed of an adulterer after the manner of Hosea (57:3-10). They trust in their own righteousness
which is altogether unacceptable to God (v. 12 compare 64:6).
They are to be judged and have no hope (v. 13a).

In contrast, God is pleased with those who put their trust in
him (57:13b). He demands a people humble and contrite in
heart, who recognize their sinfulness and helplessness to save
themselves (v. 15). This is what is meant by *repenting* (compare
Psa. 51:17). Such people put their trust in God and seek refuge
in him (v. 13b). This is what is meant by *believing*. God promises
to revive such people, to lift them up (v. 15). Here we can compare the same truths as were declared by Hannah, the mother of
Samuel long before (1 Sam. 2:1-10) i.e., God judges the proud
and comforts the humble.

The concept of peace, mentioned in 54:10, is here recalled.
There will be peace to the believers near and far (Jew and Gentile) (compare Rom. 5:1), but no peace to the wicked (those who
do not see their need of God) (57:19-21).

In chapter 58, the Lord shows specifically what is expected of
the believer. The old man (the sinful practices of the past) must
be put away so that their lives truly glorify God. Such a process
can be painful, for even in their attempts to please God they sin,
not observing the Law as God requires and intends it to be kept
(58:1, 2).

As examples he notes their method of fasting (vv. 3-9) and of
Sabbath observance (vv. 13, 14). They fast and wonder why God
is not pleased (v. 3), but they fast selfishly and not to glorify God
(vv. 3-5). In their fasting their concern is with outward show and
not inward commitment. God therefore calls for a fast that will
do some good, will help the needy (vv. 6, 7). Instead of just
giving up bread for a day, let them take that bread and feed the
hungry. Instead of giving up some pieces of clothing and putting on sack cloth, let them use their clothing to cover the naked.

If they do this, they are really fasting as God desires and God will be glorified and their communion with God will be sweet (vv. 8, 9a). Compare Jesus in the Sermon on the Mount as he deals similarly with such acts of worship as fasting (Matt. 6:2-18).

In other words, God's people ought to examine their present practices and life to determine what pleases God and what does not. They ought to cease doing evil and begin to do good (vv. 9b-12). In doing so they will be a light that shines in the darkness of this world (v. 10) (compare Matt. 5:14-16). They will also be a blessing to others like a well-watered garden (v. 11—compare Psa. 1). Finally, they will be like the repairer of a breach, makers of peace (v. 12—cf. Matt. 5:9).

As for Sabbath observance, this too is to be done to God's glory. Therefore the objective is to seek not what pleases self but what pleases the Lord on that day (v. 13). It is the only way we can give that day to God for his glory.

Note that the day is to be a delight to God's child. When one can spend that day in pleasing and serving the Lord and consider it a delight, then he is truly glorifying God and truly getting ready for the eternal Sabbath with the Lord and his people.

In chapters 59-62, we have a summary of the whole message of comfort given through Isaiah. That message is both summarized and analyzed. It begins with the recognition of Israel's sin and its consequence: separation from God (59:1-8). Their works cannot save them, indeed their works condemn them (vv. 6, 7). The fault is not God's (v. 1) but because they cannot do God's will (v. 8).

Those who look to the people for the answer to their needs look in vain (59:9-15). There is no hope, no savior among men.

God too knows this: therefore he provides that salvation which men can never accomplish in themselves (v. 16). Here we see that great doctrine already expounded in chapter 53. The armor noted here (v. 17) is the same armor listed in Ephesians 6:13ff. It constitutes the garments of salvation provided by God (compare Rev. 7:14; 19:11-16). The Redeemer who will lead God's people into triumph is described in 59:20, 21. God's covenant of grace and mercy is sure because it is based on the works of the Redeemer and the Spirit of God and the sure Word of God put into the mouths of God's people. These then are a people born of God's Spirit.

Here in chapter 60 begins the song of triumph of the people of God. It is creation all over again. Light shines out of darkness (60:1, 2), a symbolic way of expressing the inevitable triumph of God's grace in the hearts of so many (compare John 1:4, 5; 2 Cor. 4:6; Isa. 9:2). Verse 3 simply harkens back to chapter 2 again.

We see the glorified Jerusalem, the new Jerusalem of God's people forever (60:4-22). It is a glorious city (compare Rev. 21:2-27). Verse 10 seems to point to the prophesy of Noah long before, that the seed of Canaan (the unbelievers) would serve the seed of Shem (the believers—see the discussion of Gen. 9:25-27).

Jesus applies the opening words of chapter 61 to himself (Luke 4:18, 19). Again we note the comfort theme (61:2). Verse 6 recalls the covenant of God with Israel as expressed at Sinai (Exod. 19:6 cf. 1 Pet. 2:9). These blessed ones, the citizens of the glorified city of Jerusalem, Zion, are the seed of woman, the remnant, the true people of God (v. 9 cf. Gen. 3:15 etc.).

Once more (61:10—62:12) glorified Zion is portrayed, this time as a bride adorned for her bridegroom. This figure is also used in Rev. 21:2. God will have his holy people (62:12) as he purposed before creation (Eph. 1:4), and as he said to Israel at Sinai (Exod. 19:6).

We come now to the third and final section of the latter part of Isaiah. This deals with *God's Word, the judgment* (chapters 63-66).

There is judgment against the nations that do not believe and which oppose God's people (chs. 63, 64). The figure of red blood and the judgment on the nations (63:1-6) reminds us both of the song of Deborah (Judg. 5:30, 31) and the judgment of Christ portrayed in Rev. 14:19, 20; 19:13-16.

God, after pronouncing judgment on the sinful people of the world, reviews the way in which he has dealt with Israel, his chosen people. He notes first his own dealing with them in mercy and love (63:7-9) and then their stubborn resistance to his goodness (63:10).

Nevertheless, God's grace triumphed as he recalled his covenant from of old and set about to save his people in spite of their sin and stubbornness (63:11—64:12).

The call here is to wait on the Lord (64:4). That theme noted so often before (Isa. 8:17; 25:9; 26:8; 30:18; 33:2; 40:31) recurs throughout the Old Testament as synonymous with "putting trust in the Lord." There is a clear reminder that our righteousness cannot save us (64:6). The whole section closes with acknowledgment that we are what we are by God's grace alone (64:8, 9). In spite of the present situation of decay expressed in verses 10 and 11, there is a remnant that shall survive.

In the next chapter, 65, the Lord moves into a rebuke against those in Israel (the visible church) who are not obedient. On the one hand, those who are not Israelites (Gentiles) shall come to know the Lord (65:1) while those to whom God had revealed himself for so long (the Israelites) have shown indifference to the Lord (65:2-7). But God will save from Israel a remnant (v. 8). They are the seed, God's chosen people (v. 9).

To the rest of Israel, the unrepentant, he gives words of judgment (65:11, 12). While his own are blessed, those who reject God will be cursed (65:13-15). The new name referred to in verse 15 is perhaps that name given in Acts 11:26, "Christian" instead of "Israelite."

Chapter 65 concludes with another view of the final glory of God and his church. Here are introduced terms by which the Christian hope is expressed in the New Testament. He speaks of the new heavens and the new earth (65:17 cf. 66:22; Heb. 12:26, 27; 2 Pet. 3:13; Rev. 21:1). He speaks too of the new Jerusalem (v. 18; compare Rev. 21:2ff.). The promises connected with this heavenly home of God's chosen ones is in terms of long and blissful life (v. 20), and houses and vineyards not surrendered to others (vv. 21, 22) and of labors not in vain (v. 23). In other words, the opposite of the old covenant under which Israel had not persevered in Canaan because of her failures.

This chapter closes with a picture of peace like that found in Isa. 2:2-4 and 11:6, 7. The curse on all creation placed at the time of Adam's sin (Gen. 3:14-19) will be reversed (v. 25). This is similar to what Paul declares about creation in Romans 8:20-22.

Inasmuch as there is a visible church (Israel) and an invisible church (the elect and truly faithful) and the two are not the same, until the day of judgment God's true people will suffer persecution (ch. 66).

The true believers are those contrite in heart who regard God's work, taking it seriously (66:2—cf. Psa. 51:17; Isa. 57:15). The unbelievers in the church will reject them, despising them. They will persecute them while claiming to be glorifying God (v. 5). But joy and peace belong in the end to God's true people, the remnant (vv. 10, 12, 13). For the others, the fire of God's judgment remains (vv. 15-17).

Yet out of the pagan nations God will also take a people to be part of his kingdom of priests (vv. 18-21cf. 61:6; Exod. 19:6; 1 Pet. 2:9).

The final scene of the book of Isaiah therefore leaves before Israel the two great alternatives of eternity: heaven or hell. Those who attain to heaven, God's true seed, shall remain forever in blessings and glory before the Lord (in his presence) (vv. 22-23). The rest, those who sinned against God and did not repent, shall face an eternal hell where suffering has no end (v. 24). Thus, the book closes as it began: either look to God in faith or be damned forever (compare 1:24-31).

MICAH

Micah was a later contemporary of Isaiah. Micah's prophecy was much shorter than that of Isaiah, but it was addressed generally to the same people. He did prophesy before the fall of Samaria inasmuch as the message concerns both Samaria and Jerusalem (v. 1). The kings mentioned here are all of Judah, since by this time there were no kings of any consequence yet reigning in Israel. Micah himself is mentioned also in Jeremiah 26:18 as a predecessor of Jeremiah.

The message is addressed to the capitals since it deals primarily with the guilt of the leaders of the people and their sins. The first part (1:2—2:11) summarizes the sins of the people in general and God's displeasure with them. Then before centering in on the leadership and their failures, he hints of the hope to follow for the remnant (2:12, 13). The remnant theme would be later developed by Micah.

In chapter 3 he develops the case against the leaders: kings, prophets and priests. And again from 4:1 through chapter 5, he expands the doctrine of the remnant and the real hope of the people of God.

From 6:1 through 7:6, the people and leadership of the land are put on trial and found wanting so that as a conclusion, Micah gives his own personal testimony in the Lord for whom he will wait (7:7-20).

Let us now return to the beginning and study each section in more detail. *First,* we see *God's own witness against this people* (1:2—2:11). God's witness is from his holy Temple reminding us of the beginning of Isaiah's vision from the Temple (Isa. 6) and also of the later prophecy of Habakkuk in which God is declared to be in his holy temple (Hab. 2:20). The holiness of God is always put over against the exceeding sinfulness of the people.

God is seen here as very angry, treading like a lion about to destroy his prey (1:3, 4—cf. Joel 3:16; Amos 1:2) or like a mighty man of war (Isa. 42:13). The reason for his anger is the sin of Israel (north and south). That sin is concentrated in the capitals where the leadership is (v. 5). The judgment pronounced recalls to our minds Hosea's description of judgment against Israel like that against a harlot (vv. 6-7).

In the verses that follow (8-16) Micah laments and builds pun upon pun as a device to impress on the people the certainty of God's judgment. Most of his puns are lost to us in the translation but an example or two will suffice. In verse 10, *Beth-le-aphrah* and "dust" are related, i.e., *aphrah* means "dust." In verse 14, *Achzib* and "deceitful" are pronounced alike in Hebrew. This

device is often used by the Hebrew prophets. (Compare Isa.
5:7.)

The description of her wounds as incurable (1:9) reminds us
of Isaiah 1:6.

As a consequence of her sins, sure judgment will follow (2:1-
11). Using the same somber, frightening word "woe" used by
Amos (Amos 6:1) and by Isaiah numerous times, he pronounces
solemn judgment on the people for their sins. These people lie
awake at night thinking about the evil of the next day on their
schedule (2:1). The sins are similar to those which Amos pointed
out to the Northern Kingdom (Amos 8:4).

Again we note that God, in a way similarly expressed in Isaiah
45:7, is the cause of evil (judgmental evil) on those who do evil
(moral evil). Thus, as the people devise evil in their hearts, so
God purposes evil judgments against the people.

Particularly significant here is the warning that these sinners
shall not cast the lot in the assembly of the Lord (2:5). The
imagery here harkens back to the time when the lot was cast in
Canaan for all of the tribes, each getting its share. But now God
will disinherit these people.

The depths to which the people have fallen spiritually is seen
in the last paragraph of this section (2:6-11). The people refuse
to hear God's true prophets and prefer to listen to drunken
prophets who tell them lies (vv. 6, 11). They have become God's
enemies (v. 8—cf. Isa. 1:24). They oppose God's people, having
no mercy (v. 9—cf. Amos 4:1). Their preference for drunken
prophets is a symptom of their corruption (cf. Isa. 28:7f.).

But lest the believers in Jerusalem despair, Micah holds up
hope at this point (2:12-13) when he mentions the remnant,
God's flock which shall be led by God as the Great Shepherd.
Here the imagery recalls such passages as Isa. 40:9-11 and is
tantamount to the Lord saying, "Remember the words of comfort spoken through Isaiah. Do not lose heart."

After this, in *chapter three,* he gets to *the heart of the message against
the leaders in Israel and Judah* who have so greatly failed the Lord.

The first denunciation is against the heads, presumably the
kings (3:1-4). Their responsibility under God was to execute
justice (v. 1) but instead they perverted all justice because they
hated what God pronounced good. Their hearts, being evil, love
evil (v. 2). The examples of their conduct here (vv. 2, 3) remind
us of Eli's sons (1 Sam. 2:12-17). What Samuel had warned of
when he gave them the king they wanted, has now come to pass
(3:4—cf. 1 Sam. 8:18).

Next, in 3:5-8, he denounces the prophets. He had already

said that the people preferred drunken prophets to those who would speak the truth. These false prophets are here further described. They were entrusted with the oracles of God but have instead caused the people to err. Their false message of peace gives to the people a false security (v. 5). In Jeremiah's prophecy we shall see a more expanded denunciation of those who cry "peace" when there is no peace (Jer. 6:14, etc.).

The picture of prophets who oppose those who do not support them reminds us of the conduct of Eli's sons. This conduct will bring stiff judgment (3:6, 7). They will lead the people back into spiritual dark ages as it was during the period of the Judges (cf. Amos 8:11).

In stark contrast to these false prophets, Micah stands out as faithful (3:8). His words remind us of Paul's letters to Timothy, a New Testament minister of the Word (2 Tim. 1:7) or of Jesus' words regarding the Holy Spirit (John 16:8-11).

In conclusion of this section, he brings a ringing condemnation on all the leadership of the land: kings, prophets and priests (3:9-12). All serve not God, but mammon (v. 11—cf. Matt. 6:24; 1 Tim. 6:10). Yet they are brash enough to claim that God is with them (cf. Amos 5:14; Isa. 48:1, 2). The result of such false leadership is that Jerusalem will come to an unhappy end. The church which allows evil leaders to gain power and influence cannot serve God and will be set aside. So read the letter to the Christians of Asia-Minor in the days of John the Apostle (Rev. 2, 3).

Micah, before concluding the case against the people, now (in chapters 4 and 5) turns to develop that *theme of the remnant hinted at in 2:12, 13*. He begins by quoting at length from Isaiah's prophesy (4:1-3—see Isa. 2:2-4). That portion of Isaiah had served to give hope to the remnant who put their trust in the Lord in the midst of apostasy.

The words in verses 4 and 5 recall scenes of the blessings of the days of David and Solomon when the people had prospered under sound leadership (see 1 Kgs. 4:25). This then became symbolic for the bliss God had in store ultimately for those who come to him as their refuge.

The remnant would be made up of the downcast and contrite who realize their weaknesses and need for God's help (4:6-8). We are reminded of Paul's description of the believers in his first letter to the Corinthians (1 Cor. 1:26-29). God is their King as he has always been over those who serve him: the Lord reigns (Exod. 15:18—cf. Isa. 33:22).

The climax of this prophesy of hope is attained in the passage from 4:9—5:5. Here he develops that hope of a child to be born which was first given in the garden of Eden (Gen. 3:15) and then often repeated to God's people. In Isaiah we recall that the prophet spoke of that child frequently (Isa. 7:14; 9:6-8; 11:1-5, etc.).

In the next chapter, the birthplace of the child is given, the one who shall be the true King of Israel (5:2) and the true shepherd (5:4). He will bring true peace (5:5). The New Testament teaches us plainly that this is a prophecy of the birth of Jesus Christ, the Savior (Matt. 2:6; compare Luke 2:4). The people must wait for the fulness of time (5:3) even as Paul later taught (Gal. 4:4).

The remainder of chapter 5 shows that the remnant so saved by God through the Great Shepherd who leads them, is saved in order to be a witness to the nations. Therefore, they will be a blessing to those who believe (5:7), and a judgment on others who do not respond (5:8). Here we may compare Paul's description of his witness for Christ (2 Cor. 2:14-17). Those nations not responding will feel the full force of God's judgment (5:15).

At last, *the case against Israel is completed* (6:1—7:6). The language is in legal terminology as though a trial was in progress. The mountains surrounding Jerusalem serve as judge and jury. God is the prosecuting attorney, making his case (6:1-16).

God calls first for any accusations against him by Israel (v. 3). We are reminded of similar passages in Hosea 4:1 and Isaiah 1:18. God desires to reason with his people, to give them every chance to acquit themselves. The Lord recalls his own love shown to them (vv. 4, 5—cf. Exod. 20:1; Amos 2:10).

There follows a response from the people (6:6-7). The response is arrogant, as if to say, "What do you want from me?" God had already taught that it was not sacrifices he desired, but a contrite heart (v. 6—cf. Psa. 51:16, 17). Certainly the example of Solomon's multitude of sacrifices and later multitude of sins show that it is not a multitude of sacrifices that God wants (v. 7a). The last offer, human sacrifice, after the manner of the pagans, was an insult to the Lord and a mockery of God's grace so long before shown to Abraham (Gen. 22; 6:7b).

Then comes the verdict, as the mountains seem to respond now, giving their judgment (v. 8). The answer is echoed throughout Scripture (Deut. 30:15-20; Hos. 6:6, Jas. 1:27). The only way the people can acquit themselves is by confessing their sin as David did (Psa. 51) rather than denying it or seeking to cover it as Saul did.

Since they did not repent, their sins shall be judged (6:9-16). Their sins are obvious (v. 11) and have been long before condemned in Scripture (Lev. 19:35-36; Hos. 12:7, 8). Judgment is, therefore, inescapable (6:13-15). They are no better than Omri and Ahab whose kingdom was cut off long before (6:16—cf. 2 Kgs. 9:7-10).

There is no hope therefore, in man. It is vain to search for a man who can lead Israel out of her plight (7:1-6). The upright are gone from among the leadership in the land (v. 2). All do evil so that the best is a curse (vv. 3, 4). No one can trust any other, all are suspect (vv. 5, 6). The picture of the state of affairs in Jerusalem at this time shows why the city must soon fall. It warns us too that the church today can drift so far that only judgment from God can solve its problems.

This recognition of the church's deplorable state in Micah's day leads the prophet to a personal testimony as he closes his book (7:7-20).

Since there is no hope in men, Micah looks to the Lord and thereby calls all who live in his day to do likewise. Though he sits in darkness he hopes for that light of which Isaiah had earlier spoken (v. 8—cf. Isa. 9:1, 2).

Micah does not deny his own sin but, like David, confesses it (v. 9). He desires the Lord not as his prosecutor but as his defense attorney (v. 9—cf. ch. 6). He hopes in the righteousness of God, not his own righteousness (Isa. 61:10; 64:6). Thus, he will not fear any enemy (vv. 10-13).

What Micah confesses here must always be the confession of God's people. It is futile to trust in man or in his own righteousness. One must look in faith to the Lord alone.

He sees the Lord as his shepherd (7:14—cf. 5:4). He sees also the inevitable defeat of his enemies, the unrighteous (7:16, 17). The reference to the serpent as like his enemies no doubt goes all the way back to Gen. 3:15, where victory over the serpent (Satan) is first promised.

In conclusion, Micah, recalling the revelation of God given in Exod. 34:6, 7, looks to God's mercy and compassion as the basis for his faith. All men may be liars but God is true to his Word (vv. 18-20).

11

THE SEVENTH CENTURY
PROPHETS

JEREMIAH

THE PROPHET JEREMIAH ministered in the latter days of the
Southern Kingdom, Judah. His ministry covers the time from
the thirteenth year of Josiah, the last good king of Judah, until
the eleventh year of Zedekiah, the year of Jerusalem's fall. This
would be from about 626-586 B.C., some forty years (1:2, 3).

We know more about the background and life of Jeremiah
than of any other writing prophet. He tells us that he is of the
family of priests living in Anathoth (1:1). From 1 Kings 2:26-27,
we know that Abiathar the priest who was with David through
his years of hardship and triumph, was removed from his office
by Solomon as he began to reign. He was sent back to his home

in Anathoth. Solomon did this because Abiathar had joined those who supported Adonijah as king instead of Solomon (1 Kgs. 1:7). Presumably then Jeremiah was of that priestly family.

The kings who ruled after Josiah are few in number: Jehoahaz, Jehoiakim, Jehoiachin, and Zedekiah. This was the period of the rapid decline of Judah. Josiah was the last good king and he died comparatively young. The others all disobeyed God and were failures in every sense.

In 1:4-10, we find *the call of Jeremiah* to be a prophet. We shall make five specific observations about this call.

First, before Jeremiah was born God had a specific purpose for him (4, 5). God both knew and sanctified Jeremiah according to his own purpose. The word "knew" used here is in accord with similar usage in Genesis 18:19. It is not knowledge by observation (i.e., human knowledge) but by choosing, predetermining (divine knowledge), so Jesus, in reference to those to be saved and rejected (Matt. 7:23). The term "sanctified" indicates that God set aside Jeremiah according to his purpose in order that he should be exclusively God's possession and serve God as prophet to the nations. The word "to sanctify" means to set aside for God.

Second, the Lord designed Jeremiah in order that he should fulfill this purpose of God. Nothing was left to chance. God formed Jeremiah (1:5). He was truly a God-made man. All in his background and family and place of birth were in accord with the purpose God predetermined, that he should be a prophet.

Third, Jeremiah, confronted by this call showed true humility (1:6)—we are reminded of Moses' similar reaction to his call (Exod. 3:11), and of Solomon (1 Kgs. 3:7). There is nothing improper with such a reaction in the face of a call, so long as it does not result in an excuse or refusal to serve. What is important to note is that God's reply to Jeremiah's response (as Moses') was "I am with you" (1:8—cf. Exod. 3:15; Josh. 1:5). It is well to be humble, but that should lead to confidence in the Lord. We too, like Jeremiah, face the awesome task of being Christ's servants (Matt. 28:19, 20a). We too, do well to realize that the faithful accomplishment of this is far too great a task for us. But Jesus' answer comes back as it did to Moses and Jeremiah—"I am with you" (Matt. 28:20b).

Fourth, God makes clear just what the mission is (1:9-10). It is two-fold: negative and positive. On the negative side he will be required to pluck up, break down, destroy and overthrow that which displeases the Lord. It is the prophet's function. This function no doubt derives from the fact that God's Word is also given to do just that in the lives of men. In 2 Tim. 3:16, 17 we read that God's Word is profitable for reproof (knocking over) and correction (disciplining). Scripture, therefore, calls the Word a hammer and fire (Jer. 23:29). The New Testament likens the Word to a sword (Heb. 4:12). We keep in mind also that the Word of God is the Sword of the Spirit (Eph. 6:17), and the Spirit who inspired the prophets had as his function convicting men of sin, righteousness and judgment (John 16:8).

On the positive side his mission would be to build and plant (v. 10). This too, is in accord with the function of God's Word which, as Paul says, instructs us in righteousness so that we may be perfect, thoroughly furnished for every good work.

We can readily see therefore, that Jeremiah's mission in the Old Testament was not unlike that of every child of God today as he bears witness through the Word of God written.

Fifth, Jeremiah's call was to be involved in suffering. This comes later in the chapter, but is an aspect of his call so we consider it here (1:17-19). Jeremiah's faithful exercise of his mission would bring stiff opposition. This is also quite similar to what Jesus taught his disciples who would follow him (Matt. 16:24).

The visions which accompanied Jeremiah's call evidently pointed to the major aspects of his mission (1:11-16). In the first he was taught by seeing a rod of an almond tree, that God's Word is sure (vv. 11, 12). In a way similar to Amos' vision (Amos 8:1-3) God used here a play on words, for the words for "almond tree" and "watch over" sound quite similar in Hebrew.

In the second vision, he sees a boiling pot with the face from the north indicating that God's judgment would come from the north just as Joel had indicated long before (1:13-16—cf. Joel 2:20).

After this introduction including Jeremiah's call, we come to the first major section of the book, a series of messages from God through Jeremiah (chs. 2-35). These messages vary greatly in length, addressee, and content. They are not in chronological order, but the first three are the longest messages. The titles and addresses of each message follow.

1. *Message to Jerusalem in Josiah's day* (chs. 2-6).

This is very like those messages already given by the preceding prophets, speaking of God's love for Israel and the people's refusal to obey and concluding with warnings of judgment to come from the northern army. It recalls many passages from other prophets: 2:2 (Hos. 2:14); 2:5 (Mic. 6:3); 2:9 (Hos. 2:2; Mic. 6:1; Amos 7:4); 2:25 (Hosea); 2:26 (Micah); 2:32 (Isa. 1:3); 3:15 (Isa. 40:11; Micah 5:4; 7:14); 3:17 (Isa. 2:1ff.); 4:5-7 (Joel,

Amos); 4:14 (Isa. 1:16); 5:21 (Isa. 6); 6:14 (Mic. 3:5).

2. *Message in the gate of the Lord's house* (chs. 7—10).

This message warns particularly against false hope (7:4ff.). The tendency to trust in the making of offerings rather than in obedience to the Lord in life (7:21-23) recalls Saul's sins (1 Sam. 15:22) and David's faith (Psa. 51:16). The tendency to refuse to hear God's prophets (7:25-26) recalls the pronouncement of judgment found in 2 Kgs. 17:13. The lateness of the hour for Jerusalem is effectively expressed in 8:20. It points to the bankruptcy of Israel's spiritual power. How similar to God's message through Isaiah is Jeremiah 10:23-24! Man's hopeless plight without God is the closing theme of this message (10:23).

3. *Message for the men of Judah and inhabitants of Jerusalem* (chs. 11, 12).

These words call Jerusalem to task for forsaking their covenant with the Lord (11:3-8). There are also forbodings of the troubles Jeremiah would suffer later because of his faithful stand (11:18-23). In a way similar to Habakkuk later, Jeremiah here is disturbed by the sin that prevails in Jerusalem as any righteous person should be (12:1ff.). God assures of both judgment and mercy to come in a way similar to Jeremiah's mission of destruction and rebuilding (12:14-17).

4. *Message pertaining to the linen girdle* (ch. 13).

By a symbolic destruction of a linen girdle, God shows to Jeremiah the certainty of Jerusalem's pride being marred (vv. 1-9). All of the leadership will be judged (v. 13), even as Micah had warned. God's mercy revealed in Exod. 34:6, 7 is now turned away from the people (vv. 14). The impossibility of the people changing their own nature and so escaping God's wrath is declared here at the conclusion of the message (vv. 22, 23).

5. *Message concerning the drought* (chs. 14, 15).

In a manner similar to Joel, Jeremiah speaks on the occasion of a great natural catastrophe in the land. When locust ravaged the land, Joel warned that worse would come if the people did not repent (see our discussion of Joel, ch. 1). Now Jeremiah during a severe drought in his day, declares that the iniquities of the people have brought on this terrible day (14:1-7). He intervenes on behalf of the people much as Moses had done in the wilderness, but this time God refuses to allow his intercession (14:8-12).

So severe is God's denunciation of the people and the false prophets (14:14-15), that Jeremiah almost despairs (14:19, 20). He can only wait for the Lord who alone can give hope (14:22, cf. Isa. 25:9; 26:8; 40:31; 49:23).

An indication of their plight is seen in God's statement that not even the intercession of Moses and Samuel, both of whom had interceded successfully before, could now avail anything (15:1 compare Exod. 32:11-14; 1 Sam. 12:23). The reason for God's refusal to hear now is that Manasseh, the son of Hezekiah, had gone too far from God for the people ever to return (15:4). There can now be no pity. Repenting now would just be a farce (15:5, 6).

In a most moving scene, Jeremiah now cries out because of his own suffering (15:10, compare Job 3:1ff.). He finds it difficult to see how God is still with him (vv. 15-17). The Word he had loved as he partook of it has become bitter inside (vv. 16, 18). This is perhaps similar to John's partaking of the bitter-sweet gospel (Rev. 10:9). Repeating what was said in chapter 1, God assures Jeremiah that he will preserve him (vv. 20, 21).

6. *Command to Jeremiah not to marry or have children* (chs. 16, 17).

So hard will those later days of judgment be in Jerusalem that it will be better for Jeremiah not to have a family (16:1-9). It is a day of no grace from God (v. 13). A second exodus is necessary to bring the people back to their senses and this means a second bondage in a foreign land, i.e., Babylonian captivity (16:14, 15; 17:4).

In the midst of condemnation of the land, Jeremiah knows to turn to the Lord and look to him alone as Savior (17:14).

Finally, in a manner similar to Isaiah in Isaiah 56 and 58, Jeremiah holds up Sabbath observance as a test of the spirituality of God's people (17:20-22, 24-26). Obvious violations of the Sabbath day were being allowed in Jeremiah's day (17:23, 27). A cessation from such evil would give indication of the people's good faith.

7. *Message at the potter's house* (ch. 18).

At the potter's house the Lord gave to Jeremiah insight into his sovereignty. As the potter has complete control of the clay in his hands, so God controls all nations (18:1-10).

Here we see the principle by which God warns of evil and impending judgment on those he purposes to destroy. If they repent, he will not carry out the judgment (18:8). On the other hand, if God declares his intent to build up a people but they do not obey him, God will not do the good he had promised (18:9, 10).

God uses the term "repent" here to describe his change of action from that which he had before declared. This simply means that God often deals with individuals and nations conditionally. That is, if *they* repent from evil, he will not bring the judgment by which he had threatened them. On the other hand, if *they* turn from obedience, he will not bring the blessings he had promised.

In illustration of this principle, we can go all the way back to the pre-flood days when God repented of making man (Gen. 6:6). He made man to glorify and obey the Lord, subduing all creation to him. When man failed, God's pronunciation of judgment indicated his displeasure. Man was made on condition of obedience.

Again, in the wilderness, the Lord threatened to destroy Israel on one occasion (Exod. 32:7-10). But after Moses' intercession he did not (Exod. 32:11-14). We see similar instances of God's repenting elsewhere in Scripture (1 Sam. 15:11; Jonah 3:9, 10). We must remember that for the Lord, repentance does not mean a regret or change of mind due to error as it does when applied to men. God does not make mistakes so that he must correct himself. He does not repent as men repent (1 Sam. 15:29).

At times, God declares that he will not repent, which means that the judgment pronounced or the promise given is not conditional (see Jer. 4:27, 28). This is the basis then of the certainty of final judgment on evil and the certainty of the final salvation of those who are God's children.

God's dealing with Israel is a prime instance of God's conditional promises and conditional judgment. Here the Lord threatens evil (compare Isa. 45:7), but calls them to repent (18:11). But the people refuse (v. 12) and go so far as to oppose God's servant who bears God's message of warning (18:18).

All of this led Jeremiah to pray for the judgment of God against these people (18:19-23). This may seem harsh, but we must remember that God had forbidden him to pray for them (14:7, 11; 7:16; 11:14). God had made clear his purpose to judge them (15:1). For Jeremiah to pray otherwise now would have been contrary to God's will. As the Psalmist discovered, so must Jeremiah: God's enemies are the enemies of God's people (Psa. 139:21, 22). Even in heaven, there is a time to pray for the destruction of those who are opposed to God (Rev. 6:9-11).

8. *Lessons from the potter's vessel* (ch. 19).

By means of an audiovisual aid, Jeremiah is instructed to proclaim the destruction of Jerusalem. The picture of the dead bodies of those judged (v. 7) recalls Isaiah's closing words (Isa. 66:24) and is the basis for a grim scene given in the book of Revelation (Rev. 19:17, 18).

9. *Message on the occasion of encounter with Pashhur* (ch. 20).

When Jeremiah was attacked personally by Pashhur the priest and imprisoned, he became very discouraged (20:1-3). The very name by which he called Pashhur ("Magor—Missabib") meant "terror on every side" and indicated the way Jeremiah felt, surrounded by his enemies (ch. 20:3, 10). He was hurt because he was mocked (v. 7) and because his friends denounced him (v. 10). Yet, when he thought of holding his tongue he could not hold back from speaking God's Word so burning was that Word within him (v. 9).

Jeremiah on the one hand could affirm his unswerving faith in the Lord as his protector (20:11-13). Yet, so bitter was the opposition which he had to endure that he could also wish that he had not been born (vv. 14-18). In this, he was expressing the same feelings expressed by Job (compare Job 3:3-6). He is so involved with God that he feels the brunt of opposition to the Lord.

Before we are too quick to condemn Jeremiah or Job, we should remember that few men have ever been called on to endure what Jeremiah and Job had to endure for such a long time. It is not, therefore, a mark of their spiritual failure, but their spiritual stature that God would allow them to be tempted so greatly!

Keep in mind that God had declared that he called Jeremiah and formed him while yet in the womb of his mother, purposing him to be his witness (ch. 1). No doubt the recollection of this Word of God at his time of call comforted him in this hour. With Paul, he could be comforted in the realization that in his suffering God was glorified (compare 1 Pet. 4:13; Phil. 3:10; Rom. 8:17). At any rate, Jeremiah was able to survive this trial and continued to preach God's Word.

10. *Message when Zedekiah sent for comfort* (ch. 21).

Jeremiah had reason for comfort since he was in the will of the Lord, but not Zedekiah. Zedekiah hoped for deliverance of Jerusalem from Nebuchadnezzar as God had once saved Nineveh and later Jerusalem in Hezekiah's day (21:2), but such was not to be. God promised the three curses by which he often judged the sinful kingdoms of the world: pestilence, sword and famine (21:7—cf. 2 Sam. 24:13, 14; Rev. 6:3-8). In the end, they would go captive to Babylon (v. 7).

We see how the failure of the old covenant changed the circumstances for Judah when we compare 21:8, 9 with Deut. 30:15-19. In the Deuteronomy passage "the way of life" meant blessings. Here it meant only escape from the sword.

11. *Messages to the kings and leaders of Judah* (chs. 22, 23).

First, in a general way, the Lord addresses the kings of Judah calling for righteousness and justice in their leadership (22:3). Failure to do this, he tells them, will bring severe judgment and an end to the kingdom of Judah (22:5-9).

After these introductory remarks addressed to all of the kings, the Lord specifically addresses the kings one by one.

The first is Shallum also called Jehoahaz (22:10-12). He was the son of Josiah. His reign was brief and sad. He ruled three months and then was carried away captive to Egypt (2 Kgs. 23:31-33). His fate, therefore, was similar to that of Jeremiah himself who later would be carried away unwillingly into Egypt (Jer. 43:5-7).

The second king is Jehoiakim, who was Josiah's son also and whom the king of Egypt made king in his father's place (22:13-23—see 2 Kgs. 23:34). He was accused of making gains for himself at the cost of doing evil and unrighteous deeds, the very opposite of his father (vv. 13-17). His record was one of oppression and bloodshed (compare 2 Kgs. 23:37—24:4). For this, his burial would be shameful (v. 19—cf. 36:30). Among his most heinous deeds was his attempt later to destroy the Word of God written by Jeremiah (ch. 36). No doubt his deed there reflected his reaction to hearing these words of Jeremiah condemning him.

The third king, Coniah, also called Jehoiachin, would be carried away as a captive to Babylon and never return (22:24-30). We read of these events in 2 Kings 24:10-17. Together with Jehoiachin, 10,000 others were carried away at this time (2 Kgs. 24:14) among them Ezekiel (Ezek. 1:1-3). After thirty-seven years of captivity, Jehoiachin was taken from prison and favorably treated by the king of Babylon then reigning (2 Kgs. 25:27-30).

After three personal messages, which warned the people against hoping in any king, the Lord rebukes all of these leaders for their failure to be good shepherds (23:1-2). Then he promises to be himself the Good Shepherd of his people in accord with Isa. 11:11-16; 40:1, 11 (23:3, 4).

He points to the coming of the righteous Branch, of the family of David, who will actually do what God had required of the other kings (23:5, 6—cf. Isa. 11:1-5; 53). All hope therefore will rest on this One to come who *is* the righteousness of God's people i.e., the one by whom they shall have a right relationship to God (v. 6—cf. Isa. 45:24, 25; 54:17). Verses 7 and 8 recall Jer. 16:14, 15.

Most of chapter 23 is a denunciation of the other leaders in Judah, namely the false prophets and priests (23:9-40). They are both profane (v. 11). They cause the people to err (vv. 13-14). They preach a false peace that will not come (vv. 15-17). By this they show that they are not God's true prophets. They have never heard God's Word which he reveals to his true prophets (23:18-22 cf. Amos 3:7). God disassociates himself from those whose message is not in accord with his own Word (vv. 23-32). This applies to the "prophets" of Jeremiah's time and also to the "preachers" of today who do not preach in accord with God's will (compare 2 Tim. 4:3, 4).

God will no longer allow false prophets to use phrases which had been used by true prophets. Phrases like "burden of the Lord," once used by legitimate prophets, can no longer be allowed because they have been used by false prophets so much that they are now meaningless words (23:33-36 cf. Isa. 13:1; Nahum 1:1; Hab. 1:1). What is important is what God indeed has spoken through the true prophet, not a pat formula (vv. 36-40). God warns sternly here against hypocrisy on the part of those who pretend to be speaking God's Word when they are not (v. 40).

12. *Message of the vision of two baskets of fruit* (ch. 24).

This message came after Jehoiachin had been carried away captive (24:1—cf. 22:24ff.). By means of two baskets of fruit, one filled with good fruit and one with bad fruit, the Lord taught the people that those carried away (such as Ezekiel, Daniel and Daniel's three companions) would be blessed and built up and preserved (24:2-7). They would be God's true children in accord with his plans stated in Exod. 19. God would give to them a new heart (cf. Jer. 31:31-34). But the rest who resisted God's will, like bad fruit, would perish (24:8-10).

This revelation recalls the very essence of Jeremiah's call (v. 6—cf. Jer. 1:10). The threefold punishment to the disobedient is as mentioned in 21:7 (24:10).

The whole use of fruit to describe those with whom God is pleased and displeased is first seen in Isa. 5:1-7 and is further developed in the New Testament (Matt. 7:16; John chapter 15; Jas. 3:12 etc.).

13. *Message in the fourth year of Jehoiakim* (ch. 25).

Jehoiakim was an evil king whose ignominious death Jeremiah had predicted (22:19). During Jeremiah's twenty-three years of preaching the people had not responded (25:3). Therefore, God again promised judgment by captivity into Babylon (vv. 8-11).

At this point he specifically predicted seventy years of captivity before return to their home (v. 12). Later, Daniel would seek from the Lord further meaning in the number 70 (Dan. 9:2ff.). Yet, God will bring judgment against the nations used by him to punish Judah. The fall of the nations is declared in vivid imagery similar to parts of Daniel and Ezekiel and the book of Revelation which is called apocalyptic style (revelation by symbolic language, concerning the last times).

The principle applied by God in his judgment of the nations is stated in Isaiah 10:12-15. They are used by God to punish God's people, but because they become proud in their victories and do not do their deeds to obey or please God, they too will be punished. The principle is clearly stated here in Jer. 25:29, and by Peter applied to God's judgment against all nations and men (1 Pet. 4:17, 18).

14. *Message in the court of the Lord's house* (ch. 26).

The time of Jehoiakim was particularly hostile to the Lord and therefore, to his servant Jeremiah. Right at the beginning of his reign, there was an attempt to kill Jeremiah as is related in this chapter. We see the bravery of Jeremiah in the face of death (26:8-15).

His brave words persuaded the princes and people that the prophets and priests were wrong about Jeremiah (26:16). Micah, the prophet, was cited in proof of Jeremiah's right to preach as he did (vv. 17-19). In the end Jeremiah was saved from death (v. 24).

15. *Encounter with Hananiah* (chs. 27, 28).

As early as the time of Jehoiakim, God had begun to tell Jerusalem that Judah would fall and go into bondage to Babylon (27:1-11). Then, in the day of Zedekiah (the last king) these things began to be fulfilled (vv. 3ff.). Jeremiah is a dramatic gesture sought by visual aid to illustrate the reality of impending captivity (27:2). The only escape from God's wrath was by submission to this yoke which God was forcing on Judah (vv. 7-11). Therefore, to Zedekiah, Jeremiah spoke, calling him to surrender to God's will (vv. 12-15).

Similarly, Jeremiah called the false prophets and priests to repent and look to God (vv. 16-22).

However, Hananiah, one of the false prophets in Zedekiah's reign, by an equally dramatic gesture sought to counter Jeremiah's prophecy (28:1-4). When rebuked by Jeremiah and challenged to prove his false words (28:5-9), Hananiah again gestured by breaking the yoke on Jeremiah's neck (vv. 10-11).

At first Jeremiah was nonplussed (v. 11b) but he returned evidently with other bonds made of iron instead of wood and challenged Hananiah to break those (vv. 12-14). Because Hananiah had made the people believe a lie, he was punished with death (v. 17).

16. *Letters to Jews in captivity* (ch. 29).

We recall that certain Jews in the days of Jehoiachin already had been led into captivity. Now Jeremiah wrote a letter to them (29:4-32). In the letter he encouraged them to expect to stay awhile. Indeed, they must pray for Babylon and its peace, since their own affairs would be tied to the affairs of that kingdom for a time (vv. 5-7).

Apparently there were false prophets and leaders among the captives also (vv. 8, 9). They were promising a quick return, although Jeremiah had said they would be there seventy years (v. 10—cf. 25:12).

The counsel of peace given to the captives was taken seriously by some such as Daniel and Ezekiel, as we shall see. God would give those in captivity both peace and ultimately safe return. But those in Jerusalem would feel the full wrath of God (v. 17—cf. 24:8-10).

In Daniel's prophecy we learn of faithful prophets in Babylon. But here we learn that in those same days false prophets are named (29:21, 22). Apparently their end (roasting in fire) was like the death Nebuchadnezzar had prepared for the three friends of Daniel, but since they were true to God, Daniel's friends were protected by God in the midst of the furnace (Daniel 3).

A third false prophet among the captives, Shemaiah, even wrote to those in Jerusalem, urging them to rebuke Jeremiah (29:24-28). In response, Jeremiah predicted his punishment similar to that of Eli the priest in Samuel's day (vv. 31-32 cf. 1 Sam. 2:30-34). We see then what the Lord meant by the words of his call to Jeremiah (1:17-19).

17. *Command to write all in a book* (30:1-3).

18. *Message concerning Israel and Judah* (30:4—31:40).

In the midst of these passages which warn of war and the ravages of war, the Lord, the Prince of Peace, begins to address those in Israel and Judah, who did respond to God's call and put their trust in him. For these there is a message of hope.

God promised to save them from their enemies (30:4-11). Nevertheless, they must go through a time of purging in Babylon out of which his true believers will come and be God's people (vv. 21-22).

God's everlasting love will triumph in the end (30:23—31:6). Here, in a way reminiscent of Isa. 2:3, he promises that Zion (the city of God) shall be exalted in the end (v. 6). Clearly, these promises are directed not to all Israelites but to the remnant (v. 7).

We see again the Shepherd motif (31:10—cf. Gen. 48:15; Num. 27:17; 1 Kgs. 22:17; Psa. 23:1; Isa. 40). The terminology of Exodus is also found here: ransomed and redeemed (v. 11).

God's goodness will win out in the end, that goodness which he revealed long before to Moses (vv. 12-14—cf. Exod. 33:18, 19; 34:6, 7).

All here pointed to final working out of all things according to
God's will and power. In the meantime Rachel (figurative for the
remnant) must weep (v. 15). In the New Testament this passage
is quoted in reference to the slaughter of so many children in
Bethlehem by Herod (Matt. 2:16-18). In this way, that slaughter
is representative of all of the suffering God's people must endure at the hands of their enemies. But in the end, there is hope
(v. 17).

The prayer of Jeremiah in verses 18, 19, recognizing the
necessity of God's turning us if we are to be truly changed spiritually, reflects the necessity for new hearts which God promises
in the new covenant (31:31-34).

God promises that as he broke down and plucked up the
people (v. 28) so he will now build and plant. Thus, the terms
"build" or "a building" and "plant" or "growth" are terms that
describe God's people hereafter. The Lord is the builder and the
farmer, we are the building and the plant (see Matt. 7:24-27;
16:18; 13:1-9; John 15:1-5; Eph. 4:11-16, etc.).

In the old covenant, as we saw, the people would persevere in
Canaan so long as they kept God's Law (had regard for it). If
they failed, they would be removed.

Now in the new covenant (31:31-34), they would be given new
hearts to obey God, and since it was God's work it would not fail.
Therefore, as Isaiah had said before, God would never remember their sins again (v. 34—cf. Isa. 43:25). All of this points
to the New Testament work of Christ by which men are given
new birth through the Holy Spirit (John 3). Then they are enabled to believe in the Lord. Later Ezekiel in his prophecy (chs.
36, 37) will develop more fully this promise of new birth.

The certainty of these promises rests on the sovereignty of
God who directs all things according to the pleasure of his own
will (31:35-40).

19. *Message in Zedekiah's tenth year* (chs. 32, 33).

This message was given in the last year before the fall of
Jerusalem (v. 1). Jeremiah was in prison because of his faithfulness to the Lord (v. 2). While confined, he was given opportunity
to buy a field in Anathoth which was his by right of redemption
(32:8). Since the Lord had foretold this event, Jeremiah bought
the field in order to express his confidence in the Lord that God
would bring his people back to the land in safety (v. 15).

Jeremiah did not do this without much prayer and in full
realization of the extreme distress of those days (32:16-25). On
this occasion the Lord once more assured Jeremiah and all who
put trust in him of the days of return to come, not a return
physically only, but a return to a right heart (so especially

32:36-40). The whole matter concludes with a promise of the Savior to come in a way similar to Isa. 11:1-5 and Jer. 23:5, 6; 30:9 (33:15-18). In all such promises the Lord assures of peace and pardon (33:6, 8). The work will be God's work, the righteousness of the Lord imputed to us (v. 16—cf. 23:6). In short, it is clearly the gospel promise of the New Testament which is here foreshadowed (compare Rom. 5:1, etc.). The Christ will fulfill perfectly the offices of priest and king (33:17, 18).

The certainty of this promise is once more given (33:19-25—cf. 31:35-37). Clearly the Lord sees these latter promises in harmony with his original promise to Abraham to bless his seed (v. 26—cf. Gen. 12:1-3; 22:18).

20. *Message during the siege of Jerusalem* (ch. 34).

During this time the Lord sent Jeremiah to Zedekiah, the last king of Judah before the fall (v. 2). The message was a warning of impending captivity and hardship unless Zedekiah obeyed the Lord (vv. 3-5). There was evidently an attempt on Zedekiah's part to get the people to obey God's Law, particularly concerning the freeing of servants after seven years (vv. 8-15—cf. Exod. 21:2), but soon after releasing them, they took them back, thus mocking God's Law (v. 16). They went through the ceremony of cutting a calf, which was symbolic of making a covenant with God (v. 18—cf. Gen. 15:10), but since it was all an outward show and not sincere, these people would be punished (vv. 20-22).

21. *Message concerning the Rechabites* (ch. 35).

In the days of King Jehu of Israel, there was one family, the family of Jonadab, the son of Rechab, which was loyal to the king (see 2 Kgs. 10:15-24). Jonadab taught his children and they in turn their children to observe Jonadab's rules about drinking. So strict was this family in carrying out Jonadab's wishes, that in Jeremiah's day, 250 years later, they were still faithful to their forefather (35:14a). Try as he might, Jeremiah could not get them to drink wine (35:3-11).

God used this example of great loyalty to a man's commands to contrast with Israel's own unwillingness to obey the Lord (v. 14b). God commended the loyalty of these descendants of Jonadab and said that, in essence, of such is the kingdom of heaven (v. 19).

This concludes the long series of messages which God gave to Jeremiah concerning Judah in her last days. It is difficult to follow much order of development here. Nevertheless, there are some major themes running through these messages which we shall look at before going on.

First, is the theme of the *heart.* God shows that the thoughts of

the heart do matter to him. He will not accept outward conformity but insists on right hearts. We see this in 3:10 where the
Lord rejects the reforms in Josiah's day because the people did
not really return to the Lord in their hearts. But God requires
that those who serve him love him with their whole heart, nothing withheld (Deut. 6:5).

In the same chapter he implies that the people now live according to the stubbornness of their evil hearts (3:17). It is a way
of life with them. Their hearts are unclean because though, as
Jews, they may be circumcised in the flesh, their hearts are yet
uncircumcised (uncleansed) (4:4, 14—cf. Deut. 10:16; 30:6).

As with the heart, so with their ways. Their ways are cor-
rupted because they have corrupt hearts (4:18). They have
therefore reached the state which was described to Isaiah in his
call: they have eyes to see but do not see and ears to hear, but do
not hear. They are without heart (5:21—cf. Isa. 6:9, 10). Note
here that the word sometimes translated "understanding" means
"a heart for God."

Not only does their heart do nothing to please God but indeed
it rebels against him (5:23). There is no fear of God in their
hearts (i.e., no faith) (v. 24). This promotes hypocrisy in the
church so that outwardly they speak peaceably with one another
(i.e., act as believers) but inwardly they plot evil against others
(9:8—cf. 12:2).

Frequently here their condition is described as walking (living)
after the stubbornness of their hearts (9:14; 11:8; 13:10; 16:12;
18:12; 23:17). Their life is such that in reality there is no distinction between those who are supposed to be God's people and the
rest of the world (9:26).

Their prophets are no help, for the false prophets themselves
have similar hearts and indeed speak out of the deceit of their
own hearts (14:14; 23:16-26).

Judah's sin, therefore, is no light matter. It penetrates to their
hearts. Indeed, it is engraved on their hearts indelibly as if
someone had written in stone with an iron pen having a dia-
mond point (17:1). This shows the extent of the meaning of
their having stubborn hearts, hardened like stone.

The description of the heart reaches its peak in 17:9. It is
deceitful and exceedingly corrupt. We are reminded here of
Jesus' own words concerning the heart. In Mark 7:20-23, he
gives a graphic description of what is in the heart of the natural
man before he is saved.

Jeremiah asks the question, "Who can know it?" (v. 9), and
then answers it in the next verse: "I the Lord, search the heart"

(v. 10). Men deceive themselves about their own hearts and none naturally are willing to admit that they are totally corrupt within, but God who sees rightly says that they are! Only by God's Word, therefore, can men know their own hearts (compare 20:12).

The case is made. Man is totally corrupt in his heart and therefore unable to change his heart. Sin is indelible in him. Therefore, the only solution if ever he is to have a right heart, one that pleases God, is for the Lord to give to him a new heart, one that will obey. And this is just what the Lord through Jeremiah promises to do (27:7). God will then put his law in their new hearts and write indelibly on their hearts so that they will be truly God's people, all that he had purposed for them to be from the beginning (31:33—cf. Exod. 19:5, 6). They will know the Lord (have faith) because they have new hearts according to a new nature. This is, of course, the promise of rebirth of which Jesus spoke (John 3). Compare also Jer. 32:38, 39.

We see then here the theme of the heart beautifully developed from the exceeding sinfulness of the natural heart to the regenerated heart given to God's children by the grace of God.

A *second theme* is closely related. It is *the theme of peace.* At first Jeremiah is confronted with a dilemma. He recalls that the Lord had said to his true people through Isaiah that they would have peace (Isa. 9:7; 26:3, 12; 53:5; 55:12). Yet, in Jeremiah's time there was anything but peace. The armies of Nebuchadnezzar, king of Babylon, were besieging Jerusalem, and its fall seemed imminent (Jer. 4:10). It seemed as though God had deceived.

The Lord had to show to Jeremiah that the peace God promised to his own in this world was not external, but internal. Those who promised external peace to believers were false prophets, promising a peace that could never come. It was a false gospel! (6:14; 8:11; 14:13, 19; 23:17).

This external peace then, a freedom from external trouble, was deceptive and never lasting. What really mattered was peace with God, a peace through knowing God and having a right relationship to him. That was the peace that was really lost and *that* no amount of external peace from wars could ever recover. God took from this people the true peace—his loving kindness and tender mercies (16:5). Such peace, i.e., to know the Lord as loving and merciful is truly peace that passes understanding. It is a peace that the world cannot know and cannot give or take away (compare John 14:27; Phil. 4:7). This is the peace of which Isaiah had spoken in Isaiah 26:3.

But the Lord will bring peace to those who are his children.

God's thoughts are peace to them (29:11). God will establish by
his love and mercy, peace with his own who put their trust in
him (33:6).

Two illustrations of that peace with God in the midst of the
turbulent external conditions of this world will help here. In
Habakkuk we see the prophet troubled and external conditions
of war even as was Jeremiah. God shows him that it is necessary
to purge the people. But those who trust in him shall be righteous and survive. After this Habakkuk understands that as a
believer he must go through great trials on earth, but that he can
do so in peace with God.

In the New Testament, on one occasion Jesus is with his disciples in a boat on the Sea of Galilee. He is asleep. A storm arises
and the disciples are frightened. They wake him up asking him
to do something about the storm. Jesus calms the storm but then
rebukes them. They had Jesus; why was that not enough? True
peace enables God's children to be at peace in the midst of the
raging storms of life (Mark 4:35-41). In a sequel we see Paul at
peace in the midst of a storm, and though the ship failed to hold,
nevertheless Paul and those with him were saved. He had peace
while the storm raged around. So it should be with every child of
God (Acts 27:14-26).

A *third theme,* also related to the others is *the theme of trust.* The sin
of the people was a misplaced trust. They trusted in lying words
of false prophets. These prophets promised that since the temple was in Jerusalem and represented God's presence, nothing
evil could happen to the city (7:4, 8, 14). But God warned that
even as Shiloh, the former site of the Ark of God, had perished,
so would Jerusalem. Those who put trust in things, even religious symbols, are sure to fail.

Nor can men put trust in other men (9:5—cf. Mic. 7:5). Since
men's hearts are corrupt, men cannot save the world, nor even
themselves! Trust in lies and promises of men can only bring
shame and defeat (13:25, 26).

Therefore, those who put their trust in men are cursed (17:5).
They trust in the arm of flesh which cannot hold and cannot
save. Their hearts have abandoned God. On the other hand,
those who put trust in the Lord shall be blessed. God will not fail
them (17:7). They are like a tree planted by water. They will
prosper (compare Psa. 1).

Finally, there is *the theme of the remnant.* Who will trust? Who will
have peace? Who will have cleansed hearts?

First, we see the answer negatively. Those who continue to

protest their innocence will not know God (2:35). Repentance and acknowledgment of sin is imperative! (3:13). A true confession such as Jeremiah gives here is what is needed if one is to have peace (3:25). But many in Jerusalem refuse to be convicted and harden themselves (5:3). They refuse to believe that evil could befall the city (5:12).

Their refusal to repent is hard-core pride and wickedness (8:6, 8). Such pride will be the downfall of Judah (13:9, 10).

They pretend to be innocent but are evil minded, really blaming God for all of their trouble (16:12). They set their course to follow their evil purposes (18:12) and even oppose godly men like Jeremiah (18:18). They have the audacity to quote Scripture and make a mockery of God's Word by living evil lives and yet claiming to be God's people (18:18). Such people will not see God's Kingdom. They must be purged.

Those who do survive, who trust in the Lord and are his people are therefore called the remnant. Jeremiah is not the first to use this term. It is a term generally used by the prophets to describe those who are indeed God's children in the visible church.

As Amos had indicated (Amos 9:8b ff.), God will not utterly destroy the people of Israel (4:27; 5:18). Of those who oppose God and his servants then, there shall be no remnant at all (11:20-23—cf. Amos 3:12). But after captivity, God will spare some on whom he has had compassion (12:15).

This remnant will be like a scattered flock whom the Good Shepherd gathers together again (Jer. 23:3—cf. Isa. 11:11-16; 40:10, 11).

Thus, the real people of God to whom the promises belong are the remnant of Israel, those who have trusted in him (31:7). They shall go through the impending captivity and survive as God's people throughout history, a people within a people, the true church within the external Israel, surviving after the external Israel has fallen.

Leaving now this first major section of Jeremiah (chs. 2-35) we shall turn next to the second major section, the historical events of those days (chs. 36-44).

The next few chapters cover *historical events* in *the last days of Judah* as they pertain to Jeremiah, one of God's few faithful servants there at that time (chs. 36-44). Chapter 36 in particular tells of Jehoiakim's attempt to destroy the words Jeremiah had written.

In this chapter we gain insight into the way God's Word was written. Jeremiah was commanded to write in a scroll all that

God had spoken to him up to that time, the fourth year of Jehoiakim (36:1, 2). Presumably it included most of what is found in chapters 1-35, though not all since some was written after this date (36:32).

Jeremiah in turn dictated his words to Baruch, who wrote them down (36:4). Then he had Baruch read them in the Temple, since he was unable to go himself (36:6). We are reminded of Paul's words later as he was writing from prison (2 Tim. 2:9).

When the people were in a worshipful mood, in Jehoiakim's fifth year, Baruch read the words in the hearing of the people (36:9, 10). The words caused quite a stir and finally reached the ears of the king (v. 21).

The act of the king in cutting and burning the Scripture, and the indifferent way in which those around him acted, shows the depths to which the spiritual state of Judah had fallen by then (36:23, 24). It is interesting that not only did Jehoiakim fail to destroy God's Word, but in fact he unwittingly caused it to be increased (36:32). What was added apparently included all that is dated after Jehoiakim's fifth year (chs. 24, 27, 28, 29, 32, 33, and 34, at least).

This was neither the first nor the last evil man who would seek to destroy God's Word, but all have been unsuccessful. It is notable that the source of this written Word is declared to be threefold: the Lord, Jeremiah and Baruch. Each had his part (36:4) but the true author is clearly the Lord.

The remaining chapters of this section record the swiftly moving events of the last days of Jerusalem before and after the captivity proper in 586 B.C. (chs. 37-44).

In those days Zedekiah, the last king, sought from Jeremiah an encouraging word from God, since the Egyptian Army had caused Nebuchadnezzar to retreat temporarily (37:5). But Jeremiah did not alter his earlier predictions that Jerusalem would fall.

At this time, Jeremiah went to see the property he had purchased (37:11, 12—cf. 32:8, 9). His act was taken as an act of treason and he was once more imprisoned (vv. 13-15). Yet, amazingly, Zedekiah still sought from him some word of hope (v. 17).

The feeling of Jeremiah's enemies was strong against him. They called for his death (38:4). The king, though sympathetic to Jeremiah, was weak, and he was willing for Jeremiah to perish (38:5, 6). Only at a servant's insistence did Zedekiah do anything to help Jeremiah (38:7-13). Evidently he hoped for a more favorable word from Jeremiah after this deed (vv. 14-16). If so, he was disappointed, since God's Word was still "surrender or perish" (vv. 17-23).

Chapter 39 records the fall of Jerusalem including the sad end of Zedekiah, who refused to follow God's Word, and the gracious treatment of Jeremiah by Nebuchadnezzar.

As a kind of footnote, we find here a special word of comfort for Ebedmelech who had aided Jeremiah in his time of distress (39:15-18). It indicates the concern of God for all of his own and recalls the later words of Jesus (Matt. 10:40-42; 25:40).

After the fall, Jeremiah chose to remain in Jerusalem (40:1-6). There, events occurred which made his stay shortlived (40:7—41:18). The treacherous act of Ishmael in murdering the good governor, Gedaliah, brought on a time of terror in the city which led to the flight of many into Egypt.

At first, those remaining sought God's will through Jeremiah. Their requests seemed sincere (42:1-3). Jeremiah, for the first time in a long time, felt free to pray for them. They appeared to submit to whatever the Lord should direct (vv. 5, 6).

God's answer was of blessing and not cursing, of planting and not plucking up, if they would obey him (v. 10). They were warned against going into Egypt (vv. 15-16). But apparently even as Jeremiah spoke God's Word, they murmured against him, for Jeremiah knew that they would not obey (v. 21). Not only did they flee to Egypt but they took along Jeremiah and Baruch as captives (43:6, 7).

What follows indicates that not only could God's Word not be destroyed or bound, but it could not be escaped either. In Egypt, Jeremiah went right on declaring God's Word and warning of judgment to come (43:8—44:30).

The Jews in Egypt committed grave sins against the Lord and indeed went back into Egyptian bondage spiritually as well as physically, out of which God had long before led them by Moses (44:15-19). The vain reasoning of the people was like that of the sinful Hebrews who murmured against Moses; paganism and bondage are better than serving God (44:19).

It is interesting that as a footnote to this history, God declared that his name would be no more be known by these Jews in Egypt (44:26). Archaeologists reveal to us that a group of Jews settled in Elephantine, an island on the Nile far to the South. Presumably these were remnants of those who had fled at the fall of Jerusalem. Their religion was a mixture of Judaism and paganism and their god's name, Yaho, was similar to but not the same as Yahweh, the true God of Israel.

That colony suddenly disappeared after some years and is never heard from again. Neither does the Bible ever mention them again.

After a special note of comfort to Baruch (ch. 45), the remainder of the book contains a series of messages to the nations similar to those found in other prophets (ch. 46—51:58). Remember that Jeremiah was called to speak to the nations (Gentiles) as well as to his own people (1:10).

The nations mentioned are listed in a kind of chronological order as they had played a part in Israel's history. First is *Egypt* (chapter 46). Egypt had played an important role in Israel's history very early as the nation that held them in bondage for four hundred years and as the nation which the Lord judged severely at the end of those years of bondage. The prophecy tells of the battle at Carchemish between Egypt and Babylon which was fought in 605 B.C. Egypt was decisively beaten (46:2).

On his way north to meet Nebuchadnezzar, Pharaoh-Necoh was intercepted by Josiah who was himself killed in the battle, a seemingly premature death (2 Kings 23:29; 2 Chron. 35:20-24).

The prophecy here stresses the decay and downfall of Egypt (46:13, 17). Egypt like other nations is judged because of her vain pride (v. 8).

In the prophecy is also hope for God's people. In the fall of their great enemy, the righteous can see the inevitable defeat of all of God's and their enemies (46:27-28). The latter part of verse 28 reminds us of God's revelation of himself to Moses—gracious, merciful, but not overlooking sin (Exod. 34:6, 7).

Next is *Philistia,* Israel's chief opponent after conquering the land of Canaan (ch. 47). The prophecy makes clear that the days of distress to come on Philistia and her cities is not by chance, but the deliberate judgment of God (vv. 4, 6, 7).

Then follows the pronouncement of judgment on *Moab, Ammon,* and *Edom* (ch. 48-49:22). These three are kin to Israel in history, as we saw in Amos 1. *Moab* is judged for her trust in her own works and belief in Chemosh (her god) rather than in the Lord (48:7, 13). These descendants of Lot turned from the God of Lot who was himself faithful (2 Peter 2:7). Moab in pride was exalted against God (vv. 26, 29) and had ridiculed Israel in her distress (v. 27). In the end Moab must be destroyed and lose its identity as a people (v. 42). Yet the prophecy closes on a note of hope for the latter end of Moab (v. 47), perhaps because of Lot and Ruth. From Ruth of Moab came Christ.

Ammon similarly shall be overthrown (49:2). Her god Malcam shall be shown to be no god at all (49:3). Yet too, there is hope for Ammon.

Edom will be brought down for her pride (49:15—see the book of Obadiah). These descendants of Esau, secular in heart, like Esau, would surely perish as Sodom and Gomorrah did (v. 18).

Then follows a brief condemnation of *Syria*, an enemy of Israel's middle and latter history (49:23-27). In a way similar to Amos chapter 1, Jeremiah tells of the overthrow of Damascus (v. 27).

After this *Kedar* and *Hazor* are mentioned briefly (49:28-33). These children of the east (v. 28) may have been kin to Job, the righteous ancient man (Job 1:3—cf. Judg. 6:3). They were to the east of Canaan, toward Arabia, perhaps bordering on Ammon (see Ezek. 25:4, 10). The Lord decreed their destruction perhaps because, as nomads, they were complacent, at ease, thinking that they were a law unto themselves (49:31). The Lord in singling them out for judgment declares that even they are accountable to him (vv. 32, 33).

Next, *Elam* draws judgment (vv. 34-39). The Elamites were one of the oldest continuous peoples still identifiable in Jeremiah's day (see Gen. 10:22; 14:1). Their location was beyond Mesopotamia, very remote from Israel, and later part of the Persian empire. Hope is extended to these people as to Ammon and Moab.

Finally, the major portion of these messages referring to the nations is directed to *Babylon* (ch. 50:1-51:58).

This prediction of the fall of Babylon came while Babylon was at the peak of its power. The fall would come in the form of an army from the north (ch. 50:9). The reason is that they were *glad* when they destroyed Israel (v. 11). They had been God's instrument of judgment, but the fact that they enjoyed doing so, condemned them as an evil people!

God's passion on his people whom he had punished is clear in verse 17. Israel has been run over long enough. God will begin to deliver (vv. 18, 19).

The fall of Babylon as in Isaiah 21:9, becomes symbolic for the fall of the earthly empires before the Lord and his Kingdom and is so used in Revelation 14:8; 18:2. The instrument of her fall is finally named, the Medes, and ultimately the Persians (51:11). It is that north country mentioned earlier (50:3, 9). Thus the Lord shows that he is sovereign over the nations, disposing of them as pleases him (51:15).

Then addressing the Medes, he calls them his battle ax, as earlier he spoke of the Assyrians as a razor that is hired (Isa. 7:20). This battle ax will crush Babylon because of its evil. If God is against a nation, it has no defense! (51:20-25).

In the midst of this prophecy came through a message to God's people. What is against Israel's enemies is *for* Israel. He speaks of the sure and everlasting covenant with his people (50:4, 5). He assures the remnant that they will survive because their Redeemer is strong (v. 34). While Babylon will be forsaken, God's people will not (51:5). Therefore, they must flee from Babylon (a warning not to love Babylon and identify with its evil while they are in captivity) (51:6, 9, 45).

After a short personal word to Seraiah (51:59-64), Jeremiah's words are ended. Seraiah was one who went to Babylon before the final fall of Jerusalem (v. 59). After he had read the words of Babylon's fall to come, he was to tie the words to a rock and, by a great gesture, signify the fall of Babylon in a dramatic way (vv. 63, 64).

The book closes with an appended history of those days (ch. 52, cf. 2 Kgs. 24, 25). It tells how Jerusalem was completely overthrown and destroyed. The Temple was destroyed and its wares taken to Babylon where they are next mentioned in Daniel's prophecy (Jer. 52:17ff., see Dan. 5:2-4).

Jeremiah notes three captives of Jerusalem: in the 7th, 18th, and 23rd years of Nebuchadnezzar (52:28-30). One other captivity, the first, in 605 B.C., the year of the battle of Carchemish, took some 10,000 captives (Dan. 1:1; 2 Kings 24:14). The dates for the four captivities therefore are approximately as follows: In 605, 10,000; in 597, 3,023; in 568, 832 and in 581 B.C., 745; some 14,600 in all.

In about 561 B.C., Evil-Merodach raised up Jehoiachin as mentioned earlier (2 Kings 25:27-30). This was perhaps done as an evidence that God was still with his people.

LAMENTATIONS—BY JEREMIAH

This poem of Lamentations was probably written by Jeremiah and is in our English Bible attached to Jeremiah's prophecy. It is a beautiful expression of that response which the Lord expects from his children when confronted with their sin. It is a poem of the broken heart, the broken and contrite heart which God desires in his children (Psa. 51:17).

The structure of this poem is very important to our understanding of it. It is acrostic, meaning that the letters of the Hebrew alphabet in their proper order guide the writer in the development of his poem. The first word in the verse begins with the first letter of the Hebrew alphabet, *aleph*. The second verse begins with the second letter in order in the Hebrew alphabet, and so on. Since there are twenty-two letters in the

Hebrew alphabet there are twenty-two verses in the first chapter, going, as it were, from a to z.

The second chapter is constructed in exactly the same way. It too has twenty-two verses. But chapter three alters the pattern, using the same letter of the alphabet for three successive verses. Therefore verses 1-3 in chapter 3 all begin with *aleph*, the first Hebrew letter and verses 4-6 all begin with the second letter, *beth*, etc. Thus chapter 3 has sixty-six (3 times 22) verses instead of twenty-two.

Chapter 4 reverts to the pattern of chapters 1 and 2. But the final chapter, 5, is not acrostic at all. The fact that it has twenty-two verses has nothing to do with the alphabet but was probably divided that way by those who later divided the book into verses just to keep closer to the pattern of the other chapters.

In an acrostic poem the main word in each verse is the alphabet word. It is the word around which the entire thought of that particular verse is built. It shows us clearly the emphasis intended by the writer.

Other alphabet poems in whole or in part are found in the Psalms and Proverbs. Most notable of these are Psalm 119 and the poem concerning the worthy woman which is found in verses 10-31 of the last chapter of Proverbs.

In the consideration of the book of Lamentations we shall note the key word in each verse which is the alphabet word. It will help us to understand more clearly the message of each chapter. The poem is in part an expression of Jeremiah's sorrow and in part a personification of the city of Jerusalem as it lies in ruins after the fall of the city to the Babylonians.

How (aleph), verse 1. This word begins the entire poem. It expresses the terrible feeling of despair in Jeremiah as he looks on this city, desolate, as a widow abandoned.

Weeps (beth), verse 2. This key word expresses the feeling of the city personified and of all of God's children who see the city destroyed and who love her. The mention of her lovers of course recalls Hosea's message.

Captivity (gimel), verse 3. This single word communicates all of the distress of Judah. The people are no longer free to serve God. The city is empty because all of her people have been carried away.

Ways (daleth, etc.), verse 4. Even the paths leading to the Temple and the city itself are empty. None pass through her gates.

Are, verse 5. Here the verb "to be" with Jerusalem's enemies as the subject summarizes the situation. No longer do God's people rule the city. Instead, enemies do. The young children taken away remind us of those like Daniel and his three friends or Ezekiel.

And, verse 6. The conjunction adds pain to pain. Not only is she desolate but all of her beauty is gone. Her leaders of the past are all put to flight in shame.

Remember, verse 7. At a time like this God's people remember the good life they once had. The present hardships they are under wake them from the stupor of sin under which they lost the blessings of God.

Sinned, verse 8. Again in the manner of Hosea's prophecy, sin and is consequences come to mind. The clear and only explanation for her present plight is her past persistence in sin.

Filthiness, verse 9. Added to sin is its effect in Jerusalem's life. She is defiled and there is none to comfort.

Hand, verse 10. The enemy's hand is against the city and its people. Those whom God formerly defeated before Israel now have overthrown the city, even the Temple.

All, verse 11. None is immune to the suffering and hardship among the citizens of Jerusalem, not even the righteous, such as Jeremiah.

Nothing, verse 12. While God's people in Jerusalem, personified here, suffer such affliction, strangers pass by and show no concern.

From on high, verse 13. God's people must recognize that this affliction which they now suffer is not an accident of history but God's punishment on a disobedient people. It came from God, from on high, not from men.

Is bound, verse 14. The passive voice of this verb expresses the plight of the criminal in the hands of the punisher. God has put Israel as a prisoner in the hands of her enemies. She is led where her enemies please.

At nought, verse 15. All that Israel trusted in, her mighty men, are as nothing now. All which Jerusalem treasured and was proud of is reduced to zero.

For, verse 16. The cause of weeping is now evident. The preposition here simply focuses attention upon the cause of Jerusalem and Jeremiah's sorrow. The comfort promised to Israel (Isa. 40) is far from the people now. They who by God's promise (Gen. 3:15) had hoped for victory over their enemies were presently being vanquished instead.

Spreads, verse 17. Though the people pray for help, yet none comes to comfort. As Isaiah warned, their prayers are of no avail because of their sinfulness (Isa. 1:15).

Righteous, verse 18. Yet none of this indicates that God has been unfaithful in keeping his Word. It is because the people have disobeyed and ignored God for so long.

Called, verse 19. The perfidy of Jerusalem is shown here in that, while in distress, she did not call on God but on humans to aid and comfort her. They did not help though, being too busy looking out for themselves.

Behold, verse 20. Now Jeremiah perhaps on behalf of Jerusalem calls on the Lord for help.

They have heard, verse 21. The enemies have heard of Jerusalem's trouble and are glad. This is in accord with what we have seen throughout God's revelation. The enemy of God and his people always rejoices at the fall of God's people. They too therefore displease God and shall be judged (cf. Isa. 14:5, 6; Jer. 30:16).

Come, verse 22. The plea of the prophet is on behalf of God's people, that God's justice may be done also to those enemies as his justice has fallen on Jerusalem, his city.

In chapter 2, beginning again at the first of the Hebrew alphabet, the prophet by the alphabetical key words expresses God's judgment against Jerusalem. Beginning again with the word "how," he is awed by God's anger toward his people (v. 1). He expresses by the key words in these verses how the wrath of God has fallen against Israel and Jerusalem. He has *swallowed up* (v. 2), *cut off* (v. 3) and *bent* his bow against them (v. 4) like an enemy.

Indeed, the Lord has *become* as an enemy to Israel (v. 5—cf. Jer. 30:14). *And* (verse 6) added to this, he has removed his sanctuary (symbolic of his presence) from Jerusalem as Hosea had warned against Israel (see Hos. 9). God has therefore *cast off* his altar (the means of reconciliation) (v. 7) and *purposed* even the destruction of her walls (v. 8). As the gates *sink* (v. 9) and the elders *sit* silenced on the ground (v. 10) only dismay is left in the hearts of those who remain. What Hosea had warned would happen has now come to pass (v. 9—cf. Hos. 3:4).

Verses 11-19, still in alphabetical order, express the varied reactions to Jerusalem's plight by Jeremiah, by the citizens and by his enemies. The *failing* of Jeremiah's eyes (v. 11) and pleas of the children *to their mothers* for food (v. 12) give us a very heart-rending picture of how it was in that sad day of Jerusalem's fall. Note the great contrast between the insurpassable sorrow of present Jerusalem and her past praises of the insurpassable glory of her God (v. 13). We recall Jeremiah's earlier words when we read here of Jerusalem's wounds (Jer. 30:12-15).

In verse 14 he puts much blame for Jerusalem's plight on her false *prophets* who gave false and groundless hope to the citizens in her latter days.

The responses of Jerusalem's enemies are described by the verbs *"clap"* (v. 15) and *"open their mouths"* (v. 16). While God's people sorrow when the church is disgraced, Satan's children rejoice. Yet all is not by accident. The prophet retains his conviction of the sovereignty of God through all of this. What has happened, God warned would happen long before (see Deut. 28:15ff.). Therefore though enemies overrun the city now, all must know that God has *done* it (v. 17).

Verses 18, 19 exhort the people to call on the Lord now for help. A repentant and broken heart is what God calls for. They must *cry* (v. 18) and *rise* to cry some more until God shows mercy (v. 19).

In these final verses he completes the sad picture of the people *lying* desolate in the streets (v. 21). In calling God to *see* (v. 20) he is pleading for God's mercy now. God has *called* (v. 22) *forth* the terror that has stricken the hearts of the people, now perhaps he will call for mercy on the remnant.

In chapter 3, (the acrostic poem that uses *three* successive verses for each letter of the alphabet rather than one verse), verses 1-3 all begin with *aleph*, the first Hebrew letter. In verses 1-18 the prophet, speaking for Jerusalem as a whole, expresses the feeling of helplessness in the hearts of the people as they realize that all that has happened has been by God's intention.

In verses 19ff., however, he calls to *remembrance* his affliction and from it remembers God's love and faithfulness. In a fashion similar to Isaiah 1:9, he realizes that but for God's love, they would be altogether destroyed, so great is their sin and deserved judgment (v. 22).

This leads to the introduction of the call to wait on the Lord (to put trust and hope in him) after the manner of other prophets before (Amos, Hosea and Isaiah). All of these repeatedly called on the people to put trust in the Lord, i.e., to wait on him, for in the Lord alone is the answer to our greatest needs (v. 25).

There follows in the rest of the chapter, continuing on the theme of God's goodness (v. 25), a plea to do good in response to God's goodness (vv. 26, 27). What we have in the following verses is a true theology of crisis showing God's people how they must behave in times of distress while God's wrath is being poured out on the church for its sins.

In such times God's people who go through tribulation with the unrepentant sinners must bear what comes, waiting for the

Lord to work out his purposes and not despairing as though this crisis is the end of all things. It is not (vv. 26-30)! The Lord has his purpose in all such tribulation (vv. 31-32). When God afflicts, affliction is not the end but is discipline to the end that his church be purged and his true people be strengthened (vv. 32-36). The Lord metes out both good and bad but he is always in control and all injustices will be punished (vv. 36-39).

If this is what God calls for in crisis, our looking to him and waiting, then it is our part to acknowledge him in the midst of the tribulation, confessing our guilt and pleading for God's mercy (vv. 40-54). Verse 53 is particularly reminiscent of Jeremiah's own expereince (cf. Jer. 37:16).

Now in recalling God's past deliverances of his people from former distresses, Jeremiah can be assured that this crisis, too, will pass and the enemies of God and God's people will be duly punished by God (vv. 55-56).

Chapter 4, also an acrostic poem, recalls once more Jerusalem's plight but closes again with assurance first that God's wrath has an end (v. 11) and that God's enemies will all in the end be punished (vv. 21, 22).

In much the same style as Isaiah 40:2, he is assured that the end of the church's punishment, for now, is near (v. 22—cf. Jer. 33:7, 8). The end of Jerusalem's suffering will foreshadow the punishment of her enemies (v. 22—cf. Jer. 25:29; 1 Pet. 4:17).

The final chapter is not an acrostic poem. It does fully review the whole. It concludes by offering the only real hope for God's people at any time.

The seventh verse reflects the despair of the people who conclude that the paths of their fathers have led to the present tragic circumstances. We compare Jeremiah 14:20. Yet there is no attempt to acquit themselves or to blame it all on their fathers. Plainly the people of God have through this tragedy, come to see clearly their own guilt (Jer. 16:12; 31:29, 30). Later, when some in the land did attempt to push the blame off wholly to their parents, God through Ezekiel sternly rebuked them (Ezek. 18:2).

Verse 8 seems to be a reverse of the prophecy given by Noah so long before. Now instead of being served, the people of God are having to serve those who ought to have served them (cf. Gen. 9:25-27).

This final chapter also offers the only real answer to Judah's plight or the plight of any sinner caught in his own web of deceit and lies. "Turn thou us unto Thee, O Lord, and we shall be turned" (v. 21). So enmeshed in sin were the people that they were captives and helpless to help themselves. Only by God's grace and power could they turn back to the Lord (cf. Jer. 31:18, 19).

ZEPHANIAH

The ministries of four other prophets in Jerusalem are contemporary with Jeremiah. These are Zephaniah, Nahum, Obadiah, and Habakkuk. We shall now look at these prophets and their particular messages, recognizing that each spoke against the same background that obtained in Jeremiah's day.

Zephaniah repeats much that has been said already, yet in his own unique way. First he deals with the Day of the Lord (1:2-18); then he calls men to seek the Lord (2:1-3). He expands on the meaning of the Day of the Lord as a day of wrath for all sinners in 2:4-3:7. Finally, he closes with a message that the righteous must wait on the Lord in such days (3:8-20). He wrote in the days of Josiah, who, you will remember, sought to lead the people back to the Lord (1:1). Yet Jeremiah had already declared the revival a failure because the people had returned only feignedly, not with their whole hearts (Jer. 3:6-10).

The prophet himself tells us more about his heritage and family than most do. It is quite unusual for a prophet to trace back his lineage four generations as Zephaniah does. The most reasonable explanation is to assume that the Hezekiah referred to here (1:1) is *the* King Hezekiah. Thus, he is a prince from the royal line of Judah and, as was Jeremiah, of priestly descent. Zephaniah probably prophesied from about 650 to 600 B.C., toward the latter part of that period.

The prophecy begins with a very thorough denunciation of all sinners: the less obvious as well as the more obvious ones. The Day of Wrath will be terrible for all sinners (1:2-18).

In verses 2-6 he builds up to a climax of soul searching proportions. The statement at the beginning, "I will utterly consume all things from off the face of the ground," is expanded below.

We note that the order of destruction of the creatures in verse 3 is just the reverse of the order of creation (cf. Gen. 1), as if God were saying, "I shall undo all my work." From this we learn again the lesson that in man's prosperity all creation prospers, but in his curse, all is cursed (so Gen. 3:17; Rom. 8:20-22).

The picture of God's hand of judgment stretched out is by now a familiar one to us in Scripture (cf. Jer. 6:12; 15:6; Ezek. 6:14, etc.). We see here a progression in the objects of God's wrath from the more obvious Baal worshipers and worshipers of idols and stars to those who have simply turned from following the Lord and even those who have neglected seeking his will (vv. 4-6). Not only the more blatant idol worshipers, but even those who still profess to be worshipers of the Lord, while neglecting to seek the Lord in their lives, will feel God's wrath. We know that in Josiah's day the judgments began (1 Kgs. 23:4, 5). We know, too, that God was equally displeased with those who professed him with their lips but did not turn to him (seek him) in their hearts (Jer. 3:10).

The term "Day of the Lord" was introduced by Joel long before. Since then it has always been described by the prophets as a day of terror for all unrepentant sinners. We feel the horror of that day as the cries of the perishing resound from one part of the city to another (vv. 9, 10). The thoroughness of God's searching out the sinners is graphically portrayed (v. 12). Men seek to hide their sin in their hearts but cannot hide it from God (cf. Jer. 17:9, 10).

In verses 14-18, Zephaniah describes this coming, awful day in a manner similar to Joel 2 and Amos 5:18ff. Darkness shall prevail then. God will bring to an end the sinners in the land (v. 18). No doubt he is pointing to the time of the fall of Jerusalem in 586 B.C., but that fall and the tragedy connected with it point beyond to the final judgment of God on all sinners everywhere. Thus there are in history many lesser "Days of the Lord," but all point to that great climax in history, the final overthrow of all that is evil and rebellious against God.

It is quite expected and usual, in the style of the prophets, that before Zephaniah goes on to develop the doctrine of the Day of Wrath he issues a call to sinners to seek the Lord (2:1-3). In the manner of Amos, he calls for them to seek the Lord (v. 3—cf. Amos 5:6). After the manner of Isaiah 11:4, he particularly addresses the meek of the earth, i.e., the brokenhearted and truly repentant, who hope in God alone.

The next major section of this prophecy declares the coming Day of Wrath on those who are not reconciled to God, whether in the nations of the world or in Judah (2:4-37). Having pronounced woe on the foreign nations: Philistia, Moab, Ammon, Ethiopia and Assyria, he then turns to Judah in the style we saw in Amos 1 and 2.

Rebellious Judah failed to respond either to God's teaching or his correction (3:2). She failed to trust in her God. Rulers, prophets and priests are all guilty (vv. 3, 4). But they must now deal with a righteous God who will not overlook iniquity (v. 5—cf. Exod. 34:6, 7).

What does this mean for the righteous in the land who do seek the Lord and trust in him? Zephaniah gives testimony in the concluding part of the book (3:8-20).

The answer is that God's people, in the midst of the coming trials because of Judah's sins and disobedience, must wait (v. 8)! God will in the end execute justice on all nations. The call to the remnant to wait can be traced throughout the writings of the prophets (Hos. 12:6; Isa. 8:17; 40:31, 49:23; Mic. 7:7; Jer. 14:22; Lam. 3:25, 26). God will save those who look to him in hope. He will turn hearts to him (v. 9—cf. Jer. 31:33, 34).

Purging of the church must come (v. 11) but when the church is purged God will leave the poor who have waited, the remnant (vv. 12, 13). Thus God's true people, even in the midst of trials and seeming defeat, can nevertheless rejoice (v. 14ff.). Here we have in essence the answer to the sadness expressed in Lamentations.

Once more, as with Moses so long ago (Exod. 3), God comforts his people by assuring them that he will be with them (v. 17). God will rescue his afflicted ones, a promise that those who trust in him and suffer for it in the world will in the end be vindicated (vv. 19, 20).

NAHUM

Although the prophet Nahum does not give us the date of his writing, the fact that he is concerned primarily with predicting Nineveh's fall dates him at about 630, prior anyway to 612 when Nineveh fell. This would make him contemporary with Jeremiah and Zephaniah.

He begins with a general pronouncement of God's judgment against his enemies (ch. 1). The Lord is seen from two standpoints as he has revealed himself in history. First, he is jealous, avenging and full of wrath (v. 2). This is the way he always appears to his enemies, those who do not believe in him. But he is also slow to anger. He does not destroy quickly. God exercises great patience with his enemies (v. 3—cf. Exod. 34:6, 7). When he judges nations, therefore, it is because men and nations have, over a long period, refused him. None can then expect mercy (v. 6).

But to his friends, to those who take refuge in God, he is a shepherd, a stronghold, a place of escape as we saw in Zephaniah (v. 7). Each man therefore faces God either as God's friend or his enemy (vv. 7, 8).

The balance of chapter 1 simply shows that God's judgment is thorough. He will purge out all evil but at the same time proclaim the message of peace to those who look to him (vv. 9-15). In verse 15 he quotes from Isaiah 40 verse 9, the beginning of God's message of hope through Isaiah.

Having pronounced judgment in general, he now focuses in upon Nineveh (chs. 2, 3). We can see from chapter 1 how God's slowness to anger is applied in his dealings with Nineveh, capital of Assyria. Some two hundred years before, the Lord had seen Nineveh's wickedness and had had compassion on her. He therefore sent Jonah to warn her of judgment. Through Jonah's warning he led her to repent. The feet bringing good tidings of peace had walked the streets of Nineveh once.

But God will not always be patient. A time of judgment does come on those who continue to rebel. Now Nineveh's time has come. From 2:8, we learn that this message of wrath falls upon Nineveh.

We are reminded of Isaiah's word earlier against Jerusalem (3:1ff—cf. Isa. 1). Some of the words are similar to God's words through Hosea to Israel (3:4, 5—cf. Hos. 2:2, 3). The same kinds of judgments threatened against Israel's earlier enemies are now threatened against Nineveh (3:13-15—cf. Amos 1).

In words reminiscent of Joel's description of the northern army (Assyria) as like locusts, so here Nahum acknowledges that Nineveh has indeed been like a locust plague (3:16, 17). Now God's sun of judgment shall rise and all of these locusts shall flee (v. 17).

He speaks of grievous wounds in Nineveh as Isaiah earlier did to Judah (Isa. 1). But the great contrast in the two messages is that there is no hope offered to Nineveh though hope was offered to Judah. Nineveh's time has come to be judged. There is no escape.

The book is therefore a commentary on Genesis 3:15. God will defeat all of his and our enemies if we trust in him and wait, as Zephaniah had also exhorted.

OBADIAH

We can date this book to the same period as Jeremiah, principally from the internal evidence. In verse 11 is mentioned the day of Jerusalem's fall or captivity. The message pertains to the period of seeming defeat for God's people. It is the shortest Old Testament book of prophecy. It deals with the judgment of God to come on Edom (v. 1). The first nine verses in particular speak of the cause of that judgment—Edom's pride. Edom, to the southeast of Jerusalem, is the biblical nation that descended from Esau, the first son of Isaac and twin brother of Jacob (Gen. 25:19-26). Before the two were born, the Lord foretold that Esau and Jacob would be the fathers of two nations. The struggle in Rebecca's womb foreshadowed the struggle that would occur between the two nations in their history. But Jacob, the younger, who became the father of the Israelites, would prevail. In the end Esau, father of the Edomites, would serve him.

But more than just the history of two nations was involved here. We see very early that though born of the same parents and even in the same conception, Jacob and Esau are of two distinctly different families. Jacob is of the seed of God, the righteous, and Esau of the seed of the evil one, Satan. Their nature is revealed quite early as we noted in studying Genesis.

This fact, that the two are determined as to their destiny before they are born, is called to the attention of the Jews in the post-exilic period by God through the prophet Malachi. It is illustrative of God's love for Jacob (Israel) (Mal. 1:2, 3). Thus God's love for Jacob and choosing his descendants and not those of Edom demonstrates the functioning of God's election, i.e., his choosing according to his own good purpose.

Paul, in Romans 9, develops this further. He shows that on the basis of God's electing mercy, while the two children were still unborn and had done nothing good or bad, God's purpose stood not on the contingency of what they might do, but on God's choice and action (Rom. 9:10-12). In Paul's great chapter on election (Rom. 9), the illustration of God's choice of Jacob and rejection of Esau demonstrates to me that the ultimate decision of who are to be God's children rests with God and not with man. In Hebrews, therefore, where Jacob is mentioned as a man of faith (11:21), Esau is called profane (12:16), i.e., unholy, worldly.

In Malachi later, when God teaches Israel about his love of Jacob and his hate of (rejection of) Esau, Esau becomes illustrative of God's treatment of the nations that reject him (Mal. 1:3-5).

This helps us to see why Obadiah was written. Esau (Edom) is the profane nation, illustrative of all nations which exalt themselves against the Lord. Edom is proud and self-sufficient as was Esau (v. 3). Reference to their dwellings in the rock (v. 3) may refer to the ancient site of Sela (Petra), which means "rock."

This site, later developed by the Romans, was in the land occupied by Edom at this time. It is first mentioned in Scripture in 2 Kings 14:7. About 300 B.C., control of the site moved from Edom to the Nabataean Arabs and then in A.D. 105 to Rome.

Most of the beautiful remains there today are carved in the rose colored rock of that area and date from Roman times. However, some caves in the rock, carved in the great cliffs, which are so characteristic of that site, date back to the ancient days, even before Edom. The city could be entered only by the narrow entrance way which could be easily defended. It is easy to see why inhabitants of Sela would feel arrogantly proud and self-secure as did the Edomites (Obad. 3). But God would and did overthrow them, as we have seen (vv. 4, 8, 9).

In verses 10-16, *the reasons for God's judgment against Edom* are declared. *First,* there are the *specific judgments against Edom* (vv. 10-14). Precisely, it is the violence done to Jacob (Israel) by Edom (Esau) (v. 10). That violence was mentioned earlier in the prophets (Joel 3:19; Amos 1:11). To that violence God now adds charges against her actions on the occasion of Jerusalem's fall and captivity (vv. 11-12). They not only stood and watched as in a theater (v. 11) but probably rejoiced as well that Israel suffered (v. 12), a thing God would not tolerate.

They are warned against rejoicing or taking part in the spoiling or blocking the way of those who seek to escape (vv. 13, 14), even though God had warned those in Jerusalem not to try to escape (Jer. 38:17, 18, 39:4ff., 42:10-17).

Next, general pronouncements against all nations are given (vv. 15, 16). This shows that the specific warning against Edom has application to all the proud and profane peoples of earth.

The book of Obadiah concludes with *a section exalting Israel,* the remnant, the true people of God (vv. 17-21). The mention of Mount Zion recalls Isaiah 2:2ff. and 4:2, 3. The "escaped" here (v. 17) are the remnant mentioned in other passages. As Isaiah said, the remnant shall be holy, the holy seed, God's own possession (cf. Isa. 6:13).

In words similar to Amos 2, now Jacob shall be a fire itself instead of being consumed by fire (v. 18). Esau's being compared to stubble is like Jeremiah 5:14.

In Esau (Edom) the profane people, there will be no remnant (v. 18), just as there is no remnant from Nineveh (cf. Nahum 3).

In the end, as God said from the beginning, God's people shall triumph in the Kingdom of God (v. 21, cf. Gen. 3:15).

HABAKKUK

This prophet probably wrote at about the time of Jeremiah's last days in Jerusalem, just prior to the fall of Jerusalem. We surmise this from the mention of the Chaldeans in 1:6, describing them as an army about to invade the land.

The book of Habakkuk is concerned with a problem common to the eighth and seventh century prophets: the problem of sin in the church (Israel), and the seeming triumph of iniquity in Israel. Habakkuk introduces his book by a complaint about this (1:1-4). There follows an answer from God to the prophet's complaint (1:5-11). However, God's answer raises another problem to Habakkuk which troubles him more (1:12-2:1).

After this, God gives to Habakkuk a response to his second complaint and that answer of God is the heart of the book (2:2-20). Finally, after contemplation of God's answer, the prophet responds beautifully in praise and commitment, being assured and comforted through God's Word (3:1-19).

We shall now look in more detail at the message of Habakkuk. Habakkuk's *first problem* is expressed in 1:1-4. He is disturbed because though he has often cried out to God on behalf of the righteous in the land who are being oppressed by the unrighteous, God has not seemed to hear (v. 2). All around is violence, yet the Lord apparently is not doing anything about it.

He enumerates the acts of violence. He sees iniquity and perverseness, destruction and violence, strife and contention (v. 3). The law of God is ignored and justice is not done (v. 4). It seems that everywhere in the land the wicked are in control and their brand of justice prevails.

This is the typical picture we get of the state of affairs in Israel and Judah from the time of Amos to Jeremiah. Habakkuk is one more in the series of prophets who cried out against such evil in the church, among the people of Israel. Like Jeremiah and others, Habakkuk was rightly disturbed and he mourned as every true believer ought.

To his complaint God gave *a forthright answer* (1:5-11). In essence God showed to the prophet that he already had been working to deal with the iniquity in the land (v. 5). Specifically, he had raised up the Chaldeans (Babylonians) to punish his people (v. 6). Thus, in a style reminiscent of Joel, he described the frightening warlike character of this great army machine (vv. 6-11).

In other words, as God had foretold through Isaiah and Jeremiah, he was raising up these Babylonians to be the instrument in his hand to punish Judah and Jerusalem.

This caused another problem in Habakkuk's mind (1:12-2:1). He began by reciting the creed of God's people—the Lord is from everlasting. He is holy. He is above the petty errors of men. God has promised life to his people. He would never go back on that promise. The cry "We shall not die" (v. 12) expresses the confidence of God's true children in their Lord. But God sees the pagans, the people like Babylon, as stored up for judgment (v. 12).

From verses 13-17, Habakkuk describes the pagans who deal treacherously. He calls them the wicked who swallow up those *more righteous* than they are (v. 13). There follows a picture of the pagan, worshiping the works of his own hands. He is described as like a fisherman who captures men in his nets. He is proud and vain, worshiping the things that enable him to conquer, his own power and war machine. He goes on slaying the nations one by one (v. 17).

Habakkuk is here portraying the typical pagan power that threatened God's people from time to time. Surely God would not permit these heathen powers to overrun Israel, which was at least more righteous than the pagans (v. 13)! Habakkuk felt his point was well made. He would wait to see how the holy God could answer this one (2:1).

The answer received was a classic one (2:2-20), a basis for the later New Testament development of the great doctrine of justification by faith alone.

First, the Lord stressed the importance of what he was about to say. It was so important it should be posted on the billboards of that day (v. 2). It would be an answer well worth waiting for (v. 3).

He begins in verse 4. "His soul" apparently refers to the soul of the unrighteous mentioned above, that is, whoever is not upright. The characteristic of all the unrighteous (those not upright) is that they are puffed up and proud. This is true of *all* the wicked. By contrast, the *righteous,* those upright before God, live before God by faith alone.

God says here that two kinds of people exist in the world: the wicked who are not at all upright before God, and the righteous who are righteous by faith in God alone, just as was Abraham (Gen. 15:6).

The importance of this in reference to Habakkuk's problem then was that in this sense there is no such thing as the "more righteous" or the "less righteous." One is either righteous by faith in God or he is not righteous at all. In this sense we find no *degrees* of righteousness. Either it is reckoned by faith or we do not have it at all. The proud who think that they are justified by their works are merely puffed up. Such a one is like a drunk man, haughty but staggering through life into hell itself (v. 5).

In answer to Habakkuk's plea that only God's people who trusted in him should live (1:12), God therefore says, "Yes, by faith!"

Beginning in verse 6 to the end of this chapter we have a

taunting proverb which shows that it matters not whether the unrighteous one is in the church (Israel) or outside the church (pagan). All of the unrighteous displease God and shall be punished.

In a series of woes he teaches this (vv. 6-16). *Woe* to the pagan nation that plunders other nations and works violence to cities. It will be plundered in the end (vv. 6-8). But also *woe* to the individual who gets an evil gain for his house. He does his plundering on a smaller scale but God will not overlook it (vv. 9-11).

Woe to the nation that builds cities with blood (the ravages of war) and goes from conquest to conquest without thought of God's glory (vv. 12-14). But also *woe* to the man who gives his neighbor drink to make him drunk and act lewdly. He might as well be uncircumsized. God will surely punish him (vv. 15-17).

Thus God will judge all violence: that of the pagan nation which had so concerned Habakkuk but also that of the sinners in Jerusalem which also had concerned the prophet. All unrighteousness wherever it is will be ferreted out by God and punished. All idolatry: pagan or Israelite (vv. 18, 19) is equally heinous in God's sight and will be judged.

He concludes with a picture of God in his holy Temple before whom all the world is guilty and therefore put to shame. None have any righteousness at all of their own with which to boast to God. All are put to silence before the holy God (2:20—cf. Rom. 3:19).

After this marvelous answer from God, Habakkuk responds with a great hymn of praise and commitment to the Lord (Habakkuk chapter 3). It is the song of the believer, an affirmation of faith in the God who has revealed himself as the Lord has revealed himself to Habakkuk.

First, he contemplates the glory of the Lord in creation and providence (vv. 1-11). He sees the wrath of God to come because of Israel's sin and pleads for mercy (v. 2). Finally, he concludes that as God has explained, he marches through the earth judging nation after nation and overthrowing strongholds (v. 12). But he does it for a purpose. The rise and fall of nations in the course of history does have meaning. God does it all ultimately for the salvation of his people (those justified by faith) (v. 13). The latter part of verse 13 no doubt has reference to Genesis 3:15, the ultimate victory over the serpent (Satan).

As Habakkuk realized that the awful judgment must fall on Jerusalem and that even the righteous must go through it, he trembled (v. 16). But he understood too that he must accept it and wait quietly for it. He was resigned to the tribulation to come.

Though he suffer the loss of all things (v. 17), yet he can still rejoice! Why? Because he knows that God is with him and will give him the victory in the end (vv. 18, 19)! It is a great affirmation of faith and one echoed later by Paul in Romans 8:28.

Thus all believers are taught that when the church sins it will go through judgment, and though God's children must share in this judgment with the unrighteous, they will be preserved and survive. Thus the remnant, God's people, can go through the storm, in the confidence that God is with them.

12

THE TIME OF
PURGING
586-400 B.C.

THE HISTORY OF
THE PERIOD

BEFORE CONTINUING our survey of the prophets it is well to look at the history of the period of the exilic and post-exilic writings. This was a very active period in the ancient world. We can survey only briefly some of the more important events and activities of that time.

It was a time of the formation of some of the great religions of the world whose effect is still felt today. Zoroastrianism was being formed by the great Persian prophet Zoroaster, of whom very little is known, even his exact period of activity. At the same general time Confucius in China and Buddha in India were coming to the fore in the establishing of the religions to be known ultimately by their names. All of this was at the time of the emergence of Judaism among the Jews in captivity. Radical changes began to take place among the Jews because of the Temple's destruction and their being scattered among the nations. In order to maintain their traditions and faith, traditional doctrine began first to be taught and then later written down, giving structure, unity and meaning to Judaism throughout the world after the exile.

In the political world we have seen the superiority move from Assyria to Babylon already. During this period it would change again. For the last time, Semitic peoples akin to the Jews would have dominance there in the ancient world. The Babylonians were the last Semitic people to dominate Mesopotamia. The Medes and Persians after them were not Semites. There followed the Greeks and Romans, who ruled at the time of Christ. At the time of the end of the period (400 B.C.), the Persians were still in control, but the Greeks, eventually to be led by Alexander the Great, would take over the area before the end of the next century.

The Babylonian Empire which brought the downfall of Jerusalem was primarily the empire of Nebuchadnezzar. He was its dominant figure. In 612 B.C., Nineveh, capital of Assyria, fell. It was the first great campaign of Nebuchadnezzar and was led by his father whom he succeeded shortly. Later Haran, the last stronghold against Nebuchadnezzar, fell in 610 B.C.

As Nebuchadnezzar rose in power Pharaoh Necoh of Egypt, also ambitious, went to meet Nebuchadnezzar. The two armies met and fought at Carchemish in 605 in one of the great battles of the ancient world. Necoh was defeated and Babylonian dominance of the whole Bible world was assured. It was during this campaign, as Necoh went north to meet Nebuchadnezzar, that Josiah, the last good king of Judah, went out to intercept Pharaoh Necoh and was killed (see 2 Kgs. 23:29).

In those same days, Nebuchadnezzar swept down into Palestine to demonstrate his dominance in the area, taking some captives of the Hebrew children including Daniel and his three friends (see Dan. 1:1-2). This was about 605 B.C. during the reign of Jehoiakim in Jerusalem.

Later, in 597 B.C., Nebuchadnezzar came again and took Jehoiachin captive together with a large number of Israelites. Among those taken away this time was Ezekiel (Ezek. 1:1-3). From 588-586 B.C. Jerusalem and two outlying towns (Azekah and Lachish) were all that remained of Judah. They are mentioned in Jeremiah 34:6, 7. In the so-called Lachish Letters, recently discovered, exchanges between these cities and their last days have been brought to light by archaeologists. They give a graphic picture of what life was like under siege by Babylon.

Jerusalem fell in 586 B.C. The last stronghold in that part of the world, Tyre, held out twelve more years but finally fell in 574 as both Ezekiel and Jeremiah foretold (Jer. 27:1-11; Ezek. 26:1-28:19; 29:18-20).

At this point let us review the last days of Judah. Jehoahaz, the son of Josiah, ruled only three months and was deposed by Pharaoh Necoh (2 Kgs. 23:33). His older brother, Eliakim (Jehoiakim), was appointed by Necoh and ruled in his stead. He died in office as Jerusalem lay under siege. The next king, Jehoiachin, ruled for three months and was taken to Babylon in 597 B.C. Ezekiel went also in this first phase of the captivity. Jehoiachin remained a prisoner in Babylon until his release thirty-seven years later in the days of Evil-Merodach (2 Kgs. 25:27-28). The last king, Zedekiah, Jehoiachin's uncle, ruled eleven years. Most of that time Jerusalem was under virtual control of Babylon until it actually fell in 586 B.C.

The Babylonian Empire under Nebuchadnezzar thrived. After his death the kingdom lasted only twenty-three years. He was succeeded by Amelmarduk (Evilmarduk in Scripture). He was assassinated by his brother-in-law in his second year of rule 560 B.C. In quick succession four kings ruled from 560 to 539 B.C. The last two were father and son who ruled part of that time together. Nabonidus began to rule in 556 and his son, Belshazzar, with him in 553 B.C. Belshazzar was in command in the city of Babylon when in 539 it fell to the Persians while his father was out of the city.

In the time of Babylonian power, the Jewish exiles for the most part lived in or near Babylon. The history of the Jews who remained in Jerusalem after the fall is lost to us. All attention in Scripture is focused on those who lived in exile.

In Babylon, the problem the exiles faced was the challenge to their faith brought on by the seeming defeat of their God by the Babylonian army. It was the task of the prophets who went into captivity to show that the end of Judah did not mean the end of the people of God or the defeat of their God. Daniel and Ezekiel were God's spokesmen for God's people in exile and by their example and prophecy the true faith was taught and exemplified for the Jews.

Finally, as we noted, Babylon fell to the Persians in 539 B.C. The next year, Cyrus the Great, ruler of the Medes and the Persians, gave orders granting the Jews permission to return to Jerusalem and rebuild the temple destroyed by Nebuchadnezzar. We know that it was Cyrus' policy to repatriate the deserted lands and that he was instrumental in many such returns of peoples to their native lands. Nevertheless, it was God who stirred him to do this so that God's Word through Jeremiah could be fulfilled.

Expenses for the return were met out of the Persian treasury. All Jews who so desired could return. The sacred vessels carried away by Nebuchadnezzar were ordered returned to their rightful place.

Leadership of those returning was in the hands first of Shesh-bazzar and then of Zerubbabel.

About fifty thousand returned in this first group. They had as their first responsibility the rebuilding of the Temple. They found the land desolate and the Samaritans hostile. These were the descendants who were brought in by the Assyrians after the fall of Samaria.

In the meantime, as they struggled to rebuild the Temple, there was political upheaval in Persia. Cyrus was killed in 528. Two years later Darius the Great emerged as king. The Temple, because of opposition from the Samaritans and the political unrest, lay unfinished.

Finally, God, through the prophets Haggai and Zechariah, stirred the people to finish the Temple. It was done in 516.

Some fifty-nine years of history are lost to us from 516 to 457 B.C. Then Ezra, a Levite and scribe in the days of Artaxerxes of Persia, returned to teach the people in Jerusalem the Law. About 1800 men and their families accompanied him. He found those in Jerusalem spiritually weak, worldly and intermarried with foreigners.

He led them in confession of sin, and though resented by many of the Jews, he taught the people once again the Book of the Law of Moses. He had the Law read and interpreted to them. The Jews, no longer a nation, became the people of the book.

Then in 444 B.C., while the same Artaxerxes ruled, Nehemiah, hearing distressing news from Jerusalem, was given permission to return to Jerusalem and build the walls of the city for its protection. He, together with Ezra, completed the task of bringing the people back to a consciousness of their relationship to God.

Religious life was restored to a more biblical base. The rich had taken advantage of the poor. Nehemiah forced them to right past wrongs. After the walls were finished he returned to Persia for two years.

On Nehemiah's return to Palestine he found the situation had deteriorated again. Together with Ezra he led them back to God. Intermarriage with pagans was stopped. Sabbath observance was enforced. Samaritans were forced out of their places of control in Jerusalem.

Meantime, back in Persia, in the time of Xerxes, 486-465, (Ahasuerus in the Bible) Esther, a Jewess, became wife of King Xerxes. She was instrumental, together with her cousin Mordecai, in saving the Jews from extinction.

In these days of exile and return, the Jews became, even away from Jerusalem, a religious community. There was an increasing interest in and study of Jewish Scriptures. The entire Scripture: law, prophets, and the other writings began to take form as one Book of Authority. Synagogues arose both in exile and in Judah wherever there were Jewish believers. Aramaic became the most used language of that day, an international language, and as a result Hebrew fell into general disuse gradually.

For this reason, translations and explanations of Scripture became necessary. At first these were oral, then later written down, and were known as the Targums. Gradually, the Jewish religion began to have an impact on the non-Jewish world.

We turn now to the Scriptures pertaining to this era.

EZEKIEL

Ezekiel, like Jeremiah, wrote both before and after the fall of Jerusalem. But while Jeremiah wrote from Jerusalem, Ezekiel wrote from Babylon.

The book of Ezekiel falls into two major parts: that written before the fall (chs. 1—33:20) and that written after the fall (chs. 34-48). These two sections are joined by a brief account of the arrival of the news in Babylon of the fall of Jerusalem (33:21-33).

Writings Before Jerusalem's Fall (Ezekiel 1-33). The first section, the revelations before the fall (1:3-33:20), is quite different from the latter part. It deals primarily with the sins of Israel that are bringing on the coming judgment.

We date his writing as beginning in the fifth year of the captivity of Jehoiachin (1:2), which would be about 592 B.C. At this time Ezekiel tells us that God began to speak to him (v. 3).

The first division of this first section relates the great vision of divine glory shown to Ezekiel. It is apparently *a vision of God's activity and involvement in man's history* (1:4-28).

Out of the north (where all of God's judgments have come from, against Israel) comes a mysterious cloud and fire (v. 4). He sees four living creatures (v. 5). What he sees therefore is much like what John later relates having seen while he too was in exile (Rev. 4).

Both visions are descriptions of heaven and heavenly glory. From the book of Revelation we can ascertain that the four living creatures represent various aspects of Christ in his mission and glory. This would seem to be the explanation here also; however, it is clearer from Revelation than from Ezekiel. Later they are identified as Cherubim (10:15). And we know that the Cherubim guarded the way to the tree of life (Gen. 3:24) and in the Tabernacle, hovered over the ark itself (Exod. 25:18-22).

Beginning in verse 15 he tells us that the living creatures controlled wheels which extended to the earth. When the creatures moved, so did the wheels (v. 19). The spirit of the living creatures was in the wheels (v. 20). By this we can conclude that the vision shows that all that is happening on earth (the wheels) is controlled by the living creatures in heaven: the invasion from the north, the fire that comes and judges nations, even reaches to Jerusalem and Judah and is under God's control. What happens therefore on earth is determined in heaven.

Beginning in verse 22, to the end of the chapter we get a glimpse of heaven itself. It shows God's throne with one like a man (Christ?) on it (v. 26). We are told that Ezekiel saw the appearance of the likeness of the glory of the Lord (v. 28).

Since all of this was seen as over the head of the living creatures (v. 22), we see symbolized here the truth that God who is over all things is in control of all that is happening in these days, and that all is according to God's plan and purpose. God is not dead. He lives and is still in control even though his people are now going through very difficult times. This is the very heart of the message which God was speaking to Israel, his people, in those difficult days by Ezekiel, Daniel and Jeremiah.

Chapters 2 and 3 tell of *the call of Ezekiel*. After the introduction of the vision just seen, Ezekiel is assured that his ministry is controlled by God in heaven.

God addresses Ezekiel as "son of man," a term unique in Ezekiel but applied by Christ to himself in the New Testament (2:1). His mission is to go to Israel, described as a rebellious people (v. 3). We see a clear relationship between Ezekiel's call and the calls of Isaiah and Jeremiah. In all of these calls they are warned that the hearers will rebel and not receive what they say.

Whether they believe or not, they at least will know that a prophet has been there (v. 5).

Ezekiel, like Jeremiah, is comforted by the words "Be not afraid" (vv. 6ff.). Then Ezekiel is warned not to be rebellious himself (vv. 8ff.). He is to obey God, not men, whether or not they will listen to him.

The incident of the eating of the roll of the book (2:9—3:3) is similar to that recorded by John in Revelation 5:1-10; 10:8-11. Again, from this we ascertain that the book pertains to the message of God for the world, a message sent to God's people but with bitter repercussions as they bear that message to hostile men.

Ezekiel is sent primarily to Israel (3:4-11). In contrast, if like Jonah or Daniel, he had been sent to peoples of a strange tongue he might have been heard, but instead he goes to Israel and they will not hear (vv. 5, 6). Their predicted resistance to God's Word (v. 7) reminds us of the people whom Jeremiah faced. It would be a difficult task indeed (cf. Jer. 1:18).

In verse 10, Ezekiel is told that he too must take God's Word to heart. The messenger must believe the message. It was a tough mission and the prospects ahead for Ezekiel were not pleasant. No wonder he went in bitterness back to his people, aware of the life ahead (vv. 14, 15).

Again, God encouraged Ezekiel after giving him time to reflect on his call (3:16-27). He would be like a watchman whose job was to warn. If the people listened, well. But if not, he had at least done his duty. He would fail in his mission *only* if he failed to give the warning (v. 21).

Once more he saw God's glory (v. 23) and afterwards was told of impending hardship to befall him as it fell on Jeremiah. Nevertheless, God would give him boldness to speak (v. 27).

In chapter 4, the message proper begins. A characteristic of Ezekiel's preaching was to be that he would act out many of God's messages before the people. Other prophets did this occasionally, but Ezekiel did it frequently. The first message was *a portrayal of the siege of Jerusalem* (ch. 4).

He was to take an iron pan and set it up as a wall. He was to lie down by it and act out the siege of a city. We can imagine how startled the people would be to see such a thing. He was to do this each day for three hundred and ninety days on his left side and for forty days on his right (4:4-7). We assume that each day he would go out and act out this portrayal, for four hundred and thirty days in all!

These days, we are told, each represent a year of Israel's iniquity (v. 5). If we count back from the year of Ezekiel's call, 592 B.C., for three hundred ninety years, we arrive at a date in the 900's or about the time of Solomon. The added forty years perhaps represent the years of disobedience in the wilderness. This is not certain. God is saying by this that while he has been long-suffering in the years of Israel's disobedience from the time of Solomon on, he will now bring judgment on the land.

Ezekiel also acts out the famine and scarcity that shall come on the besieged city (4:9-17).

Another portrayal or visual aid message is seen in chapter 5. Taking his own hair he graphically portrays the coming judgment of God: fire, the sword and captivity (scattering to the winds) (vs. 1, 2). The horror of those days to come on Jerusalem (v. 10) reminds us of the siege of Samaria in Elisha's day (2 Kgs. 6:29—cf. Jer. 19:9). Like Jeremiah, Ezekiel pronounces the quadruple threats of God's judgment on the land: pestilence, famine, the sword and captivity (v. 12). Here we could also refer to Revelation 6 and the four horsemen, representative of forces that are cut loose on man in history.

Chapter 6 is a prophecy directed toward the mountains of Israel. We recall that in Micah 6, the Lord called on the mountains to judge between him and Israel. Now he directs a prophecy toward the mountains themselves, where the high places are (6:3ff.). This properly will be compared to another message to the mountains given in chapter 36. Like Hosea, Ezekiel rebukes the people for not knowing the Lord (v. 7).

Beginning in verse 8 we find a note of hope. He will leave a remnant. Some will escape (vv. 8, 9). Only when they see how sinful they are in God's sight will they truly begin to know the Lord (vv. 9, 10). He brings home to the people this message by mighty stomping of his foot (v. 11).

As we could expect, Ezekiel concludes this series of prophecies by prophesying the sure end of Israel (7:2). It is near (7:8). Much of Joel is reflected here (7:14). The evil of the nations which will overrun the land recalls Habakkuk's problem (7:24). At such a time as this people will wish for a word from God and none will come. (Remember, Jeremiah the prophet of that day was carried off to Egypt—cf. Amos 8:11.)

The next three chapters, 8-10, record *a vision given to Ezekiel of the sins of Jerusalem.* In this vision he is transported spiritually from Tel-abib in Babylon to Jerusalem (8:3). He sees the image of jealousy in the Temple (vv. 3, 5, 6). It is full of abominable things in God's sight (vv. 9-11). You remember that the Lord declared himself to be a jealous God, having zeal for his name and truth and not allowing any rival in the hearts of his children (Exod. 20:4-6; 34:12-17).

What was Ezekiel actually seeing here? In verse 12 we have the answer. He was being given, spiritually, in this vision, a glimpse into the very hearts of those who lived in Jerusalem, in the chambers of their imagery—i.e., their evil hearts, as God saw them. This tour of the Temple in Jerusalem in Ezekiel's day was in actuality a tour of the hearts of those who worship there. This is made clear when we read Ezekiel 14:4. A unique revelation in Scripture, it gives us a view of the sinful hearts of unbelievers unlike anything else in Scripture. No wonder God speaks so often of the sinful heart and the need for it to be cleansed.

On his tour, Ezekiel sees hearts full of idolatry and vain worship (8:14-18). Finally, God declares that only those who mourn over such conditions will be spared (9:4—cf. Rev. 7:2, 3). We are reminded of Jesus' words: blessed are they that mourn. Judgment must begin at the house of the Lord (9:6) even as we read elsewhere (Amos 3:2; Jer. 25:29; 1 Pet. 4:17). Ezekiel is moved by this to deep emotional concern for the people (v. 8—cf. 11:13). Nevertheless, God warned that his wrath would not be turned away this time (9:9-11).

The series of visions of the hearts of the people closes with a continuing view of God's glory (ch. 10) in a scene similar to that with which the book opens in chapter 1. The glory of God cannot tolerate such iniquity in the hearts of men.

Next, chapter 11, shows Ezekiel *the vision of evil leaders*. We know that Jeremiah faced such men as he sought to tell the truth (11:2). Ezekiel is called to prophesy against them (11:4). The judgment is severe (11:5-8). As a result of his prophecies, one of those he saw in the vision did die (v. 13—cf. v. 1).

Earlier, Ezekiel had asked God's mercy when judgment began (9:8). Now again he cried to God (11:13). The first time God did not respond, this time he did.

Beginning in 11:16, God declared a word of hope to Israel. Promising to protect them while in captivity (v. 16), he also assures Ezekiel that he will bring them back to their homes after ridding them of all that is evil (vv. 18ff.). In words similar to Jer. 31:31ff., God promises a new spirit and a new heart to the remnant (11:19). God's purpose as expressed in Exodus 19, to have a holy people, will be realized (v. 20). But for those who remain in sin, no hope is offered (v. 21—cf. Amos 9:8bff. and Isa. 66:24).

With this note of assurance, the series of visions begun in 8:3 is concluded (11:24).

Once more, in chapter 12, Ezekiel is told to act out Jerusalem's captivity before the people (vv. 1-6). In doing so he is to be very dramatic, acting out the fear that will be in the hearts of those in Jerusalem in that day (vv. 17ff.).

Apparently, because God had delayed to fulfill his Words through such prophets as Jeremiah concerning the fall of Jerusalem, some made a proverb saying that the visions of the prophets had failed (12:22-25). But God will not now delay (vv. 27, 28).

The false prophets who falsely comforted the people in Jeremiah's day, saying that the time of judgment was far off, became Ezekiel's target now (13:1ff.). Only woes are stored up for them (v. 3). God declares war on them (v. 8). They will have to eat their words of peace (v. 10—cf. Jer. 8:11, 14:13, etc.).

He also turned to rebuke the vain women in a fashion similar to Amos (13:17ff.—cf. Amos 4:1ff.).

Even the elders of the captivity are rebuked. In accord with what we saw in 8:12, these elders have idols in their hearts (14:4). God rebukes and punishes all false leaders to the end that God's true people may not defile themselves (14:9-11).

Nothing can avert the judgment about the fall (14:13-14—cf. 2 Kgs. 23:26, 27). Not even great men of God such as Noah, Daniel, and Job could help if they were there. The name *Noah* brings to mind the great flood judgment when only Noah was righteous. The name *Job* brings to mind the ancient patriarch who so pleased God that Satan could not shake him. *Daniel* of course was a contemporary of Ezekiel's generation and was living at that time in Babylon. All knew directly of his piety. Yet these could not help Jerusalem out of her trouble (v. 14). The theory that the Daniel mentioned here is not the biblical Daniel but another known in the ancient literature of Ugarit, located on the Mediterranean coast, is unlikely. There is no reason why Ezekiel should not appeal to the well-known, godly contemporary Jew.

Again, note the use of the four kinds of judgment: famine, evil beasts, sword (war) and pestilence (14:12, 20). But as before, God offers hope to the faithful remnant (14:22, 23). In a way similar to Isaiah 5, Ezekiel speaks of Israel as like a worthless vine (ch. 15).

Chapter 16, still addressed to the faithless elders, reminds them that their origins are not so noble (16:1-5). Their origins as an identifiable people began in Canaan, to which God called Abraham in order to make of him a distinct family. The combination of Amorite and Hittite (v. 3) certainly points to their pagan origins (see Josh. 24:14, 15). Abraham's ancestors were

Amorites. Perhaps "Hittite" refers to Bathsheba, wife of Uriah, who became David's wife.

The description of Israel as like a child adopted and like a wife nurtured and loved recalls Hosea's words in the early chapters of his prophecy (16:6-14—cf. Hos. 1-3). The beauty described (v. 14) recalls the good days of Solomon's reign but the harlotry that developed (vv. 15-29) recalls the latter days of Solomon's rule. Much of the rest of chapter 16 no doubt is intended to remind them of Hosea's similar indictment against the northern kingdom of Israel at an earlier time.

Still, God cannot forget his promise, which was even recalled in Hosea's message; namely, that he will not give up his people. God will establish in the end an everlasting covenant (16:60-63). A day of reconciliation will come!

The next few chapters, 17-24, contain *several parables,* illustrating another way in which the prophet communicated God's truth to Israel.

In chapter 17 he tells *the parable of the two eagles* and *the vine.* The first eagle planted a vine in order to bear him fruit (17:1-6), but another eagle came and the vine bore fruit for him instead (vv. 7, 8). Therefore, such a treacherous vine could not stand, it was faithless and would be uprooted (vv. 9, 10).

God explains the parable as follows: the first eagle represented Babylon which made a treaty with Jerusalem that Jerusalem should serve Babylon's king (vv. 11-14). But treacherous Judah made another treaty with Egypt (v. 15), the second eagle. Therefore, Babylon would surely punish Jerusalem (vv. 15-18). The Lord is speaking here of events which are recorded in 2 Kgs. 24:1—25:7, in the days of Jehoiachin and Zedekiah.

Then the Lord applied this whole parable to his relationship with Israel as his vine (17:19-24). This reminds us of Isaiah chapter 5:1-7. Israel, God's vine, failed him. How much more must she be punished.

Chapter 18 contains *a parable* frequently *used in Ezekiel's day,* "the fathers have eaten sour grapes, and the children's teeth are set on edge" (18:2). We see mention of this parable in Jeremiah 31:29, 30 and perhaps in Lamentation 5:7. But it was not a proper parable. God had made quite clear that this was not the case (Deut. 24:16). Some might face the consequences of their parents' sins, but they would never be held guilty for the parents' sins (18:4).

Thus the Lord, through Ezekiel, gave a series of examples showing that God held each generation accountable for its own sins (18:5-20). In verses 21-24, he introduces another concept akin to what he had just said but really *a summary of man's relationship to God.* The wicked who repent and turn to God will be justified in God's sight (having been saved by faith in God—21-23). However, if one who is trusting in his own righteousness should sin, his evil would not be forgiven because he had trusted in his so-called righteousness, not repenting toward God (v. 24—cf. Isa. 64:6).

Many evidently accused God of inconsistency here (18:25), but God shows that it is because men's lives are not consistent (righteous) that the trouble comes (v. 29). In other words, all have sinned, therefore all are guilty. None can live righteously in God's sight and therefore all must repent (v. 30). What God calls for here, a new heart and a new spirit (v. 31), only God himself can supply. And he will supply it as he said in Jeremiah 31:31ff., and as he will yet say in Ezekiel 36:26ff.

In the lamentation recorded in chapter 19, one passage recalls to our memory Isaiah 5:1ff. The planting in the wilderness (v. 13) reminds us of Hosea 2:3.

When elders came again to inquire of God through Ezekiel, the Lord refused to answer them (20:1-3). For them, the words of Amos 8:11 were about to come true. Then in a review of their history and God's past dealings with them, God showed them their past rebellions (20:5-32).

In the midst of this long summary of history, God gave insight into the purpose of the Sabbath which they had ignored: it was to be a sign that God was sanctifying them (vv. 12, 13). It should have recalled them to strive to be obedient to God through each week, seeking his good for their lives, but they ignored the purpose of God and went right on in their own disobedience.

Showing them in this historical rebuke that they utterly failed to be what God purposed them to be, he now called for a second wilderness experience, captivity among the nations, so that they could learn again to do God's will and could learn once again that God could purge his people (20:33-39).

In a style like Isaiah chapter 2, he gives hope to the remnant that do learn to trust the Lord and obey him in captivity. They will be his people after the rest have been purged out (vv. 40-44).

After having explained the necessity of the captivity and purging to those in Babylon, in exile already, the prophet now turned toward the south (from Babylon) and addressed the people still in Jerusalem (20:45; 21:2). Jerusalem was about to fall (20:45—22:31). The Lord showed that Babylon was his appointed instrument of judgment (21:18-20). The time had come to punish Judah for her sins which had been uncovered (21:24, 25). The sins in the hearts of the people had now been exposed so that even Ezekiel had seen them. The Lord shows us here that the purpose of his judgment was to purge the people of all guilt (22:15-18). Plainly there were no alternatives. No man could be found who could fill the gap between God and his sinful people. There was no mediator found (22:30, 31). Here we can compare Jeremiah 15:1, where not even Moses or Samuel would be sufficient as a mediator now. In Isaiah 59:16, God gives the only inevitable answer to this spiritual impasse. Only the Lord can come and stand in the gap, only he can bring salvation to his people.

The parable of the two women: Oholibah and Oholah (ch. 23), is a parable expressing the exceeding sinfulness of Israel and Judah from the time of Egypt on. Oholah (Israel) is so named because of her establishing her own tabernacle and worship in the days of Jeroboam I (1 Kgs. 12:26-33). The name Oholah means "her tent." Oholibah (Judah) means "my tent is in her," and has reference to the true sanctuary which was still in Jerusalem (23:4). God shows that each of the two sisters sinned and displeased God and that as the one (Oholah) had been punished already, so must the other.

The parable of the Caldron (ch. 24) again stresses the importance of the purging that must now occur in Jerusalem at the hands of Nebuchadnezzar, the king of Babylon (24:2). It is like a caldron emptied and burned out thoroughly by hot coals (see vv. 3, 6, 11).

To teach the people that they must accept this judgment of God without mourning, God brought a great personal sadness into Ezekiel's life at this point. He told Ezekiel that his own wife would die but that he must not even mourn this great loss. He must go right on prophesying (24:15-18). Ezekiel was to be an example to the citizens of Judah in the time of captivity, as they heard of Jerusalem's fall. They must not mourn (24:22-24). We see then once more how God at times led his servants through very difficult experiences in order that they might better communicate God's message to his people (cf. Hosea's tragic marriage and Jeremiah's many imprisonments).

The last major section of the first division of Ezekiel is concerned with *messages to the nations* (ch. 25-32), as we have also seen in Isaiah, Jeremiah, Amos, and Zephaniah.

Ammon is judged for laughing in the day of Jerusalem's calamity (25:3). *Moab* is condemned for ridiculing Judah (25:8); *Edom* for the cruelty to Judah (25:12) and *Philistia* for her continual enmity against the land (25:15).

Then in chapters 26-28, he gives special attention to *Phoenicia.* Tyre, her main city, boasted of her invincibility and rejoiced when Jerusalem lay under siege (26:2). Actually, Tyre did hold out for twelve years more against Babylon but did fall in 574 B.C. Tyre had been a proud city and had colonized much of the Mediterranean shoreline including Carthage in North Africa. Because she was so proud and vain, God made an example of her now (v. 3). God will bring Nebuchadnezzar against her and she will fall and not be built again (26:7, 13, 14).

In the midst of the following long lament over the city of Tyre, we find a focus upon the king of Tyre (ch. 28). Because his heart is proud and he thinks of himself as a god (28:2), he will be the recipient of special judgment from God (28:6ff.).

So great is his vanity that the king of Tyre illustrates the very pride of Satan himself (28:12-19). The words in this lamentation seem to refer to a being greater than the king of Tyre and though his name is not mentioned, Satan is evidently the object of this prophecy (cf. Isa. 14:12ff. and Luke 10:18).

The objective of God's judgment against Tyre and Sidon would be that the nations might know that there is a God to whom all are accountable (28:20-24). Like so many prophecies we have seen directed against the nations, there is here also hope offered to God's people, the remnant (28:25ff.).

Next, *Egypt* is condemned (chs. 29-32). This judgment too is in order that the nations may know that God must be dealt with (29:6; 30:8). Again, here too, hope for God's remnant is promised (29:21). The fall of once mighty Assyria is held out as a warning to Egypt of her inevitable end (31:2ff.).

In the concluding part of the prophecy is a kind of roll call of hell. Egypt will have lots of company when she goes down in judgment (32:18-32). Assur (Assyria) is there (v. 22), Elam (v. 24) and a whole host of others (vv. 26ff.) and there. Pharaoh will have much company (v. 31).

The first division of the book of Ezekiel closes with the statements regarding the watchman's duty (ch. 33) similar to that one found in chapter 3:16-21. Again, as the city of Jerusalem is about to fall, Ezekiel is taught that his responsibility before God is to warn the people. He is God's watchman over the house of Israel, to warn them (33:7). We have here then in reality an expression of the responsibility of every witness before God. We are all to bear witness to God's truth. That is our responsibility. Only God can make the message effective to those that hear. Much of what was said in chapter 18 is also repeated here (33:12ff.).

The rest of chapter 33, verses 21-33, relate *the news that Jerusa-lem has fallen.* This would be about 586 B.C.

Writings After Jerusalem's Fall (Ezekiel 34-48). Beginning in chapter 34, and going to the end of the book (chapter 48) we have the second major division of Ezekiel's prophecy—the prophecies given after the fall of Jerusalem.

After news of the fall of Jerusalem arrived in Babylon, the messages of Ezekiel from God changed considerably. He moved from warnings of judgment to messages of hope.

But first he deals with the false prophets and false shepherds of Israel who misled the people and brought them to their sorry end (34:2). Such have fed themselves instead of feeding God's flock. He uses the shepherd's imagery here both to convey their failure and to imply what the good shepherd should have done (34:4-6). We see here therefore a concept of the good shepherd, similar to that found in Isaiah 40:11, and fulfilled only in the person of Jesus Christ (see John 10). God himself will have to be the true shepherd since all under-shepherds have miserably failed (34:11, 15, 16).

The words of 34:17-20 remind us of Matthew 25:32ff., Christ judging the sheep. These words also recall Isaiah 9:7; 55:3-5 and Jeremiah 30:9 respecting the promises to David (David's greater son, Jesus) to be that true shepherd whom God will provide (34:22-24). Thus God's sheep, the remnant saved, shall know the Lord whom they have failed to know in the past. They will know that he is the deliverer (34:27), and they will know that they are his people (sheep) (34:30).

The contrasting judgment against Edom found in the next chapter (ch. 35) no doubt is to remind the people of the very different way God has dealt with Edom (Esau) in contrast to Israel (Jacob) after the fashion of the later prophet Malachi (Mal. 1:2-4). Edom is the perpetual enemy of Israel (35:5—cf. Amos 1:11) and therefore continually represents that element of the church which is secular and out of God's grace. As did Obadiah, so Ezekiel warns Edom of judgment because they rejoiced at Israel's tragedy (35:15).

In chapter 36 God begins a great message of hope for his people. It is addressed to the mountains of Israel as was chapter 6, but is quite different. In chapter 6 the Lord had rebuked the mountains (the people of Israel) for their sin and warned of judgment, but here he brings the gospel of hope.

Because the enemy has rejoiced over the downfall of God's people (36:2), God will now punish Israel's enemies (36:5-7).

God will now make his people fruitful (v. 8—cf. Isa. 11:1ff.).

Israel's own righteousness and works were defiled when they dwelt in the land of Israel (36:17—cf. Isa. 64:6). God had to punish and purge these people, but when the nations ridiculed Israel and their God because of her suffering, the zeal of God for his name prevailed (36:20, 21).

The Lord therefore makes the point here that he will save Israel from her shame not because she deserves it but for his own name's sake, i.e., for God's glory before the nations (36:22-24).

The word of salvation which God will accomplish is to sprinkle (cleanse) his people from their sins in their hearts as he had earlier shown to Ezekiel (36:25—cf. ch. 8-10). This is in accord with the promise through Isaiah (Isa. 43:25).

In words similar to Jeremiah chapter 31:33, the Lord promises to give to the people a new spirit and a new heart (36:26). He will do this by the work of his Holy Spirit in them (v. 27—cf. Joel's promise long before, Joel 2:28, 29).

Then the people will obey. They will have hearts to obey when God has worked his great work in them (v. 27). Then they will dwell in their place in peace and blessings which will not end and will be fruitful (vv. 28ff.).

This is no less than the promise of the new birth by God's Holy Spirit. The same truth is seen taught by Jesus to Nicodemus (John 3). It is also the doctrine expressed by Paul in Titus 3:5. This is the washing of regeneration and renewing work of the Holy Spirit.

Again, he reminds them that it is not for their sakes (because they deserved it) that he will regenerate them, but because of God's glory (36:32ff.).

Chapter 37 is a vision in which the doctrine of regeneration is illustrated. Ezekiel sees a valley full of dry bones (vv. 1, 2). He emphasizes their dryness (deadness). The question is put—"can these bones live?" (v. 3). Obviously they cannot do anything themselves. They are quite dead. Ezekiel wisely answers that only God knows (v. 3).

Now God commands to him a very strange thing. Ezekiel is to preach to these dead bones and call them to hear the Word of the Lord (v. 4). Obviously this makes no sense from the human standpoint. If they are really dead they cannot hear or respond.

But the Lord reveals to Ezekiel that as he preaches, God will cause his Spirit (the word in Hebrew used here is the same as in 36:27) to enter them and give them life (v. 5). Again we see the doctrine of regeneration taught quite clearly. They will live and *know* that the Lord is God (v. 6).

Thus we recall God's words to Elijah after he had seen his efforts to convince Israel of their sin fail. God showed to Elijah that men would be changed only by the still small voice, God's Word, working by his Spirit in them (see our comments on 1 Kgs. 19:9-12—cf. Zech. 4:6).

Ezekiel obeyed the Lord and the result was exactly what God said it would be (37:7-10). Here, words sometimes translated wind or breath are all the same word found in 36:27—*spirit*—and ought to be so translated. The point is, new life, regeneration, is the work of God's Holy Spirit.

The lesson taught here is exactly the same as in Ephesians 2:1-10. We were all dead in sin by nature (Eph. 2:1-3), but God in his mercy and love made us alive when we were dead and helpless (Eph. 2:4-9). He did this that we might live and glorify him by the work we now do in his name (Eph. 2:10—cf. Ezek. 36:27).

The Lord shows that this is the way hopeless Israel shall have hope (37:11-13). They will live because God has put his Spirit in them, to dwell in them, God's new holy temple (see Eph. 2:21).

The rest of chapter 37 illustrates how this plan of redemption is the only one and the one by which all of God's people shall be gathered together under one head (vv. 15-28). The two sticks represent Israel and Judah (all the people—vv. 15-19). In essence God is saying here that there will be one church, one people of God in all the earth. But the children of Israel, God's seed, will be gathered from all the nations (v. 21). This is in accord with Paul's words in Ephesians 2:11-22 that from Gentiles and Jews God will make one true church. The true Israel consists of those everywhere who will believe in the Lord as Paul says again (Rom. 9:6-8; 11:25-32; Rom. 4:1-17). Likewise, Jesus in John 17 looks to the one church (John 17:20-24).

The hope of one king (37:22) recalls Hosea's words (Hos. 1:11) and in 37:24, this one is called David, pointing to the promise to David that God would establish his throne forever (see 2 Sam. 7:10-16). The doctrine of one shepherd therefore points to its fulfillment in Chrsit (34:23; Isa. 40:10—also see Isa. 9:7, Jer. 30:9; Hos. 3:5).

The everlasting covenant, one that will not fail (v. 26) is God's new covenant (different covenant) established through Christ and declared in the time of Christ (Luke 22:20—cf. 1 Cor. 11:25; 2 Cor. 3:6; Heb. 9:15, etc.). It is new in that it was made known after the old covenant failed (i.e., after it was evident that Israel could not endure in the land of promise because she could not keep God's law), but it is the ancient covenant, indeed timeless,

for in God's purpose it is the original covenant, established before the world was created (Eph. 1:4).

The next two chapters, 38 and 39, contain prophecies against
Gog, ruler of Magog, (38:2). It is not possible to identify him
with any specific individual known in history. Revelation 20:8
identifies the king and land as representative of the rulers and
nations of the world which are united under Satan against God
and God's people.

The prophecies of Ezekiel now therefore appropriately turn
to deal with the world, Satan's kingdom, which is at enmity with
God's kingdom and God's purpose. Since the Lord has just
shown how God's kingdom is to be established and prevail (chs.
36, 37), he will now deal with the kingdom of Satan and its
destruction.

God declares himself against Gog and all world rulers of Satan's domain (38:3—cf. Eph. 6:10-12). As Joel, much earlier,
had announced God's call to war against the nations of the earth
(Joel 3:9ff.), so does Ezekiel here (38:7).

The scene of battle portrayed here (38:14-16) reminds us of
Revelation 29:7-10, the attack of the world against God and
God's people. It is the final climax of that showdown which God
foretold in Genesis 3:15. The Lord will fight for God's people
(38:18, 21-22). The imagery here is like the divine judgment
against Sodom.

Again, God declares himself to be against Gog (the world
rulers—39:1). The fall of Gog and Magog is described in terms
recalling Revelation 19:17, 18 (39:4-6—cf. vv. 17ff.). The object
of this final great overthrow is that God's name may be glorified
among the nations (vv. 7, 8).

The scene of dead bodies (39:11, 12), recalls Isaiah's words at
the close of his message (Isa. 66:24). When God has destroyed
the kingdom of this world, then God's people (the true Israel)
will know that God is the Lord forever (39:21-29). God will not
leave them alone again. They will always (forever) be with the
Lord!

The final part of the book, chapters 40-48, is a vision of the new
temple. We recall that Ezekiel was given a vision of the Temple
in chapters 8-11, which was defiled. We saw there that what God
had shown him was in reality the hearts of the people, i.e. the
temple of their bodies which were evil and in which
God would not dwell.

Therefore, this temple represents the hearts of God's people also. Ezekiel goes through this new temple and carefully measures each part of it. He searches it out as God would search out the hearts of men. All is perfect. There is no flaw in it (chs. 40-42). God declares that this is the place of his throne where he will dwell forever, where his glory fills the house (the hearts of his people—43:1-9).

This Temple is God's handiwork, cleansed by him, as he reminded Ezekiel just before showing him the Temple (39:29). God will sit enthroned in the hearts of his people (43:7). They will not be defiled again (43:7).

This concept of the believer's heart as God's holy temple is developed in the New Testament (1 Cor. 3:16, 17; 6:19; 2 Cor. 6:16). For this reason Jesus points to the day when men will not worship in this or that building but will truly worship in spirit and in truth (John 4:23, 24). This is why we read in Revelation 21:22 concerning heaven, that there is no temple there. Every child of God is the Temple of God. The temples of this world only point to the ultimate Temple of God with his people.

When the people see the Temple God will build, they will be ashamed of themselves for their present sins (43:10).

None but God's children will be in God's sanctuary (44:9—cf. Rev. 21:8, 27). The Temple shows no flaw (chs. 43-48). It is holy, where God dwells forever (48:35). At this point and by way of conclusion it would be profitable to reflect on what God has shown symbolically to Ezekiel and to us.

We see clearly that the revelation of God to Old Testament saints is quite different from his revelation to New Testament saints. But all are true believers in the Lord. They differ in that in the Old Testament God speaks in terms of what he *will do*. But in the New Testament he declares what he *has done* in Christ.

All Old Testament saints and New Testament saints, are saved by belief in the same Lord. *In the Old Testament,* God's people learned by the symbolic signs which God gave, i.e., the tabernacle, the sacrifices, etc., how to approach God in faith, recognizing their sinfulness and with broken hearts, learning to trust him alone for salvation. *In the New Testament,* God's people see Jesus, the fulfillment of all that is symbolized in the Old Testament signs, the only true way to God, the only true life.

In the Old Testament, God's children are reborn by God's Spirit even as in the New Testament. This is evidenced by the faith in them. By their faith they are shown what God will do, symbolically, for their redemption, and they trust in the Lord to do it. *In the New Testament,* God's children are reborn by God's Holy Spirit which is also evidenced by their faith in the Lord. By their faith they come to know what God has done in Christ, really, for their redemption and the redemption of all men, and they trust in the Lord who has done it.

In the Old Testament, the saints knew Christ (God, their redeemer) by the verbal description of himself which he gave through Moses (see Exod. 34:6, 7). *In the New Testament,* we know Christ in the flesh, the Word made flesh, a living manifestation of God.

In the Old Testament, the saints did have the Holy Spirit who gave them gifts in limited numbers and fruits also of the Spirit. But *in the New Testament* we see the Holy Spirit poured out, giving gifts and producing fruit in all believers as the Holy Spirit comes to dwell in (abide in) all believers.

In the Old Testament, the commission of God to his saints was not world wide, but the anticipation of the gospel reaching to all nations is clearly seen from the beginning (i.e., Noah's prophecy—Gen. 9:26, 27; the promise to Abraham—Gen. 12:3, 22:18). But the people lacked the spiritual power to communicate the gospel to the ends of the earth. It was a time of establishing God's beachhead in Satan's world of sin.

In the New Testament, our commission is to the ends of the earth. We are his witnesses. We have the power (Acts 1:8) and therefore we take the battle to Satan as God goes about to win out of the world his people and to spoil Satan as he binds him by the preaching of the Word, leaving him helpless to prevent God's work of salvation in all the earth.

Finally, *in the Old Testament,* the inheritance is chiefly in terms of a geographical area and in terms of a fruitful land, though God does call for fruit in the lives of the people, fruit of righteousness and justice (i.e., Isa. 5:1-7). But *in the New Testament* he speaks of spiritual fruit and of a new heaven and a new earth and of an inheritance incorruptible and undefiled that will not fade away (1 Pet. 1:4, 5).

Yet even in the Old Testament, God's children understood that the inheritance they looked for was not of this world (see Heb. 11:8, 10, 16; 12:22; 13:14). The real city of God, an inheritance of his people, has always been heaven, the new Jerusalem (Rev. 21, 22). Therefore Paul warns the Galatians not to be deceived or to look back to earthly Jerusalem for their hope (Gal. 4:21-31). Our Jerusalem also is above and is free. Our hope is on the new Jerusalem which is above, not on the earthly city of this world!

DANIEL

The book of Daniel was written by the prophet Daniel during the exile in Babylon. We are told that there were brought into Babylon from Jerusalem some of the treasurers from the house of God in the third year of Jehoiakim (Dan. 1:1, 2). This would be about 605 B.C. Presumably, at this same time, some of the Israelites were also carried to Babylon (1:3, 4—see also 2 Kgs. 24:1; 2 Chron. 36:5, 6).

In the first six chapters Daniel records events in the life of Daniel and his three friends. The messages contained here pertain largely to the nation of Babylon and the witness of Daniel and his friends, the children of God, to that nation in which they were held captive. The messages are therefore to the pagan world. But they are included in God's book to his people and are therefore profitable to us who believe as well.

The latter six chapters contain various visions and revelations given to Daniel which expand somewhat on what was revealed to the pagans and which pertain primarily to the ultimate triumph of God's kingdom and his people. Here are found some very specific prophecies relating to the coming of Christ and the final accomplishments of God's purpose.

The part from chapter 2:4 to 7:28 the text is in Aramaic, a language akin to Hebrew and the primary language of communication in Babylon at that time. The reason this section is in Aramaic is probably because the message was primarily directed to the Babylonian world and the world at large. Even chapter 7, in the second division, deals largely with the development of Nebuchadnezzar's dream which had been recorded in chapter 2.

Let us now look at the message of Daniel.

Chapter 1 introduces us to Daniel and his friends. All were among those selected by Ashpenaz, the servant of Nebuchadnezzar, because of their fine appearance and skills. They were thus the cream of the crop among the Israelites brought captive into Babylon (1:3, 4). They, together with other Jews and youths from other lands, were to be taught in all of the learning of Babylon and in the Babylonian language which would have been the difficult Akkadian language with its numerous syllables (v. 4).

The course was to last for three years in which time these youths would be favored and fed. The fine food and dainties from the king's own menu were to be given to them (v. 5).

The four Hebrew children mentioned as among those youths all bore names which glorified God (1:6, 7). Daniel's name

means "God is my judge." His name was changed to Belteshaz-
zar, which means "Bel protect his life." Hananiah's name means
"the Lord has been gracious" and Hananiah's name was
changed to Shadrach, which means "command of Aku (the
moon God)." Mishael's name means "who is like God?" It was
changed to Meshach, which means "who is like Aku?" Finally,
Azariah's name means "the Lord has helped" and was changed
to Abednego which means "servant of Nebo." We see from all of
this then that there was an attempt to Babylonize these Jewish
young men and by renaming them to take glory from the true
God and give it to the pagan gods of Babylon.

It was on this occasion, when placed in a situation where their
whole background as Jews and as God's children was challenged,
that Daniel and his companions took their stand. They were
faithful to God in seeking to maintain a diet in accord with God's
law (1:8). Daniel, the obvious leader here, made a heart commitment to seek to glorify his Lord. Perhaps he kept in mind the
words of Proverbs 23:3-6. Clearly he sought not merely outward
conformity to God's Word, but heart commitment to the Lord.

As we saw with Joseph in a similar relationship to Pharaoh, so
here God blessed Daniel who put his trust in the Lord (v. 9). God
opened the door for Daniel's stand in faith to lead to greater
service in God's Kingdom.

We note how Daniel proposed that his faith and that of his
friends be tested. For ten days they would eat only some herbs
and water. If at the end of that time they did not have a better
countenance than the others, then they would resist no more (v.
13).

We note two things here. First, in their own act in faith they
did not wish to cause hardship on others, i.e., Ashpenaz (vv.
10ff.). Likewise, Abraham when he refused the rewards of the
king of Sodom did not block others who might wish to have their
rewards (Gen. 14:24). Our own acts in faith should not be im-
posed on others.

Second, the test was to establish who had the finer
countenance—Daniel and his friends, or the rest, eating the
king's dainties (v. 13). The term "countenance" has to do with far
more than the fatness or leanness of the face. That in itself was
incidental. The term really refers to one's attitude and general
feeling of happiness or bitterness or whatever may be in the
heart. A fair countenance means a heart that is right, an evil
countenance means that evil lurks in the heart. Cain, for example, showed before God an evil, fallen countenance which had to
do with his attitude, not fatness or leanness (Gen. 4:5).

When tested, the four proved to have fairer countenances,

i.e., better attitudes in spirit than the rest. Besides, they were even fatter, i.e., more healthy looking (vv. 14-16).

In this stand in a little matter, they proved faithful and therefore God entrusted to them much more. As Christ said, "He that is faithful in a very little is faithful also in much" (Luke 16:10). Many are entrusted very little in God's Kingdom because they have not proved faithful in the little things (see Luke 16:11, 12; 19:17).

God therefore gave to Daniel and his friends much knowledge and wisdom by which they would go on to glorify the Lord before the whole secular world (1:17-21). The reputation of Daniel quickly spread so that even in the time of Ezekiel, a contemporary of Daniel, the wisdom of Daniel was used as a superlative expression of wisdom among men (Ezek. 28:3) and Daniel was ranked with Noah and Job in his fame and righteousness (Ezek. 14:14, 20).

Chapter 2 tells *of a dream of Nebuchadnezzar and its interpretation* by Daniel. After his dream, the king called in his specialists in dream interpretation (2:2). This may be why Daniel and his companions were not called in. His reputation in interpretation had not yet been established. In verse 4 the Aramaic language takes over as the rest of the account is given. It is not clear from the Aramaic here whether Nebuchadnezzar had forgotten his dream or simply wanted to be sure that what the interpreters said was correct. Probably the latter (2:5, 7, 8). The severity of the punishment indicates that he suspected they were frauds which is of course what they were (v. 9).

The response of the Chaldeans to this strange demand paved the way beautifully for the glorifying of God through Daniel— by their admission, none but God could do what the king demanded (2:10, 11).

It is interesting that though Daniel and his friends had not been called in, yet when the order went out to kill all the wise men of Babylon, Daniel and his friends were sought out first (vv. 12, 13). This shows again how the enmity of the world is directed against God's children.

Arioch's kindness to Daniel indicates again how God often gives favor to his own in the eyes of their enemies (vv. 14-16).

Note how Daniel first shared the problem with his friends and then called for prayer. In times of trial he knew where to turn, as did David and Hezekiah before him (2:17, 18).

No sooner did God reveal the dream and its meaning to Daniel, than he responded in praise to God (2:19-23). He praised God's name, the hope of Israel, and God's wisdom and might (v. 20). He saw how in the dream God revealed his absolute control of all men and kingdoms (v. 21). The God of Wisdom and Might had now given wisdom and might to Daniel (v. 23).

We see too how others benefited from God's blessings on his own children (v. 24). Daniel, taking over where the Chaldeans left off, showed clearly that only his God, the true God, could do what was asked (vv. 27, 28—cf. 2:10). Daniel saw to it that only the Lord received the glory for what he was about to do (v. 30).

The dream itself recalls several other Old Testament passages. The reference to the stone that crushed the image recalls both Genesis 3:15, the crushing of Satan, and Isaiah 8:14, 15 and 28:16. In those passages, Christ is clearly the Stone that will crush Satan and his empire. The debris left after the crushing is described as chaff (v. 35). This calls to mind Psalm 1, and that same description of the unrighteous. The mountain which grows (v. 35), points to Isaiah 2:2ff., Mount Zion, the city of God. Thus we can understand that once Daniel was shown the dream by God, he could, from Scripture itself, surmise the meaning. It is important to see that God reveals truth by truth already given. We note five parts to the image: head, breast and arms, belly and thigh, legs, feet (2:32, 33).

In the interpretation Nebuchadnezzar learned first that the kingdom he had and his place at the head of the kingdom (king of kings) was by God's gift alone (vv. 37, 38). As the head of gold, Nebuchadnezzar's kingdom represented the first of a series of kingdoms on earth. Each succeeding kingdom is less in quality (value) but greater in strength (vv. 38-40). The fifth part of the image is the feet, i.e., the foundation of all of the kingdoms of men (v. 41). This would point to the fact that all human kingdoms rest on the base that cannot hold (iron and clay mix which will not hold together). In the end they fall apart (vv. 42, 43).

Meantime, God sets up his Kingdom which will last. His Kingdom outlasts all human kingdoms. It stands forever (v. 44).

Thus Nebuchadnezzar is shown what must surely come to pass. His kingdom and those which succeed it will all crumble, based on a faulty foundation, and in the end God's Kingdom will triumph (2:45).

As to the identity of the other kingdoms, we can reasonably assume that they represent the Medio-Persian Empire (silver), the Greek Empire of Alexander (brass) and the Roman Empire (iron). Later, two of these are certainly identified (8:20, 21) so that we are not here speculating.

What we see here then is God's prediction of the powers to come and the ultimate triumph of Christ's Kingdom already

foretold by the earlier prophets. Of course, all human kingdoms, those of this world, are but manifestation of Satan's kingdom. He is elsewhere in Scripture described as the god of this
world or the prince of this world (John 12:31; 14:30; 16:11;
2 Cor. 4:4; Eph. 2:2 and 6:12). In short we see here declared to
men that their kingdoms in the end will be overthrown because
Satan shall fall.

Nebuchadnezzar was greatly impressed by the feat of Daniel
and his God (v. 47). He showed his feelings by making Daniel
high in government, together with his friends (vv. 48, 49). But
one does not see here that Nebuchadnezzar really understood
what God was saying to him. This dream and its interpretation
ought to have brought him to his knees before God, but, as we
see in the next chapter, it did not.

In *chapter 3,* we have *an account of some kind of statue of gold erected
by Nebuchadnezzar.* Apparently, all he got from the dream was
that he was the greatest and his kingdom the greatest and so he
proceeded to require all men to worship his image of gold (no
doubt because the head of the dream image was of gold) (3:1).
Its dimensions suggest that it was not a statue of a man but it
clearly symbolized Nebuchadnezzar's greatness (3:1-5). The
penalty for not worshiping the image at the signal was to be
death in the furnace (v. 6). Thus Nebuchadnezzar showed his
vain pride. He pushed down the truth in unrighteousness as
natural man always does (see Rom. 1).

The conformity required here and displayed by most of the
people reminds us of Revelation 13:14ff., and the day yet to
come when men will conform to the demands of pagan powers
allied with the pseudo-church.

There were perhaps many who did not conform. Nevertheless, as we saw in 2:13, the enemies of God's people quickly
sought out those of God's people against whom they were jealous and sought to slay them (3:8ff.).

We see again the vanity of Nebuchadnezzar when he learned
that the three friends of Daniel would not conform. We do not
know why Daniel was not mentioned. Perhaps he was away from
the city at the time (3:13). Nebuchadnezzar's giving to them a
second chance was more out of his own vain pride than out of
any kindness in him (vv. 14, 15). His boast (v. 15) reminds us of
the boast of the king of Assyria in Hezekiah's day (Isa. 36:20).

The answer of the three brave men is classic. It was a great
display of true faith. They felt obligated and answerable only to
the Lord in this matter (v. 16). They knew their God was able to
save them from the furnace, nevertheless, whether he would or

not they did not know (vv. 17, 18). No matter, they would never deny him.

After Nebuchadnezzar carried out his threat (vv. 19-23), he saw someone with them, and all four were walking about in the furnace (vv. 24, 25). The identity of the fourth person is interesting. Nebuchadnezzar thought he looked like the son of the gods. Was it Christ? We cannot know. The judgment that it looked like one of the sons of the gods was a pagan evaluation.

After they came out, unhurt, all were amazed and again God was glorified (v. 27). Again Nebuchadnezzar did not profess his own faith in their God but he did commend *their* faith in their God (v. 28). He would no longer tolerate any opposition to their God, a remarkable decree to come from a pagan of that era (v. 29). Again, God raised his faithful ones to great position over their enemies as pleased him (v. 30).

The *fourth chapter* is *the last about Nebuchadnezzar.* In it we see *the final humbling of the king* in his own confession that there is a sovereign God who rules and controls men and kingdoms and does as pleases him.

First we have his proclamation (4:1-3). In it he acknowledges the greatness and superiority of God's Kingdom over all, even his own. Then in verses 4-36, he relates how he was humbled because of his pride after he refused God's warning (v. 27). He was so self-centered that he took all glory for himself (v. 30). Therefore, all that the dream had forewarned came true (cf. 4:20-26 and vv. 31-33).

After his humbling ordeal in which he was apparently driven mad, Nebuchadnezzar humbled himself before God (v. 34). He did acknowledge the truth God demanded of him (see vv. 17, 25, 34).

When he regained his senses. Nebuchadnezzar then not only acknowledged God's greatness but made proclamation that all should so acknowledge him (vv. 36, 37). In all of this we note two other things: first, Daniel was bold to exhort this pagan king to live righteously. He was not afraid to speak the truth in love even to secular powers (v. 27). Neither should we be. God does expect of them righteousness and mercy and holds them accountable when they fail. It is therefore proper for God's people to speak against unrighteousness in high places. It is in fact their duty.

Second, Nebuchadnezzar spoke of God in such a way as to seem to be a believer himself in the end (v. 37). What he said there is not different from what Hannah said of the Lord in 1 Samuel 2. Whether he believed, we cannot know nor must we decide. That rests in God's hands. The fact that secular history neither records Nebuchadnezzar's humbling nor his praise of Israel's God need not surprise us. The records of men constantly blot out things in their midst that glorify God.

Chapter 5 tells of *the last days of the Babylonian kingdom* which did not last long after Nebuchadnezzar's death. Belshazzar himself was only recently known to secular history. For a long time historians and liberal biblical scholars considered this whole chapter to be fictitious. They claimed that there never was a Belshazzar and that the last king of Babylon was Nabonidus. Then records of Nabonidus in which he mentioned his son Belshazzar were found. Evidently, Belshazzar was second under his father and co-regent. At the time of the fall, Nabonidus was out of the city of Babylon and Belshazzar was in charge. This would have been about 539 B.C.

Belshazzar and his guests were one evening enjoying a great feast. To add to the festivities, he ordered the vessels taken by Nebuchadnezzar from the Temple in Jerusalem to be brought in for drinking vessels (5:2). We read of this in 2 Kgs. 24. Here the term "father" applied to Nebuchadnezzar means ancestor, not literal father, just as Abraham might be called "father" by Jews much later or David "father" of Hezekiah, etc., Belshazzar's actual father was Nabonidus.

They profaned the holy vessels of God's Temple and even praised their own gods as they drank. Whatever Nebuchadnezzar had learned of God was clearly not communicated to his children and descendants (v. 4).

At this point a hand appeared and wrote on the wall (5:5ff.). It was enough to strike fear in the heart of the king and his guests. His offer to reward the reader and interpreter of the message written included the offer to be third in the kingdom (v. 7). The offer of third place was of course because his father, Nabonidus, was first and he second. He offered the highest honor he could give (v. 7).

The queen, mentioned in verse 10, was doubtlessly his mother, the wife of Nabonidus. She would have remembered Daniel from Nebuchadnezzar's days. Her praise of Daniel makes clear the impact he had had on that generation although she was evidently far from a believer in Daniel's God (5:11, 12).

Belshazzar's offer to Daniel was ludicrous (v. 16) inasmuch as his kingdom would end that night. Daniel's refusal reminds us of Abraham's refusal of the rewards offered by the king of Sodom (Gen. 14).

Again, Daniel showed his strength in faith as he took opportunity to rebuke Belshazzar for not being able to learn from the experiences of Nebuchadnezzar that all men and especially kings must honor the true God (vv. 18-24). The particular sin of Belshazzar was in desecrating the vessels of the Most High God (v. 23). As God had done earlier to the Philistines who dese- crated the ark, so here too, God alone would punish those who did not honor his name (cf. 1 Sam. 5, 6).

For the first time, in verse 25, we learn what was written by the hand on the wall. It was in Aramaic and the words would be understandable to the king. However, the meaning was not. It said "numbered, weighed and divisions." Daniel's interpretation simply reflected what had before been said by Isaiah and Jeremiah, that the kingdom of Babylon would surely fall. The next kingdom of Nebuchadnezzar's dream (the Medes and Per- sians) was about to take over (v. 28). The word *Peres*, meaning *divided*, was probably also a play on words for it even named the conqueror—Persia.

The reward to Daniel by the king is, as we said, ludicrous. It was little honor to be made third in a kingdom which would soon fall (vv. 29, 30).

The mention of Darius the Mede (v. 31) raises some problems. His identity is not yet known from any secular source. He was a relatively old man at the time and apparently one of the generals in the Persian army, a Mede himself.

By this time the Medes and Persians were one empire though originally they had been separate. Apparently, this Darius was in charge of the army actually taking Babylon, though Cyrus was the real king over all the Persians. Darius then for some time functioned as ruler of the city of Babylon and the outlying dis- tricts and suburbs.

Chapter six tells of *how Darius honored Daniel* in his reorganization of the government of the city. The organization described here is the typical Persian organization (6:1-3). The elevation of Daniel would naturally provoke jealousy as similar treatment had in Nebuchadnezzar's day (6:4).

The tribute to Daniel as a faithful servant to the king does not mean that Daniel in any way compromised his faith. In fact, just the opposite. It was only in matters where his allegiance to his God would be tested over against his allegiance to the king that he could be accused (v. 5). No one came before the Lord in Daniel's life, not even the king.

The plot of the rival presidents against Daniel was not Darius' will but perhaps in those busy days of reorganization he simply signed what was put before him without due thought (v. 9).

Daniel's reaction was to go on living as he always had (v. 10).

He made no show of religion here, but the spies soon found out that he still worshipped. It was his practice (v. 10b).

When Darius knew the truth of what had happened he deeply regretted but was caught in the legal web he had inherited. Darius was not the head of the empire and could not change the laws, only Cyrus could do that (6:12-15).

Darius nevertheless displayed remarkable faith in Daniel's God (v. 16). And when Daniel was protected from the lions, Darius was glad. As God had visited the friends of Daniel in the fiery furnace, so now God's angel was in the lion's den with Daniel (see 3:25). Daniel's trust in God never wavered, he was a true child of God (v. 23—cf. Isa. 12:2, 26:3).

The punishment of those who sought to destroy Daniel was severe (v. 24), but no more severe than the punishment of Korah in the wilderness when he led a rebellion against God's chosen leader (Num. 16:28-35).

Thus Darius sent out a decree similar to the one by Nebuchadnezzar (6:25-27—cf. 4:1ff.). The honor to Daniel in Darius' day again shows how the Lord entrusts much to those who are faithful to him in a little. The mention of Cyrus in verse 28 does not mean that he succeeded Darius as king but that simultaneous to Darius' rule over Babylon, the city, was a rule of Cyrus over the entire empire. This ends the first major division of the book. We go now to the final division, chapters 7-12, a series of visions and revelations given to Daniel during the days of his activity in Babylon.

The *first vision* is recorded in *chapter 7* and is dated the first year of Belshazzar which would have been before the events of chapter 5. Daniel's dream is similar to Nebuchadnezzar's dream in that it apparently showed the same truth. Instead of four parts of an image, however, the four kingdoms were symbolized by four beasts (7:3-7). Here we learn something about the nature of the four kingdoms. The first (Babylon) was like a lion, the most majestic, the king of the beasts (v. 4). The second (Persia) would be powerful and fearful like a bear (v. 5). The third (Greece) would be like a leopard (v. 6). The four heads represented the four divisions of that empire after Alexander's death. The fourth beast was very terrible and enduring (v. 7). The mention of iron teeth identifies this beast with the iron portion of the image of Nebuchadnezzar's dream (cf. 2:40).

The image of the beast, to represent the secular powers of the earth, is later picked up by the book of Revelation. In Revelation the forces of evil on the earth are symbolized as beasts (see Rev. 13). The ten horns here (v. 7), as in Revelation, apparently represent the successive kingdoms after Rome (Rev. 12:3, 13:1). The rest of Daniel's vision really begins where Nebuchadnezzar's left off and elaborates upon the overthrow of the kingdoms of this world and the triumph of God's Kingdom. Much found here is later seen also by John in Revelation. The description of the ancient of days (v. 9) is very much like the description of Christ in Revelation 1. The wheels remind us of Ezekiel's vision (Ezek. 1). The open book of judgment reminds one of Revelation 20. The slaying of the beast is also shown in Revelation 20 (Dan. 7:11).

The night vision of Daniel revealed the coming of the Son of Man, a term used and applied by Jesus to himself (v. 13). Jesus describes his own coming in just these terms (Matt. 26:64—cf. 1 Thes. 4:17). What Daniel was seeing in this vision was an elaboration on the theme of the triumph of God's Kingdom as introduced earlier in Nebuchadnezzar's dream. Included were visions of the defeat of the kingdom of men, the judgment of all men and the return of Christ. Verse 14 has many New Testament companions (1 Cor. 15; Eph. 1:20ff.; Phil. 2:9, 10, etc.). Here Christ is shown as the stone of Nebuchadnezzar's dream who will crush all earthly powers.

In verses 17 and 18 the vision is interpreted and the emphasis on the triumph of God's Kingdom and his saints is clear. It shows that in reality there are just two kingdoms among men: Satan's kingdom (the four beasts) and God's Kingdom. All believers belong to the Kingdom of God and will triumph with Christ.

The horns described in verses 19-21 reflect the human successors to the kingdom of Rome, the fourth beast, the succeeding rulers of this world, all under Satan. In the end they always seek to destroy God's Kingdom and God's saints. It is their nature (see Rev. 12:17; 17:13, 14).

The promise that in the end the saints will possess the Kingdom (v. 22) points to the revelation of John in Revelation 29:7-9. In the final showdown Satan and his seed are overthrown.

The portrayal of Babylon and Rome as the beasts, and symbolic of kingdoms of this world against God's Kingdom, is also seen in the New Testament Revelation. Revelation 17 and 18 speak of Babylon as the representative of earthly power that must be overthrown. And the scarlet beast of Revelation 17:3ff. is doubtlessly intended to point to Rome with its famous seven hills (17:3, 9).

The personality described in Daniel 7:25 sounds very much like the lawless one of 2 Thessalonians 2:3-12 (cf. Rev. 13:7). The expression "a time and times and a half time" (v. 25) is also found in Revelation 12:14 and there it seems to me to represent the years of the church in history between the two comings of Christ, i.e., from Jesus' ascension until his second coming.

The thought of the whole vision of chapter 7 is summarized in verse 27. It declares the inevitable triumph of God's Kingdom.

No doubt there was still much here which Daniel did not understand and was not permitted to understand (v. 28). This would be in keeping with the words of Peter (1 Pet. 1:10-12).

Chapter 8, the *vision* in the *third year of Belshazzar* is an elaboration on the duel between the second and third beasts or nations. The *ram* moved from the east toward the west, north and south (8:4). He represented Persia (v. 20). The *he-goat* was in the west and moving over the whole earth (8:5) and represented Greece (v. 21).

We know that Xerxes of Persia did attempt to move west toward Greece but was stopped. Later, Alexander the Great ruled over Greece and spread his empire over all the world of that day, defeating Persia in the end.

The mention of the magnificence of the he-goat (v. 8) is in accord with Alexander's own exaltation of himself to the place of a god. The replacement of the empire of the he-goat by four divisions is also in accord with what happened to Alexander's empire when he had died. It broke up into four kingdoms ruled by generals in Alexander's army.

Particular attention is given in this vision to one little horn (ruler) who was pompous and profane (vv. 9ff.). Particularly his atrocities in relation to God's sanctuary are noted (vv. 11, 12, 24, 25). The duration of his rule in Jerusalem is given as about three and a half years or 1,150 days.

All of this fits quite well the rule of Antiochus Epiphanes who ruled from 175 to 163 B.C. in one of the divisions of the Greek empire after Alexander. During his reign he sought to Hellenize (make a Greek city of) Jerusalem. He robbed the Temple and set up a statue of Jupiter in the Holy of Holies. He ordered swine sacrificed on the altars, anything to desecrate God's worship. So accurate are these predictions of chapter 8 that unbelievers and liberal biblical scholars as well have considered them written after 163 B.C. instead of in the time of Daniel (the 500's B.C.).

Chapter 9 tells of Daniel's desire to understand better the meaning of *seventy years* mentioned by Jeremiah (9:2—cf. Jer. 25:11, 12 and 29:10). We have here therefore a prayer of Daniel as he seeks greater wisdom. The number seventy obviously meant that Jews would be in exile seventy years, but Daniel searched for further meaning in the symbolism of the number seventy. The number seven in Scripture frequently conveys the concept of completeness.

We see here the fervent and devout life of prayer which Daniel lived (vv. 3ff.). We see his readiness to confess his sin and those of his people (vv. 5, 6, 8, 11). Yet, as David, he desired God's mercy and forgiveness (v. 9). He showed too his allegiance to the Law of Moses, the Word of God (vv. 11, 13).

He made great intercessory prayer on behalf of Jerusalem though he was far away from the city (vv. 16-19). He prayed in Darius' first year (9:1) which was also the first year of Cyrus. Therefore, when in that year (539 B.C.) Cyrus decreed the return of Jews to Jerusalem (see Ezra 1:1), it may well have been an answer to Daniel's prayer.

We note also in the prayer how Daniel grasped the message of God's relation to our righteousness and our need for God's mercy (9:18—cf. Jer. 23:6; 33:16; Isa. 64:6).

God responded at that time to Daniel's prayer by sending Gabriel who had appeared to him earlier (9:21; 8:16). This same Gabriel later appeared to Zacharias (Luke 1:19) and to Mary (Luke 1:26) to announce the birth of Jesus. His appearance here to Daniel was for the same purpose.

He showed that the number seventy also represented seventy weeks, or the time to finish God's work of destroying sin and establishing righteousness and to fulfill all prophecy relating to Christ (9:24). References to the going forth of the commandment to restore Jerusalem (9:25) would at first seem to mean the time of Cyrus' decree (539 B.C.) or the first return under Zerubbabel in 538 B.C.

We know from Ezra and Nehemiah that there were three returns. The first was in 538 under Zerubbabel. The second in 458 under Ezra and the third in 445 under Nehemiah. The point of the prophecy in verse 25 is to show that sixty-nine weeks must elapse between the commandment to return and the time of the anointed one, the Messiah. If we assume that he is speaking here of the coming of Christ to accomplish redemption, then the time would be over 400 years.

If we take the days each to represent a year on the basis of Ezekiel 4:6, then 483 years are required (sixty-nine times seven). In such a case 538 B.C. could not be the beginning point since 483 years from then would place us at 55 B.C. This would be far too early. But if the point of reference be the time of Ezra's return, 458 B.C., then we come to A.D. 25, and the appropriate time of Jesus' ministry.

There is much to be said for setting the time of Ezra's return as the beginning point for counting the 483 required years. Zerubbabel's return was not meaningful in bringing a spiritual revival to the land. Ezra's was. It was a spiritual return, as we shall see when we study Ezra. It was the time of the return of the people to God's Word, the true return to God.

Reference to the cutting off of the Messiah points probably to his death (v. 26). This would have occurred around A.D. 25 when we realize that Jesus was born 7 B.C. and not in the year 1. The error of the counting of the years of Jesus' birth has been long known. Herod the Great, active in the earlier years of Jesus' life, died himself in 4 B.C.

Reference in verse 27 to the ceasing of the sacrificial system, would refer to the accomplishing of all that the sacrificial system and the sacrifices symbolized, by the death of Christ. The tearing of the veil of the Temple at the time of Jesus' death indicated the end of the usefulness of the sacrificial system, the Temple, and all they symbolized. It had now all been accomplished (Matt. 27:51).

Chapters 10-12 allude to *the great warfare* between Michael and his angels and Satan and his angels (10:1). We know more of this from Revelation 12:7-9. When it occurred we are not certain. Since this revelation occurs after the revelation concerning the work of Christ (ch. 9), we can assume that it is in connection with that great event. Revelation 12:13, also indicates that Satan was cast out of heaven to be confined to the earth after Christ's death and resurrection (see Rev. 12:5). Jude 9 also indicates that there had been a long contention between Michael and Satan. Jesus too speaks of the casting down of Satan in connection with his own work and ministry (Luke 10:18).

Evidently, Satan had access to heaven until Christ's work was finished, to accuse God's children and to contend over the dead (cf. Job 1, 2), but after Christ's finished work, he was hurled out of heaven.

Michael therefore appeared to Daniel to assure him of what God would yet do for his people who trusted in him (10:12-14).

Chapter 11 is much like chapter 8. It tells of the struggles between Persia and Greece (11:2). It is an expansion of chapters 8, 9ff., telling of the little horn (Antiochus Epiphanes) who made himself king.

Here Antiochus Epiphanes becomes symbolic of all rulers who raise themselves against God and his people (11:28-39). Here we find many allusions to the last days and to the wars and rumors of war to precede them (v. 31—cf. Matt. 24:15 and 2 Thes. 2). It speaks of the falling away of many from the faith (v. 34—cf. 2 Tim. 3:1ff.).

The prediction of trouble to come for God's people (12:1) parallels New Testament revelation (Matt. 24:15-22). In the last days before the coming of the Day of the Lord there will be hard times for the people of God.

Reference in 11:31 to the abomination of desolation in the days of Antiochus Epiphanes was used by Christ in Matthew 24:15 to be indicative of the pagan defilement and profanation of God's people by the pagan world.

The closing words of Daniel, chapter 12, give great hope to the people of God, both in Daniel's day while they were still in exile and for the future, so that God's people would look toward God's ultimate triumph.

The promise of deliverance was to those whose names were written in God's book, the Lamb's book of life (12:1—cf. Rev. 20:12; 3:5).

The resurrection of all of the dead, some to go to eternal life and others to eternal punishment (12:2) is in full harmony with Isaiah 66:22-24 and Revelation 20:12-15.

The emphasis here is on God's children, in the meantime, till these things are accomplished, being busy in witnessing to the truth God has proclaimed, shining as lights in a darkened generation (12:3—see Phil. 2:15).

In verse 4 we are told that many years must pass and much history to accomplish the purpose of God. "Many shall run to and fro, and knowledge shall be increased" is a good summary of human history.

Daniel, as all believers, desired to know how long (v. 6). God never says. His answer to Daniel was like that later to John (12:7—see Rev. 12:14). It simply means that God will not say.

Verse 10 pictures history in the meantime to be a time of many being redeemed from sin into God's Kingdom while many others continue to live in sin and do wickedly. Once more God calls for his people to be patient and to wait (v. 13).

ESTHER

The book of Esther tells of God's protection of his people in the time of Ahasuerus, known in secular history also by the name Xerxes. The events which are recorded here occurred in the first half of the fifth century B.C. prior to the return of Ezra in 458 B.C. (1:1).

The unusual characteristic of the book of Esther is that nowhere in it is the name of God found. Nevertheless, the activity and control of God over all that happens here is quite evident.

Chapter 1 tells of *the deposing of Vashti,* the wife of Xerxes, from being queen. The occasion was a feast of which we have seen other examples in Daniel 1:3-7). It is evident that there was considerable liberty in his era (v. 8) which is perhaps mentioned here in contrast to the usual custom of kings.

The king's command regarding Vashti was wrong (v. 11). We have to commend her for her refusal. But by it the way was made for Esther to become queen, because the king, following the advice of his counsellors, deposed Vashti and began to search for another queen (1:15-22).

Chapter 2 relates the way in which Esther was chosen to be queen. She was a Jew and this would have been against her becoming queen. Nevertheless God overruled. This chapter makes that clear.

Mordecai, Esther's cousin and foster father, is introduced in 2:5. His ancestors had been with those carried to Babylon in the reign of Jeconiah (Jehoiachin). This would have been 597 B.C. in the time when Ezekiel too was carried captive (Ezek. 1:2).

His cousin, Esther, was chosen as one to compete for the honor of being queen (2:8). As with Joseph and Daniel, so with Esther, she gained favor with those who cared for her. Thus the presence of God was with her (v. 9).

At this time a series of events began which could not be reckoned to chance. Though God's name is not mentioned, it is evident that his hand guided all of this long chain of events to its culmination and to the salvation of the Jews from their enemies.

1. *Esther did not make known her Jewish background (v. 10).* This was significant for the later history.

2. *When Esther appeared before the king she pleased him most (2:15-17).* This led to her being in a strategic place where she could be of service to God and her people. We see, too, that though she was in such a high place she nevertheless was subject to the spiritual guidance of her cousin Mordecai (v. 20). This, too, would be significant later.

3. *Mordecai learned of a plot to kill the king (2:21-23).* Mordecai was in the king's gate, the center of political activity. He had his ears open and learned of the plot. He duly reported it and the men were apprehended and punished.

4. *These events were recorded but not rewarded (2:23).* Strangely, though Mordecai was given full credit for the report that saved the king's life, he was not then rewarded. This too proved to be significant later.

Before going on with the series of events leading up to the rescue of God's people, we are told of the background of the threats to the Jews' welfare.

A man named Haman rose high in Xerxes' kingdom (3:1). He had the praise and glory of all men except Mordecai. Like Daniel, Mordecai loved God too much to bow to men or show them reverence (3:2). Again, while the Lord's name is not mentioned, the similarity between these events and Daniel chapter 6 are so clear that it is quite obvious that Mordecai honored the same God as Daniel and risked his own life in the same way.

This led Haman to hate not only Mordecai but all Jews (3:3-6). He plotted their destruction as many since, including Hitler, have done.

From this the plot of Haman against Mordecai and all Jews began (3:8-15). The cooperation of the king in all of this simply follows the pattern of Nebuchadnezzar and Darius the Mede in putting too much trust in their advisors. So at the time of the casting of Pur (the lot) (v. 7), a decree went out over the kingdom, over the king's signature, that all Jews should be slain (v. 13). This caused no small concern among the Jews (v. 15).

Mordecai sent word to Esther (4:1-4). Mordecai further told her to help her people by going to the king on their behalf (v. 8).

Her hesitation was understandable. She had risen from captive to a high place in the kingdom, as Joseph earlier had done and as Moses had done in his first forty years in Egypt. She knew that any act on her part might precipitate her downfall. Then she certainly could not help her people. She may well have reasoned this way (4:11).

Mordecai's reply is classic. He showed her that her exaltation was not for her own advantage but for her people. To act selfishly now would not save her (v. 13). Furthermore, Mordecai here expressed great faith in God by implying that the people would be delivered whether or not she consented (v. 14). The words "who knoweth whether thou are not come to the kingdom for such a time as this?" expressed the greatest faith in a God who is sovereign and directs the course of men. Surely nothing which led to her being queen had been coincidental.

Esther is to be commended for her brave resolution to be willing to try to save her people (4:15-17). Again the call to fasting indicates a people of faith.

Now we take up again the series of events which led to the saving of the Jews from their enemy Haman.

5. *The queen received favor in the eyes of the king (5:2).* The first hurdle was over, but she still had to convince the king of the evil of Haman whom he trusted and the righteousness of her cause.

Wisely, she did not attack Haman openly but played for time to work out a plan (5:4). The invitation to proud Haman to eat with the king and queen flattered Haman and put him off guard.

6. *The king was desirous to please Esther (5:5, 6).* He offered to grant her petition without even knowing what it was. Again, she wisely moved slowly, deliberately, giving time for the situation to develop. She learned to wait on the Lord (5:7-8).

7. *Haman, pleased with himself, grew angry at Mordecai, being self assured of his own success (5:9-14).* Encouraged by his wife, Haman decided to move against Mordecai, thus acting prematurely. If God's children would just learn patience, how often God will deal with their enemies in his own way.

8. *The king that very night had a sleepless night (6:1).* While Haman plotted Mordecai's death, God took sleep away from the king.

9. *The king determined to remedy his sleeplessness by having the boring chronicles of the kingdom read to yim (6:1).* This was the same kind of action that one might pursue today who would select a dull book to put him to sleep if he was having trouble going to sleep.

10. *The place in the chronicles from which the reading was taken turned out to be the place which had recorded Mordecai's good deeds on behalf of the king earlier (6:1, 2).* Of all the pages that could have been read, it was no coincidence that this place was selected.

11. *Again, the fact that no reward had been given Mordecai at that time was significant (6:3).*

12. *Haman was getting ready to see the king to tell of his intent against Mordecai.* This occurred just at the time the king most deeply appreciated Mordecai (6:4-7).

13. *Haman in his vanity thought the king desired to honor him (v. 6).* This led to his advice that the man the king honored be greatly honored as he described it (vv. 8, 9).

It would have been interesting to see Haman's face when he learned that it was Mordecai whom the king intended to honor and not Haman (6:10). The prophecy of his wife and friends to Haman was very true (6:13). His world quickly fell apart.

The account in chapter 7 is a classic. It contains great drama and is exciting to read.

14. *Esther's petition* was *revealed* concerning her people (7:3-5). She appealed for herself and for her people. Only when the king asked the identity of the people did she give it (v. 6).

15. *The thoroughly frustrated Haman foolishly appeared in a compromising position with respect to Esther before the king's very eyes (7:8).*

16. *Haman was executed on the gallows he had built for Mordecai (vv. 9, 10).*

We see in this long chain of events that God was in control of all and that he moved on behalf of his people for their salvation. None of these events can be called a mere coincidence. All was guided by the hand of the Savior, the Lord.

The rest of the book is anticlimactic and shows how all Jews, like Mordecai, were delivered from destruction that day. Again, 10:3 reminds us of the latter days of Daniel. In this book as in the book of Daniel, the Lord assured his people that he was indeed able to deliver them from their enemies even while they remained in exile.

13

THE RESTORATION
AND FUTURE HOPE
OF GOD'S PEOPLE

IN 538 B.C. God stirred the heart of Cyrus, king of Persia, to allow his people to return to Jerusalem to rebuild the Temple of their God and to settle again in the land of Canaan. They would no longer be an independent country nor would they have a king but they would be in their own land.

This return was primarily a physical return. For the most part the people did not grow spiritually during these days. Their primary task was to rebuild the Temple and even this was accomplished only slowly and after God's prophets spurred them on to complete it. The world was still very much with them.

The period covered by this chapter is from 538 B.C. until approximately 400 B.C., a time period in which 1 and 2 Chronicles, Ezra, Nehemiah, Haggai, Zechariah and Malachi all appear.

1 AND 2 CHRONICLES

When the people were returning to their homeland after more than a generation in captivity, their needs were many. They had lived in the midst of paganism, most of them born there. They had been without the Temple and without the sacrificial system. They also, for the most part, had been without any leadership in those days among their own people.

There were no more kings to lead them. Most of the prophets were now silent. And the priesthood had fallen into disgrace during the latter days of the kingdom and most of its priests had utterly failed God.

The great need then as the people contemplated return was for a spiritual revival. Such a revival would have to be accompanied by a rise of respect for the priesthood and by a fresh understanding of the place and importance of the Temple and the sacrificial system because all of these things had deteriorated before the very eyes of the people in the latter days in Judah.

The books of Chronicles have as their purpose primarily to recall the people of God back to those institutions which God had first given to his people so that they could once again be a people contrite of heart, understanding the importance of holiness, righteousness and justice, so that they could understand their need of God and the way they must come to him, having their sin dealt with in the proper manner. All of this was connected with a fresh understanding of the place of the priesthood and the sacrificial system and the Temple in the lives of God's people.

The Chronicles are not another history, parallel to Samuel and Kings, simply giving another account. Neither should the Chronicles be read together with Samuel and Kings. They are separately written for the purpose of showing how, in God's dealing with his people, great emphasis had been placed on the priesthood and sacrifices and the Temple.

Therefore the fact that the Chronicles give great attention to David's interest in the Temple but do not mention his sin in regard to Bathsheba is not dishonesty. It was not the intention of the author of Chronicles to relate another history per se. The people already had Samuel and Kings, so there was no need to repeat that content. Chronicles was written for one purpose, to bring the people back to a respect for the means of spiritual leadership which God had established in the beginning—the priesthood and all that related to it. Once they had established this respect, then the grounds for spiritual revival so greatly needed would have been laid and could be built upon.

The term "priest" occurs in the Chronicles more than a

hundred times, more than in any other book except Leviticus. "Levite" occurs about a hundred times, more than in any other book without exception. This gives some idea of the emphasis of this book.

1 Chronicles opens with a genealogy beginning with Adam (1:1). The genealogy covers the first eight chapters. Then chapter 9 deals with the post-exile residents of Jerusalem, primarily the priests. The remainder of 1 Chronicles covers the life of David from his rise to power until his death.

2 Chronicles picks up at this point and covers the life of Solomon in the first nine chapters. The rest of the book traces the kings of Judah from Rehoboam until the fall and the decree of Cyrus for the return.

Let us now return to 1 Chronicles and note its emphasis. The book begins with a record of the genealogies of Israel (chs. 1-8). The first name is Adam (1:1). Adam is rarely mentioned in the Old Testament outside of Genesis chapters 2-5. In addition to this passage he is mentioned only in Deuteronomy 32:8 and Job 31:33 and possibly in Hosea 6:7 though it is disputed whether or not the word in Hosea should be translated "Adam" or "man."

Adam's place here both supports his historicity as an individual and shows that through him the line of grace through Seth began.

Chapter 1 traces from Adam through Seth, Shem, Abraham, Isaac to Jacob who is here referred to as Israel. In addition, the descendants of Japheth and Ham as well as of Esau are traced to several generations as in Genesis.

Chapter 2:1—4:23 gives great attention to the genealogies of Judah's descendants, on down through David (3:1) and Solomon (3:10).

From 4:24 to 5:26, the genealogies of Simeon, Reuben and Gad are traced, including a brief account of the fall of the northern tribes of Reuben, Gad and the half tribe of Manasseh, before the forces of Tiglath-Pileser (5:25, 26).

Chapter 6's eighty-one verses are given exclusively to the descendants of Levi, the priestly tribe, including their duties and the cities in which they lived in the land, thus establishing their rightful place among God's people. Chapter 7 briefly traces the descendants of Issachar, Benjamin, Naphtali, Manasseh, and Asher. Chapter 8 focuses exclusively on Benjamin, probably because the Benjamites were eventually joined to Judah as one people. Chapter 9 records the names of some who returned in the first resettling of Jerusalem after the exile. Here primary attention is given to the priests who returned (9:10-44).

The *remainder of the book* is devoted to *the time of David* (chs. 10–29).

After a brief account of Saul's failure and death (ch. 10), David and his supporters are noted (chs. 11, 12). In the next four chapters great detail is given to David's bringing the ark into Jerusalem (chs. 13-16). His attention to the Law and the place of the Levites in this act gets considerable emphasis (13:2, 3; 15:2, 15ff.).

The keeping of the ceremonial law and the appointing of Levites to care for the ark once it was placed in Jerusalem is recalled in 16:1-6. Then David lifted a hymn of praise to God by Asaph, the chief of those priests who were appointed to care for the ark (16:7-36, cf. 16:5). In this hymn are included parts of Psalm 105 (8-22); 96 (23-33) and 106 (34-36). The chief responsibility for the care of the ark was then left in the hands of Asaph and his brothers (16:37-43).

Chapter 17 records David's great desire to build a permanent house (temple) for the ark. The material here is similar to that in 2 Samuel. The next three chapters review David's successes in his reign over Judah, his military victories and spiritual leadership. Then in chapter 21, we learn of David's sin in numbering the people which is also recorded in 2 Samuel 24:1-25. The primary purpose in recording this particular event seems to be to prepare the way for the very long account of David's attention to the preparation of the building of the Temple by his son Solomon.

It was the sin of numbering the people that led to David's purchase of the Temple site (21:18—22:1). This site is later identified as Moriah (2 Chron. 3:1), where Abraham had built an altar on which to sacrifice his only begotten son, Isaac (Gen. 22).

Beginning in chapter 22 of 1 Chronicles and going to the end of the book, great attention is given to David's preparation for Solomon's building of the Temple. The whole matter is introduced in 22:2-5. This tells of the gathering together of materials and supplies for the building itself.

The rest of chapter 22 contains the charge of David to Solomon concerning the building of the Temple. There is much emphasis on hard commitment to the task. David saw it as a primary work of Solomon in his reign (22:9, 10, 14, 19). He also urged obedience to God's Law through Moses upon Solomon (22:12, 13).

Chapters 22-26 provide considerable detail of the various offices which David prescribed for the Levites including their duties. Only after this, was the political organization of the people mentioned (ch. 27). This shows where David's interest lay, in the Temple and the Levitical laws pertaining to it.

Chapters 28 and 29 contain David's addresses concerning the Temple and his explicit instructions to Solomon on how to build it, together with exhortations to Solomon on spiritual commitment (28:9). Offerings were taken from the tribes for financing the building (29:1ff.) and finally David prayed before all concerning the work to be begun by Solomon (29:10-19).

The book closes with a notation of David's death and the beginning of Solomon's rule (29:22-28). The histories mentioned in 29:29, 30 are probably what we call the books of Samuel.

2 Chronicles continues to trace the rule after David with great attention to Solomon's reign (chs. 1-9) and particularly to his efforts in Temple building. Chapter 1 tells of his wisdom and glory and then through the bulk of this section, through 7:10, relates his efforts in building the Temple. The rest of chapter 7 plus chapters 8, 9 close the section on Solomon with attention given to Solomon's fame. The rest of the book records the rulers of Judah from Rehoboam to the end. In all of these chapters we see continual emphasis and attention given to the priests and the sacrificial system and their part in history.

In *chapter 1* we learn of *Solomon's worship at Gibeon,* where the Tent of Meeting was, although the ark had been moved to Jerusalem. That night the Lord appeared to Solomon and promised him wisdom (1:7-13).

In *2:1–7:10,* we read of *how Solomon set about to build the Temple.* Great attention was given to detail of structure and to furniture. Finally, when it was completed the ark was brought in (5:2-10). Chapter 6 contains Solomon's prayer of dedication of the Temple as is also recorded in 1 Kings chapter 8.

After God's glory filled the Temple (7:1-3), the people worshipped there. Then the Lord appeared to Solomon with promises if he obeyed, and with warnings if he was not faithful (7:11-22).

Chapters 8 and 9 conclude the life of Solomon and note particularly his fame. They do not mention his sins which brought such disgrace in his latter years. The record of Solomon's latter years was made clear in 1 Kings. The purpose of this book was to show the purpose of the Temple and all that pertained to it. The Temple and not Solomon was the primary subject here.

Chapters 10–36 record *the kings of Judah in succession.* Great emphasis is seen on the part played by the priests in this history.

In Rehoboam's reign, chapters 10-12, we learn how the priests from the north fled south when Jeroboam departed from the ordained worship. The priests in fact led the way and set the example for any faithful ones living in the north (11:13-17).

In Abijah's reign (ch. 13), the priests led in prayer bringing rescue by God when, on one occasion, Judah was threatened by Jeroboam of Israel (13:13-16).

In Asa's reign (chs. 14-16) note is made of the absence of priests in the northern kingdom and how this greatly affected their spiritual state (15:1-5). In Jehoshaphat's reign also (chs. 17-20) spiritual revival and return to faith occur by the leadership of the priests going about the land teaching God's words (17:7-9).

When Jehoshaphat was rebuked by the Lord through Jehu the prophet for his alliance with Ahab (19:1-3) Jehoshaphat repented and set priests over the affairs of Jerusalem to give better spiritual leadership (19:8-11). Again, later when the people were threatened by Ammon, their enemy, Jehoshaphat called people to great faith in the Lord and his servants the prophets (20:20—cf. Isa. 7:9; Hab. 2:4; 2 Pet. 1:19). At this time two singers (priests) led in worship and praise to God (20:21). Then in the reign of Jehoram (ch. 21), son of Jehoshaphat, an era of evil began. Jehoram slew all of his brothers who were rivals to the throne, a wicked thing to do. In this time a message from Elijah came to Jehoram warning him of judgment to come because of his sin (21:11-15). The Lord followed through with the judgments he had forewarned of (21:18ff.). No mention of priests or their centrality is made in this evil period. But God was active, destroying those who had rebelled against him and those tainted by the blood of wicked Jezebel, the wife of Ahab. Remember that Jehoram had married the daughter of Jezebel and Ahab, Athaliah (22:7, 8—cf. 2 Kgs. 8:18).

Athaliah (Jezebel's daughter and the wife of the deceased Jehoram) attempted to take over the kingdom. She sought to secure her position by killing off all rivals and possible rivals (22:10). However, one of Jehoram's daughters, the wife of the priest Jehoiada, managed to hide one son of Jehoram named Joash (22:11).

When the child was seven, Jehoiada the priest presented him to the elders of the land and Athaliah was overthrown (23:1ff.). Thus we see how Judah and the line of David were saved by a priest from destruction. Joash himself was greatly influenced for good as long as Jehoiada the priest lived (24:1, 2). He restored the Temple (24:4) and raised funds to finance its upkeep (24:8).

However after the death of Jehoiada, Jehoram reverted to the evil ways of his father (24:17-19). When Zechariah, son of

Jehoiada the priest, rebuked the king for his evil, Joash had him killed (24:21). So dastardly was this deed that Jesus mentioned it in his discourse on the evil times in which he lived (Luke 11:49-51).

In the reign of Amaziah, Jehoram's son (25:1ff.), he began as a good king but later led the people into idolatry (25:14ff.). He too was punished with death at the hands of conspirators (25:27).

Uzziah's reign was good. He sought to please the Lord (26:1ff.). He was influenced by the life and martyrdom of Zechariah, son of Jehoiada the priest (26:5). Yet he too became vain and usurped priestly duties as Saul, the first king, had done (26:16). For this he was punished severely. We note how the priests of that era were faithful guardians of the things of God (26:17, 18). For his sin, Uzziah had leprosy the rest of his life (26:20).

Jotham, Uzziah's successor, was afraid to enter the Temple after his father's experience (27:2). Apparently he just left the religious matters to the priests. His son Ahaz therefore was a sceptic about religious matters and showed no desire to follow the Lord (28:1ff.). In his reign he made an alliance with Assyria and hired them to fight his enemies Syria and Israel, the northern kingdom (28:16ff.).

Because of his concern for the things of the Lord, the reign of Hezekiah the son of Ahaz, occupies the next four chapters. He called the Levites to clean up the Temple (29:5). This action was duly noted (29:12). The sacrificial system was restored (29:24). The Levites were restored to their duties as in David's day (29:25, 30). It was an era of true revival (29:31ff.). It was also an era of evangelism. In Hezekiah's day word was sent to the north inviting those of Israel to join those in Judah in true worship of the Lord (30:5, 6). This was just before the fall of Samaria and the last opportunity for God's children in the northern kingdom to join those in the south (30:13-16). Again we see the key part in all of this played by the priests (30:26, 27). The entire 31st chapter is devoted to laws concerning offerings and tithes.

The reigns of Manasseh and Amon were evil for the most part (ch. 33). Therefore no priestly activity is noted here. Then with chapters 34 and 35, we see again the reign of a good king, Josiah, great-grandson of Hezekiah. He, too, called on the Levites and priests to aid in cleaning up the Temple and repairing it (34:9, 12, 14).

Once more, attention was given to the Law of Moses, and the rightful spiritual leadership of the priests was restored (35:1-3—cf. verses 9, 10, 18).

After Josiah's premature death (35:24) there came a succession of four kings all of whom did evil. Not only did they do this but also the priests fell away from God (36:14). With their fall came the beginning of the fall of the whole city of Jerusalem and the captivity in Babylon (vv. 19, 20).

The book closes with notice of Cyrus' decree that the people of Judah who would could return to Jerusalem to rebuild the Temple (36:22-23).

We see then that the overall message of Chronicles is that when the priests are faithful and the kings and people follow their spiritual leadership, the people of God are blessed. But in years of neglect of the priestly matters or indifference to the Law of Moses, evil arises and causes great suffering for God's people.

Therefore Chronicles was written to stir the hearts of the people to a return to the old foundations which had been laid by Moses long before. These foundations of faith in the entire Word of God are still the only valid way God's people can truly return to a right relationship to their God.

EZRA

The book of Ezra is a continuation of 1 and 2 Chronicles. It starts where Chronicles leaves off, with the decree Cyrus made in 539 B.C. (Ezra 1:1—cf. 2 Chron. 36:22-23). In Ezra 1:3, 4 we find additional words not found in the Chronicles record which tell of the financing of the return.

After the record of Cyrus' decree is given, the book of Ezra divides easily into two basic parts: *the first return* under Sheshbazzar and Zerubbabel (1:5—6:22) and *the second return* under Ezra (chs. 7–10). These two returns were separated by some eighty years.

In the record of *the first return* we are told first of the favorable response to Cyrus' decree given by the people of God (1:5-11). Again, we note emphasis on the priesthood and its part in the return (1:5). The initiative both for Cyrus' proclamation and the people's good response came from the Lord (1:1, 5). Included in the things carried back to Jerusalem were the vessels which Nebuchadnezzar had taken from the Temple and which Belshazzar had defiled (1:7—cf. Daniel 5:2ff.).

Sheshbazzar, mentioned as the leader of the return (1:8) was quickly overshadowed by Zerubbabel whether because he died or because he was old and unable to lead. He quickly faded from the scene. In *chapter 2*, a list of the families who returned is given. Again we note considerable attention given to the Levites

(2:36ff.). Some who claimed to be of the priestly family could not prove it and were not allowed to function as priests (2:62, 63).

A total of 42,360 plus 7,337 servants are listed as returners to Jerusalem (2:64, 65).

When they arrived, many of those gave willingly of their wealth to restore the Temple (2:68). We see here a spirit commended by God in giving (cf. Exod. 35:29; 2 Cor. 9:7). Once more Levites appeared as significant among those returning (v. 70).

Chapter 3 records the resumption of the sacrificial system and other laws pertaining to the Law of Moses (3:1-7).In the second year after they returned, they began to rebuild the Temple. This would be about 537 B.C. (3:8). By that time Zerubbabel was clearly the leader. Oversight of the work of building was given to the Levites (3:8). Jeshua, the priest, had charge of all (3:9). All was done in accord with Levitical law and as David had directed (3:10—cf. 1 Chron. 6:31).

The mixed emotions of many, noted here as work began, reflects the concern of many that this house could not match the glory of Solomon's temple (3:12-13). Later Haggai would deal with this pessimism (Hag. 2:3-9).

In *chapter 4* we begin to see external opposition arise to the work which the Jews were doing. The opposers were the inhabitants of the land, the Samaritans who had been established in Canaan since the days of the Assyrian conquest of Samaria (4:2). We read of these people in 2 Kings 17:24-41. They are described as ones who feared the Lord and served their own gods (2 Kgs. 17:32, 41). They settled in the land with a syncretistic religion, an amalgamation of paganism and Jehovah worship.

Their offer to assist the Jews was therefore an offer to compromise. Zerubbabel and Jeshua did well to refuse them (4:3).

They avoided the error of Joshua which led to so much compromise when Israel first came into Canaan (Josh. 9:3-27—cf. Judg. 1:27, 28, 32, 33; 2:1-3). The cost of refusing the compromise however was that their enemies sought to interfere with all that they did. When we stand against God's enemies, we draw the fire of Satan and his seed (4:4-5).

The mention of Ahasuerus' name (4:6) raises a problem for us. It is not clear who is the Ahasuerus who is mentioned here. From secular chronologies we learn that Cyrus ruled until 530 B.C. After him Cambyses ruled til 522, then Darius the First until 486 B.C. The Ahasuerus we know is from Esther 1:1—the Ahasuerus known also as Xerxes. He did not rule until 486 B.C. Mention of him here was simply in connection with this earlier resistance to the Jews in Zerubbabel's day as if to say that the resistance continued on down to Ahasuerus' day (486 B.C.) or for more than fifty years.

The Artaxerxes of 4:7 is known in secular history as Cambyses and he ruled, as we noted above, from Cyrus' death in 530 B.C. until 522 B.C. During his reign, the enemies of the Jews in Jerusalem became sufficiently strong to get work on the Temple stopped. They wrote to the king Cambyses (Artaxerxes) in Aramaic (Syrian) as all official letters were written (4:7).

Here the Scripture quotes the letter at length and so from this point, as in Daniel, the Scripture is in Aramaic (Ezra 4:8—6:18). Since this whole section contains much correspondence between the king and other officials and concerns the official procedures relating to the Jews, it is understandable that the whole section is in Aramaic. Then beginning in 6:19, when attention is focused once more on the worship and conduct of God's people, the Hebrew language is used.

The letter was an accusation against the Jews. It misrepresented the facts in that it accused the Jews of being rebellious and seeking to build up the walls to have independence from the Persian king. In short, they were accused of perfidy (4:12, 13, 16). By implying their own interest in the king, the writers sought from him a favorable answer to their request that the work on the city be stopped (vv. 15, 16).

Though they had lied in this respect concerning Jewish activity, their lies were successful in getting work on the Temple stopped (4:24).

In 522 B.C. Darius came to power in Persia. For some time now work on the Temple had ceased. It lay there unfinished while the Jews busied themselves with their own houses and affairs.

It was important to the glory of God that the Temple be finished and also to the good of the Jews. The Temple represented the presence of God with his people and pointed the way to the finished work of God on behalf of his people. God had promised to give them a new Temple (heart) through Ezekiel, as you recall (Ezek. 36, 37, and the vision of the new Temple). The rebuilding of the Temple therefore expressed the faith of the people in the faithfulness of God to perform his promises. To leave it unfinished was an expression of indifference to the greatly needed work of God.

Using the occasion of Cambyses' death evidently, two prophets arose to stir the people to resume building. Haggai and Zechariah wrote messages which we shall study later (5:1). Their work was effective and Zerubbabel and Jeshua began again work on the Temple (5:2).

When questioned by authorities about their work (5:3, 9) they told in detail their history and what was behind the effort (5:11-16). Appeal was made to Darius to resolve the matter (5:17).

It is apparent from the answer of Zerubbabel and the others that they understood their past history and its meaning and that they had been duly humbled by God's dealings with them (5:11, 12).

Darius' men found the decree of Cyrus relating to the house of God at Jerusalem (6:1-5). Darius' answer therefore to the authorities in Jerusalem was most favorable for the Jews. Not only did he permit work to resume but ordered financial aid for them (6:7, 8). The desire for their prayers on behalf of the king recalls the words of God to Jeremiah earlier relating to the exiles in Babylon (Jer. 29:7—cf. also Ezra 7:23; Rom. 13:1-7; 1 Tim. 2:1, 2). The letter was quite effective in stopping all enemies of the Jews from interfering (6:11).

Thus by God's blessings the work was finished and the Temple completed (6:14). The date of completion, the sixth year of Darius (6:15) would be about 516 B.C. It had taken over twenty years, as the primary life's work of Zerubbabel and Jeshua.

Once more we see emphasis given to the leadership of the priesthood as the priests led the people in proper worship in accord with God's Law (6:19-22). The use of the name Assyria (v. 22) simply reflects the habit of calling the area by its old name, as one might refer to Zaire as the Congo.

This completes the record of the activity of Zerubbabel and those with him. In chapter 7 we begin *the second half of the book of Ezra* pertaining to *the work of the priest Ezra* in bringing the people spiritually back to the Lord (chs. 7-10).

Some fifty-eight years passed from the events of chapter 6 to the events of chapter 7. In the meantime all of the spiritual leaders of the former era presumably had died and the people in their living had reverted to the practice of mixed marriages which threatened the very continuance of an identifiable people of God as it had so often before.

In the time of Artaxerxes of Persia, God raised up from among the exiles a group of believers led by Ezra, who is described as a ready scribe in the Law of Moses (7:6). This was in the seventh year of Artaxerxes which would be about 458 B.C. (7:7).

Ezra can be compared to Daniel as he set his heart to serve the Lord (7:10—cf. Dan. 1:8). We note his threefold goal: to *seek* (learn) God's Law; to *obey* it; and to *teach* it. Ezra is also often compared to Moses and considered in many respects to be another Moses, so well acquainted with the Law had he become and so devoted to it. His commitment to the Word of God is very much like what Paul called for in the life of Timothy (2 Tim. 2:2).

Artaxerxes' long letter is also in Aramaic (7:12-26). It is a letter of recommendation. The letter granted to Ezra considerable freedom and power (7:21, 22).

Again we note the Persian king's desire to win the favor of all gods (7:23—cf. 6:10). Also, we see once more great emphasis on the importance of the priesthood to Israel's return to God. Ezra was himself a priest descended from the line of Aaron, Eleazar, and Phinehas (7:1-5). Chief among those who went with him were priests (7:7). Special protection was granted to the priests accompanying him (7:24).

In this letter we also get insight into Persian justice and the levels or degrees of punishment meted out: death, banishment, confiscation of possessions, or imprisonment (7:26).

As with all other great spiritual leaders so with Ezra, all glory is given to the Lord for what has been accomplished (7:27ff.).

After a brief genealogy of the heads of families of those accompanying Ezra (8:1-14), we have Ezra's personal account of the trip back to Jerusalem. When he did not find any Levites among those going he sent for them (8:15-20).

Ezra's desire to return unescorted by the king's men was a desire to glorify God and express great faith in him (8:22). His faith was rewarded (vv. 33, 34).

After arrival Ezra was confronted immediately with the continuing threat of the integrity of God's people, mixed marriages (9:1, 2). Ezra's reaction was that of a truly devout man who mourned over the sins of the people (v. 3—cf. Matt. 5:4).

He wisely began not by open rebuke, but by seeking out those who were subject to the authority of God's Word and who desired to obey the Lord (9:4). With these he prayed (vv. 5ff.).

Ezra did not act sanctimoniously in this matter, but in his prayers included himself in the sin and guilt of his people, i.e., "our iniquities" (v. 6). He recognized that the survival of any remnant to this point in history was solely by God's mercy and not by anything deserved (9:8—cf. Isa. 1:9). He expressed great gratitude to the Lord for everything God had done for those people (9:9). In the midst of discouragement he was able to see much to be thankful for. His chief point of concern was the mixed marriages and here his petition centered, that the evil which had been done might now be undone (9:13-15).

In this action and prayer of Ezra we see an excellent example of spiritual leadership. Pastors of congregations could learn much about patience, meekness and humility from this man, and the development of these attitudes can go far in healing the evil of any congregation.

As Ezra and those few devout ones gathered in prayer, others joined them (10:1). True revival was beginning to have its effect. The people were led to repentance (10:2, 3). First the spiritual leaders made commitments to obey God (10:5), then they called together all the people to rectify the wrongs done (10:6ff.).

As the people gathered, their faith was tested. They faced great and radical changes which made them tremble inside. After this it started raining as they awaited Ezra's leadership (10:9).

Ezra called for action commensurate with their confession of sin. They were to separate from their foreign wives (v. 11). If this seems radical, it is because the very continuance of the holy seed was at stake. God had always warned against marriage with unbelievers. Wherever that had been ignored, great and serious consequences had fallen to God's people.

Because of the enormity of the task and the hard rain that fell, the people determined to appoint a committee to deal with the whole matter (10:12-14). So far as I can discover, this is the only Scriptural warrant for the very popular practice of church courts today to appoint and refer matters of business to committees.

Included among those of mixed marriages were many priests and Levites. These were dealt with first (10:18-24), then the others (10:25-44). The book closes therefore with the evident record of the peoples' action to back up their verbal commitment.

NEHEMIAH

Thirteen years after Ezra had come to Jerusalem, Nehemiah, back in Babylon, received word that things were not going well among the returned exiles (1:1-3). As Ezra had done, so Nehemiah mourned for the situation and confessed his own and their sins before God (1:4, 6, 7). He, like many before, recalled God's great revelation of himself (Exod. 34:6-7) and on that basis called on God's mercy now (1:5, 8). He appealed particularly to the promises of Deuteronomy (1:9—cf. Deut. 30:4).

Nehemiah's position in the Persian government was high. As cupbearer to the King (1:11) he would be one of the most trusted servants of the King and probably an advisor. His sad countenance was noted by Artaxerxes (2:2). When God opened the door, Nehemiah was ready. After an ejaculatory prayer (v. 4) he made request to return for a time to help his people. Evidently, unlike most who returned, he had not purposed a permanent move but only a trip, a mission to meet a specific need in Jerusalem. We note again how God moved the hearts of kings to do his will (2:8—cf. Prov. 21:1).

There are two major parts to the book of Nehemiah: first, *the rebuilding of the wall,* the great need Nehemiah saw while still in Shushan (2:9—6:19); and second, *the rebuilding of the people spiritually,* the great need he, together with Ezra, saw after he arrived in Jerusalem (chs. 8-10). It is around these two great works that the ministry of Nehemiah centers.

As with Zerubbabel and the first return, so with Nehemiah, as soon as he arrived, enemies also arose to oppose his efforts (2:10). Nehemiah, like Ezra, showed good and wise leadership in not openly declaring his attitude but gathering a few with whom to share his concern (2:11-12—cf. Ezra 9:4). He led the men to initiate the rebuilding of the walls (2:17-18). Nehemiah exemplified great faith in undertaking the work at the cost of ridicule from their enemies (2:19-20).

Chapter 3 relates the details of building. It was a well-planned procedure and wisely carried out, each man preparing the wall closest to his house, thus assuring that each segment would be carefully done (3:28).

Chapters 4-6 detail some of the problems encountered by the determined builders. The first problems were external coming from their enemies (ch. 4).

First they were ridiculed (4:1-3). Nehemiah took this to the Lord in prayer (vv. 4-5). The people were encouraged by God and continued to build in spite of the ridicule (v. 6).

Next, their enemies tried force and threats (4:7-8). Again the people prayed (v. 9) and this time Nehemiah met force with force and armed his people to protect themselves (4:10-14). He encouraged the people by exhortations not to fall back before the enemies (4:14, 20).

There were also problems which arose from within the camp of Israel (ch. 5). Among the Jewish people, the rich were taking advantage of the poor (5:1-5). The old sins of the eighth and seventh centuries were reappearing. Nehemiah was greatly disturbed (5:6).

These sins were strictly forbidden in God's Law (verse 7—cf. Exod. 22:25; Lev. 25:36). Here we see application of God's Law to a very real situation (v. 8). Nehemiah's strong exhortation to obey God had its effect (5:9-12). The people were now becoming more submissive to God's Law.

It is important to see that Nehemiah, who had been appointed their governor, himself set the example for his people (5:10, 14-19). Nehemiah's repeated prayer to be remembered by God for the righteousness he had done, was not an expression of works-righteousness, but of righteousness *unto* good works (v. 19). He continually desired, as did others we have studied for God to receive all the glory.

When the wall was about finished, once more the enemies of the Jews tried to stop this work. This time they tried trickery (6:1-14). Sanballat at first tried to lure Nehemiah away from his work to do him harm, isolated from the other Jews (v. 2). Nehemiah's commitment to the work the Lord had given him to do spared him from this evil plot (v. 3).

Next, the enemies threatened to have the work stopped by letters to high officials (vv. 6, 7). This did not work either (vv. 8, 9).

Finally, they sought to get at Nehemiah by a friend turned traitor (vv. 10-14). Once more Nehemiah by wisdom avoided their attempts to get him to compromise and the wall was completed (v. 15). The impact on all their enemies was great and to the glory of God (v. 16).

Chapter 7 has reference to the genealogy presumably that was mentioned in Ezra 2:1-70 (7:5). Many decades had passed since that first return and a renewal of the genealogy was in order. Again, special note was made of the Levites and priests among those coming to Jerusalem (7:39-56, 73).

After the work was finished, concern now moved to the rebuilding of the people spiritually (chs. 8-10). In this Ezra was the leader (8:1). Ezra, the ready scribe in God's Law, was ready for this occasion and he read and taught the people day after day (8:2-8). We note here several interesting things. First, we see the people's respect for God's Law in that they stood attentive for several hours a day to listen (8:3-5). Second, Ezra read and spoke from something much like our pulpits today (8:4). Third, the Word not only was read, but also explained (8:8).

We see here what, no doubt, became the practice in the synagogues of that day and after. In Jesus' time a similar pattern was followed (Luke 4:16-22—cf. Acts 13:14-42).

As a result of the teaching of God's Word the people sought to be doers of that Word, keeping its laws (8:13-18).

Finally they came to a time of public confession before God (ch. 9). In this revival the Levites were the spiritual leaders (9:4-5). They led in great prayers of confession (9:5-38).

This prayer is worthy of careful study since it shows how a people of God, taught by God's Word, came to a broken and contrite heart. They began by praising God according to his revelation of himself: Creator and Preserver (v. 6); Caller of his people through Abraham (v. 7); Maker of an eternal covenant with his people (v. 8).

There follows in the prayer a long review of God's gracious dealing with his people in spite of their sinfulness and stubbornness (vv. 9ff.). Their hope remained in God's revelation of himself as One ready to pardon and who is gracious (vv. 17-31, cf. Exod. 34:6-7). In the end their petition was for God's help and their own commitment to a sure covenant with God, to obey (v. 38). Again the leadership of the Levites and Priests is prominent (v. 38).

Chapter 10 contains the list of signers of the covenant representing all the people (vv. 1-27) and the content of the covenant itself (vv. 28-31). After this they followed through with actions reflecting their intent to obey God's Law (vv. 32-39).

Chapters 11 and 12 contain chiefly the census of priests and their establishment in places of leadership among the people together with provisions for their allotments.

Chapter 13 contains the account of the rectifying of whatever practices still obtained among the people which were inconsistent with the Law of God. One example is the discipline meted out to Eliashib the Priest who permitted an Ammonite, Tobiah, to live in the Temple court (13:7).

Another example of abuse of the Law was in withholding those portions from the Levites which were their due (13:10-14).

Still another violation was in regard to the Sabbath (13:15-22). We recall how the prophets had stressed the importance of observing this law (cf. Isaiah 56:1ff, 58:13ff.).

Finally, there were still some who were marrying foreigners (13:23-24). Nehemiah dealt with these as a threat to the future of God's people (v. 25). He held up Solomon as a bad example in this matter which had led to much sorrow (vv. 26-27).

All whose lives were compromising in any way were disciplined (v. 28). The work of Nehemiah was finished. He had indeed been faithful to the Lord and a worthy ally and a great aid to Ezra the Scribe in accomplishing the spiritual task (vv. 29-31).

HAGGAI

Haggai and Zechariah were prophets who were mentioned in Ezra 5:1 in the time of Zerubbabel. They were raised up by God to stir the people to resume the building of the Temple in the days of Darius I of Persia. The second year of Darius would be about 521 B.C. (1:1).

The message of the prophet is directed to the leaders responsible for rebuilding the Temple: Zerubbabel and Joshua (Jeshua) (1:1).

Evidently, after the death of the king of Persia, Cambyses, who had stopped the building, the Jews did not again attempt to resume building. In the years when they were forbidden to build they had become occupied with other things. This attitude became one of procrastination (1:2).

Yet, it was a dishonor to God's name before the pagan world for his people to live in finished homes while the Lord's house lay in ruins or incomplete (1:4).

The Lord, therefore, asked the people to consider their ways (1:5 etc.). This became the basis for Haggai's message.

The problem faced was that God's house lay incomplete. Day by day as the Jews went about their labors, to and from their fields and houses, they passed by the wastelands of the Temple. That Temple had meant to them the very presence of God and the very portrayal of how they were to come to him. Had not God promised by Ezekiel that he would bring them back to a new temple? Did it really matter that this temple lay in ruins?

The answer lay in a good look at their daily life (their ways) (1:5-7). The people were certainly working hard in their fields and at home but were getting nowhere (1:6). The solution to their problem lay in putting God first in their lives. If they would take up again their first task and their primary purpose in returning to Jerusalem (1:8-9), then God would bless them and not send more droughts which had hurt them so much lately (1:10-11). It is the simple lesson of learning to put God first (Matt. 6:33).

Haggai's message was effective (1:12-15). The people resumed the building and the Temple was completed. This people were spiritually alert to God's voice. They obeyed. And the Lord assured them once more that he was indeed with them (1;13).

The *result* of their endeavors to put God and his will first was that *the Lord was glorified* (2:1-9). There had been some who had remembered the old Temple (2:3—cf. Ezra 3:12). They had had mixed emotions since the new Temple did not match the splendor of the former one. The danger was that this new house would be despised (2:3). Yet as with men, so with temples, men look on the outside but God looks deeper (see 1 Samuel 16:7).

The Lord assured Zerubbabel that he would be with his people (2:4) and that he would fill his Temple with glory (2:7). It was not the amount of silver and gold that made it glorious but God's presence and blessing (2:8—cf. Matt. 23:16-22).

Indeed, the Lord promised more glory to this latter temple than to the former (2:9). This said a great deal about Solomon and all his glory as compared to the simple work of simple men of faith (cf. Matt. 6:28-29).

The people were required once more to learn the lesson that God is not glorified by our good works alone, i.e., what we can do for him. Our works and efforts in reality all fall far short. They are unclean (2:10-14—cf. Isa. 64:6). What is required for God to be glorified before his people is that they repent and turn to God, putting him first, acknowledging their need of him (2:17, 18). It is only then when he is first in their hearts that their works can be called good works which glorify God (see Matt. 5:16 and Eph. 2:8, 9, 10). When the people had put God first, then God began to bless them. God's name, indeed, would be glorified before all (v. 19).

The message of Haggai closes with a promise regarding Zerubbabel (2:20-23). Here Zerubbabel is seen as a symbol of God's rebuilding his kingdom (v. 23). The Lord will destroy all of Israel's enemies, the kingdoms of this world, in the end (2:21-22) as he promised through Daniel and will exalt the remnant of his people, personified in the obedient leadership of Zerubbabel (cf. 1:14).

Thus, in the space of three months (see 1:1, 15 to 2:10, 20) Haggai completed his work of prophesying God's Word to the people, but it was effective to the completion of the Temple and the glorifying of the name of God.

ZECHARIAH

Zechariah was a contemporary of Zerubbabel and Haggai. He too was raised up to stir the people to resume building the Temple in the second year of Darius (1:1). However his message is quite different in style and content from Haggai. His writing contains much apocalyptic material (symbolic writing), as do the books of Ezekiel and Daniel in the Old Testament and the book Revelation in the New Testament.

This book of Zechariah falls basically into two parts. *The first part* contains visions shown to Zechariah in order *to call the people to their task of rebuilding* (1:7-6:8). Then in the *latter half* (6:9-14:21) we find primarily *prophecies given to Zechariah* for God's people *to give them hope concerning the future.* Zechariah's ministry covered more time than did Haggai's, at least into the fourth year of Darius (7:1).

Zechariah's message opens with a lesson from the past (1:2-6). As Haggai had done, so Zechariah called the people to return to the Lord, i.e., to put him first in their lives (1:3—cf. Hag. 2:17-18). The fathers before exile had not learned that lesson (1:2, 4), and had suffered bitter consequences for not learning it (1:6). In essence Zechariah, like Haggai, was calling them to consider their ways because God would deal with them in accord with their ways toward him (1:6).

After this, Zechariah records *a series of visions and revelations* given to stir the people on to greater commitment to the Lord (1:7-6:8).

The first vision was of *a man on a red horse* (1:7-17). The red horse and others are explained as those sent by the Lord to walk about on earth (v. 10). There is in Revelation 6:1-8 a comparable vision of horses. In Revelation the message is apparently related to the forces of history which are let loose on earth. Here it may mean the same thing. The horses suggest conquering armies as we have seen in many prophets (compare Joel 2:4ff.). The angel seems to interpret the vision as symbolic of the affliction that has afflicted Israel for the past seventy years (that is, the period of captivity—1:12).

At this point the Lord confronted Zechariah with reassuring words that God now intended good for his people (1:13ff.). As he had through other prophets (Isaiah, Jeremiah, Ezekiel), so here he expressed his displeasure with those nations such as Assyria and Babylon, Edom and Moab, and others which had been merciless in their dealings with his people. God revealed, however, that he did not intend to punish his people with the severity which those pagan peoples meted out against Jerusalem.

For this reason, it was important now that God show his mercy on his people and restore them to a right relationship with him (v. 16). It was therefore important that the Temple, the symbol of God's presence and blessing on his people, be completed (v. 16). Once more God's people would have an inheritance (this is the meaning of "the line stretched over Jerusalem"—cf. Jer. 31:38-39). The words of Isaiah for God's people long ago would be carried out (1:17—cf. Isa. 40:1ff.).

The *second vision, 1:18-21,* is of *four horns and four smiths.* It teaches much the same thing we saw in the first vision. It clearly tells in a symbolic way that the forces which brought affliction to Jerusalem will be destroyed (v. 21).

The *third vision* is of *a man with a measuring line* (2:1-13). It is no doubt related to Ezekiel's vision of the new Jerusalem (2:2). God's promise to be Jerusalem's wall and Jerusalem's glory is in accord with the message of Haggai 2:7 (v. 5, cf. Isa. 4:5). It is an expansion of the theme of the first and second visions, namely, that God will bless his people in the end (2:6-10).

Added to what the other visions told, this one hearkens back to earlier messages, giving promise of blessings on other nations as well, as they come to the Lord and God's people (v. 11—cf. Mic. 4:2). As had been said by Hosea, the Lord will be known by his people (v. 11). As God had said through Moses, his people would be his inheritance forever (v. 12—cf. Deut. 32:9).

As in Isaiah, Micah and Habakkuk, so here God speaks from his holy Temple, putting all to silence before his holy presence (2:13—cf. Isa. 6:1-5; Mic. 1:2; Hab. 2:20).

The *fourth vision* is of *Joshua the high priest* (ch. 3). This Joshua or Jeshua was Zerubbabel's co-worker in leading the people back to Jerusalem to rebuild (Ezra 5:2; Hag. 1:1). The presence of Satan as his adversary suggests a similar scene in Job 1 and 2, which we shall look at later (cf. 1 Chron. 21:1). Satan's frequent appearances in heaven before Christ's completed work on the cross and subsequent resurrection have been commented on before (see our remarks on Ezek. 28:11ff.). Joshua here, the high priest, clearly represents all of God's people, the true remnant, plucked as a brand from the fire (v. 2—cf. Amos 4:11). Like all men, Joshua is clothed with filthy garments (his own unrighteousness) (v. 3—cf. Isa. 64:4).

God in his mercy, takes away Joshua's filthy garments and clothes him with clean garments (righteousness by faith) (3:4—cf. Isa. 53; Rev. 3:4-5; 4:4; 6:11; 7:9, 13; 19:14; etc.). The restoration of Joshua to the priesthood (3:6ff.) no doubt points to God's desire for the priesthood of all believers (Exod. 19:6; 1 Peter 2:5, 9; Rev. 1:6; 5:10).

Thus the righteous one of Joshua's day is a sign of the coming Christ, the Branch (3:8—cf. Isa. 11:1; Jer. 33:15). The closing scene of peace is often used in Scripture to express the ideal peace on earth to God's people, the day when all evil is past and only God's people remain (3:10—cf. 1 Kgs. 4:25; Isa. 36:16; Mic. 4:4; etc.).

This vision lifts the people beyond their present difficulties and helps that generation to see what God has planned for their latter end. This too would motivate them to rebuild, to express their faith in God's promises.

The *fifth vision* is of a *candlestick and olive trees* (ch. 4). Zechariah saw a golden candlestick with seven lamps and beside it two olive trees (vv. 1-3). This vision communicated the truth that God's work was to be accomplished not by might and power of men (i.e., the swords of men) but by the Spirit of God (v. 6). The truth therefore was similar to that revealed to Elijah as seen in 1 Kgs. 19—not by earthquake, winds, and fire, but the "still, small voice."

The lesson was immediately applied to the building of the Temple in Zerubbabel's day (v. 9). It had been started by the stirring of God's Spirit who moved Cyrus to decree the building and the remnant to return and build (cf. Ezra 1:1, 5). No amount of human force could stop God's Spirit now from seeing its completion. So God raised up the two olive trees (the two witnesses, Haggai and Zechariah) to move Zerubbabel and Joshua to finish the task they had begun (vv. 11, 14).

The same attitude as seen in Haggai's message is noted here too. There were some who would ridicule the efforts of these Jews as a small insignificant thing (v. 10). But if God ordained it, it was not insignificant and God would see it through. In Revelation 11 is a similar vision to this one.

The *sixth vision* is of *a flying roll* (ch. 5). The roll itself would be identifiable as God's Word written, the Book of God (cf. Jer. 36:2; Ezek. 2:9). God showed to Zechariah that its truths were applicable to all men and that all would be judged by it (5:3, 4). Thus as Habakkuk had been shown, so now Zechariah sees that God's standards are applied to all and that God's Law will search out and judge every sinner, no matter where he is.

As illustrative of the scrutiny of God's judgment God shows to Zechariah a vision of a gigantic ephah (measure), large enough for a woman to sit in it (vv. 6-7). Amos had rebuked the people for making the ephah small (cheating their brothers by dishonest measures) (Amos 8:5—cf. Hos. 12:7; Mic. 6:11). But God would take the secret sin and enlarge it and swallow them up in it as he did here symbolically with the woman (vv. 7, 8).

Her transportation to Shinar (a term sometimes used for Mesopotamia and beyond), that realm which was at this time controlled by Persia (5:9-11), pointed to the deportation to Babylon of the sinners in Israel.

As a second illustration of the scrutiny of God's judgment, Zechariah sees four chariots drawn by horses of various colors, similar to the horses seen in 1:8ff. (6:1-8). Here the horses are described as the four winds going forth over all the earth (vv. 5-7). By this God simply symbolizes the penetrating judgment of God which, like the wind, blows in all directions over the whole earth. This seems to be the meaning of the similar vision in the book of Revelation (Rev. 6:1-8; 7:1).

In this series of visions God has spoken to his people showing them symbolically the meaning and significance of those days. God was at work purging his people and judging the world. The call to rebuild the Temple and finish was not of men but from God, therefore it was important. It must be finished.

This concludes the first main division of Zechariah. In *the second part*, Zechariah is given *a series of messages* in a way similar to other prophets of God pointing to the past judgments of God on his people and the future hope of the remnant who look to God for salvation *(6:9-14:21)*.

First, God commanded *the crowning of Joshua the high priest* (6:9-15). Here we may compare chapter 3. God instructs Zechariah to have Joshua crowned (v. 11) presumably as a symbol of God's exalting his people through the one called the Branch or Bud who will spring up and build God's True Temple (vv. 12-13).

Several passages come to mind here. First the Christ, David's greater son, is described as a Branch in Isaiah 11:1, one who shall branch forth out of Jesse's stock. Then in Isaiah 53:2 the Christ is similarly described as a root out of dry ground. He is seen as both priest and king (v. 13). As priest he shall build God's Temple and as king he shall rule God's kingdom (cf. Isa. 9:6-7).

In the New Testament we see the words about Jesus pointing both to his mission to build God's True Temple (Church, John 2:19-21—for the Church is the Body of Christ) and to rule the nations (cf. Acts 7:35; Matt. 2:6; Rev. 2:27; 12:5; etc.).

Here in Zechariah 6:13, his mission is described as one of peace even as in Isaiah 9:6.

This passage (6:9-15) therefore serves a double purpose. On the one hand it would spur the people on to rebuild the Temple in their day as an expression of their faith in God's promises regarding the glorious Temple of God that was to be in the end (cf. God's message through Ezekiel in the latter part of that book). At the same time it pointed to the greater work of the coming Prince-Priest (the Christ) in accomplishing God's purpose to build an everlasting temple (Christ's Church).

The *second message* (7:1-7) pertains to *the true fasting of God's people.* As Isaiah had done (cf. Isa. 58:3-7) so Zechariah is here concerned with true fasting lest the religious act become just an act with no real significance. Significantly here the Lord taught that one could not fast to the Lord if he did not eat and drink also to the Lord (7:5-6—cf. 1 Cor. 10:31). All we do should be to God's glory! Thus we learn frequently in God's Word that God is concerned that all worship, including fasting, be to the glory of God. He is concerned with an attitude of heart, not just the act (see Matt. 6:16-18; John 4:23).

The *third message* pertains to *the former judgment of God* meted out *to Judah* for her sins (7:8-14). God had expected true justice in the lives of his people (7:8-10—cf. Gen. 18:19; Isa. 5:7), but they refused (v. 11). This is why God had brought strong judgment on the land (v. 14).

Yet in the *fourth message* (8:1-17) God explains *why he has caused a remnant of Israel to return* to the land *and rebuild.* In this section God expresses his determination to have an obedient people in spite of their past failures. God is returned, therefore there is hope for his people (8:3). The holy mountain (God's Church) shall yet survive and be built up (v. 3—cf. Isa. 2:2-4). The description of an era of peace (v. 5) recalls God's promise in Revelation 21 and 22 of the New Jerusalem, the hope of all God's people. It is a picture of universal peace for the remnant, God's true people—the survivors of God's judgment by faith (v. 6).

Again we see how this passage was designed to spur the people on to complete the Temple, an expression of their faith in God to do what he had promised (v. 9). The vine which once disappointed God (Isa. 5:1ff.) will yet blossom and bear fruit (v. 12). But these promises were only for the remnant, God's true children (v. 12).

We take note also that God does not change his requirements for the conduct of his people (8:16-17—cf. 7:8-11).

The *fifth message* promises to that remnant *a true restoration of joy* in worship and blessing (8:18-23). Here we ought to keep in mind that Joel had long before spoken of the need for joy in worship of God (Joel 1:16; 2:18-29). In those days, the era of God's pouring out his blessings on his Church, many would come from the Gentiles to the people of God and seek those same blessings (8:23).

The *sixth message* carries through chapters 9-11, and tells both of *the sure end of Jerusalem's enemies* and *the coming of her King.* Here Tyre is symbolically representative of all of God's enemies. She is overthrown (9:3-4). Similarly God deals with the Philistines and all of God's enemies (9:5-8).

The Lord will do this by the King who is to come (9:9-10). Here the Christ is described in terms both of his glory and humility. The passage is applied to Jesus in the New Testament (Matt. 21:5). He will sit upon an everlasting and worldwide kingdom (v. 10—cf. Daniel's message, Dan. 2:44-45).

The remainder of this chapter points to the great victory through the Christ who will come—the King of God's people. By his shed blood and the blood of the covenant, he sets free those who are imprisoned (v. 11—here see also Gen. 22, God's promises of a lamb for the burnt offering; John 1:29; Heb. 10:29;

1 Cor. 11). God will protect his people (9:15).

In chapter 10 allusions are made to Daniel's figure of the he-goats (Greece—see Dan. 8:21; 9:13) and the shepherds, all who had failed God (10:3). The shepherds referred to those leaders of Israel who sinned (cf. Jer. 50:6; Ezek. 34:10). When men fail, God's mercy enters in and he will lead his people (10:6). It will be like a second exodus for the remnant (10:8-12).

In chapter 11, God as the great Shepherd of his flock, will feed the pitiful (the ones who know their poverty and need of God) (11:4-10). The true sheep of God—the poor of the flock—would know God's voice and follow (v. 11—cf. John 10:1-6).

The alternative to hearing and obeying the true Shepherd is to be shepherded by hirelings who will not help but harm the sheep (11:15-17). They are shepherds like those described in Ezekiel 34:2-10 (cf. John 10:12-13).

The *final message,* the *seventh,* is concerned with *the suffering and death of the King* but *also with his final triumph* (chs. 12-14). Here the Lord speaks as creator (12:1). He will allow the nations to come up against his Church (12:2-3—cf. Rev. 20:7-9), but God will in the end smite them (12:4-6—cf. Rev. 20:9b) and save his people (12:7-9).

But even in the midst of this picture of final triumph the Lord once more reminds them of the cost to God for their salvation as he did in Isaiah 53 (Zech. 12:10-14). He clearly speaks here of their Savior's suffering and death in order to show his grace to them (cf. John 19:37). Thus as in chapter 9:9, so here, they are shown that together with glory there is to be suffering before the final triumph of their Savior over their enemies.

Chapter 13 continues to speak of the Redeemer's shed blood, a fountain to cleanse their sin and uncleanness (13:1). Those guilty of afflicting the Savior will be those of his own people (13:6). Specifically here the wounds in his hands are mentioned (cf. Luke 24:39, 40 and John 20:24-27).

Again prophesying of the Savior's suffering he describes him as the smitten Shepherd (13:7—cf. Matt. 26:31). In his suffering and the hard life of those who follow him the faults are purged out so that the refined ones, the remnant only, will survive and be saved—that is the people of God (vv. 8-9).

The last chapter returns to the words of 12:1-3 and the picture of the nations gathered against God's Church (14:1-2). Again God declares his intention of entering the battle on behalf of his people and winning the victory for them (14:3-8—cf. Dan. 12:1; Rev. 20:7-9). The expression "at evening there shall be light" (v. 7) points to the hope that when things seem darkest for the people of God then God will return and turn their night into day.

God will then reign as King of Kings (14:9—cf. Rev. 1:5-6). Again we note that all the nations will be judged but from them a remnant will be saved also, the true Israel, the true seed of God (14:12-16). God's city and people shall be thoroughly purged of all unbelief and all sinners in that day (14:17-21—cf. Rev. 21:8, 27). There will be no room in the tents of Shem for the Canaanites in that day (14:21—cf. Gen. 9:25-27; Isa. 54:2-3; Jer. 30:18; Zech. 12:7).

We see then from Haggai and Zechariah how important it was for God's people at that time to be active in completing the Temple. In that temple was symbolized the promises of God to be with his people and given them triumph in the end. At that time they best expressed their faith in the Lord and his promises by completing the task which the Lord had given them to do.

MALACHI

The writings of the prophet Malachi came toward the end of the Old Testament revelation, probably a generation or two after the days of Ezra and Nehemiah. He is generally dated at about 400 B.C.

It is evident from the context of Malachi's message that since the reforms of Ezra and Nehemiah at the middle of the fifth century B.C., the Jews had once more deteriorated spiritually. This is particularly reflected in their questions which God so patiently answered in the book.

From *chapter 1 through 3:15* we find *a series of questions asked* apparently by the leaders of the people who did not believe what God had been teaching them through his Word. Each question is preceded by a statement from God assessing the spiritual state of the people in that day. There follows the doubtful questioning by the people and finally God's answer. After this series of questions and answers, the message proceeds to *a clear delineation between the righteous* and their future *and the unrighteous* and their future (3:16-4:3). A final exhortation for God's people closes the book (4:4-6).

God opens his message by *declaring his love for the Jews of this post-exilic era* (1:2-5). As he had in the beginning with Israel at the time of the exodus, God shows here too that he loves them (v. 2—cf. Deut. 4:37). Yet they doubt his love and question it (v. 2).

The answer of God is to have Israel look at history. Jacob and

Esau were brothers of the same parents. Yet God did not deal with them in the same way. In choosing Jacob, God rejected Esau. The choice was clearly God's. As a result Esau did not succeed. Left to his own evil devices he rebelled against God but could never defeat God or God's people (1:3-5).

If we think back we recall that Esau was a carnal man, thoroughly materialistic (see our discussion of Genesis 25-27 and 33). He showed evidence of a pride against God. Later his descendants, the Edomites, also resisted God and were proud against all men. God through Obadiah foretold of their sure fall. (See our discussion of Obadiah.)

God here is showing that because Israel is still blessed of God and is still his people while Esau and his descendants are under God's curse, this proves God's love for them. Here God's love means that he has chosen Israel and his hate means that he had rejected Esau.

Later Paul uses this example in writing to the Romans in chapters 9-11 to show that the salvation of all men depends on God's grace and on election, not on works (Rom. 9:10-13). Neither Jacob nor Esau deserved to be blessed. If God had left Jacob to his own devices he would have ended up like Esau. That is the point. He did not end up like Esau and the only reason is that God had loved him.

Next, *God rebukes* the *priests for not honoring him but despising his name* (1:6-2:9). We recall that the priest and priesthood had been revived after the exile, and that that revival was instrumental in the reformation among God's people in the days of Ezra and Nehemiah. Now apparently the priests were once more departing from God's Law (1:6). They were heading back toward the state of affairs that had developed in the days of Eli and his two evil sons (cf. 1 Sam. 2:12-17).

Yet the priests asked "How have we despised your name?" (v. 6). God's answer was that in the first place they offered to God the leftovers, keeping the best for themselves (v. 7). They treated God with contempt by offering him what they would not dare give to the governor of the land (1:7-8). God refused to accept such gifts. He called them to repent and offer true offerings (vv. 9-10). The situation was much as it had been in Isaiah's day when God had also refused the worship of the Israelites (Isa. 1:11-15).

God was jealous for his name and his glory among the Gentiles even if the priests were not (1:11-12). What is more, they found the whole worship of God boring and wearisome (1:13). Their offerings dishonored God. He warned that he would not allow this (v. 14). God said he would send a curse on them, setting them aside from being priests (2:1-3).

At this point God expressed the ideal priesthood in terms of his original covenant with the tribe of Levi (2:4-7). When God originally set up the priesthood in the time of the exodus, he chose Levi's tribe (and in particular Aaron and his sons) to be his priests. The early priests revered God; they respected his name (v. 5). They knew God's Law and taught it, living in accord with the righteousness which God demanded (v.6). Therefore they were effective spiritual leaders, bringing many to God (v. 6).

Verse 7 beautifully expresses what God always intended the priests to be. They were to teach God's Word. They were to be the source of learning God's Law for the whole people. In short they were God's messengers, supposed to be apt to teach all spiritual truth from God. The best example of this is seen in the man Ezra (Ezra 7:6).

In contrast to what they ought to be, these priests in Malachi's day had turned from God's will. Instead of helping they had caused the people to stumble (2:8). As a result these priests had lost the respect of all the people (v. 9).

Next, the Lord rebuked the people for *their treachery shown toward one another* (2:10-16). They were supposed to be spiritual brothers of the same godly family (v. 10). But instead they had dealt treacherously in their relations with one another and had therefore profaned and disgraced the covenant which God had made with the families of Judah.

The people again asked in what way they dealt treacherously and profaned God's holiness (vv. 11-14). God's answer was to point particularly to their marriages, their covenant family relationships. They had as it were profaned God's holiness by marrying the daughters (worshippers) of foreign gods (v. 11). For this cause they could not worship God acceptably (vv. 11-12). Because they had profaned the covenant seed, having no regard for God's holiness, and married idol worshippers, they could not expect God to accept their offerings not even with tears (v. 13).

Evidently, these people so accused had divorced their wives of faith and had married pagan wives (v. 14). Yet God had never willed such a thing. He made them male and female to marry and become one flesh (Gen. 2:24). The home was to be a sound place where godly parents were to teach their children God's Word and will (Gen. 18:19). They were themselves to live as a godly example (Deut. 6:4-9). We see how in Abraham God sought a godly seed refusing Ishmael and choosing Isaac. We see also how Abraham, understanding God's will to have a godly holy people, refused the daughters of Canaan for his son's wife and sent his servant to find Isaac's wife among those of his own family (Gen. 24).

The Lord, as Jesus himself showed, never willed that his

people should destroy their marriages by divorcing wives who were believers. God viewed such a putting away of one's wife as an act of violence, like ripping apart a garment sewed together to stay together (v. 16—cf. Matt. 19:3-9).

Following this, the *Lord declares* that *the words of the people now wearied him* (2:17-3:6). Yet again they ask, "Why is this so?" (2:17). The words of which God spoke were their moral judgments which disregarded God's truth and declared evil to be good and profaned God's name by teaching that God would approve their evil deeds. In other words they had actually doubted the existence of a God of justice (2:17).

At this point the Lord expressed his purpose to send a messenger before he came in judgment against the people (3:1-6). The coming of this messenger would precede that of the Lord himself. But his coming would not be pleasant, it would be frightful; for he came to convict the people of their sins lest when the Lord did come they would all be consumed (3:6). The coming of the messenger then was to cleanse the people by calling them to repentance (vv. 2-3). All who did not repent would be swept aside in judgment (v. 5).

This prophecy points to John the Baptist (Matt. 11:7-19). Like the message of Joel the prophet, he warns of the coming awful day of the Lord (cf. Joel 1:15ff.). The very purpose of John's coming was to prepare the people to receive their Lord. Had he not come and by the baptism of repentance in that day prepared the people, then when Jesus came, all would have been judged and swept aside. John's was a unique and greatly needed mission, without it all would have been consumed (v. 6—cf. Matt. 3:1-12; Luke 3:1-20). Only the fact that God is gracious and merciful could save the people (v. 6—cf. Isa. 1:9).

The Lord *then rebuked the people for turning aside from the Lord* and *not keeping his ordinances* (3:7-12). They doubted this accusation too, saying "How shall we return?" (v. 7). God showed them one specific way. They could return to God by once again giving God his tithe. They had been robbing God by denying him what was rightfully his (v. 8). God promised a gracious blessing on them if they would show their love of him by giving to him the tithe (vv. 10-12). Their love of money had brought a curse on them and prevented their coming to the Lord (v. 9—cf. Luke 18:18-25).

Yet instead of responding to God as he had asked, *the people had been stout against God* (3:13-15). Once more the people asked incredulously, "How is this so?" (v. 13). God showed them that in their words they murmured against God as the Israelites had done in the wilderness (v. 14). They envied the proud and wicked, supposing that such people flourish and get away with their sin (v. 15). God had called those who were obedient to him happy (3:12) but these people had declared that sinners and doers of evil were happy (3:15), thus setting aside God's judgment.

With *verse 15,* the series of questions and God's answers come to an end. Malachi then moves on to stress the clear-cut distinction between *the righteous and the unrighteous, the blessed and the cursed* (3:16-4:3).

The righteous are here as elsewhere described as those who fear the Lord (v. 16). They are the true believers (cf. Prov. 1:7; 9:10; 19:23; Psa. 34:9; 112:1; etc.). Their names are recorded in God's book of remembrance (v. 16—cf. Isa. 4:3; Dan. 12:1; Rev. 17:8; 21:27).

God claims these for himself, his own people (v. 17). In God's saving this remnant, he will make a clean distinction between the righteous and the wicked (v. 18). As he had declared through the Psalmist (Psa. 1:4-6) so here again he makes clear that all the wicked who have refused to believe in him will be destroyed (4:1). On the other hand, those who have feared the Lord and are assured of God's blessing, have the Sun of righteousness shining on them, to heal their sins (v. 2). This no doubt points to the work of Christ to save those who believe.

This section closes with the promise of victory over the enemies namely the wicked seed of the serpent, Satan (4:3—cf. Gen. 3:15; Rom. 16:20).

The message of Malachi closes by calling God's people to continue to obey God's Law through Moses, expecting and eagerly awaiting the coming of the Lord who will be preceded by Elijah (John the Baptist) (4:5—cf. Matt. 11:14). Only his coming will save the people from being smitten when the Lord comes (v. 6).

With this the Old Testament prophecies end. They end by pointing back to the foundation of the Old Testament faith, the Law of Moses, and also by pointing ahead to the coming of the Lord to save his people.

Some four hundred years would pass in silence, with no word from God until suddenly in the days of Tiberius Caesar of Rome and Pontius Pilate of Judea, John, the son of Zachariah, heralded the imminent coming of the Lord Jesus Christ.

14

THE BOOKS OF DEVOTION AND PRACTICAL LIVING FOR THE PEOPLE OF GOD

THREE BOOKS of the Old Testament remain to be studied. They are Job, Psalms, and Proverbs. In these three the faith and life of the people of God are to be found. They deal with the great issues of Christian faith and living. They are also timeless in terms of their dealing with issues which people of every generation must face. We shall begin with Job.

JOB

We know very little of Job outside of this book. He is mentioned in Ezekiel as being on a par spiritually with Noah and Daniel (Ezek. 14:14, 20). All three were known for their righteousness.

In the New Testament book of James, Job is held up as an example of patience (Jas. 5:11).

Job presumably lived about the time of the patriarchs Abraham, Isaac, and Jacob; yet Job is not identified as a Hebrew but as one of the children of the East (Job 1:3), a term applied broadly to those living east of Canaan.

When the book itself was written, we are not told. Job may have been written during a period in Israelite history when wisdom literature was being written, because the book speaks much about wisdom. We could place it sometime after Solomon's time, probably around the time of Hezekiah. However, as we noted, the book is timeless in regard to its great themes.

The book of Job is divided into the following major parts: *a prologue* narrative telling of Job and his suffering, chapters 1 and 2; an *expression by Job of his great problem,* chapter 3; a *long dialogue* between *Job and his three friends,* chapters 4-31; a *long monologue by Elihu,* a fourth rebuker of Job, chapters 32-37; *God's answer to Job's problem,* chapters 38-41; *Job's response* to God's answer, 42:1-6; and *finally,* a *brief narrative* telling of *God's blessings on Job* in *his latter days,* 42:7-16.

The prologue narrative (chapters 1 and 2) tells *first of the man Job.* He was from Uz, of which we know very little except that it was a place recognized in Jeremiah's day and was linked with the nations of the Philistines, Edom, Moab, and Ammon (Jer. 25:20). It was particularly linked with Edom, which was to the southeast of Israel, south of the Dead Sea area.

Job was well-pleasing to the Lord, described as perfect and upright, a God fearer who turned from evil (1:1). He was therefore like Noah in his generation (Gen. 6:9), and like Abraham he sought to live before God (Gen. 17:1).

He was also prosperous, having ten children and an abundance of property (1:2, 3). Above all he was devout, not only a faithful worshiper of God, but very careful and anxious about the spiritual state of his children (1:4-5).

After those five introductory verses we move suddenly from the man Job to *a scene in the presence of God* (1:6-12). We are not told who the sons of God were who were mentioned in 1:6. Most have concluded that they were some kind of angelic beings. However, the term "sons of God" in Scripture generally refers to believers among mankind (Gen. 6:2-4; John 1:12; etc.). These may have been those who had already died in faith and who were in some sense in the presence of God.

It is surprising to see Satan also in such an assembly. Scripture seems to imply some sense in which Satan was allowed in God's presence prior to Jesus' work of redemption. After that, he was said to be cast out of heaven and confined to earth (see Luke 10:18—cf. Rev. 12:7-9; John 12:31; Isa. 14:12-20; Ezek. 28:2-9).

Satan's activity included going about the earth, seeking to accuse God's servants on earth (Job 1:7—cf. Rev. 12:10; Zech. 3:1; Luke 22:31).

The Lord approves of Job, describing him in terms elsewhere applicable to the patriarchs Noah and Abraham. Satan's challenge to God's judgment concerning Job says in essence that one serves God only for what he can get out of it for himself in this life (v. 10). Satan challenges God to take away his blessings from Job, predicting Job's defection from God in such a case.

In response, and for his own glory, the Lord permitted Satan to take all from Job. Nevertheless, in his sovereignty, God would not permit Satan to touch Job's body (v. 12).

The trials against Job from Satan at God's consent came in the form of natural catastrophies and human atrocities: raiders (vv. 15, 17); perhaps lightning (v. 16); and strong winds (v. 19). Satan's control of these natural forces can only be understood as by God's permission since ordinarily in Scripture they are under God's control. The raiders were simply acting under the order of their father, the devil.

Job's acceptance of these tragedies, though grief-stricken, gives the lie to Satan's accusation (vv. 20-22). Clearly Job showed himself to be a faithful child of God.

In chapter 2 we find a similar account, this time with Job suffering physically (2:1-8). Even his wife added to his woes by encouraging him to denounce God and die (v. 9). Once more Job's faith and integrity shine through clearly (v. 10). He accepts whatever befalls him with steadfast love and faith toward God.

From all of this we can safely conclude that the problem of this book is not "Why do the righteous suffer?" since that question has already been answered. The righteous suffer in this world for the glory of God and to show their true faith in God. Nor was this the problem that troubled Job. It is clear that he did not ask God why God allowed these things to happen. He freely recognized God's right to deal with him as it pleased God. He did not suspect or accuse God of any wrongdoing in all that happened to him. For the answer to the question of the main problem or concern of this book, we must go farther.

However, we must recognize that we have gained great insight already into God's dealing with his children. At times he may require them to suffer for his glory. In such times he may not make clear to them why these things have happened. But he expects them to accept whatever happens without accusing him or complaining.

We learn also much about the nature of Satan. He is indeed as a roaring lion going about seeking whom he may devour. He is an enemy of God, for he seeks to take away from God's glory. And he is the enemy of all believers, for he seeks to destroy and discredit them.

Chapter 2:11ff., introduces us to the setting for the long debate that was to follow. Three friends of Job from places distant from his house received news of his tragedies. They came to comfort him (v. 11). However, they were undoubtedly unprepared for what they found. They were amazed at the misery of Job (v. 12). They were in fact speechless (v. 13). We see Ezekiel in a similar circumstance (Ezek. 3:15).

Chapter 3 contains *Job's complaint,* and here we are approaching the real problem of the book.

Few men have suffered and had their faith tested as had Job. The way in which he began his speech may seem shocking to us, but we must remember that he was not complaining about the suffering. This has already been demonstrated. His complaint was about something else.

The strong words of Job 3:3-19 are matched perhaps only once elsewhere in Scripture—by Jeremiah (Jeremiah 20:14-18). There is much in common between Job and Jeremiah. Both suffered greatly for their faith without complaining. But both were very lonely, having no human comforters. Both were denounced by their friends (cf. Jeremiah 20:7-10). Both sought to see God's hand in things as an assurance that all was well (cf. Jer. 20:12).

Thus Job's desire to die in order to escape his trials is not unique, but it came only as his own faith in God was tested to the limit. Neither Job nor Jeremiah denied the Lord, but both asked to be released from their trials by death.

What then was Job's real problem? We see it first expressed in 3:20-26. He considered his way to be hidden from God. He felt hedged in, shut off from God (v. 23). He could endure suffering physically, but the spiritual pain of having no fellowship with God, of not being able to sense God's presence, was too much. It was a problem with which he could not cope. All his life he had fear of such a broken communion, of not being able to find God (3:25—cf. 1:5). He had no rest, no spiritual peace, but only a troubled heart because he could not find the Lord in this time of loneliness, when all had forsaken him or were at a loss to know how to comfort him.

In essence Job was saying in this third chapter, "If I cannot have fellowship with God it is better for me to die. If indeed men are cut off from fellowship with God, it *is* better to be dead."

At this point we begin *the three cycles of debate between Job and his friends: Eliphaz, Bildad, and Zophar (chapters 4-31—cf. 2:11).* The *first cycle* covers *chapters 4-14* and includes *statements from all three friends* and *by Job in response to them.*

Eliphaz speaks first (chs. 4 and 5). He also sets the pattern for all of the speeches of the friends. Though he begins with a seemingly complimentary description of Job (4:3, 4), yet he quickly rebukes Job and begins to develop the basic charge against him which is simply repeated and amplified by each friend in succession (vv. 5-9). In essence what they all say is that only the wicked suffer, therefore if Job suffers it is because he has sinned against God and he had better get right with God (vv. 7-9).

We can see how these friends all say essentially the same thing (cf. 5:6-8; 8:4-6, 13, 14, 20; 11:2-6; 11:12, 20). The more Job protested his innocence before God, the more denouncing and derogatory the friends became in their statements. We note that they made many true statements regarding God and the nature of man (5:9-13, 17, etc.), yet they sought to make themselves as God and sought to judge and condemn Job, thus misapplying the theology they had. Here is a clear-cut example of how one with a perfectly sound and orthodox theology can nevertheless be very wrong because he cannot apply it to life. He is not truly humbled by it. He is like Eliphaz, Bildad, and Zophar, proud and vain in thinking and in theology but of no use whatever in helping others, and very wrong in judgments concerning others.

Job also responds to the friends in much the same way each time. Three things are noticeable in this answers: (1) He persistently denies his guilt before the Lord, he knows of no sin which he has not confessed and been forgiven of. He believes strongly in justification by faith in the Lord. He will not accept the argument of the friends that all is not right between him and God. (2) He returns time and again to his original complaint. He wants fellowship with God but does not feel it. (3) He shows signs of increasing bitterness as the three "friends" badger him mercilessly, but he never is overcome with bitterness.

Looking at each of these, *first we note how consistently Job protested his innocence.* He affirmed vehemently that he had not denied the Holy One (6:10). He challenged his friends to show unrighteousness in him (6:28-30). He did not claim sinlessness but did affirm that all of his sins had been dealt with by God. He knew that God had pardoned his sins and did not hold them against him (7:20, 21).

Job affirmed strongly his righteous state before the Lord, meaning of course, righteousness by his faith in the Lord (13:18). He also seemed fully confident that this precious doctrine of righteousness which he held to would be vindicted in the end (17:9).

Job was confident too that his own righteous stand before God in faith would stand the test of God and be proven (23:10). In the end Job knew that the doctrine he held to of justification by faith was right and that he could not concede to his friends that his faith in God was of no value (27:4-6). Job understood that far more was at stake here than winning an argument. At stake was the whole basis of man's relationship to God through justification by faith.

To the end, Job never wavered in this conviction. He would not accept the charges of his friends that he lived a life contrary to God's will. He showed both righteousness and justice in his dealings with all men (29:12-14). We have no reason to doubt him, for God had already affirmed the integrity of Job (1:1, 8; 2:3). His very last words were again a denial of the charges brought against him by the three men who accused him wrongly (ch. 31).

There is never really any doubt, or at least there should not be any doubt, that Job was right and his friends wrong. Job was not claiming sinlessness but a right relationship with God as every true child of God who can claim that he stands justified by faith in God.

The friends, on the other hand, increase in error as they persist in their charge that Job has displeased God and is suffering because of that. We know of course from the first two chapters that their whole thesis is wrong. Yet they persist.

Gradually their accusations became increasingly cruel and erroneous. Bildad threw the death of Job's children into his face, condemning Job of being nothing but wind (8:2-6). Indeed he impugned the very faith of Job (8:13, 14). Zophar was judgmental and harsh in his words (11:1-6). But it is Eliphaz who changed most in the course of the debate from a rather reserved beginning to a final denunciation of Job which became, in fact, a list of false charges which could not at all be sustained (15:1-6; 22:5-10). The latter charges of 22:5ff. are outright lies with no basis of fact. Evidently as Eliphaz talked he became increasingly frustrated and resorted to whatever words he could find to degrade Job whether they were true or not.

The friends never did really understand *what bothered Job,* though *he persistently expressed his feeling of being cut off from God, not able to find God.* After stating it in 3:23 he often expressed the same thing in other words and ways. He felt that since he could not know God's nearness, he was without help and without wisdom (6:13). He knew God must be near but he could not find him (9:11). Over and over he pled for some word from God (10:2, 3). He was assured that the answer to his problem lay with God and God's Word, but he could not reach God (10:12, 13).

Once he had known close fellowship with God and in those days when he called, God always had answered, but now it was different and Job was bewildered (12:4). To him the horror was that God seemed to hide his face from Job with whom in the past Job had had sweet fellowship (13:21-24). He longed for the days of the past when he heard God and responded in sweet communion (14:15). He knew that if God would answer him God would fully vindicate him before his accusers (16:19, 20, 21).

Job consistently felt frustrated that his cries to God for an answer, a response, seemingly were not heeded by God at all (19:6-8). It seemed as though God had built a wall between him and the Lord. No one understood. Not even his friends came to comfort Job (19:13-22). Nevertheless, Job continued to affirm that in the end God would fully vindicate him. Because he was right with God, he would in the end triumph though his present circumstances seemed to be to the contrary (19:25-27).

Job's great problem was that he did not feel God was near. He did not sense any fellowship with God. He could not find his Lord (23:3-5, 8-9). He longed for those days past when he walked with God and felt God's presence and knew God as a friend who was always near him (29:2-5).

In essence, Job's problem was like that of most believers at some time in their Christian experience. At times we feel God's presence very near us and our communion with God is sweet and precious to us. But sometimes, without warning, God seems far away. Our prayers seem to fall back upon us and not reach him. When we read his Word it is like brass and seems cold. It does not stir us or warm us. It is a common experience for Christians, when we do not feel God near and we do not know why. This was Job's problem.

As his friends continued to badger Job, we see increasingly a note of bitterness developing in him *toward his friends and even toward God.* Job sensed that very bitterness himself (9:18-24, 28-29). He at times wondered whether it was worth anything to be faithful when the wicked seemed to prosper (12:6). In this feeling he had an experience in common with the psalmist (see Psalm 73). No doubt every believer at times wonders whether the suffering for righteousness' sake is worth it in the light of the prosperity of the wicked. Yet such feelings come when our vision is on earth rather than in heaven, when it is temporal rather than eternal. The psalmist came through it (Psalm 73:17ff.) and so did Job.

Though Job said many things out of a bitter heart as his friends continued to hurt him with their cruel words and as he continued to be frustrated at having no answer from God (13:21ff.; 14:1ff.; 16:9ff.; 21:4-15), yet in the end he would not accept the way of the wicked and turned from any thought of being like them (21:16).

While we cannot excuse Job's bitterness, we can certainly understand it. In the end he continued to believe that his cause was just and he desired simply a confirming word from God.

After the long period of debate between Job and his three friends nothing was settled between them. Suddenly, unintroduced, though apparently listening in to their conservation, *Elihu,* a fourth accuser of Job *began to speak* (chs. 32-37). He had already decided that Job and his friends were wrong and gave promise of saying something significantly new (32:1-10).

Elihu was a brash young man who felt he knew all the answers. He ridiculed the friends (32:15) and at the same time sneered at Job's claim of innocence (33:8-12). Apparently he believed all that Eliphaz had said against Job without investigating it (34:7-8). He even wished for more pain to befall Job to teach him a lesson, thus proving to be even more harsh and cruel than the friends (34:35-37).

Indeed, Elihu revealed the height of arrogance when he supposed himself to be speaking for God (36:2). But in the end he said nothing different from what the three friends had already said (36:11-13). As for Job's desire for a word from God, Elihu seemingly said that God is above all and has no need to answer anyone (36:26ff.). He clearly did not know God himself and had not experienced fellowship with God as Job had.

When Elihu had finished his long and meritless speech, God quickly dismissed all that he had said by describing his counsel as dark and without knowledge (38:2).

Then God began his answer to Job (chs. 38-41). In essence in God's answer we see the Lord take Job on a verbal tour of the universe. He shows Job the creation of God and his providence. By asking Job whether he can provide the daily needs of all of these creatures, the Lord is in essence saying that surely God does. All creatures great and small are God's concern. Without Job's help the Lord has been and continues to meet their every need. This Job can see if he will open his eyes.

God's answer left Job speechless (40:3-5). When God was

through, Job affirmed that all was of God and could now affirm that he saw with his eyes clearly what before he had only heard with his ears, i.e., his doctrine of God was now much clearer (42:1-5). In the face of such overwhelming evidence of God's watchcare over all of his creatures, Job was overcome with a feeling of his own smallness ever to have questioned God's concern for him (42:6).

What in fact was God's answer? It was certainly not, as Elihu had contended, that God is above all and has no need to answer men. Elihu had said this (36:24-32) and God had called those words, "words without knowledge" (38:2). What God said to Job in his long answer was essentially what Jesus pointed out to his disciples—the God who provides so abundantly for all of his little creatures, will he not also take care of you? (see Matt. 6:25-34).

Job had gone on his feelings instead of depending on the truth of God's natural revelation. If he had opened his eyes and seen that God was still providing for all of the creatures around Job and was still guiding his whole creation, then Job would not have been anxious. He would have been assured, as Jesus pointed out to his own disciples, that God will even the more provide for his children all that they need! Job was anxious because he went by his feelings rather than by God's clear revelation.

Communion between God and Job was never really broken. All creation and providence declared that fact. The answer then was all around Job all that time but he turned inward toward his own feelings and therefore missed the answer.

This book therefore has an important message for all of God's children. We must go not on what we feel but on what God's truth reveals. If we do not feel God is near, or if we do not feel that he hears us, then we must know that such feelings are not reliable. God's truth revealed in his Word speaks even more clearly to us today than the natural revelation did to Job. We have an even better reason not to be anxious but to be assured that God is near, he does care and he will provide our every need.

We are told that Job was right in contending for the faith and justification by faith against the erroneous counsel of the friends. What he spoke, God said, was right, while the words of the friends displeased God (42:7).

In order to show to all what he had said to Job, God poured out rich blessings on Job in the end (42:10-16). But we know that Job was satisfied before the latter blessings. They therefore were not for his sake but for the sake of the friends and for us that we should all see that indeed God was pleased with Job and still favored him.

PSALMS

The book of Psalms is a collection of 150 hymns of worship of God's people. They express the gamut of the religious experience of God's people as they worship God individually and corporately.

Attempts have been made to arrange and rearrange the psalms according to some meaningful scheme, but no such attempts have succeeded. They are divided into five books which some have compared to the five books of Moses. But this too is not easily demonstrated.

Trying to establish the setting and period of each psalm also is hazardous. Some have titles which indicate a setting, but even those are not certain, having been apparently added at a later time and not part of the original words.

It is best therefore in studying the psalms to assume that they are the timeless expression of the worship of God's people in a way acceptable to God. If they record the people's feelings and faith toward God, they are nevertheless the expression which God has desired and approved, therefore they are a real part of God's Word and part of the infallible Word of God, containing great revelations concerning God and man and the way of salvation.

The proper introduction for the book of Psalms is Psalm 1. In it we get what may be called the proper context for the entire Psalter and for every psalm. We shall therefore give special attention to Psalm 1 and then see how it is the context for all the rest of the psalms.

Psalm 1 begins by speaking of *the blessed life.* The very term *blessed* requires some thought. It is an expression more like an exclamation: "Oh the blessedness of . . ." It pertains to the life which pleases God, i.e., the life of God's children.

Without making an exhaustive study of the word we can nevertheless note that it describes the blessed life as consisting of these three basics: knowing yourself as God knows you; living as God desires you to live; and taking refuge in the Lord as Savior and Protector from your enemies.

The term "blessed" first occurs in Deuteronomy 33:29, in reference to Israel as God's special people, saved by the Lord and triumphant through him.

In respect to *knowing ourselves as God knows us,* the Word teaches that the blessed life involves being reproved by the Lord, i.e., shown by him in his Word that we are sinners and need his help (Job 5:17). The blessed life insists that we not hide our sin or ignore it but rather that no deceit be found in us (Psalm 32:1-2). This is the only basis of the true forgiveness which is the only basis for happiness or the blessed life (cf. 1 John 1:8, 9, 10). We must be honest with God. God's Word chastens and teaches us and therefore we are blessed. He deals with us as with his own children (Psa. 94:12—cf. 2 Tim. 3:16-17).

Regarding *living our lives as God desires us to live,* we are taught that God expects us to be not only hearers of the Word but doers also (Jas. 1:22; Matt. 7:24ff.). Psalm 1 declares that the blessed life of the righteous is seen in his not walking in the way of sinners but rather finding his delight in God's Word (Psa. 1:1-2—cf. Psa. 112:1). Moreover, the blessed life calls for our performing God's will in accord with the standards he has always held before his children: righteousness and justice (Psa. 106:3—cf. Gen. 18:19; Isa. 56:1-2; etc.). Or to put it another way, we are to walk in God's Law (Psa. 119:1; Prov. 29:18) to find the blessed life. This means of course that we love God and our neighbor, giving thought and concern to the poor and the weak (Psa. 41:1; Prov. 14:21; Jas. 1:27).

Finally, *the blessed life* includes our *taking refuge in the Lord,* both from our enemies when we seek to live as pleases God, and from our sins when we acknowledge them and plead to God for forgiveness (Psa. 2:12; 34:8; 40:4; 65:4). This concept of taking refuge in the Lord is expressed both as trust in the Lord (Psa. 84:12) and as waiting for him (Isa. 30:18).

This is the blessed life. As we compare these Old Testament passages concerning the blessed life with the words of Jesus on the same subject (the Beatitudes of Matt. 5:3-12), we see a great similarity. *The first three beatitudes:* "blessed are the poor in spirit; blessed are they that mourn; blessed are the meek" all point to our realizing our sinfulness and need of God, i.e., knowing ourselves as God knows us.

The second three beatitudes: "blessed are they who hunger and thirst for righteousness; blessed are the merciful; blessed are the pure in heart" express *the kind of life God expects us to live.*

Finally, *the last three beatitudes:* "blessed are the peacemakers; blessed are those persecuted for righteousness' sake; blessed are those persecuted for Christ's sake" *all speak of our taking refuge in God,* being at peace with him and finding in him *hope* in the face of enemy persecution (cf. Rom. 8:18).

Returning now to *Psalm 1* we find the blessed life described here in terms of *the righteous man and his righteousness* (1:1-3). In contrast, the wicked man has no place among God's people (1:4-5). The closing verse, 1:6, shows the *contrasting ways* and ends *of the righteous and the wicked.*

Returning now to *the first part of the psalm, the blessed life of the righteous* is first expressed *negatively,* that is, in terms of what he will not do. From this we see that as one is right with God he will be found in opposition to the counsel, ways, and position of the world of sinners (1:1).

The *counsel of the ungodly* is to know ourselves without reference to God. We live and plan our lives without any concern for God. This was Satan's counsel to Adam and Eve (Gen. 3). It was also the counsel of the people at Babel when they proposed to build a city without any mention of God at all (Gen. 11:3-4). Man, because of pride, sees no need of God because he does not see himself as God sees him, a sinner, dead in trespasses and sins. Therefore, he plans his life and lives it without acknowledging God at all.

The *way of sinners* therefore is to do what pleases them, not what pleases God. They set their sights on the glory, fame, riches, and rewards of this world as did Esau. They are profane and cannot see or accept the spiritual goals of God for his children.

The *seat of scoffers,* the inevitable end of the sinner's life, is without any hope. Rejecting God, in the end he cannot find any meaning to life. Since all men were created to have fellowship with God, rejecting that great end, man ends in bitterness and despair.

But there is also a positive side to the righteous life. He delights in God's Law (will). He therefore meditates on that Law all the time. His attitude toward God's law is quite opposite from that of Satan's children (see Jeremiah 6:10). One's very spiritual state is indicated by his attitude toward God's Word.

By the word "meditate" we mean more than some dreamy-eyed reflection on the Bible. To meditate is to apply God's Word, his truth, to every facet of one's life. It is to be a doer and not only a hearer of God's Word (cf. Deut. 6:4-9; Josh. 1:8).

Such righteous ones who are permeated spiritually by meditation on God's will have their lives changed, made alive and fruitful (v. 3). They are likened to a tree that is transplanted beside the source of life. Their roots go deep into God's life-giving and life-sustaining Word (cf. Jer. 17:8). They, unlike sinful Israel, are faithful, showing spiritual fruit of righteousness and justice in their lives (cf. Isa. 5:1-7; Gal. 5:22-23). Their leaves *do* not wither (die) because they live eternally. In all things they will prosper—if not in the eyes of men, surely in the eyes of God (Josh. 1:8; Rom. 8:28). A godly life cannot fail!

In stark contrast, the wicked or unrighteous has no stability whatsoever. The figure of chaff as dry and dead is an appropriate figure of the unrighteous (v. 4—cf. Matt. 3:12). For this reason the wicked will fall in the day of judgment no matter their seeming prosperity in the world. They have no place in the congregation of the righteous, no matter that they were in this world members of the visible church, perhaps even preachers in it (v. 5). God will purge his Church of all unrighteousness. No sinner will have part in the true Church (Rev. 21:27; 22:14-15).

In conclusion, God shows once more as he has so often done before from Genesis 3:15 on that there are but two families of men—the righteous, whom God has known (chosen to be his); and the wicked or unrighteous, whose way shall perish (1:6—cf. John 3:16).

In this psalm are introduced all of the major themes of the entire Psalter, which are: the righteous and his righteousness; the unrighteous and his wickedness; *and* the inevitable end of each. *Also implied here is the theme of* the enmity that exists between the righteous and the unrighteous.

The Psalter therefore expands on the righteous life, the praise of and meditation on God's Word, the faithful life spiritually of God's children, the fact that the righteous never withers (does not perish) and that in the end all he does will prosper. The Psalter also details the wickedness of the wicked, his unstable life, and his ultimate judgment and overthrow by God. In addition the Psalter frequently speaks of the enmity of the unbeliever toward God and God's children, an enmity expressed in hostility and cruelty toward God's children. It also teaches the importance of the believer's knowing and dealing with his enemy, the unrighteous one, as an enemy, without compromise and without hypocrisy.

We shall find one or more of these themes in each psalm. Our point of reference in studying any psalm should always be the perspective of Psalm 1.

We shall now look briefly at some of the psalms, noting particularly what themes are interwoven in each.

Psalm 2 shows how the unrighteous in contrast to the righteous mediate or apply vanity to their lives (v. 1). They express their enmity against God and his children. Yet God by his Anointed (the Christ, his Son) has given victory to all who take refuge in him (v. 12).

Psalm 3 shows the righteous under attack by the ungodly (vv. 1-2). Nevertheless he finds God his refuge and is assured of

God's deliverance out of the hand of his enemy. God and not man decides the believer's salvation (v. 8).

Psalm 4 stresses the peace of God's child who puts his trust in the Lord (vv. 3, 4, 8) in the midst of the vain living of the ungodly.

Psalm 5 expresses God's displeasure both with the sinner and with his deeds (vv. 4-6), and his blessing on those who come to him in trust (vv. 7-8).

It contains an assessment of the wicked (v. 9) and the believer's prayer for God's justice upon the wicked (v. 10). This latter prayer is in perfect conformity to God's own view of the wicked (vv. 4-6). Finally, assurance for those who take refuge in God closes the psalm.

Space will not permit us to analyze each psalm, but as we see in these first five, the themes all emanate from Psalm 1 and simply expand upon it.

We shall now look at a few selected psalms from the rest of the Psalter.

Psalm 19 beautifully expresses the wonders and effect of that Word of God upon which the righteous are to meditate. The first six verses speak of God's natural revelation about which God taught Job. It is evident that great truth about God is taught by all which God has made and by all which God does in providence day by day (cf. Gen. 1; Rom. 1:20). Yet there is an even greater revelation of God in his Word. It is this about which the psalmist particularly speaks here (vv. 7-11).

He speaks of *the names of God's Word;* the law of the Lord, the testimony of the Lord, the precepts of the Lord and the commandment of the Lord (vv. 7-8). Each of these terms has its special meaning. "Law" refers to the entire body of God's Word, all that is taught. "Testimony" refers particularly to the Ten Commandments as the summation of God's law. "Precepts" refers primarily to the application of God's law to life, the law in its application. "Commandment" refers to the specific Word of God for any given situation as Christ used it in dealing with Satan's temptations (see Matt. 4:4, 7, 10).

He speaks also of *the character of God's Word* (vv. 7, 8). It is perfect, it is sure, it is right, it is pure. By "perfect" he means complete, lacking nothing (cf. Deut. 4:2; 12:32; Rev. 22:18-19; Prov. 30:5-6). By "sure" he means that it is dependable, steadfast. The word here used is the same as the word from which the Old Testament concept of "faith" or "to believe" comes. See our discussion of "faith" in Genesis 15:6. By "right" he means, by the true standard of what is right, God's judgment. And finally, by "pure" he means without a flaw, in contrast to the higher critics and doubters of our own day who claim that the Bible is full of errors.

Finally, he speaks of *the effect of God's Word* (vv. 7, 8). It restores the soul, makes the simple wise, rejoices the heart and enlightens the eyes. It restores the soul by giving life to those who were dead in sin, converting them by God's Spirit unto God. It makes the simple wise (by faith in Christ) as they are led and nurtured on God's Word and grow spiritually into spiritual wisdom from God (compare 2 Tim. 3:16-17; 1 Peter 2:2). It rejoices the heart, making God's child rejoice at its truth as one might rejoice when a good meal is set before him or when he takes his bride unto himself or when one wins a victory over strong competition. The word "rejoice" is used in all of these contexts elsewhere in Scripture. It enlightens the eyes as spectacles to a nearsighted man, enabling us to see life honestly and at the same time from God's perspective.

The psalmist next speaks of the incomparable value of God's Word (v. 10) and its practical use to the believer in his present and future life (v. 11). By God's Word we are taught truth about ourselves which we cannot otherwise know (v. 12). This enables us to live more pleasingly to God. God's Word is the only infallible guide both for the words of our mouths and for the serious application of that Word in our lives (meditation). Only by following God's Word can we hope to be found acceptable to him. Psalm 119 is similar in nature and content.

Psalm 22 also deals with the suffering of the righteous at the hands of the unrighteous. It reckons with the same problems that faced Job, the sense of God's forsaking the psalmist, the failure to hear God's answer (22:1-2).

Unlike Job, the psalmist can and does appeal to God's written revelation regarding those who trust in God. He draws strength from the assurance that God is near and will hear him though he is despised by men (vv. 3-11). While he suffers much, as Job did, nevertheless he senses God's nearness and in the end is comforted so that he in turn can comfort others (vv. 12-24). The close of the psalm looks to the proclamation of God's goodness to the ends of the earth (vv. 27-31).

This psalm was particularly precious to our Lord in the hours of his agony on the cross (Matt. 27:46). We can see in it both Jesus' sense of God's leaving him in the hour he took on himself our sins, and at the same time Jesus' assurance as he put himself in the hands of his Father, assured by this very psalm that God would not be far off (vv. 19, 24).

We have looked already at *Psalm 51*, David's great psalm of confession of his sin regarding Uriah the Hittite (see our comments on 2 Samuel 12:13ff.).

Psalm 69 is one of the imprecatory psalms which have troubled many and by some have been called "unchristian." But far from it, the imprecatory psalms express the thoughts of every true Christian who understands the real issues involved in that enmity between the righteous and the unrighteous.

The psalmist here is quite amazed by his enemies and their hostility against him (69:1-4). Yet on the basis of his assurance that the righteous shall prosper as God has promised in Psalm 1, he looks to God in hope (vv. 5-6). He feels keenly that his suffering is for righteousness' sake (vv. 7-12). In time of such distress he knows that God is his only refuge (vv. 13-18).

This whole psalm must be seen in the context of Psalm 1. He knows that God knows him and that God knows how he suffers at the hand of his enemies (vv. 19-21). His prayer, therefore, for their overthrow is fully in accord with God's announced intent to destroy the wicked (vv. 22-28—cf. Psalm 1:4, 5, 6).

It is noteworthy that the description of these unrighteous ones is in the New Testament applied to the crucifiers of Jesus (v. 21—cf. John 19:29); to those rejecting Jesus (vv. 22-23—cf. Rom. 11:9-10); to Judas Iscariot (v. 25—cf. Acts 1:20); and to the unclean and abominable (vv. 27-28—cf. Rev. 21:27).

Here the psalmist is treating the enemy as the enemy. Following God's lead, he recognized the inevitable end of the ungodly. To pray otherwise would have been contrary to God's will! The psalmist is not rejoicing at the overthrow of the ungodly but he is recognizing that it is God's will (cf. Job 31:29).

This is clearly not a personal enmity which the psalmist expresses, but that clear-cut enmity which God has established between his seed and the seed of Satan (Gen. 3:15). It is deceitful to give comfort to God's enemies who in the end will perish. The psalmist knows hope only for those who love God's name (v. 36).

Psalms of a similar nature (and equally misunderstood by many) are *Psalms 137 and 138*. In 137, verses 8 and 9 do not express the attitude of the psalmist as happy because of the judgment to fall on the Babylonians but rather he declares that those who crush their babies under foot (i.e., the Persians) will be happy in their doing of it. Psalm 139, in the latter part, again declares that the psalmist hates his enemies. But this is not a personal hatred, it is based on the fact that God's enemies have become his enemies (vv. 21-22). Since they are God's enemies, once the psalmist put his trust in God, they became his own enemies. To make peace with those who are opposed to God would be sin and rebellion against God, the act of a Judas!

Returning now to *Psalm 73*, this psalm deals with the seeming prosperity of the enemies of God, the wicked. The psalmist is greatly troubled by this and tempted to turn from God in search of earthly prosperity but his knowledge of God's truth taught in Psalm 1 regarding the end of the wicked turns him from such a sin against God (vv. 17ff.).

In *Psalm 94* the psalmist appeals to God's vengeance as he considers the prolonged wickedness of the ungodly (vv. 1-11). He is comforted in the knowledge that God will strengthen and support the righteous and not let them be overcome (vv. 12-19).

We close by looking at *Psalm 150*. This psalm is filled with the refrain "hallelujah" or "praise the Lord." It shows that the task of God's people is to claim all for God and make all things praise God. It is truly the "hallelujah chorus" of the Psalter.

All of these psalms which we have observed point back to Psalm 1 and find their context there. They must be seen in the light of the themes introduced there so that they may be seen in proper perspective. What we see in these few psalms can be seen also in the rest of the Psalter.

PROVERBS

The book of Proverbs, along with Job and Ecclesiastes, is called wisdom literature primarily because these books deal with true wisdom from God as over against the human wisdom of men which cannot lead to God. Before we go into the content of this book therefore it will be well to consider briefly the biblical view of wisdom.

Scripture makes clear that there are two kinds of wisdom among men: general and special (or natural and supernatural).

Natural wisdom comes with experience, to men of maturity who gain from experience certain wisdom about living (Job 12:12). Such wisdom is passed on from generation to generation, gradually accumulating. Most ancient cultures had bodies of wisdom literature. While it is better than force, yet because of the sinful nature of man, natural wisdom's effectiveness among men is weakened (Eccl. 9:16-18). Above all, human wisdom falls short in that it cannot lead to God. It is earthbound (1 Cor. 1:20-2:5).

Paul in the same context (1 Cor. 1 and 2) leads us into a consideration of supernatural wisdom, wisdom from God, for believers. This wisdom comes only by revelation, through God's Word by God's Holy Spirit (1 Cor. 2:6-16).

In the Old Testament much is taught about this supernatural or special wisdom. First we learn that it comes only from God, not out of the hearts of men. It is a gift of God (1 Kgs. 4:29). Furthermore, the gift is given in order that men might better do the work and carry out the responsibility which God has given to them (Exod. 28:3; 36:1).

This supernatural wisdom from God is imparted only through his Word. Our wisdom from God comes not simply in knowing God's Word but in keeping it (Deut. 4:5, 6). This means that wisdom consists of more than knowing facts. It comes by application of God's truth to our lives. True wisdom is to know and to do God's will (cf. Matt. 7:24-27).

Thus by having wisdom we are enabled to please God by our living, by doing what he expects of us—doing righteousness and justice (Gen. 18:19—cf. 1 Kgs. 3:28). In the New Testament God's desire for our lives is described in terms of spiritual fruit. James shows that wisdom from God is productive in the fruits of the Spirit (Jas. 3:17-18—cf. Gal. 5:22-23; Psa. 37:30).

Finally, wisdom from God enables us to know ourselves as God knows us, being shown by his Word our real selves so that even in the most secret area of the innermost being God's Word may reveal all hidden sins in us (Psa. 51:6, 16-17).

The Old Testament teaches that our wisdom from God begins with trusting the Lord and in his Word, i.e., the fear of the Lord. Eve's folly occurred when she determined that wisdom came apart from the Word of God (Gen. 3:6).

Job expresses most clearly the relationship between true wisdom and God's revelation (Job 28:12-28). The term "fear of the Lord" means "trust in the Lord." The psalmist uses this term frequently to express the concept of one who is a "God-fearer," which means "believer" (cf. Psa. 115:11-13).

In Proverbs 1:7 we read that the fear of the Lord (trust in the Lord) is the beginning of knowledge. Later in 9:10 we learn that "fear of the Lord" is the beginning of wisdom. In these two sentences the word for "beginning" is different in the Hebrew. In the first case (1:7) the word translated "beginning" has the sense of the beginning as one looks toward the end, the final outcome. Thus faith in the Lord is essential as we look toward the working out of knowledge in wisdom (the application of the knowledge of God's Word to our lives).

In the case of Proverbs 9:10, here the word translated "beginning" means the beginning as the first step. Thus, to believe in the Lord (fear him) is the first step in the whole process of that wisdom which is to come.

What then is the end or final goal of wisdom? Again in Proverbs we find the answer (Prov. 3:13-18). Here we learn that wisdom is the key to the truly blessed life. To gain wisdom is better than the gaining of silver and gold or rubies (cf. Psalm 19:10; 119:72, 127). In short to have wisdom from God is incomparably greater than anything this world can offer. Whatever men have desired: length of days, riches, honor, pleasantness, peace, life, happiness, all are exceeded by wisdom from God.

Let us now go to this great book of wisdom, Proverbs, in order to gain from it further understanding of the ways and blessings of wisdom.

The purpose of the book is stated first (1:2-4): to know wisdom and instruction, to discern words of understanding, to receive instruction in living wisely in righteousness, justice, and equity (cf. Gen. 18:19). Thus we are equipped to give prudence to the simple and teach knowledge to young men (cf. 2 Timothy 2:2). We see then that the book is designed to equip us fully to do the work of God, teaching us until we in turn are able to teach others.

The goal of the book is given in Proverbs 1:5-6. By it the wise increase in learning and are given insight into God's dark sayings, i.e., the mysteries of the kingdom of God. There is in Proverbs therefore an inexhaustible supply of knowledge and growth in wisdom if we take it seriously. By it we can all grow spiritually.

Before we begin a study of the book let us first note the structure.

First, we find *an essay* introduction *in praise of wisdom* (chs. 1-9). It is written from the point of view of a parent giving instruction to his son. Parental instruction is the proper context here (1:8-9—cf. Deut. 6:4-9). Here the son is urged to fear the Lord (1:7; 9:10). This is a challenge to believe in the Lord, thus choosing God's wisdom above the lures of this world.

Next, we have *the first group of proverbs per se* (chs. 10—22:16). These are Solomon's proverbs dealing with the contrast between righteousness and wickedness (the wise and the foolish). It also contains a section on man's great problem and its solution, a kind of tract (16—22:16).

After this there follows *the words of the wise* (22:17—24:22), apparently proverbs by the wise men of a period after Solomon, *then an appendix* to these *words of the wise* is joined to it (24:23-34).

Next, we have *an additional collection of Solomon's proverbs* gathered in the days of Hezekiah (chs. 25-29). These deal in particular with lessons in conduct and the alternatives of life.

Finally there are two brief sections titled "*The Words of Agur*" (ch. 30) and "*The Words of Lemuel*" (ch. 31). This is the outline we shall follow in the study.

An essay in praise of wisdom is the first part of the book of Proverbs. It serves as *an introduction to the whole book* (chs. 1-9). The title of the book as a whole, "The Proverbs of Solomon," is a general description of the content though clearly it does not mean that Solomon wrote all that is contained here. The proverbs of Solomon, specifically chapters 10—22:16 and chapters 25-29 were the framework and basis for the whole collection. Probably in the days of Hezekiah the whole collection was compiled (25:1) and an introduction (chs. 1-9) was written.

The first section begins properly at 1:7. We have already noted the relationship between the fear of the Lord and faith (1:7; 9:10). The whole section is couched in the concept that knowledge and wisdom begin truly only as we fear the Lord and learn from him.

The proper context for this long essay in praise of wisdom is the parental instruction of believing parents toward their son (1:8—cf. Deut. 6:1-9). Both parents are mentioned here, though the first nine chapters are particularly concerned with the father-son motif. It is interesting to note that the book of Proverbs opens with the father's instructions to his son, while the book closes with the son's praise of his mother and then of his wife (the mother of his children) (ch. 31).

First, the father challenges his son to take a stand against the sinner's way, much as we saw in Psalm 1 (Prov. 1:10-19). In fact, the context for this instruction seems to be Psalm 1. The son is to guard against being enticed to follow the sinner's way or counsel (1:10-19). This way leads to death (cf. Psa. 1:1, 4-6).

Then in 1:20 he begins the main body of instruction which has as its objective to persuade him to guard his heart against the deceits of the world and to give his heart to wisdom (1:20-9:18). The father does this by describing wisdom as a fine lady, and by describing the lures of the world as a harlot. We shall call them Lady Wisdom and Mistress Evil.

In the *first subsection, 1:20-3:12, Lady Wisdom and Mistress Evil are introduced.* They battle for the heart of the young man and his father exhorts him to guard his heart above everything else (4:23). The heart is so very important because out of it comes the life of the man (the issues of life). By this he means that what is in the heart is what ultimately will guide and direct the life to its final outcome.

Jesus teaches similarly in Matthew 15:18-20. There Jesus

shows that it is what comes out of the corrupt heart of a man that truly defiles him and his life.

Lady Wisdom is introduced by the father (1:20-33). She is plain-spoken and aboveboard. She addresses young men as simple ones (v. 22) which is what all men are, simple, susceptible to the wiles of Satan. They need wisdom to be rightly guided in life. That wisdom comes from God's Word which Lady Wisdom here offers (vv. 21, 23—cf. Psa. 19:7). She warns clearly that the alternatives which each man faces are calamity or security (vv. 24-33). There are no alternatives beyond this, follow her (with wisdom) into true security or reject her and fall into disaster!

The father strongly counsels his son to seek her and embrace her (2:1-10). Then he warns against *the wiles of Mistress Evil,* whose path leads to death (2:11-22). She is called a strange woman, a foreigner, whose words flatter (v. 16). We see how her flattery works when we note that even Joshua was taken in by her in the affair of the Gibeonites (Joshua 9:3-15—see our commentary there).

The father then counsels his son to trust in the Lord, to fear him and honor God (3:1-12). He must depart from evil (Mistress Evil) so that his life may prosper (3:7). The son will show his fear of the Lord by honoring God with his whole substance, all he owns (vv. 9-10). He will grow as God teaches him, through chastening, what pleases and what displeases the Lord (vv. 11-12).

At this point *the father moves into a praise of Lady Wisdom (3:13-4:27).* First he speaks of her incomparable value (3:13-18). Then he shows how following her will lead to paths of practical living (3:19-35). He must seek to do good to his neighbor and not envy evildoers who do evil to gain for themselves (vv. 27-31). He contrasts the ways of the perverse and the ways of the upright (vv. 32-35). The final goals of each are respectively shame or glory (v. 35). Again we can compare here Psalm 1, which seems to be the background for what the father is teaching.

Chapter 4 contains the exhortation of the father to his son to follow Lady Wisdom. He appeals to his own experience of how he was instructed by his father (4:3-4). He stresses how he has both taught his son the right way and also lived that way before his son as an example (v. 11). Again he makes the point that there are just two ways to go, the path of the righteous which leads to God's goal for him, or the path of the wicked which leads to increasing darkness (vv. 18-19).

After challenging the son to guard his heart, he shows that to guard the heart will mean to control his whole body and all of its parts: his mouth, his lips, his eyes, his eyelids, his feet (4:24-27).

This is what is meant by the issues of life. It is what the heart dictates that the hands and feet, the eyes and ears, the mouth will do.

The next three chapters (5-7) are concerned with *warnings against the wiles of Mistress Evil.* As we noted above, she is described as a harlot, a seductive woman of the streets. Perhaps this choice of a personification of evil is because to a young man a woman of the streets can be a fascinating thing. Her lips seem to drop honey (5:3), but in the end she gives a bitter taste of life (v. 4). Her ways lead to hell (v. 5). The consequences of indulging in the harlot's appetizing invitation are clearly delineated here (vv. 7-23).

Next, in a practical way, the father warns the son against earthly entanglements which lead a man into the snares of Mistress Evil (6:1-19). One way to become involved with sinners is to speak without thinking, to speak too hastily, to commit yourself and your life to a sinner (6:1-5—cf. Jas. 1:19). Another way is *to be idle,* thus giving opportunity to Satan to utilize your idleness for his service (6:6-11). There is no neutral position in this life, one who is not for the Lord is against him (cf. Matt. 12:30). Finally, *failure to control the body:* the eyes, the mouth, the feet; is to lead to calamity (6:12-19—cf. 4:23-27). God hates the life in which the members of the body are not subject to and under the control of the Word of God. Such lives by the action of their eyes, their hands, their feet show that the heart does not belong to God (vv. 16-19).

Again the father returns to parental instruction and the Word of God taken seriously as the way to avoid a life dominated by evil (6:20-24). Without it we are susceptible to the wiles of Mistress Evil and are easily seduced by her to our own destruction (6:25-35). If a man can be enraged with jealousy when a young man lies with his wife in adultery, how much more the Lord when we are seduced by evil (vv. 32-35—cf. Exod. 20:5; Hos. 2:2-7).

Chapter 7 relates the only way to avoid the lures of Mistress Evil; namely, to embrace Lady Wisdom (7:1-4). There follows a very graphic picture of a simple man (without wisdom) being seduced by Mistress Evil. He is like putty in her hands. If he does not have Lady Wisdom at his side he cannot resist the seduction of Mistress Evil (7:5-23). Again the father warns that her ways lead to death (7:24-27).

The last part of the introduction gives an invitation to follow Lady Wisdom (8:1-9:12). It also gives Mistress Evil's counter-call (9:13-18). Lady Wisdom's call is the call to life by fearing the Lord, trusting in him, putting faith in him (8:13). She cries publicly for all to follow her (8:1-4; 9:3-6).

Mistress Evil's call is the call to death itself by going on in your own way, pleasing yourself and not God (9:15, 18).

With this the introduction closes. Both Lady Wisdom and Mistress Evil have given their final calls to the young man. If he heeds Lady Wisdom and fears the Lord, he has taken the first step toward true wisdom which is imparted by the words to follow in the book of Proverbs (chs. 10-31). If he is lured away by Mistress Evil, then what follows in the rest of Proverbs is of no value to him, it only condemns him.

Following the instruction we find *the Proverbs of Solomon* per se (10—22:16). This is the first main section of the book, hence the separate heading (10:1). This section was in all probability the nucleus of the book of Proverbs around which the rest of the book including the introduction was built.

This section is subdivided into *two basic parts:* chapters 10-15 and chapters 16—22:16.

In the *first part* is a collection of Solomon's proverbs dealing with the theme *the righteous contrasted with the unrighteous.* The *righteous* are *described variously* as the upright, the perfect, the wise, the diligent, those who love, heeders of correction, the lowly, the truthful, the slow ones to speak, and the tranquil. In contrast the *unrighteous* are *described* as the wicked, the foolish, the slothful, those who hate, the proud, liars, those who speak rashly and the envious. Here we are taught many things concerning the righteous. *In regard to eternity* he is delivered from death (10:2; 11:21; 14:32). This means more than simply living eternally. He has a quality of life in all he does. As Psalm 1 declares, his leaf does not wither. His memory is blessed by those who have known him (10:7) and he has a sure reward (11:8—cf. 1 Peter 1:4). For this reason his house shall stand in contrast to that of the wicked which shall fall (12:7—cf. Matt. 7:24-27). He shall never be removed from God's presence (10:30).

In regard to this present life he does not famish but flourishes as a leaf (10:3; 11:28—cf. Psalm 1). This means that his hope turns to gladness, i.e., it is never frustrated (10:28; 13:9, 25—cf. Matt. 5:6). His root yields fruit (12:12—cf. Psa. 1; John 15; Gal. 5:22, 23). The quality of his days increases (10:27). This means that he gets far more out of life, no matter how many days he lives on earth.

In regard to the goal of his life, his desire is granted (10:24). He knows what is acceptable to God and prays accordingly (10:32; 15:8), being assured that the Lord will hear him (15:29).

In regard to others, he is a blessing. He is an everlasting foundation, his life being strength for others (10:25). When he speaks it

is to the good of others (10:20, 21; 12:26). When all goes well
with him the citizens of his city rejoice (11:10-11). He guides his
neighbor toward good (12:26). Even his beasts are better off
than those of the unrighteous (12:10—cf. Rom. 8:19-23).

In regard to God's Law, the righteous controls his thoughts so
that they are just (12:5), meaning that they are in accord with
God's will. He has righteousness or a right relationship with God
by his faith and this assurance guards him (13:6; 11:6). He is
delivered from evil by his knowledge of God and God's will
(11:9—cf. Christ in his temptations, Matt. 4:1-11). Fearing the
Lord (being a believer), he hates all which is opposed to God
(14:2; 13:5—cf. Psa. 5:4-6; 139:19-22).

This is the righteous, and *God is well-pleased with him.* God loves
him (15:9) and is for him (19:29—cf. Rom. 8:31-39). He is the
Lord's delight (11:20).

In these chapters we could follow in a similar manner the
other related themes. We could gain insight into the meaning of
being wise or foolish, diligent or slothful, loving or hating, cor-
rigible or incorrigible, lowly or proud, truthful or liars, slow to
speak or speaking rashly, tranquil or envious. I commend such
studies to you as a profitable way of knowing yourself as God
knows you.

One significant theme discovered as one meditates on these
verses is the subtle threat to a righteous life by the entrance of
the traits or companions of unrighteousness into one's life in the
form of far less sinister looking clothing than unrighteousness or
wickedness. While we recoil from such terms as "wicked" in our
lives, yet we may not so respond to envy or rash speaking or
perhaps even to lying or pride or sloth. We must examine ourselves to see if any of these traits are found in us for where they
are, wickedness is not far away.

The *latter half of Solomon's proverbs* (16—22:16), contains proverbs of a different sort. Here instead of a miscellany of proverbs
dealing with the righteous and the unrighteous we find again a
kind of essay developed along one particular subject or theme.
Much that was taught in the first half is found also here, but here
it is related to a particular theme: *the way of man and the way of
God.* Here the way of man which was introduced in the first
section and leads to death is developed and the way of God is
also expounded (14:12; 16:25).

The problem is that the way of man seems right in his own
eyes (16:25). But man sees defectively. His heart is corrupt. Left
to himself, man cannot know the extent of his own sinfulness
(16:2—cf. Jer. 17:9-10). He needs a revelation of God regarding
himself. This is of course the whole point of chapters 10-15 of

Proverbs, to show us men as God sees them. Therefore the themes introduced there are in this section interwoven into the primary theme of man's way versus God's way.

As 16:2 declares, *it is the Lord who is the final judge.* To him alone all men are accountable. This idea is variously expressed in these chapters: the Lord tries the hearts of men (17:3). God is the maker of the eye and the ear, therefore his judgment has precedent over what we see, hear, or think (20:12). The Lord searches the hearts of all men (20:27). God the knower of the heart is the final judge of the heart (21:2). In the end God according to his judgment preserves or overthrows man (22:12).

This then is *the problem.* Man sees things one way (thinking he can do himself what is good enough for his own salvation) but God sees quite a different way (all are sinners and totally unable to choose the right).

God is in control ultimately so that the way which God approves, and not man, will be the triumphant way. This idea too is expressed in various ways. A man may plan to do according to his own will but God overrules and actively directs where man will go (15:9). God disposes all things according as it pleases him (16:33). Man's plans have no standing when opposed to God's counsel. God's counsel will prevail every time (19:21). Whatever way a man actually goes, whether he willed it or not, God works all according to his own pleasure (20:24; 21:1—cf. the book of Jonah). In short, there is no counsel of men which can overrule God's will (21:30).

Since therefore God is in control and all goes according to God's counsel and plan, and since man cannot help himself or change his evil nature as God sees it (20:9), then man can see his own problem solved only as he learns to commit himself into the hands of the Lord (16:3). This is clearly a call to trust and faith in the Savior God.

The solution to our sins which lead us in the way to death is *God's mercy and truth* shown towards us (16:6). Truth tells us how very sinful we are, and points us to trust in God who shows mercy to those who look to him in true repentance and despair in themselves. The fear of the Lord called for here is, as we have shown, a call for faith in God as a refuge for the sinner.

We must therefore *give heed to God's Word* (as chapters 1-9 have already exhorted) and learn to trust in the Lord (16:20). This is the way of true happiness (compare Psa. 1).

Once we have found him *we must run to him with diligence* (18:10). He is *our only sure refuge* from sin, death, and Satan. He alone can destroy these enemies (Gen 3:15; Rev. 20:9-14; 1 Cor. 15:26). Just as the way of man leads to death, so the way of the

Lord, fear of him, tends to life (19:23). To such a one who believes is given assurance of abiding satisfaction and protection from that evil which haunts every man born into the world. The Lord and he alone can save us (20:22).

This is the formula of these chapters (16—22:16). Upon this formula we can hang all of the rest of the wisdom found in this section.

Beginning in 22:17 we have a new section, *the Sayings of the Wise* (22:17—24:22). This section was evidently appended to the Proverbs of Solomon at an early date and contains the wisdom which God gave through others than Solomon. This section is marked by many couplets or pairs of verses which contain exhortations followed either by reasons for the exhortation or consequences if one ignores them.

The goal or purpose of these couplets is to make the believer's life pleasant, i.e., in harmony with what pleases the Lord (22:18-19).

The first couplet is a good example of the style found here (22:22-23). It teaches our responsibility to the poor, reflecting much of what has been said by the prophets. Here we again need to remember that the term "poor" refers not only to the poor materially but to the poor in spirit, i.e., the humble (cf. Matt. 5:3).

The next couplet teaches how we must act toward those who are wrathful (22:24-25). This reminds us of Psalm 1:1. Other examples of couplets and what they teach are as follows: 23:1-3, conduct before a king; 23:6-7, conduct before the enemy; 23:10-11, dealing with the fatherless or helpless; 23:17-18, fearing the Lord rather than envying the sinner (cf. Psa. 37:1-4); 23:20-21, avoidance of drunkards and gluttons; 23:26-27, choosing Lady Wisdom rather than Mistress Evil (cf. chs. 1-9); 24:1-2, warnings against evil doers; 24:15-16, the triumph of the righteous over the wicked; 24:17-18, attitude toward a fallen enemy; 24:19-20, the inevitable end of the wicked.

In the midst of this section is a very graphic portrayal of a drunkard which should be studied by all who indulge in potent whiskeys and strong drinks in our days (23:29-35).

Appended to these *sayings of the wise* is another brief collection of the same (24:23-34). Among these verses are many New Testament favorites: 24:23, cf. Jas. 2:1-13; 24:29, cf. the "golden rule" of Christ, Matt. 7:12; 24:30-34, cf. "by their fruits ye shall know them" (Matt. 7:16).

With chapter 25 we begin a *new collection of proverbs of Solomon* (chs. 25-29). These are distinguished from the former ones by being those collected in the days of Hezekiah and his men (25:1). It was probably in this time that the entire book of Proverbs was finally compiled and completed.

The collection is subdivided into two major sections: the *lessons in conduct* (chs. 25-27) and the *antithetic proverbs* (chs. 28-29).

Various themes all relating to the righteous conduct before differing categories of men is the subject of this first part: conduct before kings (25:1-7); conduct toward neighbors (25:8-20); conduct toward one's enemy (25:21-28); conduct before fools (26:1-12); conduct toward sluggards (26:13-16); warnings against strife (26:17-25); and finally warnings against pride (ch. 27). Among other things we find here are several passages alluded to in the New Testament, i.e., 25:7 regarding our seeking the lower place (cf. Luke 14:7-11) and regarding our heaping coals of fire on the enemy's head (25:21-22—cf. Matt. 5:44 and Rom. 12:20). The meaning of this latter term would seem to be that when one does kindness to an enemy, he throws him into utter confusion as when a man heaped coals of fire on the head of another.

In 26:4-5 we find two verses that at first seem to be contradictory. But they are not. In essence they show that there is no way to answer a fool to his own satisfaction. Since he is a fool, then he lives as though there is no God. If one seeks to answer him on his own premise, i.e., there is no God, then he has conceded to him too much and has no sure foundation from which to make his own position (v. 4). But if one does not answer him at all, then the fool goes away thinking that he is right, so that in the light of his folly, the believer must answer him on the basis of the certainty of God's Word, which the fool will not accept but nevertheless which the believer must affirm before him for the sake of God's glory (v. 5).

The *last section* of the *appendix to Solomon's proverbs* (chs. 28-29) contains several *antithetic proverbs* or statements showing the contrast between the righteous and wicked. Here the conjunction "but" occurs frequently. The content here is quite similar to that found in the first part of this section (chs. 10-16).

Leaving now the Proverbs of Solomon, we find in *chapter 30, the words of Agur* of whom we know nothing except what is said here (30:1).

Agur gives to us first *his own personal testimony* (vv. 1-10). He believes in the complete dependability of God's Word (vv. 5-6).

He asks only his daily needs from God, not too much or too little (vv. 7-9). He therefore is in harmony with what the Lord taught in the Lord's Prayer and in the Sermon on the Mount (see Matt. 6:11, 24-34).

Next he describes *the faithless generation* which is apparently his own generation (30:10-33). There is here a clear relationship between 30:11 and verses 15-17; and between 30:12 and verses 18-20; and between 30:13 and verses 21-23; and between 30:14 and verses 24-28.

In conclusion he *exhorts* men *not to rise against the King (the Lord's anointed)* but to make peace with him lest his wrath be poured out (30:29-33).

The final section of Proverbs is titled "The Words of King Lemuel; the Oracle which His Mother Taught Him" (31:1-31). It is in two parts: the words of his mother (vv. 2-9); and an acrostic poem in praise of the worthy woman (vv. 10-31).

The mother's counsel which he records here is primarily dealing with warnings against the righteous king taking strong drink (vv. 2-7—cf. Isa. 5:22; Hosea 4:11; Hab. 2:15; Deut. 16:19). To do the job God expects of him (31:8-9), the king must be sober (cf. Mic. 3:1-4).

The closing part, verses 10-31, is a beautiful alphabetical poem extolling the attributes of a godly wife. Such a wife has her husband's trust (v. 11). She is diligent in providing for her family, she is capable of making important decisions regarding the finances of the household, she even works in the market, selling her goods (vv. 12-19, 24). Yet she has time to be concerned for the poor (v. 20) and time to make beautiful things for herself (v. 22). She is strong, dignified, and wise but above all she is kind (vv. 25-26). She is never idle but always thinks of others, especially of her own household (v. 27).

For this reason she is praised by her children and by her husband (vv. 28-29). She is not concerned for the social graces or for beauty but for being a God-fearer. She commends herself to them (vv. 30-31).

It seems quite appropriate therefore that this book which begins with a father's counsel to his son should end in a son's and a husband's praise of his mother and wife. Thus once more we see the whole of the book of Proverbs couched in the family context, in the home which God ordained (Gen. 2:24) and through which God has purposed that evangelism and instruction in the truth of God should begin (Deut. 6:4-9).